SHAKESPEARE
& ME

ALSO EDITED BY SUSANNAH CARSON

A Truth Universally Acknowledged:
33 Reasons Why We Can't Stop Reading Jane Austen

SHAKESPEARE & ME

38 GREAT WRITERS, ACTORS, AND DIRECTORS ON WHAT THE BARD MEANS TO THEM – AND US

Edited by Susannah Carson

Foreword by Harold Bloom

ONEWORLD

A Oneworld Book

First published in Great Britain by Oneworld Publications 2014
Originally published in 2013 in the United States of America as *Living with Shakespeare* by Vintage Books an imprint of Random House

Copyright © Susannah Carson 2013
Foreword copyright © Harold Bloom 2013

ISBN 978-1-78074-426-1
eISBN 978-1-78074-489-6

Printed and bound in Great Britain by TJ International, Cornwall

Oneworld Publications
10 Bloomsbury Street
London WC1B 3SR
England

CONTENTS

Foreword: Who Else Is There? by Harold Bloom   vii

Introduction: The Tygers Hart by Susannah Carson   xv

BILL WILLINGHAM	A Little Monkey Business	3
SIR ANTONY SHER	Speaking Shakespeare	12
CAMILLE PAGLIA	Teaching Shakespeare to Actors	26
SIR BEN KINGSLEY	The Architecture of Ideas	45
CICELY BERRY	*King Lear* in Retrospect	56
TOBIAS MENZIES	Method and Madness	67
RORY KINNEAR	Character and Conundrum	75
MATT STURGES	I Know a Hawk from a Handsaw Regardless of the Weather, but That's Pretty Much It	90
JAMES EARL JONES	The Sun God	104
EAMONN WALKER	Othello in Love	141
BARRY JOHN	*Othello: A Play in Black and White*	162
JESS WINFIELD	Re-revising Shakespeare	178
BRIAN COX	"I Say It Is the Moon"	199
RALPH FIENNES	The Question of *Coriolanus*	220
RICHARD SCHOLAR	Trial by Theatre, or Free-Thinking in *Julius Caesar*	228
STANLEY CAVELL	Saying in *The Merchant of Venice*	251
F. MURRAY ABRAHAM	Searching for Shylock	262
FIASCO THEATER	Boldness Be My Friend	275

KARIN COONROD   Killing Shakespeare and Making
                          My Play   290

DOMINIC DROMGOOLE   Playing Shakespeare at
                          the Globe   299

ANGUS FLETCHER   Tolstoy and the Shakespearean
                          Gesture   316

J. D. McCLATCHY   The Red Scarf   330

GERMAINE GREER   Spring Imagery in Warwickshire   335

JAMES PROSEK   What's in a Name? or Unnamed
                          in the Forest   341

DAVID FARR   The Sea Change   352

ALAN GORDON   Looking for Illyria   356

ELEANOR BROWN   Shakespeare's Siblings   370

EVE BEST   "A Star Danced"   377

DAME HARRIET WALTER   Two Loves, or the Eternal Triangle 389

JANE SMILEY   Odd Man Out   407

DAME MARGARET DRABBLE   The Living Drama   412

JOYCE CAROL OATES   The Tragedy of Imagination in
                          Antony and Cleopatra   418

MAXINE HONG KINGSTON   War and Love   433

PETER DAVID   On the Terrible and Unexpected Fate
                          of the Star-Crossed Lovers   440

CONOR McCREERY   Shakespeare and Four-Colour Magic 444

JULIE TAYMOR   Rough Magic   466

JAMES FRANCO   *My Own Private River*   483

ISABEL ALLENDE   Enamoured with Shakespeare   489

Index of Plays and Characters   493

Permission Acknowledgments   499

Harold Bloom

———

FOREWORD
Who Else Is There?

In my long career as a teacher, I have found that students, interviewers, and fellow readers keep asking me, "Why Shakespeare?" It seems a question as necessary to ask as it is impossible to answer, unless you respond, "Who else is there? Who but Shakespeare has influenced so many creative intellects?" The genealogy includes Milton, Austen, Dickens, Keats, and Emily Dickinson, and many of the strongest writers of our own generation. Who besides Shakespeare has perfected expressions of experience, and broadened and defined the horizons of human possibility? He has given us, through thirty-seven plays, 154 sonnets, and four longer poems, a secular religion.

His is the most capacious of consciousnesses. He comprehends and apprehends realities that are available to us but beyond our ken until he manifests them.

If you run any mode of criticism, whether historicism—old or new—or analytical, through Shakespeare, you find it is Shakespeare who illuminates your mode of thinking and not the other way around. His is an electrical field. Anything entering it will light up, but Shakespeare powers the illumination.

There is no God but God, and his name is William Shakespeare. Yahweh is not God. William Shakespeare is God. Heinrich Heine said, "There is a God, and his name is Aristophanes."

On Heine's model, I again remark: there is a God, there is no God but God, and his name is William Shakespeare.

Shakespeare did not set out to create a religion, or to define us. We can never know his motives—presumably to fill seats, write good parts for his actors, stay out of the sight of Walsingham, Elizabeth's Chief of the Secret Service, and so avoid the fate of Thomas Kyd, who was tortured, and Christopher Marlowe, who was stabbed to death. In the plays, we find traces of Shakespeare's evolution as an artist. He swerves from the influence of Ovid, Chaucer, and Marlowe, and discovers that the only opponent worthy of agon is the writer of his own earlier plays. Not Shakespeare as man, but Shakespeare as playwright was the source of his own continued artistic struggle to break free of self-overdetermination.

Paul Valéry, great theoretician of influence, said we must learn to speak of the influence of a mind upon itself, a very rich insight which I have adapted to my own understanding of Shakespeare. After a large book on Shakespeare called *The Invention of the Human* and a shorter one devoted to *Hamlet* called *Poem Unlimited*, I explored the influence of Shakespeare's mind upon itself in *The Anatomy of Influence*, which provides some radically new readings of the elliptical qualities in *Hamlet*, in *The Tempest*, and of Edgar in *King Lear*. The only significant influence on Shakespeare, in the end, was Shakespeare himself. Increasingly in his work, what he leaves out becomes much more important than what he puts in, and so he takes literature beyond its limits. He transforms himself, a victory for art, and yet his own position as poet and as self-precursor resulted in an internalization of the conflict and an unresolvable ambivalence.

The result is a panoply of characters who possess inner lives so very intricate that, although they are finite on the page, to us they nevertheless remain infinite in faculty and endless to meditation. The more elliptical the renderings, the more complex, illusory, and transformative the result. Shakespeare invented the depiction of inwardness in imaginative fiction, and with these characters he shows us how to overhear ourselves think and, by so doing, become richer, more complex, and more sensitive human beings. We learn about ourselves in these plays, and at the same time we enter their worlds to overcome our loneliness. These are our friends, our lovers, our enemies, our parents, our children, and the characters we encounter only briefly in the course of our daily lives.

Ralph Waldo Emerson said that Shakespeare wrote the text of modern life, which means that we are all of us, each in turn, a kind of amalgam of various Shakespearean roles, though I would prefer to call them people. Shakespeare is people, and I write about them not only as roles to be performed, but as more real than you and I. If this is an eccentricity, at least it is a useful one for many actors, and for readers who look to literature for more than confirmation of their own critical agendas.

Old Bloom likes to identify with Sir John Falstaff, but another part of him secretly and inwardly identifies with the Black Prince of Denmark, and another part, rather yearningly, doesn't identify with, but wishes he were on warm terms with, Cleopatra of Egypt. Many years ago, in London, I saw a production of *Macbeth* with Michael Redgrave as the hero, and the marvelously fierce, sexually intense actress Ann Todd playing Lady Macbeth. When she cried out "Unsex me here!" Miss Todd grabbed herself in the crucial area and doubled over. Many men in the audience were highly activated.

My favorite fantasy is that Falstaff did not allow himself to be done in by his murderous adopted son, the dreadful Prince Hal, and instead Shakespeare let him wander off to the Forest of Arden. There he sat on one end of a log, with the beautiful Rosalind on the other, and the two matched wits. Orson Welles had a fantasy in which he remarked that Hamlet did not go back to Elsinore but voyaged on to England, where he eliminated poor Rosencrantz and Guildenstern, stayed on, grew old and fat, and became Sir John Falstaff. Welles played a splendid Falstaff in the movie *Chimes at Midnight*, with Jeanne Moreau as Mistress Quickly.

We are used to characters breaking loose from Shakespeare. You cannot confine these figures to their own plays. They become instances of what was said of Spenser's *Faerie Queene* by Gabriel Harvey: that Hobgoblin had run off with the garland of Apollo. Shakespeare kills off Mercutio, since otherwise who would pay attention to Romeo? Juliet is marvelous enough, so people would keep admiring her. It became a choice between Mercutio and the play, and Mercutio had to go. In the same way, what can you do with Falstaff? He is larger than the play. He is life itself. Shakespeare may not have intended Sir John to turn into this comprehensive vision of immanence, but his is the outstanding instance of the real presence in all literature. He appears again in the beautiful Cockney prose elegy of Mistress Quickly in *Henry V*, but that isn't Sir John anymore. The impostor in the unforgivable play *The Merry Wives of Windsor* is not Falstaff either. It is in *Henry IV*, Parts 1 and 2 that he triumphs.

My book *Hamlet: Poem Unlimited* shows the Prince escaping from Shakespeare and writing his own play. He loathes the story that is unworthy of a majestic and marvelous mind. Shakespeare and Hamlet fight it out in the play. That sounds like Bloomian fantasy, but the more deeply you absorb *Ham-*

let, the more you realize that the Prince has cut loose from Shakespeare. I can understand anyone not much liking Hamlet. I remember a conversation with the learned scholar Alastair Fowler in which he said to me that it wasn't right to call Hamlet a hero-villain, for he is rather a villain outright. Hamlet is responsible for eight deaths, including his own. He destroys everyone in the play who has a speaking part, with the exceptions of Horatio, the fop Osric, and the dunderhead Fortinbras, who marches in with his army at the close—and so pragmatically Hamlet is very bad news indeed.

And yet he raises for Shakespeare, for me, and for you, a problem that we can't, I think, escape. One of the strangest ideas in Freud, expressed in his letters and by anecdotes concerning him, is the belief that great souls who are able to sustain a thorough psychoanalysis can emancipate their own thinking from its sexual past. When Freud is at his most reductive, he is sometimes strongest. It is the very small child's immense curiosity about gender difference that is the origin of thinking in every one of us, and almost all of us never transcend this. Thought never does get emancipated from its sexual past, and so we are caught in an endless moody brooding. Hamlet escapes, and I do not know whether that is his triumph or Shakespeare's. Hamlet has freed thinking from its sexual past. He does not know, we do not know, and perhaps Shakespeare does not know, when the actual sexual relationship began between Gertrude and Claudius. This leaves the unnerving possibility that Hamlet is the natural son of his uncle. If you protest how unlike he is from Claudius, reflect that he scarcely resembles that great basher of heads in battle, his putative father King Hamlet.

In *Hamlet*, and perhaps also throughout his canon, Shakespeare seems to have liberated his own thinking from its sexual past. He produces the uncanny detachment of the Sonnets.

They are a different mode than the plays, for they do not invent human beings. Lyric rather than dramatic, the narrative they offer is dangerous if employed to reveal the historical man. The poet of the Sonnets is Shakespeare, and yet he is also outside Shakespeare, revealing and concealing himself. Sonnets 1 through 126 possess a distanced erotic intensity, and the Sonnets from 127 on show an indisputable and heated erotic rancidity, although both the earlier poems concerning the fair young man and the later poems dealing with the dark lady are unified by their ironic stance. Shakespeare is so advanced in irony that we never will catch up. There is but one Sonnet in the sequence which is beyond irony, and that is 129, "Th'expense of spirit in a waste of shame," which affrights us but will not let us go. Here, perhaps nowhere else, the force of Shakespeare's sentiment becomes just as strong as his craft. He is one with the Sonnet's speaker, momentarily and deliberately giving in to madness as perhaps the last defense there ever can be against the lure of that perilous imbalance. There may be elements of Shakespeare himself in Hamlet and in Falstaff, and perhaps traces of the same rancidity in the later plays, most notably in *Measure for Measure* and *Troilus and Cressida*, but in those dramatic instances the craft outlasts the sentiment.

Such rancidity is different from Shakespeare's negations, which culminate in the high tragedies. At their strongest, as in Iago, Shakespeare's grand negations are figures in a negative poetics which is a kind of dramatic negative theology. Iago is the incarnation of the spirit of modern war, which is his religion. Even Shakespeare surpasses himself, since, after he composes *Othello*, in the next fourteen consecutive months he goes on to write and revise *King Lear*, *Macbeth*, and *Antony and Cleopatra*. Had one the privilege of having a drink with Shakespeare in a tavern, no doubt in salacious company, insofar as either of us could disengage our attention from our associates and the spirits, I suppose I would have asked him: Am I right in believing that after the high tragedies that culminate in *King Lear* and *Macbeth*, and then modulate magnificently into *Antony and Cleopatra*, it had all cost you too much?

Susannah Carson

———

INTRODUCTION
The Tygers Hart

We live in Shakespeare's world, which is to say that we live in a literary, theatrical, cultural, and even psychological world fine-tuned for us by Shakespeare. Had he never lived, we would have bumbled along well enough, but he *did* live, and he did write, and those works were printed, and read, and performed, and passed on, and read some more, and performed some more, and emulated, and assimilated, and quoted, and so on. So that now, four hundred years later, we continue to read and perform and emulate his work so thoroughly and so passionately that it's difficult to conceive who we would be—as a culture, as ourselves—had Shakespeare never existed.

Shakespeare is the most widely read author in English; his *Complete Works* are second in popularity only to the Bible. In the United States, 90 percent of secondary school students read Shakespeare; 100 percent read him in Britain. But even before we come across the texts themselves, somehow we have already been infused with the themes of his thought and even snippets of his language. One is reminded of the young student who, upon seeing his first production of *Hamlet*, reported that he liked it well enough but that it was full of clichés: an apocryphal story, or does it happen all the time? Shakespeare is in many ways so near to us that his words have already found their way into our hearts and heads.

In other ways, however, Shakespeare remains distant—a shadowy figure who wore ruffs and tights and wrote with a quill. The four hundred years separating us from him have taken their toll, and so it often seems that either we have to imagine our way back to him or we have to help him find his way forward to us. In addition to the time jump, Shakespeare keeps his distance through a variety of literary and biographical puzzles. His language is often impenetrable, for his vocabulary is abstruse or forgotten or invented; his syntax is sometimes contorted out of sense by verse; and his word games—such as the tongue twister and brain twister "Light seeking light doth light of light beguile"—can make our heads spin. Furthermore, Shakespeare couldn't turn a plot for a bedtime story, and so he stole his plots, tinkered with them a bit, and then left them some mixture of lopsided, implausible, clichéd, unresolved, and (if historical) inaccurate. And then, to make matters even worse, we don't even know how much of Shakespeare was indeed Shakespeare. Whether one thinks the great Authorship Question is nonsensical or worthy of serious consideration, it has contributed significantly to the aura of magic and mystery surrounding the poems and plays.

Despite all these complexities, when we finally relax into Shakespeare's language we find those thoughts—rich and reso-nant, well-known and new—that help us make sense of our human condition. And when we slide into his stories we lose track of events and fall in with the motley crowd of impish her-oines, rakish heroes, mischievous rogues, harrowing villains, ominous ghosts, star-crossed lovers, and brilliant fools. These are fresh acquaintances, but they double as those familiar fig-ures we have met on this other side of fiction. More familiar

still, we can often recognize in Shakespeare's characters aspects
of our own selves.

The goal of this collection of essays is to reacquaint readers
with the Shakespeare they already love and to help them get
to know that other, trickier Shakespeare too. The essays cover
a broad range of experiences (reading, performing, adapting,
interpreting), and the essayists offer a wide variety of professional backgrounds (actors, directors, scholars, poets, novelists, graphic novelists, and even one naturalist-explorer). I've
attempted to bring together as many perspectives as possible,
not in order to be exhaustive—indeed, with Shakespeare, one
can never be exhaustive—but to celebrate the many different
approaches to appreciating Shakespeare that are possible. There
is no definitive response to Shakespeare, but rather a multitude
of questions, anecdotes, observations, theories, attempts, and
hopes. Together, they constitute a joyful and endless conversation. This book is part of the larger cultural exchange occurring
right now, which extends to epistolary exchanges between old
acquaintances, coffee-table talk, seminar discussions, conference panels, film production meetings, discussions between
directors and actors on the staging of difficult scenes, and—
perhaps my favorite instance—those warm debates friends
engage in as they file out of theaters.

This book is also part of a broader historical conversation
that goes back to the very beginning—starting with Shakespeare's first critic, Robert Greene, who referred to him in
1592 as having "a Tygers hart wrapt in a Players hyde"—and
no doubt this conversation about Shakespeare will be with the
human race all the way until an end we cannot now predict.
I do not think that is overstating the matter: there is indeed
something fearsome and formidable about that scope, and yet
we should not feel overwhelmed, as we should not feel over-

whelmed by the idea of genius, since it all comes down to an immediate response, a joy, a sharing, a love, a sudden finding of ourselves—and all of that is tethered by what is, at heart, nothing more than words. That scope is as large as it is small. "O! For a muse of fire." "Out, damned spot." "Do we not bleed?" "His nose was as sharp as a pen." "O, what a rogue and peasant slave am I." "Juliet is the sun." "Put out the light, and then put out the light." "A world-without-end bargain." "What country, friends, is this?" "The island is full of noises." "Let me not be mad." "I am content."

Together, the new Shakespeareans represented in this book will help readers close the four-hundred-year gap by finding the rhythms of a language that is both familiar and foreign, as well as by discovering the relevance of stories that are both legends and realities.

* * *

Most of us, for better or worse, first encounter Shakespeare in the classroom. We are assigned *Romeo and Juliet* or *Macbeth*, for instance, and then perhaps we grumble and go home and put off the reading until the very last moment, and then read through the requisite scenes as quickly as we can to make the process of imbibing essential culture as painless as possible. That the initiation of an adolescent to Shakespeare should be conducted in such a rude and unpalatable manner is a great loss.

If Shakespeare must first be encountered read, then it is a shame that the reading should be so dry. Reading can be just as exciting as attending a stage play or a film when undertaken by a reader with an active imagination. With your own powers of invention you can imagine Shakespeare just how you want him, and so he can become, in that way, entirely yours and yours alone. You can have your own *Hamlet*, your own *Twelfth Night*, your own *Henry IV.* You can be the director, and the lead actor, and the other actors too, as well as the scenery, and the costumes, and the lighting, and the audience. It is self-indulgent, never mind solipsistic, but it is entirely possible, and can be not only quite sufficient but hugely thrilling.

Reading Shakespeare affects how we live our lives in the broadest sense and, if we are writers too, then it can also affect how we write. In recent years, novels have helped us close the distance between ourselves and that distant Shakespeare. These contemporary works include Jane Smiley's *A Thousand Acres* (inspired by *King Lear*), Alan Gordon's *Fools' Guild* series (inspired by the fools in Shakespeare, especially Feste from *Twelfth Night*), Eleanor Brown's *The Weird Sisters* (inspired by all of Shakespeare), and Jess Winfield's *My Name Is Will: A Novel of Sex, Drugs, and Shakespeare* (inspired by Shakespeare's life). How can novelists such as these, writing directly in line with Shakespeare, find the space for their own voices and inventions? Does Shakespeare haunt writers like the ghost of the old King Hamlet, or does he work a strange magic which allows them to float into the deep imaginative realms of Bottom's dream?

The issue is not limited to those works that wear their Shakespearean influence on their sleeves. In addition to novels in which versions of Shakespearean characters walk the pages, there exist works in which Shakespeare's presence can be felt like a shadow in between the lines. Throughout the Western canon, and even on the borders, Shakespeare's influence is pervasive: to trace it in novels, plays, and poems would be to give the greater part of the history of literature. What is it like to be a modern nonwhite and/or non-Protestant-or-Catholic and/or female author writing in the tradition of the quintessential dead white male? What's it like to try to find a place in the English language to create, for instance, a Chinese-American novel, as has Maxine Hong Kingston? How does growing up in Chile and pasting drawings of Shakespeare onto matchsticks to help envision his plays influence the writing life of a novelist such as Isabel Allende? Is the situation any different when one is working from within the same tradition to carve out space for one's own fictional worlds, as Dame Margaret Drabble and Joyce Carol Oates have done in their novels? In their essays, these novelists reveal, in various modes and through various themes, those elements of Shakespeare they have taken in, made their own, and accepted as influence, even as they have risen above the influences to find the sound of their own distinguished literary voices.

The novel seems like a traditional genre, and yet it was a new, still unproven literary form when Shakespeare was writing (Cervantes, often credited with the first "modern novel," *Don Quixote*, died close to the same day in the same month of April 1616). What, then, about those literary forms that are new today? Has Shakespeare suffered from the rise of comic books and graphic novels, or has he been able to reinvent himself as something like an illustrated superhero? This is a medium which, like the theater, unites language and imagery to create something greater than the sum of its parts. But aren't comics just kid stuff, written by grown-up kids? Hardly. In this collection, some of the most celebrated, award-winning, well-read, literary—and, yes, playful—creators in the comics industry reflect on the influence of Shakespeare in their own lives: Bill Willingham, author of the literary comic book series *Fables*; Matt Sturges, author of *Jack of Fables* and *House of Mystery*; Peter David, prolific novelist, screenwriter, and author of *Marvel 1602: The Fantastick Four*, which features Shakespeare as a character; and Conor McCreery, author of the series *Kill Shake-*

speare, which weaves many of Shakespeare's stories together into one riveting world.

Poetry, on the more traditional side, seems to be more elite than popular these days—and yet poetry was Shakespeare's own literary form, in the Sonnets and his longer poems, as well as in the plays themselves, which are extended dramatic poems. J. D. McClatchy, poet, professor, and editor of *The Yale Review*, writes on Shakespeare's poetic influence.

The best literary criticism is an art in its own right. The scholars and philosophers whose essays appear in this collection have chosen to address a wide variety of topics. Angus Fletcher writes on how Shakespeare brought subtleties and harmonies to his language, resulting in a new music of meaning. In an essay on *The Merchant of Venice*, the philosopher Stanley Cavell reflects on the nature of justice, drawing from his own personal encounters with prejudice. The Oxford professor Richard Scholar reflects on what free-thinking and democracy mean in *Julius Caesar* as a way to get at what they mean in the world of politics today. By means of a close reading of springtime imagery throughout the plays, Germaine Greer comes to the conclusion that Shakespeare spent every Lent with his family in Warwickshire, where he accomplished so much of the writing which, it has been claimed by some, was too extensive for one man to produce.

Just as there is no single way to read Shakespeare, there is no single way to either write about him or write through his influence: as these essays show, the inspirational possibilities of Shakespeare as a written text are infinite.

* * *

Perhaps the most important circumstance to keep in mind when reading Shakespeare is that he wrote for the stage. Unlike the works of authors such as Milton or Dickens, Shakespeare's works can be considered not only in the black and white of the printed page but also in what John Gielgud once called "the pasteboard glitter of the theatre." When we watch Shakespeare as spectators, we can enjoy the dual-level experience of a deeply personal, individual response, on the one hand, and on the other a communal audience alchemy. We are alone, and we are also part of something larger than ourselves. Watching a performance or film doesn't confuse the two experiences and lessen them, but rather heightens the enjoyment of both.

A different set of questions arises, therefore, as soon as we consider Shakespeare not just as flat on paper, but in that magical, moving pop-up book of the theater, for those printed words, stamped so distinctly in black and white, have inspired countless staged productions and films. We can imagine our own Shakespeare come to life, true, but the one thing we cannot do for ourselves is imagine all those other possible Shakespeares, all those other interpretations which are beyond our ken. Encountering these other visions expands the limits not only of our own imagination, but also of our ability to respond to and fully inhabit the human condition. Those involved in the staging and filming of Shakespeare—actors, directors, playwrights, screenwriters, voice instructors—have a particular relationship to Shakespeare, since they are actively involved in making his work a living experience. How do they tap into this vital force both personally and professionally? How do they draw from it different sounds and colors? And how do they communicate this, their privileged sense of Shakespeare's energy, to their audiences time and again, across an infinite combination of plays, characters, productions, and performances?

Some of these essays address single plays, of which *Othello*

has proven one of the most compelling. What's it like to be
the first black man to play Othello at the Globe Theatre? That
would be Eamonn Walker, a pioneer in the role in 2007. What
is it like to be a part of a production that is both *Othello* itself
and an Indian rewriting of *Othello*? The legendary actor, director, and instructor Barry John writes of his experiences as a
white ex-pat in India, in *Othello: A Play in Black and White*.
And how do one's experiences of *Othello* change, after revisit-
ing the great work over the course of a career spanning no less
than seven productions? The great James Earl Jones reflects on
his past incarnations and conveys his current thoughts on how
to reinvest Othello with the status of tragic hero.

Othello, it would seem, has a strong resonance with modern audiences. The same is true of *The Merchant of Venice*. I've
mentioned Stanley Cavell's piece on justice in *The Merchant*. In
his essay, F. Murray Abraham reflects on the manner in which
he was able to portray Shylock as the sympathetic cornerstone
of the play. *Hamlet*, the greatest work in Western literature, is
correspondingly one of the most discussed plays in the collection.

Some of the essays reflect a lifetime of living with Shakespeare. Having performed in both romances, such as *The Taming of the Shrew*, *As You Like It*, and *A Midsummer Night's Dream*,
and tragedies, such as *King Lear*, *Titus Andronicus*, and *Coriolanus*, Brian Cox traces Shakespeare's pragmatic relationship with
social order. Sir Antony Sher reflects on a life of performing
Shakespeare's greatest heroes and villains, including Richard III,
Leontes, Macbeth, and Iago—and that other masterpiece of
a character who is neither hero nor villain, Lear's Fool. For us,
Sir Antony is one of the quintessential Shakespearean actors,
but in this essay he reflects on his unliterary upbringing—"To

paraphrase Hamlet, the Shers' motto could well have been, 'What's Shakespeare to us, or we to Shakespeare?'"—and the decades-long process of learning to feel comfortable in Shakespeare's language, having been born a South African of Jewish descent.

What is it like to be a female actor playing roles originally written for cross-dressing boys? What does Shakespeare tell us about how to be the heroines of our own lives in this modern world? Dame Harriet Walter reflects on her experiences embodying Shakespeare's greatest heroines, from Cleopatra to Viola to Juliet. "In all but a few cases," she writes, "I found myself as a character in competition with a man for the love of the hero." Eve Best reflects on her experiences playing Lady Macbeth and Beatrice at the Globe—two characters who seem polar opposites, but who share a similar strength.

Sir Ben Kingsley writes on the fundamental importance of encouraging younger generations to rise to the challenge of Shakespeare, insisting that "of course it's relevant. It's us. It's the birth of the greatness of our language." His colleague, the legendary Royal Shakespeare Company voice director Cicely Berry, reflects on her experience directing *King Lear* in a production which provoked a radical shift in the way the plays were then brought to life: through an awareness of how Shakespeare creates character not just with the meaning of words, but also with their very sounds. Camille Paglia, social critic and professor at the University of the Arts, writes about her years of teaching Shakespeare to young American actors, for whom, unlike for British actors, "he is an import, trailing arty clouds of glory." She encourages a deep engagement with the plays, encompassing the particularities of Shakespeare's language and the grandeur of his themes.

In addition to being a master craftsman, Shakespeare was a

popular writer whose primary goal was to delight his audiences. How can Shakespeare's sense of humor be updated to produce the same giggles and guffaws? In this tradition is the Reduced Shakespeare Company's *The Complete Works of William Shakespeare (abridged)*. In his essay, the company's cofounder Jess Winfield writes of adapting *The Complete Works* to suit the humor of different venues around the world during different times, using Shakespeare's sacred status as prime material for comedy. The members of the celebrated Fiasco Theater company reveal how they transformed *Cymbeline*, often considered a "problem play," into a riotously funny New York production. Karin Coonrod, Yale professor and director of a Public Theater production of *Love's Labor's Lost* (*sic.*) writes about helping modern audiences understand the light-hearted romantic banter of this linguistically complex play. The artistic director of the Globe Theatre, Dominic Dromgoole, writes of the specifically linguistic challenges—and opportunities—involved in staging *Love's Labour's Lost* and *Henry V.*

Having played Hamlet as well as Edgar in *King Lear*, Tobias Menzies writes about accessing these characters, both of whom adopt a form of madness, in a way that's modern and yet retains the original magic. David Farr, the playwright, screenwriter, and Royal Shakespeare Company director, explores Shakespeare's use of the sea as imagery for change. Interested specifically in the changes undergone by characters throughout and even before the beginnings of their plays, Rory Kinnear writes about his creation of Angelo in *Measure for Measure*, Hamlet, and Bolingbroke in *Richard II.*

After having been part of theatrical productions, some directors are moved to bring their favorite plays to film. Julie Taymor produced stage versions of *The Tempest* before filming her innovative production with Helen Mirren as Prospera;

in her essay, she writes of decisions inspired by the cinematic medium and of the different weight the story enjoys with a sorceress as the lead. Ralph Fiennes acted in *Coriolanus* on stage ten years before he decided to revisit the work as director and as Coriolanus himself in film. In his essay, he writes of the various ways in which he adapted the Roman setting to resonate with contemporary politics by using a modern setting and filming in Croatia.

*   *   *

The fact that there are two primary ways of encountering the plays has led to two different interpretive approaches, which, more frequently than not between Shakespeare's time and now, have remained distinct. Should Shakespeare be read? Scholars, historians, and writers tend to prefer the pleasures of curling up with a good book. Or should Shakespeare be performed? Directors, actors, playwrights, and filmmakers describe the delights of the stage. It is almost as though there are two different traditions entirely.

But is it possible to have it both ways? The essays in this collection cover both sides of this spectrum and add new dimensions as well: although some performers write about performing and some novelists write about writing, most of the essays transcend the traditional division. Actors are scholars, critics are performers, directors are readers, and so on.

Two of the contributors defy categorization from the outset. James Franco is an actor, director, writer, poet, scholar, and artist. In his essay, he writes about his recent Gagosian Gallery cinematic installation based on Gus Van Sant's *My Own Private Idaho*, which was in turn based on *King Henry IV, Parts 1 and 2*. James Prosek is an artist, writer, documentarian, and natural scientist. Drawing from his own experiences exploring South

America for new species of birds, he reflects on the nature of naming in Shakespeare's magical forests.

* * *

Shakespeare continues to be an inexhaustible source of inspiration for new creators, and just when one thinks nothing more can be done, a new work is born. There are great Shakespearean goings-on right now—but then, there always are. What accounts for his sacred eminence? His perennial celebrity? How is it that Shakespeare is always in theaters, in cinemas, in bookstores, and in our lives? And how is it that he appeals to all sorts of people? One thinks of the great literary figure Robertson Davies, who as a small child would look up admiringly at engravings of the great actors playing Antony and Portia, or of Isabel Allende with her makeshift matchstick theater, or of James Earl Jones listening to his uncle reciting *Antony and Cleopatra*. The essays in this book, it is hoped, will speak to those who have lived with Shakespeare for decades as well as to those who are just beginning their acquaintance with him. By painting portraits of their individual Shakespeares, those who have shared their favorite insights and anecdotes in the following essays are also inviting each of us to deepen, and perhaps even to discover, our own distinct and inevitably personal Shakespeares too.

A NOTE ON THE TEXT

The order of the essays loosely calls out certain themes, but other themes are interwoven throughout. Just as with any sustained conversation, while some ideas arise once, others recur and are modulated, supported, and refuted by their authors in varying contexts. Some of the authors wrote on single plays, some on multiple plays, and some on the entire corpus—thereby making any rubric impossible, and thankfully so, as one of the goals of this collection is to dissolve apparent boundaries. Since there can be no true order to such a variegated collection, any reading sequence will do. Please see the back of the book for an index of plays and characters for specific navigation.

Except where otherwise noted, the text and the line references of the citations are taken from the RSC edition of 2009, which was modernized from the First Folio; for some of the shorter citations, mentioned in passing, the line references have not been included.

Although portions of some essays have been offered previously (see the permissions page), these essays have been updated by the authors specifically for this collection. This is the first time the essays have appeared in their current form.

I'd like to put thanks in print to each of the contributors, for they took time from their busy schedules to pause, reflect, recount, and write. This book owes its existence to Bonnie Nadell. Other support and counsel, in a variety of forms, was offered by: Harold Bloom, Jeanne Bloom, Karen Carson, Brian Cox, Jordan Culver, Dominic Dromgoole, Flynn Earl Jones, Janet Dulin Jones, Angel Jiménez de Luis, Tristram Kenton, Sharib Khan, Ken F. Levin, Albert Maggini, Ben Nathan, Dawn Revett, Joshua Bower Saul, Fiona Shaw, James Sime, Dame Harriet Walter, and Sarah Williams.

SHAKESPEARE
& ME

Bill Willingham

A LITTLE MONKEY BUSINESS

A Selection of Not Entirely Random Musings on Shakespeare and Storytelling

---

BILL WILLINGHAM is an American novelist, graphic novel author, and comic artist. His series *Fables* has been the recipient of fourteen Eisner Awards. His work includes *Jack of Fables*, *Peter and Max: A Fables Novel*, *Elementals*, *House of Mystery*, *Down the Mysterly River*, *Ironwood*, *Batman*, *X-Men Unlimited*, and *The Justice Society of America*.

THE BUREAU OF INFINITE MONKEYS

You've heard about that legendary bureaucracy made up of an infinite number of chimpanzees, diligently typing away, until eventually one of them randomly produces the complete works of Shakespeare? Well, that was me. I'm the monkey that wrote the Bard's more or less complete works: the comedies, the tragedies, the historicals, and the poems. All of it.

I'm serious.

I did it, but I didn't do it randomly. After a school-sponsored, forced introduction to one of his plays (*Macbeth*) at an early age, and the astonishing revelation of just how grand such a thing could be, I set out, with malice aforethought, to see the rest. I saw every staging and performance I could get to. I hunted down the various festivals, in Ashland, Oregon, and Cedar City, Utah. I caught *Twelfth Night* first in the gym at Sunnyside High School, and then again, years later, on an open-air stage built out over the cricket-haunted shore of Lake Tahoe. I lucked into James Earl Jones's portrayal of King Lear on a tiny black-and-white TV, in Milton Tobey's college dorm room. I devoured the film adaptations, the recorded stage productions on PBS and its ilk, and if there were some I could never arrange to see, I could at least read them. I immersed myself in Shakespeare and all of his works. And in the seeing, or reading, by agreeing to be drawn into the stories, I ended up writing them too.

This is something he must have known early in life, but I came late to understanding. Like every other storyteller in history, Shakespeare always worked with a coauthor. He often admitted as much. Take this example: "Suppose within the girdle of these walls / Are now confined two mighty monarchies" (Prologue 19–20), his character Chorus says in *Henry V.*

Who's he speaking to? He's addressing the audience member, perhaps commanding with authority, or maybe requesting with humility (depending on the performance, I suppose), that the audience member does his part in the required author-viewer (or -reader) collaboration, without which no story can be told in any medium.

Chorus suggested the two mighty monarchies. That inventive fellow, or clever woman, named Audience supplied the details, daring, by means of imagination and extrapolation, "on this unworthy scaffold to bring forth / so great an object" (Prologue 10–11).

Imagine that your story requires that there be a city on a hill. If you say as much in a novel, your reader will provide it. He'll gladly and quickly build each brick and timber of it, each avenue, back alley, and public fountain. After all, that's

Reader's job as coauthor of the tale. But if you try to do his job for him, by attempting to describe each and every detail of that city, instead of only giving out the few details essential to moving the story along, you'll bog the whole thing down and smother it. You're the momentum half of the writing partnership. Reader is the details man.

If the play requires there be a city on a hill, try to actually build the thing complete. Try to find any stage that can hold such a monstrosity. It is better to simply suggest such a thing with a dab of paint on canvas and a deft turn of phrase from one of your characters. Then trust your coauthor to do the rest.

Let's return to Chorus one last time, because he does it so well. Just as Hamlet's speech to the players is often cited as Shakespeare's acting class, Chorus's prologue encapsulates the most vital need of staging:

> But pardon, gentles all,
> The flat unraisèd spirits that hath dared
> On this unworthy scaffold to bring forth
> So great an object. Can this cockpit hold
> The vasty fields of France? Or may we cram
> Within this wooden O, the very casques
> That did affright the air at Agincourt?
>
> (Prologue 8–14)

No pardon is necessary, Chorus, because the answer is an unqualified, "Yes." This cockpit can indeed hold the vasty fields of France and all the rest, because Audience has both the wit and the power to write in everything Playwright left out. Rather, nothing was left out, because both writers in the partnership knew their parts of the job and executed them masterfully.

And that's how I came to write the complete works of Shakespeare. I coauthored them with the man himself, each and every time I picked up one of his works or sat in one of his audiences.

Now, why was any of this worth mentioning, since, in hind-sight, it seems so obvious? Partly to finally put an end to this nonsense:

Revealed at Last! Who Really Wrote the Plays Attributed to Shakespeare!

I have to confess I'm not well versed in these conspiracy theories, largely because I recognized their worth early on and gave them all of the care and attention they deserve, which is not much. But I know the questions persist, with different groups offering up diverse historical personages as candidates for the true author of Shakespeare's plays. If I recall correctly, Sir Francis Bacon is one that comes up most often.

Well, they're right. Assuming Bacon attended one or more of Shakespeare's plays in his life, then he did actually write them, but, as we've settled above, only in coauthorship and only to the extent that the play (or the book, or the movie) isn't fully written until it takes place in the mind of the reader or viewer.

Who really wrote the plays of Shakespeare? He did, but then so did everyone else.

Even so, take a bow, Sir Francis. Well done.

MY SHAKESPEARE PLAYS
ARE NOT YOUR SHAKESPEARE PLAYS

Here's one of my favorite examples. I first watched *The Merchant of Venice* not two inches away from Rebecca May Baird, of Sunnyside, Washington. But, by the end, it was obvious we'd watched two different plays. In my version, the lovely and erudite Portia was clearly the villain of the story. There couldn't be any other interpretation. In fact, to this day, she's quite obviously the number one of all of Shakespeare's villains, not only out-Heroding Herod, but out-Iagoing Iago. Portia makes Lady Macbeth seem the heart of compassion. Compared to her, Don John in *Much Ado About Nothing* is a boy scout.

Look at the facts. Like many good villains she comes as a wolf in sheep's clothing, presenting herself as a peacemaker, with her famous Quality of Mercy speech:

> The quality of mercy is not strained,
> It droppeth as the gentle rain from heaven
> Upon the place beneath. It is twice blest:
> It blesseth him that gives and him that takes.
> 'Tis mightiest in the mightiest, it becomes
> The thronèd monarch better than his crown.
> His sceptre shows the force of temporal power,
> The attribute to awe and majesty,
> Wherein doth sit the dread and fear of kings.
> But mercy is above this sceptred sway,
> It is enthronèd in the hearts of kings,
> It is an attribute of God himself;
> And earthly power doth then show likest God's
> When mercy seasons justice.
>
> (4.1.184–197)

The speech doesn't work, moving every heart but Shylock's, but that's no indictment against Portia. Her base villainy is revealed later, once she has the upper hand and shows not a hint of mercy herself. In fact, she really hammers the guy:

> Tarry, Jew.
> The law hath yet another hold on you.
> It is enacted in the laws of Venice,
> If it be proved against an alien
> That by direct or indirect attempts
> He seek the life of any citizen,
> The party gainst the which he doth contrive
> Shall seize one half his goods, the other half
> Comes to the privy coffer of the state,
> And the offender's life lies in the mercy
> Of the duke only, gainst all other voice.
> In which predicament, I say, thou stand'st,
> For it appears, by manifest proceeding,
> That indirectly, and directly too,
> Thou hast contrived against the very life
> Of the defendant, and thou hast incurred
> The danger formerly by me rehearsed.
> Down therefore, and beg mercy of the duke.
>
> (4.1.353–370)

She gets him good, and then, through Gratiano and the Duke, engineers (or at least stands by and approves of) Shylock's forced conversion to Christianity. Sweet mercy indeed, lady.

But Rebecca didn't see it that way. In the version Rebecca created, in collaboration with Shakespeare and the company of players, Portia remained the heroine throughout. Granted my interpretation is spot-on, while Rebecca's version is simply wrong, but the point is made. Not only is every performance of every play a different story, every audience member co-creates his own unique story. Given that, Shakespeare turns out to be far more prolific than we imagined.

THE STORYTELLING PEOPLE
(INCLUDING, WITH ALL DUE APOLOGIES, JUST
A LITTLE BIT MORE ABOUT MONKEYS)

Finally, I'd like to pose an idea for why Shakespeare and his works are important to us as a human race in full, and not just to the small minority that actively follows his stories.

It's one of the central questions of our existence. What defines humanity? I'd like to propose that we dismiss most of the scientific designations, because they miss the mark. I'm told *Homo erectus* was all the rage for a time. *Homo erectus*? So what if we can walk upright? A bear can do as much. Monkeys, beavers, chipmunks, bugs, and birds can do it. A dozen kinds of bird, including penguins and emus, even gave up flight to do it. My cat can do it for a step or two (and let me tell you, he looks adorable when he does). Even lizards will run along on two feet to intimidate an enemy or woo the ladies.

Maybe we can do it a little better than the average bear, but the ability to walk on our hind legs doesn't make the man.

Homo sapiens, aka the "wise or knowing man," gets us a little closer. But what is it we know? We know how to make and use tools, and that used to be the gold standard for separating us from the common beasts. But that was before we discovered that chimpanzees make and use tools, and that kicked the door wide open. Studies were studied. All manner of birds and beasts were scrutinized more closely, and it turned out the animal world abounds with tool users. Even the common crow has been shown to use and make tools. Not only that, crows are secondary toolmakers, meaning they can first construct one tool to help them make the secondary tool they really need. When tool use collapsed as the protective wall separating man from beast, secondary toolmaking was quickly erected as the new, this-time-we-mean-it bastion. Now that's gone too.

So what's left?

I propose that our storytelling is what makes us taxonomically significant. What separates us from the other beasts is our never-ending capacity for spinning yarns.

We tell stories to live, to love, to prosper, and to fail. A house doesn't get built until someone—the architect or the wise old man of the village—first tells the story of how it will be built, and why, and for whom. And the architect doesn't begin his story until he first hears from the young couple—eager, scared, nervous, and excited—telling him the tale of the sort of home they want.

Stories create stories, create stories, create stories, or nothing gets done.

Money isn't real. It's a fantasy we tell each other to convince us it has worth—an agreed-upon fiction that crumbles unless everyone goes along with it. The laws we live under are the stories we tell ourselves about the kinds of people we hope and expect to be. And those stories matter. Interrupt the story by breaking one of those laws (try one of the big ones, just for fun) and you'll likely find out how important they are.

Every road and every step along it begins with a story.

It isn't just the practical side of our lives that is ruled by the stories we tell (and here we get closer to the Shakespeare connection). Our fictions move us to do great things, things worth doing for no better reason than there's poetry in us. We dream before we do.

Lincoln credited (or blamed) Harriet Beecher Stowe's entirely fictional tale *Uncle Tom's Cabin* for making war inevitable. If that's true, how much of the war's blood is on her hands? And in turn, how much of the vast human freedom that followed can be attributed to her? I don't know, but wouldn't that make a hell of a story?

Generations before we physically set foot on the moon, the storytellers got us there first. In the dim and distant past we spun tall tales about impossible lost continents like Lemuria and Hy-Brasil, and then we went out and found them in fact.

Stories precede everything we do. That's our most basic nature, and we couldn't escape it if we tried.

It can be argued then that there's no higher calling than that of the storyteller, and Shakespeare is an example of its finest realization. If those who hold up toolmakers as the apex of human achievement want to celebrate Fulton, Edison, Einstein, and Oppenheimer as their patriarchs, I give you real world-changers like Homer, Jack Kirby, and the aforementioned Shakespeare as the archangels of pure story. And I give you that small wooden stage, that most worthy scaffold, as the laboratory in which our future is being designed.

Shakespeare is important, because we, each and every one of us, are members in good standing of the species *Homo fabulae*—the Storytelling People.

Sir Antony Sher

SPEAKING SHAKESPEARE

SIR ANTONY SHER, KBE, was born in South Africa; he is an actor, author, playwright, and painter. His stage performances include roles in *Stanley*, *Primo*, *An Enemy of the People*, *Broken Glass*, *Kean*, as well as the Shakespeare plays *King Lear*, *Othello*, *Twelfth Night*, *The Merchant of Venice*, *Titus Andronicus*, *The Tempest*, and *Richard III*, for which he received an Olivier Award and an Evening Standard Award; the stage productions of *The Winter's Tale* and of *Macbeth*, with Dame Harriet Walter as Lady Macbeth, were made into films. His extensive film work includes roles in *Mrs. Brown* as well as in *Shakespeare in Love*, for which he earned a Screen Actors Guild Award. His performances have been recognized with many further distinctions, including another Olivier Award, a Drama Desk Award, and the Peter Sellers Award for Comedy. His books include *Woza Shakespeare: Titus Andronicus in South Africa*, *The Year of the King*, and *Beside Myself*.

It was in Cape Town, South Africa, that I realized I was finally at ease speaking Shakespeare. Which is not to say that I speak it perfectly, but simply that it's grown familiar and unthreatening. I'm at home in it now.

It intrigues me that this happened in my real home, the place where I was born and brought up, Cape Town. I was playing Prospero in *The Tempest*, a coproduction of Cape Town's leading theatre, the Baxter, and the Royal Shakespeare Company (RSC) in the United Kingdom. The year was 2009.

It had been forty-one years since I left Cape Town to train as an actor in London, at the Webber Douglas Academy of Dramatic Art. At that time, I had no idea that my career would mostly be as a classical actor, and mostly with the Royal Shakespeare Company, or that I would nevertheless be imbued with a sense of trespassing. Surely Shakespeare was the territory of tall, handsome, honey-voiced British actors. How could there be a place for a short, bespectacled, Jewish South African like me?

Shakespeare had not been taught well at my school, Sea Point Boys High—the plays were made to seem boring, lifeless, often incomprehensible. Local productions were rare, and these were, frankly, like those in England's regional theatres during the 1950s: a style that's been described as "all starched vowels and wrinkly tights." And literature or drama was certainly not part of my family life. Dad was a hardworking businessman, who relaxed with his 6 p.m. whisky in his den, or Saturday afternoon sport on the wireless. To paraphrase Hamlet, the Shers' motto could well have been, "What's Shakespeare to us, or we to Shakespeare?"

On the other hand, I saw Olivier's film trilogy—*Henry V*, *Hamlet*, and *Richard III*—and here was a vision of a different kind of Shakespeare: thrilling, moving, funny. But was this just the illusion and spectacle of cinema, or, as we called it, the bioscope? Could Shakespeare possibly be like that on stage as well?

Yes! I learned this one week after my arrival in London in July 1968. I travelled up to Stratford-upon-Avon to see the legendary RSC in action. It was a matinee performance of Trevor Nunn's production of *King Lear*, starring Eric Porter. Years later I worked with Porter, and he told me that he had been unhappy in the show, that it had not been well received critically, and that it hadn't even transferred to London, but I was oblivious of these things in the magical dark of the RSC's main house on that sunny afternoon. It was Shakespeare's own genius which was revealing itself to me—his genius as a playwright, not just as the much-edited author of Olivier's films—and I was also swept away by the imagination of the theatre people who were interpreting him. Lear's first entrance took my breath away. He was a hunched, white-bearded figure sitting cross-legged on a bier, carried aloft by attendants: a pagan king, a man-god, invincible. Perfect for the beginning of his story, which is a descent into powerlessness. And so the show went on. Michael Williams was remarkable as the Fool, his face permanently etched into a tragicomic mask, making crazy, dangerous jokes as he and Lear slid into the abyss. Why had the teachers at Sea Point Boys High not told me that the spirit of Samuel Beckett was already alive in Shakespeare's heart?

On the train back to London that evening, I was travelling not from Stratford but from Damascus. I'd had my epiphany. Shakespeare in the theatre, Shakespeare live, could be amazing. But was there any place in it for me?

We were taught Shakespeare excellently at drama school by the actor Nick Amer. From him I learned two things which I still practice to this day: one, that you have to paraphrase every single word, *translate* it into ordinary English; two, that, having understood it, you then have to get it up to speed. In real life we don't spell things out, we think and talk very quickly. An audience will grasp the essence of a Shakespeare speech much better the same way. I was also lucky to have as one of my drama school directors the mesmeric performer and writer Steven Berkoff. He did a production of *A Midsummer Night's Dream* with my year. I played Puck: a wild, demonic figure, leaping and clambering over the lovers. Berkoff was teaching me how physical Shakespeare could be.

This was to stand me in good stead when I joined the RSC in

1982. My first role was the very same one that had so astonished
me in Trevor Nunn's 1968 *King Lear*—the Fool. Now the director was Adrian Noble, and Lear was Michael Gambon. Through
discussions and improvisations, my Fool emerged as a strange
clown: a small, deformed man who wore a red nose and white
makeup. He did snatches of half-remembered music hall routines, sometimes double-acts with Lear himself, and, as a final
grim joke, was accidentally stabbed to death by his master in the
mock trial during the storm. It worked extremely well, but I'll
never forget Adrian once saying to me, "If only you could be as
dexterous with your voice as you are with your body."

Here was the rub. The essence of Shakespeare is the text.
The essence of good Shakespeare acting is an ability to speak
the text. There's no amount of physical showing-off which
can compensate. A fact which I ignored completely in my next
Shakespeare role—Richard III. Unlike the Fool, whose dia-
logue is often in prose, or comprised of little ditties and songs,
Richard has to speak screeds and screeds of iambic verse, pure
Shakespeare stuff. It's the third-largest role in the canon (after
Hamlet and Iago), and I feared that I simply wasn't up to it,
vocally. I trusted neither my technique nor my voice itself.
Ringing in my head was what a major Shakespeare actor should
sound like, whether of the older generation, like Olivier and
Gielgud, or the one just ahead of me, like McKellen and Jacobi.
If you think of human vocal cords as the raw, natural material
which fashions a musical instrument, then mine—with their
roots in the Jewish, Cape Townian tunes of South Africa, and
later twisted into new shapes by the "received pronunciation"
of my British drama school training—didn't seem to produce
the same timbre. And so I embarked on an elaborate way of
playing Richard III—on crutches, multi-limbed, the "bottled
spider" which Queen Margaret describes—and hoped that this

would distract people from noticing that I didn't yet possess the power or skill to do what graces the best Shakespeare performances. This is when the part is somehow born inside the actor himself (and not just the writer) and comes ringing out through his own throat. Richard III was a success for me, but I knew there was much further to go.

Shylock was next, but he didn't really force me to confront the problem. In our production he was an unassimilated Jew, a Turk in the Venetian ghetto, speaking in a thick accent. The language of the play was clearly not his mother tongue.

At the same time, I was settling into life at the RSC, and one of the perks of working there is that they function both as a theatre company and as a training school. They pay you to learn to speak Shakespeare . . . ! Surely it should be the other way round. But they've no choice: it's not just the likes of me who arrive on their doorstep with little or no sense of how to perform their resident dramatist. I thought I was especially disadvantaged because of my South African education, but not many British schools teach Shakespeare much better. And there's an added problem nowadays: many young actors are more attracted to working in films and television than in the theatre, particularly theatre in the classical tradition. But even if some are simply using the RSC as a stepping stone to movie stardom, they have to learn to do it, to speak Shakespeare.

In my early years with the company, we could not have been more fortunate in the people assigned to tutor us. Two of the great Shakespeareans of modern times: the voice coach Cicely Berry and the director John Barton. With them, we had one-to-one sessions, group workouts, master classes. The lessons they were teaching were deceptively simple in theory, but hard in practice—as with one of Ciss Berry's catchphrases, "pass the baton," where you have to reach the end of your own speech very clearly, so that, in the great rush of words which make up a Shakespeare text, the next character can pick up the thought and run with it. This isn't easy, for it goes against our modern way of communicating, which is to mumble away our sentences, trailing off with a "y'know" or "see what I mean?" One of John Barton's preoccupations is for the actor to "ask the question, really ask the question." When we ask questions in real life, we can't see the rest of the script: we don't know what the answer will be, or even if one will come. Our questions have a note of urgency. But in Shakespeare plays, when questions are part of a big speech, laid out as verse on a printed page, actors can often forget to "really ask" them, and they can sound rhetorical. Another of John's observations about Shakespeare is that, when he wants to make his most heartfelt statements, he uses the simplest language, which needs no paraphrasing whatsoever. Lear says to his Fool, "O, let me not be mad." In the depths of despair, Macbeth says, "Tomorrow and tomorrow and tomorrow." Reaching out to touch what he thinks is a statue of his dead wife, Leontes says, "O, she's warm!"

I have prickles down my spine as I write this.

In my twenty-nine years with the RSC, another factor has played an important part in my quest to speak Shakespeare well. By chance, I've performed an exceptional amount of plays by his contemporaries. They don't possess his genius with the iambic pentameter—he's like a master jazz musician, he can both keep to the beat and jam round it—and the difficulties the others experience in writing, and thereby cause the actor to experience in performance, make Shakespeare's skills easier to comprehend, and therefore to serve.

First I did *The Revenger's Tragedy*, formerly thought to be by Tourneur, now by Middleton. The language is harsh and jagged—it's like trying to hold barbed wire in your mouth.

Next I played the title role in *Tamburlaine the Great* by Christopher Marlowe. Ah, his mighty lines. They hit the iambic like a drum—stirring and bold, but ultimately monotonous; you have to use every bit of imagination to bring life to the relentless rhythm. Then there was *The Roman Actor* by Philip Massinger. The part of Domitian Caesar is one of the best I've ever played—a tremendous portrait of a psychopath—but the verse was tricky again: long, highly structured sentences which are like lawyers' arguments, and often defy any efforts to make them sound spontaneous. And then finally *The Malcontent* by John Marston. It's a riotous black comedy, but its language is bizarre: Marston makes up words, like "fubbery" and "whim-wham," or goes off on strange riffs, where the sound of the speech seems more important than its substance.

What a relief to return to Shakespeare. This was as Leontes in *The Winter's Tale* for the RSC in 1999. Some scholars say that Leontes's early speeches are incomprehensible, but this isn't true. In fact, it's a perfect demonstration of another of Ciss Berry's most firmly held beliefs—that Shakespeare is meant to be spoken, not read. Leontes's jealousy erupts in the soliloquy that begins: "Inch-thick, knee-deep, o'er head and ears a forked one!" (1.2.119). We know that "a forked one," "o'er head and ears," refers to a cuckold's horns, but what on earth does "inch-thick, knee-deep" mean? Academics sitting in their studies may frown in puzzlement, but an actor playing Leontes will leap on the line with relish. It's an ugly, visceral bubble of subconsciousness rising to the surface, as in a dream or nightmare. His jealousy is irrational: he believes his wife and his best friend are having an affair, yet we, the audience, know that they are not. In our production, we decided that he was suffering from an actual psychological illness known as Morbid or Sexual

Jealousy, where this syndrome occurs exactly as Shakespeare describes. And once you understand that Leontes is mentally unstable—as opposed to the old-fashioned view that he is "villainous" or "evil"—every one of his unfinished sentences or jumped thoughts becomes a valuable detail in creating his portrait.

For the first time in my career as a Shakespeare actor, I was discovering that by fully trusting Shakespeare, his instincts in writing the role, one could experience the text as liberating rather than intimidating.

"I have done the deed." Sir Antony Sher as Macbeth in Gregory Doran's Royal Shakespeare Company production, 1999.
Photograph by Tristram Kenton.

This was even more true in my next role, later the same year—Macbeth. I found the character very difficult to crack—probably the most difficult one I've played. Particularly in the first part, before the murder of Duncan. He watches himself, he hesitates and changes direction, he *thinks* so much. Who is this man? On the one hand, we're told that he's ruthlessly violent on the battlefield—he rips open people "from the nave to th'chops" (1.2.24). On the other hand, his wife complains that he is "too full o'th'milk of human kindness" (1.5.12). But the part gradually revealed itself to me, and it was by following the clues that Shakespeare plants in the text. In complete contrast to Leontes's language, Macbeth's is steady and ordered. This is a man who likes to keep himself in control. As any military leader must. He can give himself permission to go berserk at war, but in the calm and safety of his own home he is extremely troubled by the prospect of murdering an unarmed old man asleep in bed. And once he has "done the deed," his mind fractures. I think that Act 2, Scene 2, the scene after the murder, is one of the greatest in Shakespeare. It's written in verse, but very naturalistically, in short, shared lines between husband and wife, who try to absorb what's happened.

> LADY MACBETH: My husband?
> MACBETH: I have done the deed. Didst thou not hear
>   a noise?
> LADY MACBETH: I heard the owl scream and the
>   crickets cry.
> Did you not speak?
> MACBETH: When?
> LADY MACBETH: Now.
> MACBETH: As I descended?
> LADY MACBETH: Ay.
>
>   (2.2.14–21)

Macbeth is panicking; Lady Macbeth is trying to calm him down. It's brilliant writing. Because it feels so real, it puts you in the situation. "Yes," you think, "this is how I'd behave—veering between hysteria and the instinct to survive."

Both *Winter's Tale* and *Macbeth* were directed by Greg Doran (who is now the RSC's Artistic Director). He is another of the great Shakespeareans who have taught me. As his partner in real life, I could be accused of prejudice, but fortunately my opinion is shared by others. Reviewing his 2008 production of *Hamlet* with David Tennant, the *Sunday Times* said, "There is no better director of Shakespeare around today." While the influence of the other great Shakespeareans like Ciss Berry and John Barton has been enormous, it's another thing to be actually married to one. (We took out a Civil Partnership in 2005.) Greg's knowledge of and love for Shakespeare is so profound that I believe it has changed my own relationship to the playwright. Greg has convinced me that I have as much right to be performing Shakespeare as any British-born actor, and that his work belongs to us all.

I've stopped worrying about the sound of my voice, even if the odd South African vowel slips out from time to time. And in fact, South Africa itself played a big part in the next two Shakespeares that I did.

In 2003 I was Iago in Greg's RSC production of *Othello*, with the South African actor Sello Maake Ka-Ncube in the title role. We'd worked with Sello before, when we did *Titus Andronicus* at Johannesburg's Market Theatre in 1995: he played Aaron, I played Titus, and Greg directed. That production was done in South African accents—I was an Afrikaner, others were Xhosa, Zulu, Cape Coloured, or poor white—so it created a new, different way of speaking Shakespeare. But now in *Othello*, except for Sello, who would play the Moor in his own African accent, the rest of the cast would be British, including me.

By this stage I had lived in Britain for thirty-five years,

much longer than my youth in South Africa. I was a British citizen, I was experienced at British life, and it was no longer an issue. So playing Iago as the Regimental Sergeant Major in a British base in Cyprus—our production was set in the 1950s—was entirely comfortable to me. Nevertheless, two aspects of my South African past turned out to be useful for the role. The first was that I'd been forced to do conscription in the army after leaving school, so I was well practiced at square-bashing.* The second was that I'd been brought up in the old South Africa, Apartheid South Africa, and knew about racism at its deepest level. In the play, Othello is Iago's senior officer; outwardly, Iago has to respect him, but that doesn't mean it comes from his heart. I remember in rehearsals one day, Sello and I discussed an image from Nelson Mandela's inauguration as president in 1994: he was surrounded by a guard of honour, made up of older, white military generals, the same men who might well have ordered his death just a few years earlier.

Shakespeare writes Iago's racism in that jokey-brutish tone which soldiers use—"an old black ram / Is tupping your white ewe" (1.1.92–93), he warns Desdemona's father. The same line also illustrates another of his personality traits: he can't open his mouth without sexual imagery spilling out. There's some big problem here, and in his marriage with Emilia. Impotence? Sterility? Greg and I decided not to put a name to it, but just to place it, as a ticking bomb, at the core of this very dangerous man.

And so on to playing Prospero in *The Tempest* in 2009, which felt like the moment when the different strands of my life came together. It was, as I said, a coproduction between the

---

* Editor's note: square-bashing is a military drill performed on a barracks square.

Sir Antony Sher as Prospero in the Royal Shakespeare Company/
Baxter Theatre Company production of The Tempest, *2009.*
Photograph by Tristram Kenton.

RSC and the Baxter Theatre, and was the brainchild of one of
South Africa's top directors, Janice Honeyman. Her concept
drove the whole enterprise: the magic in the play is difficult to
realize in modern Western society, but it's natural in an African
context where the spirit world of the ancestors lives alongside
the living, breathing population. So, in Janice's production, the

sequences of magic were conjured up by ritual, by music and dance, by masks and puppetry. The members of the company were all South African: the actors, who included the great John Kani as Caliban, and his son Atandwa Kani as Ariel, as well as the musicians and the stage management. The Baxter built the sets, made the costumes, and rehearsed and opened the show before its run in Stratford and a U.K. tour. RSC's part of the bargain was to supply a lot of the funding, as well as to send over their Head of Voice, Lyn Darnley (originally South African herself), to work with the actors, and also Greg, who is increasingly adopting John Barton's role of running Shakespeare master classes.

The sessions with Lyn and Greg were held on the upper floor of the Baxter building, in a big airy room which served as foyer to their studio theatre. And it was during one of these when I suddenly found myself rejoicing in the familiarity of it all. A place of learning, with hot sunlight streaming in—this was like my childhood, like schooldays, except that the lessons now being taught were about how best to speak and play Shakespeare. All around me were South African actors of varied ages and backgrounds, all excited and probably daunted by the task of performing one of Shakespeare's great plays. I was going through it with them, and I'd been through it many times before. I knew all the exercises and routines, all the dos and don'ts—I'd spent a career practicing them—and at last I felt at ease speaking Shakespeare.

Written towards the end of his life, Prospero is thought to be the most autobiographical of Shakespeare's roles. In the play he's a magician, in real life he was a playwright, and in two speeches—"Our revels now are ended" (4.1.161) and "Ye elves" (5.1.38)—he bids farewell to his art.

I'm aware of an irony here. Just as Shakespeare says good-bye, I'm feeling welcomed. Except now I'm running out of roles.

* * *

There is Lear, of course. Greg and I discuss it occasionally, quite casually. At this point in time it's no more than an intriguing notion. What will it be like if the Fool finally gets to play the King?

Camille Paglia

TEACHING SHAKESPEARE
TO ACTORS

CAMILLE PAGLIA is University Professor of Humanities and Media Studies at the University of the Arts in Philadelphia. Her books include *Sexual Personae: Art and Decadence from Nefertiti to Emily Dickinson*; *Sex, Art, and American Culture*; *Vamps and Tramps*; *Break, Blown, Burn*; and *Glittering Images: A Journey Through Art from Egypt to* Star Wars.

Who wrote Shakespeare's plays? An actor. No aristocrat, such as Sir Francis Bacon or the Earl of Oxford, could have produced these nearly forty plays, which show such intimate knowledge of the demands and dynamics of ensemble performance. When Shakespeare was active in London, theater was borderline disreputable, denounced from the pulpit by Puritan preachers. Because of issues of public hygiene and crowd control, municipal authorities eventually forced the theaters outside the city limits—to the South Bank of the Thames, where Shakespeare's company built the Globe Theatre. While aristocrats attended plays and even sponsored theater companies, they could never have inhabited and learned from that brash underworld, from its cramped, ramshackle back stages to the volatile streets and seedy inns and taverns. Shakespeare was a popular entertainer who knew how to work a crowd. His daring shifts in tone, juxtaposing comedy with tragedy; his deft weaving of a main plot with multiple subplots; his restless oscillation from talk to action to song and dance: this fast pace and variety-show format were the tricks of a veteran actor adept at seizing the attention of the chattering groundlings who milled around the jutting stage of open-air theaters.

My approach to teaching Shakespeare departs from the norm because most of my four decades as a classroom teacher have been spent at art schools—first Bennington College and then the Philadelphia College of Performing Arts, which became the University of the Arts after a merger with its neighbor, the Philadelphia College of Art. Many of my students have been theater majors, some already with a professional résumé. In the United States, Shakespeare is usually taught as a reading experience, but my Shakespeare course is closer to a practicum, even though students neither recite nor perform in it. I approach the plays from a production angle, with stress on the range of interpretive choices available to an actor in each speech or scene. More academically structured universities have often offered Shakespeare as a large lecture course breaking out into weekly seminars led by graduate students. Students would be generally expected to read a play a week, thus sampling a third of the Shakespeare canon over one semester. That forced-march syllabus may be useful for English majors, but it does not work for actors, who must engage with the text on a far more concrete level. In guiding actors through Shakespeare, the teacher operates like an auto mechanic, taking an engine apart and showing how it goes back together again. Each internal function and connection must be grasped tangibly, as a sensory datum and not just a mental construct. Thus five Shakespeare plays have proved to be more than enough in my course, and it is still a struggle to cover them adequately. My goal is to give the actors a portable system for engaging with any of the plays, should they have the good fortune to encounter them in their careers. After two opening lecture classes, where I survey the transition from the Middle Ages to the Renaissance in art, science, economics, and politics, I turn to sequential line-by-line analysis of the plays, which occupies the rest of the semester.

Though they may have read one or several Shakespeare plays in high school, most young American actors basically come to Shakespeare cold. He is an import, trailing arty clouds of glory. In Great Britain, in contrast, Shakespeare represents history and tradition, stretching a thousand years back to early medieval kings and warriors. Many of his characters, from Lear and Macbeth to Richard II and Henry V, step straight out of royal annals, though Shakespeare enlarged, invented, and reimagined at will. Despite ominous slippage these days through competition from mass media and video games, most British audiences know Shakespeare's plays well, having seen and performed in them at school and town events since childhood. Sophisticated theatergoers in Britain are finely attuned to every innovation, even the fleeting shading of a syllable. In the United States, no Shakespeare production, even on a college campus, can assume that more than a fraction of the audience is thoroughly familiar with the play or understands most of the dialogue. Hence the American actor has an immense responsibility for communication to the audience—a task hampered by the possibility that he or she may never have seen a live performance of Shakespeare. There are three major areas that deserve special attention from actors studying Shakespeare: language, action, and politics.

LANGUAGE

Confronted with students of widely varied academic backgrounds, a teacher must break through the sometimes paralyzing reverence that surrounds Shakespeare in the United States. His often archaic vocabulary, encrusted with editorial footnotes, can be intimidating, especially to young actors working out dialogue. Thus one must stress that Shakespeare was writing at the dawn of modern English, when the language was still in flux. He was making up words and usages as he went along, so successfully that many of them ended up in dictionaries, when those were first codified in the eighteenth century. What this suggests is that much of Shakespeare's audience too may have had only a dim idea of what was happening on stage. His actors conveyed thought and emotion through tone, rhythm, and gesture. It was a period that valued virtuoso shows of verbal facility for their own sake; characters in Shakespeare are sometimes seized by torrents of words so urgent and turbulent that the speaker seems possessed. Furthermore, Shakespeare often engineers lively and at times comic effects by bouncing plain, blunt Anglo-Saxon monosyllables off the fancy polysyllabic vocabulary, derived from Greek and Latin, that had been brought to Britain by the Norman conquest.

Some American directors, as reported by my students, make the actors annotate Shakespeare's blank verse, so that they know they are playing poetry. I am highly skeptical and even disapproving of this practice, except for actors who already have prior training in poetry or Latin, where meter is parsed. It may be profitable in England, where poetry has streamed in an unbroken line since Chaucer, but I fail to see how concern about the blank verse can do anything but disorient and unnerve American actors. The power of language in Shakespeare's plays resides more in variation than in regularity. There is a robust physicality and even muscularity in his speeches, which can be as jagged and syncopated as jazz. Indeed, I recommend that actors playing Shakespeare look to music for inspiration. Some of Shakespeare's voices are lilting, melodious, or flutelike; others are relentlessly hammering and percussive; still others are rough, insolent, and zigzagging, like a bebop saxophone. To avoid monotonously "reciting" lines, the actor could borrow musical techniques such as dynamics (soft/ loud) or modulations in tempo, including overt hesitations— following the way people in real life pause and grope for words. The actor must appear to be *thinking*, an impression aided by lively eye movements.

Where sensitivity to poetry is required, however, is for Shakespeare's all-pervasive imagery. As literary critics noted long ago, each Shakespeare play can be regarded as an extended poem with its own set of emblematic images, whose recurrence produces a chiming effect that works subliminally on the audience. Examples are the four elements of earth, air, water, and fire in *Antony and Cleopatra*; the master metaphor of the "garden" in *Hamlet*, with its attendant adjectives like "green" and "rank" (meaning rotten or malodorous); and the chillingly ubiquitous "nothing" in *King Lear*—a blank zero prefiguring the wasteland of modernist alienation. The production dramaturge should assist the actors in rehearsal in identifying these key words, which are sometimes the emotional or conceptual heart of a speech. They are always universals that transcend time and place. Although postmodernists myopically deny that universals exist, these basic terms of human experience animate all great art and give it global reach. Whenever a key word occurs in a given Shakespeare speech, the actor might consider subtly highlighting it, so that it hangs or floats over the audience, who through their own life record of pain and pleasure gain a moment of clarity and access into the play's deepest themes. It may be helpful for the dramaturge to present one or two of Shakespeare's Sonnets in workshop to demonstrate the evocative power of concise imagery. Best for this purpose is certainly Sonnet 73 ("That time of year thou mayst in me behold"), with its vivid metaphors of tree, sun, and fire.

In Shakespeare's plays, quality of language equals quality of character. There is a stable, centered simplicity and nobility to the speech of his admirable, ethical characters. For example, here are the faithful Cordelia's virtually first words in *King Lear*: "Love and be silent" (1.1.53). This economical aside, with its enduring spiritual resonance, comes as a refreshing contrast to the glib, sycophantish babble that we have just heard from her treacherous sisters, Goneril and Regan. Improvisational eloquence under conditions of high stress proves substance and courage, as in Mark Antony's passionate oration over the corpse of Julius Caesar in the mobbed Roman Forum or Othello's defense at a midnight Venetian war council of his secret marriage to the young Desdemona, a mesmerizing speech whose journey through fabulous memory defuses the menacing atmosphere.

Syntax (sentence structure) is a primary indicator of mental health or psychological coherence in Shakespeare. The actor must be alert to syntactical obstructions or fractures which signal confusion, anxiety, or imminent breakdown. Claudius's first speech in *Hamlet*, for example, is disrupted and contorted by guilt as he tries to refer to Gertrude, the wife he took from the brother he murdered: the subject, verb, and direct object of his sentence are cleft apart and strewn dismembered over seven lines. Hamlet's brooding first soliloquy also degenerates from philosophical heights to syntactical chaos as he is compulsively flooded with lurid pictures of his mother's allegedly bestial sex life. When the villainous Richard III wakes up from troubled dreams before the climactic battle at Bosworth Field, where he will be defeated and killed, his speech heaves and lurches into sputtering fragments, sharply contrasting with the calm, steady, resolute address to the troops delivered by his opponent, the Earl of Richmond and future Henry VII, founder of the House of Tudor that will produce Elizabeth I. But sometimes complicated or serpentine syntax in Shakespeare arises from public rather than private ills, as in Horatio's opaque review in tortured legalese of the festering dispute with Norway that threatens war with Denmark.

ACTION

Shakespeare's bursts of action, alternating with passages of reflection and character development, seem perfectly normal to modern audiences schooled on war movies and TV crime dramas. But for a prolonged period, Shakespeare's violence, along with his trafficking in shock and horror, damaged his reputation in France, where elite taste was formed by Racine's neoclassic tragedies in the seventeenth century. In ancient Greek tragedy, action was reported by messenger speeches but never shown, even when traumatic events, such as Jocasta's suicide and Oedipus's self-blinding, have just occurred in a bedchamber on the other side of the palace doors. A cool, contemplative, philosophical distance, embodied in choral commentaries, was considered essential. Brutal business in Shakespeare, such as Hamlet stabbing Polonius through a tapestry in the Queen's bedroom or the Duke of Cornwall stomping out the pinioned Gloucester's eyes in *King Lear*, struck French critics as crude and vulgar.

High-impact physical expressiveness is a crucial component of Shakespeare's aesthetic, a masculine choreography that was sometimes neglected in sedate and tony productions of the late nineteenth and early twentieth centuries. Standards changed for both actors and audiences with the arrival

of social realist theater in the 1930s; its raw, proletarian style
inspired the Actors Studio in New York and the "kitchen-sink"
school of postwar London. Today, action is so accepted and
expected that a required course in stage combat may be built
into the theater curriculum (as at the University of the Arts,
where women actors too must take it). Once identified with
stunt work, action has risen in prestige over the past forty years
because of the global influence of Asian martial arts movies.
Explosions of action in Shakespeare are sometimes spiritually
purgative, releasing the accumulated tensions of the play: this
cathartic effect can be seen in the finales of both *Hamlet* and
Macbeth, where the protagonists escape from their doubt and
fear through bravura swordplay, thus atoning for their errors
and defiantly recovering their heroic stature before death.

American actors have a natural facility for action, as was
observed with admiration by European audiences even during
the silent film era. In the United States, posture and deportment
are more relaxed, and sports have a higher cultural status than
they do in Great Britain, where most literati still profess disdain
for them. Thanks to their spontaneity and playfulness, American actors are also good at farce, buffoonery, and slapstick—
one reason for the huge popularity of pratfalling comedian
Jerry Lewis in reserved France. Where this may pose a minor
problem for Shakespeare productions is in drunk scenes, such
as that between Sir Toby Belch and Sir Andrew Aguecheek in
Twelfth Night or between Caliban and Stephano in *The Tempest*. Characters reeling around on stage elicit such delighted
and uproarious audience response (perhaps from relief at finding something recognizable amid Shakespeare's demanding
language) that American actors may be tempted to overdo the
clowning and selfishly play to the gallery.

Other aspects of Shakespeare's staging can be classified as

action, which governs the disposition of the body. Because the
Globe had no curtain, Shakespeare devised ingenious ways of
getting the actors on and off stage (more evidence that the plays
were not closet dramas composed in a nobleman's library). Dar-
ingly, he starts scenes and whole plays in the middle of conversations: two actors stroll onstage while talking in normal tones,
forcing the audience to hush itself in order to overhear. Shakespeare expects the audience to make rapid intuitive judgments
based on characters' manner and body language. For example,
Antony and Cleopatra opens with a Roman, Philo, disparaging
Antony as a sex-addled "fool" and the dark-skinned Cleopatra
as a lustful "gypsy" and whore (1.1.10–13). But this cynical view
is immediately contradicted by the movingly poetic endear-
ments exchanged by the two fond lovers as they arrive from the
opposite direction.

　　King Lear too opens with characters entering midconversa-
tion: the Earls of Gloucester and Kent are sharing worrisome
political rumors when the subject takes a personal and indiscreet
turn. Each production of *Lear* must decide how much, if any,
of this humiliating talk is heard by Gloucester's bastard son, the
embittered and soon malevolent Edmund. Some show of over-
familiar, leaning-in body language seems implied in Gloucester's lines, as he tastelessly boasts to Kent about the "good sport"
had with a nameless pretty wench at Edmund's accidental conception. Kent's discomfort at this coarse sniggering is blatant,
as he vainly tries to restore a dignified tone. Ideally, the audience should probably read the body language of Gloucester and
Kent exactly as Edmund is reading it: Gloucester's bumptious
insensitivity met by Kent's embarrassed unease. Before we have
even heard Edmund speak, therefore, we already have a clue
about the formation of his sociopathic character, hardened by

routine discrimination and abuse—a prime example of Shake-speare's prescient anticipation of modern social psychology.

Body language is similarly cued in the scene on the castle ramparts where Hamlet, trying to follow his father's ghost, is being physically held back by Horatio and Marcellus, who fear the ghost may be a demon. Presumably drawing his sword, Hamlet threatens to kill anyone who stands in his way. This agitated scene superbly demonstrates Shakespeare's great gift for staging. What the audience sees are two men rushing for-ward and then being thrown backward, beyond the sweeping circle made by Hamlet's sword as it is pulled from its scabbard. It is a visually stunning, nearly geometrical effect that could have been designed only by a man with many years of practical experience in live theater.

Another example of implicit body language is the scene where Ophelia, obeying her pompous father's command, returns Hamlet's gifts and love letters. The mere sight of her beauty rescues Hamlet from one of his most despairing solilo-quies, and he addresses her with tender respect and hope for forgiveness: "Nymph, in thy orisons / Be all my sins remem-bered" (3.1.95–96). No matter how many times one has read or seen the play, it is hard to resist a fantasy of Hamlet and Ophelia's reconciliation at this moment. But it is not to be: Ophelia dutifully plows ahead on her father's agenda, and Hamlet reacts with pain and anger: "No, no: I never gave you aught" (3.1.103). His change of mood is so extreme that some physical recoil is surely signaled, even perhaps an abrupt jump backward. At some point in this harrowingly escalating scene, where Hamlet correctly guesses that Ophelia has become a tool of her father and that he is being spied upon, the precious mementos probably fall to the floor between them, a symbol

of their shattered romance and a foreshadowing of Ophelia's
pitiful ruin.

POLITICS

The contemporary actor's search for motivation in a Shakespeare role is complicated by alien elements in the Renaissance
worldview. Politically, Shakespeare was not a populist or demo-
crat but a monarchist who believed that government was best
led by a wise, strong ruler. The crown is a near-mystical symbol in his plays, which feature sporadic suspicions of the fickle
mob. Freedom is the watchword of modern democracies, but
Shakespeare's guiding principle was order. Lingering in popular memory were the thirty years of civil war that England had
endured a century before. For both the Middle Ages and the
Renaissance, hierarchy or "degree" in the political realm mirrored the perfection of God's cosmic master plan. A king, it was
thought, ruled by divine right. Although Shakespeare himself
may have tended toward the agnostic, there is a trace of that
religious premise in his plays in the difficulties encountered
by usurping kings like Macbeth or Claudius in asserting and
maintaining authority. Kingship is conferred but also learned,
as when Prince Hal matures into Henry V by abandoning his
youthful hedonism and severing ties with the carousing Falstaff.

Nationalism, customarily portrayed today as a crucible
of war, imperialism, and xenophobia, is a positive value in
Shakespeare. Nation-states had emerged in the Middle Ages
as a consolidation of dukedoms, an administrative streamlin-
ing that, at its best, expanded trade, advanced knowledge, and
reduced provincialism. This progressive movement of history
is the major theme of *King Lear*, where Lear's foolish choice
to divide his kingdom (which he does not possess but holds
in trust) plunges it backward toward chaos and barbarism,

reducing the king himself to a nomad battered by the elements. Unless they know European history well, most American actors rarely notice the nationalistic motifs in Shakespeare. In *Lear*, for example, the invasion of Britain by France—even though it promises rescue by the forces of good (Cordelia is now the queen of France)—creates patriotic conflicts for a British audience that Americans will not feel. Similarly, even a small detail such as Hamlet's being dispatched to England to collect overdue tribute for Denmark would stir a flicker of atavistic indignation in British hearts. Nationalism resoundingly recurs in a different context at the finale of *Hamlet*, where the stage is scattered with royal corpses. The bracingly vigorous entrance of Fortinbras marks the occupation of Denmark by a foreign power. With the self-destruction of its ruling class, Denmark has lost its autonomy and become a subject state of Norway.

Hierarchy also structures family and gender relations in Shakespeare. Fathers were law-givers, and children were expected to obey. In *Romeo and Juliet*, Shakespeare's audience would have sided with Juliet's parents, who had the right to make marital decisions for a fourteen-year-old girl. The play's power resides precisely in Shakespeare's success in shifting the audience from its default position through the captivating lyricism of Romeo and Juliet's love. Because of our own reflex bias toward romantic free choice, it's important that a contemporary production not side so completely with the lovers as to warp the play: Juliet's hot-tempered father should not be portrayed as a pasteboard ogre, nor should the aristocratic Paris, his sound choice for Juliet, seem like a callow prig. In *The Tempest*, Prospero displays a sometimes disturbing control over his daughter Miranda and her suitor Ferdinand: he puts Miranda to sleep and freezes Ferdinand in place, like a statue. This problematic manipulation of consciousness is partially ameliorated by Prospero's status as a magician whose secret arts parallel Shakespeare's spellbinding power over an audience.

Shakespeare is repeatedly critical of rigid, uncomprehending fathers. One of the haunting mysteries of his plays is how often he deletes the mothers of his young heroines, who are left undefended against the errors of obtuse fathers. Miranda has thrived in her widowed father's watchful nurture, but Cordelia, Desdemona, and Ophelia suffer severely from the absence of a mother's sympathetic counsel and intervention. Ophelia, torn between her proper deference to her father and her love for Hamlet, tries to do the right thing and ends up destroying her own and Hamlet's lives. Shakespeare worsens Ophelia's plight by sending her brother off to university in Paris and oddly even denying her a female confidante, like Juliet's jovial nurse or Desdemona's worldly-wise maidservant, Emilia. This terrible isolation, compounded by her father's death at Hamlet's hands, intensifies the emotional pressure on Ophelia and makes comprehensible her descent into delusion and madness, which Shakespeare pointedly contrasts with Hamlet's passing episodic depressions. A contemporary actor playing Ophelia must strike a delicate balance in portraying her tragedy without excess sentimentality. She is not simply a frail flower or hapless victim of rank injustice. Her father, Polonius, is arrogant and at times stupid—ignoring her hurt and need for comforting and callously broadcasting her secrets as mere data to whisk to the king—but he is solidly within his rights to determine Ophelia's affairs and protect her chastity. Ophelia makes a considered ethical choice, a courageous decision to renounce the man she loves.

The divergence of cultural assumptions between the Renaissance and today is nowhere clearer than in regard to marriage, which is glorified in Shakespeare's plays as a symbol of spiritual harmony and social order. His comedies sometimes end in a stampede of mass marriages, blessed by heaven and destined for fertile procreation. Marriage in our own time has lost much of its uniqueness and high value, partly because women now have access to jobs outside the home and can support themselves. Weddings remain popular as theatrical extravaganzas, but marriage has shrunk to just another lifestyle option, and the divorce rate has soared. Shakespeare's generation of poets, including John Donne and Edmund Spenser, was instrumental in the valorization of marriage, which had once primarily been an economic contract negotiated between a father and a prospective son-in-law. Medieval love poetry was addressed to a mistress or a distant, unattainable idol, not a wife.

The strong tilt toward marriage in Shakespeare's plays creates interpretive problems for contemporary actors. In *As You Like It*, for example, the witty and boldly enterprising Rosalind, who spends most of the play disguised as a boy, instantly falls in love with Orlando, an amiable lunk who seems nowhere near her level. He is athletic and sweet but slightly slow, like Joey (played by Matt LeBlanc) on the long-running hit TV show *Friends*. Rosalind's infatuation with Orlando exemplifies Shakespeare's favorite theme of the quirky madness of love, but it must not seem as if she is adopting and schooling a large, goofy dog. Her ritual divestment of her male garb before her wedding restores the Renaissance gender code and magically generates an approving apparition of Hymen, the guardian spirit of marriage. Rosalind's inseparable friendship with her cousin Celia is one of the few places in Shakespeare's plays where any trace of homosexuality can arguably be detected. (Another is Antonio's quick attachment and unusual generosity to Sebastian in a subplot of *Twelfth Night*.) Although his celebrated contemporary Christopher Marlowe wrote openly about a gay king in

Edward II, Shakespeare's plays are overwhelmingly committed to heterosexual love. In his private life, Shakespeare was evidently split: his love Sonnets are directed to a forceful, dusky-skinned woman and a well-born, aimless, beautiful young man.

Shakespeare is very sensitive to the dignity of women. Sexually degrading remarks about women in his plays are automatically symptomatic of a twisted, corrupted character or of a temporary state of mental disease, as experienced by Hamlet and Lear in their darkest moments. Nevertheless, modern productions of *The Taming of the Shrew* must struggle with the issue of misogyny. The play has long been the focus of feminist ire, with only the dissident Germaine Greer, a Shakespeare scholar among her other public roles, willing to stoutly defend it. The bad-tempered and violent Kate the shrew (a sharp-toothed mole) cows her inept father and breathes fire at any man who crosses her. It is possible to interpret Kate's hostility as a frustrated product of her entrapment in a world lacking any outlet for women's talents and pent-up energies except marriage. Petruchio, who frankly admits his motive for marrying is mercenary (he's on the hunt for the fattest dowry), breaks down Kate's rebellious personality by treatment that today would be classified as spousal abuse—denying her food and sleep, letting her wallow in the mud, and generally humiliating her. The actress playing Kate is confronted at the finale with one of the thorniest challenges in the Shakespeare canon: a long public speech where she declares that women are "soft and weak" and must "serve, love and obey" their husbands (5.1.176–177). After the rollicking humor of the play, modern productions are reluctant to end on a sour note, so the speech is now performed as if it is overtly satirical—whether that is true to Shakespeare's original conception or not.

The dramatis personae of Shakespeare's plays are always a

mix of social classes. Because of Britain's still-entrenched class system, with its sometimes cash-poor but highly visible landed aristocracy, British actors have little trouble in playing Shakespeare's upper-class roles. In the United States, in contrast, status is conferred solely by wealth, celebrity, or transient political power. Furthermore, since the 1960s, American authority figures, from politicians, ministers, and bankers to parents and teachers, have gradually adopted a less formal, remote, and dictatorial style. Young people today will often startlingly say that one or both of their parents are their "best friends." Dress codes have also relaxed with the spread of sportswear, sneakers, and proletarian blue jeans, even marketed by a mandarin heiress, Gloria Vanderbilt. It is now hard to appreciate why John F. Kennedy caused a sensation by not wearing a hat at his presidential inauguration in 1961.

Because of these broad social changes, American actors coming to Shakespeare have few or no direct models of hierarchical authority and class assertion. The audience must clearly perceive the class differences among Shakespeare's characters. Working-class women, for example, would paradoxically take up more space on stage than their upper-class counterparts: their movements are physically freer and their clothing looser, because designed for labor. Upper-class posture is reserved and contained, as if housed in an invisible bubble. Actors with prior training in classical ballet, which descends from the elegant seventeenth-century court, or continental equitation (called English riding in the United States) have a distinct advantage here. Even among young British women actors winning parts these days in productions of Shakespeare, Jane Austen, or Oscar Wilde, there is an irksome trend for mannish arm-swinging, which originated among the new sportswomen of the 1920s who took up golf and tennis. Until World War I, respectable ladies kept their elbows close to their bodies and their hands clasped gracefully above the waist or otherwise occupied with their skirts or some object like a fine handkerchief—an accessory crucial to the plot of *Othello*. Nor did ladies flash their teeth or grin like Huckleberry Finn, another anachronism currently epidemic in period roles.

Manners are not superficial trivialities but the choreography of social class. Manners both define and limit character and must therefore be represented in the actor's process. Without attention to class distinctions and stratification, important plot elements in Shakespeare will be blurred or missed altogether. In *King Lear*, for example, it is a violation of propriety for Goneril, who is the duchess of Albany, to be confiding private matters about her father and sister to her steward, Oswald. In *Twelfth Night*, the countess Olivia is too flirtatious with the duke's page, Cesario (Viola in drag), just as her own steward, Malvolio, is later too presumptuously forward with her. On the other hand, Shakespeare presents as evidence of Prince Hamlet's refreshing lack of snobbery his gracious affability to the visiting troupe of players as well as his easy cordiality with the gravedigger at work in the churchyard. Precedence and rank are pivotal in the banquet scene where Lady Macbeth, trying to divert notice from her husband's hysteria at Banquo's bloody ghost (which only he can see), abruptly orders everyone to leave: "Stand not upon the order of your going, / But go at once" (3.4.137–138). The ugly lack of ceremony in this chaotic mass exit represents the breakdown of social cohesion in a Scotland ruled by a criminal.

Witty banter, the signature sound of the upper-class comedy of manners, comes easily to British actors, whose culture is oriented toward verbal panache, from Oxbridge debating societies to Question Time in the House of Commons, with its scathing sallies met by laughter and applause. American actors today are overexposed to snark, the dominant style in TV comedy. With its snidely ironic put-downs, snark lacks the arch, competitive rhythm, like that of fencing, which has always characterized the thrusts, parries, and repartee of great high comedy. For help with Shakespeare's witty dialogue, I recommend to my theater students such classic film comedies as *The Philadelphia Story*, *All About Eve*, and *The Importance of Being Earnest* (the 1952 version directed by Anthony Asquith), which show how epigrammatic lines can be crisply shaped, timed, and delivered. The Mid-Atlantic accent (midway between American and British) once heard among scions of prominent, affluent families such as Franklin D. Roosevelt and Katharine Hepburn, used to be taught to actors in theater school. It was perfect for high comedy but became too affected and artificial over time. However, Sigourney Weaver, playing an imperious Wall Street stockbroker in *Working Girl*, shows how that elite accent can be subtly modified for use by American actors playing upper-class roles.

* * *

Shakespeare's plays famously survive transfer into any locale and time period. They have been set, for example, in medieval Japan, Nazi Germany, a space colony, and a suburban high school. But this amazing flexibility does not necessarily give infinite latitude to high-concept directors. In *The Goodbye Girl*, Richard Dreyfuss hilariously plays an earnest young actor struggling with a narcissistic Off-Off-Broadway director who sees Richard III as a flaming queer. Radical experiments with Shakespeare make sense in Britain, where new angles on the fatiguingly familiar are welcomed. But in the United States, live professional productions of Shakespeare are so rare that, like it or not, they are thrust into an educational role. Actors of

Shakespeare are exponents and defenders of a high culture that is steadily disappearing.

Because of the dominance of the Method in theater training here, American actors seeking their own "truth" are sometimes impatient with the technical refinements in which British actors, with their gift for understatement, are so skilled. Rehearsal is central to the Method actor as a laboratory where the ensemble merges through self-exploration. American culture, from Puritan diaries and Walt Whitman to Jackson Pollock and Norman Mailer, has always excelled in autobiography. But which is more important—the actor or the play? Shakespeare's plays are a world patrimony ultimately belonging to the audience, who deserve to see them with their historical distance and strangeness respected. The actor as spiritual quester is an archetype of our time. But when it comes to Shakespeare, the actor's mission may require abandoning the self rather than finding it.

Sir Ben Kingsley

THE ARCHITECTURE OF IDEAS

SIR BEN KINGSLEY, CBE, joined the Royal Shakespeare Company in 1967 and has been recognized with the title of Honorary Associate Artist. He has performed in theatrical productions of *Macbeth*, *As You Like It*, *King Lear*, *Troilus and Cressida*, *Much Ado About Nothing*, *Richard III*, *Measure for Measure*, *The Tempest*, *A Midsummer Night's Dream*, *Antony and Cleopatra*, *The Merry Wives of Windsor*, *Hamlet*, *Cymbeline*, *Julius Caesar*, *Othello*, *The Merchant of Venice*, and the one-man play *Kean*, based on the Shakespearean actor Edmund Kean, as well as in films of *Antony and Cleopatra* and *Twelfth Night*. His work in such films as *Gandhi*, *Bugsy*, *Schindler's List*, *Sexy Beast*, *The House of Sand and Fog*, and *Hugo* has earned him many honors, including an Academy Award and three nominations, two Golden Globe Awards and seven nominations, three BAFTAs, a Screen Actors Guild Award and three nominations, two Emmy nominations, and a European Film Award. He is currently working on a film of Christopher Rush's novel on the life of Shakespeare, *Will*.

W hen Daniela, my wife, was offered Titania in *A Midsummer Night's Dream* last year, it was her first experience performing Shakespeare. I had been in the famous *Midsummer Night's Dream* of Peter Brook as Demetrius, and so we sat in our kitchen, right before I had to go to Morocco to film, and we worked through the role of Titania—and two things absolutely delighted me. The first was that my recall, my *joyful* recall, of the play was complete and instantaneous, and very detailed.

The second was that Daniela's grasp of the poetic rhythms of Titania's way of speaking was immediate, which could be something to do with her being Brazilian and with her speaking Brazilian Portuguese. Our appreciation of rhythm is an extremely important part of how we communicate artistically, musically, metaphorically, mythologically. Rhythm in speech, rhythm in written language, is crucial to the survival of an idea, and so in exploring her Titania—which turned out to be magnificent—I realized that I myself had really taken in that John Barton key to deciphering poetic drama and turning it into an event that an audience can be moved by. The way that had stuck to my rib cage was really gratifying because it has been a while since I've performed Shakespeare, and yet it was right there, hugely I'm sure thanks to Peter Brook, to that production of the *Dream*, and to Cicely Berry, the great voice coach whom I love dearly, as everyone does.

Now, the concern with the lineage—since John Barton, Cicely Berry, and Peter Brook are of the generation that preceded my generation, and are all in their eighties—is that the thread that joins Shakespeare to us, that was twined by them, braided by them, is going to snap. I recently asked my future daughter-in-law, Anna, who sometimes works with a Shakespeare company, if there is anyone who is going to pass on this baton of how to decipher this miraculous language. It's important that people not force-feed children with it at school badly, but that when children encounter it they actually slap their foreheads and realize, "Of course! It's my mum, it's my dad, it's my cousin, it's my life, it's the war, it's today." Which of course it is. To keep banging on about Shakespeare being relevant is a bit stupid, really, since of course it's relevant. It's us. It's the birth of the greatness of our language. Using my wife as an example of the generation of younger actors who have been denied John Bar-

ton and Cicely Berry, I know that it's possible for them to grasp
the essence of that acting in the same way. I needed Daniela
to continue this wonderful work on her Shakespeare for longer
than the run of *A Midsummer Night's Dream*, because she's got
it, and it mustn't elude her. And Anna did tell me, in all sincer-
ity, that the teachers in the tradition do exist. There are people
who completely comprehend and celebrate what Cicely is doing
and they are able to pass it on, which to me is a great relief.

Now, however, the arena in which it's being passed on is
shrinking. I came through the British repertory system, and
then the Royal Shakespeare Company, and for a period that
loosely spanned eight years I was part of a company in which we
were all listening to the same beautiful voices on stage decipher
this extraordinary text and make it fresh to the audience, so that
they were standing and cheering at the end, shouting, "Please
do it again! Please do it again!" My plea, therefore, would be for
schools to adopt or invite a group of travelling players. That was
how I started, actually. It was in what's called Theatre in Education, and I was with a group of players who travelled to schools
doing Shakespeare for children. We performed excerpts from
Shakespearean plays, because we were only a group of four so
we couldn't do the whole plays. Later on in my career, whilst I
was still associated strongly with the Royal Shakespeare Company and the National Theatre, I had an opportunity to tour
American campuses with a similar small group of actors. Then,
we were with much more mature students who were in their late
teens and early twenties, but the same gasps of recognition and
understanding of a passage in a play that they were labouring
over, and that seemed totally abstract, were beautiful to hear.
Students were exclaiming, "Oh my God, of course, *that's* what
it means." I get a rush of experience whenever I come across a
passage, especially a thorny passage which tends to lie dead on

the page, which suddenly springs to life in performance. These passages have to be acted to be understood, because there's so much irony in Shakespeare, and irony doesn't translate in print. And also, if teachers are unaware of irony in a line, they're not going to pass on the irony to their pupils; they're just going to struggle with the text as it is.

I think the issue is very serious. I think that we need to examine the education system in the Western world and stop hurtling desperately into an electronic future. If there's no money for education, if there's no money for a Shakespeare syllabus, then we're all wasting our time. We're all wasting our time if nobody says, "I'm going to fund a group of actors to go into classrooms, so that that's all they do"—because it's a wonderful first job for any group of actors. They're well schooled, they love their Shakespeare, and they go into the classroom and they throw a bomb into it. *Bang*. And they perform a scene from *Romeo and Juliet* and kids are thinking, "I didn't know about *that*." I've heard that in classrooms.

But all those wonderful gasps and revelations are not going to happen unless someone says, "Here are millions of dollars for you. Let's take the money from over there and put it here instead so that our children can learn to speak to each other and learn our language." Instead, we're shoving them into semi-illiteracy and it's brutally unfair. Our heritage as humans is our language and our expressive skills, and yet we think it doesn't matter. "Just give them an iPhone. It doesn't matter, it's all they're worth." No, it's not. Our children are worth more than that. And so I urge: funding, funding, *funding*.

*   *   *

Thinking back, I can recall no specific moment when I first discovered Shakespeare. There was no moment of epiphany.

Fortunately I got into a really good school, and so I think by osmosis I realized it was a cornerstone of my culture and my language, and so it rather effortlessly just became an accepted part of my landscape as a schoolboy. And I don't know what the moment was when I realized I wanted to be a part of it all on stage. When I was in my late teens, nineteen I think it was, I fainted halfway through *Richard III*. It was a very hot day and there were no seats for sale in the auditorium, so I paid to stand at the matinee performance. The heat was so overpowering that I collapsed, but then I revived and watched the rest of the play, standing at the back and sometimes walking along the back of the auditorium as Sir Ian McKellen walked across the stage, to keep a minimum distance between myself and him. The play is probably 98 or 99 percent verse, so the iambic pentameters are remorseless and they sweep you up from the moment of the first line to the end. The exquisite rhythm of that language and its mesmerizing effect has been diluted horribly, and I think now we just have noise the way it's usually performed. But they're still related. The noise is a sort of horrible offshoot of the original, which is poetic drama. After the play, I met all the actors and vowed that I would join their company, and they said encouragingly, "Good luck" and "I hope you do."

Two or three years later, I did join them. Trevor Nunn auditioned me, and I am eternally grateful for his accepting me and then guiding me and molding me and looking after me so that I became an associate artist of the company after a year, and then in a few years, a very few years, was playing Ariel in *The Tempest* and Demetrius in Peter Brook's *A Midsummer Night's Dream*. That then gave them the confidence to give me Hamlet, and to me that was the cornerstone and a huge event in my life.

I've now done seventeen of Shakespeare's thirty-seven or so plays, and the only similarity I find in the characters is that they're written by the same great writer. They're all aspects of the same extraordinary mind. Hamlet and Feste, for instance, are both products of this huge intelligence and yet are completely unlike each other, even though both play the fool and both share a certain detached wisdom. What we lack now, in our society, in our leadership, are people who are "No" men as opposed to "Yes" men. So many people who get elected into powerful positions are around people who say, "Of course you can," "Of course you must," "You're absolutely right," rather than the all-licensed fool who says, "What are you doing? You have a brain like an egg"—and won't be shot, or sacked, or dismissed. Unfortunately, Hamlet can't be his own fool, but in a sense he has to be. That's what damns him and blesses him: he has to try to be his own fool.

In terms of commenting on my own work, of telling more about how I played Feste and how I played Hamlet, I'm hopeless. The commentator can comment on my work, but I can't, just in the way that Hamlet can't be his own fool. I simply can't, since I've really no idea other than I have a deep appreciation of language and of gracefully communicating an idea, which is shrinking so fast in our culture it's shocking. How can you gracefully impart an idea to another? Graciously, tantalizingly, in such a way that it is intriguing and beautiful? The language is collapsing at an astonishing rate. Conversation and wit and riposte and debate were a pastime for people. They actually went to coffeehouses or inns or taverns or had dinner, and they never stopped talking. Even well after Shakespeare, there were huge, wonderful architectural ideas like those of Mozart or like those of the great architects themselves in the Reformation and Restoration. The architecture and the music were ascending and awkward and confident, and I'm sure their creators' conversations were like that too: they were capping one another. And now, I sometimes get screenplays sent to me where a sequence of dialogue can be "Fuck you!" "No, no, fuck you!" "No, fuck you!" "No, no, fuck *you*!" "Oh, great," I think. "How wonderful that we've evolved to that." But it's catastrophic, really, when in the space of that many lines Shakespeare could have given you a little kingdom of intellect and challenge. "To be, or not to be" now would be "What the fuck?" And that would be it.

During rehearsals of *Hamlet*, we played with colloquializations to get into the play and help it feel modern, and then one day a curious thing happened. Buzz Goodbody, a wonderful young woman who had terrific authority and massive affection for her cast, was directing, and Andre Van Gyseghem, a senior member of the cast then, was playing Polonius. We were focusing on the relationship with the generation that played the dysfunctional parents, Polonius and Claudius and Gertrude, all of them spying on their children, all of them power-mad, all of them serving very distorted causes. As we were rehearsing, we were seduced wrongly by the fact that we were playing in modern dress and therefore thought that we had to make it modern, which is ludicrous because Shakespeare is modern anyways. If you put it in modern dress, the language doesn't need to change. Why should it? But the occasional "um," "oh," and "you know" were slipping in, which was dreadful, in the same way that you don't put twiggy bits into Mozart. And then Buzz said, "Okay, *one* of you in the cast is rehearsing in a completely appropriate manner, and is serving the text," and we all realized, of course, that it was Andre, who was performing, rehearsing, and speaking at twice the rate of anyone else in the room, and we realized that speed is of the essence when you're reading Shakespeare, just as speed and rhythm and compressed energy are of the essence when you're performing Mozart. You don't pause. If you pause, you lose the audience. The audience are running to keep up. That's what they've paid for. That is their joy. *Hamlet* is not a four-hour anesthetic. It's a two-hour challenge to the brain. Having then as a group been given this opportunity, we started to listen and appreciate Andre in a very different way, and all of us then, overnight, dropped all of our additions and colloquialisms and insertions of "um" and "uh."

Then Buzz encouraged us to have speed runs, whereby we would do the whole play at a very dangerous rate. It was nerve-wracking. A speed run forces you to be essential, to find in your speed the essence of what you're trying to communicate, and to realize how emphatical, and how repetitively emphatic, Shakespeare can be, and how that emphasis finally gets through to a rather restless sprawling audience on many, many different levels. A lot of Shakespeare's audience were illiterate. Now the plays have become quartered into some kind of elitist literate exercise. It's stupid. The plays are there to entertain and dazzle people who have brains and love language. A lot of people, the groundlings, couldn't read or write, but it didn't matter. "Let us go and hear a play," they used to say. They didn't say "Let us go and see a play," although I'm sure the blood-and-gore action on stage was amazing and thrilling to watch.

My son Ferdinand understudied Rory Kinnear as Hamlet at the National Theatre in 2010. He played Rosencrantz in that production, and his Rosencrantz was exquisitely good. As a result of his role as understudy, I was able to watch my son's own Hamlet on stage, with Dani and his sister and his brother and various other family members and all the other family members and friends and agents of the understudy cast. It's a play I find very difficult to watch, but within a few seconds I realized that even though Ferdinand is ten years too young to play it, he's already got it.

To capture Hamlet is an extraordinary responsibility. But

as I said to my son, "Don't look up, because you'll feel it's insurmountable. Don't look down, because you'll fall. All you can do is go from one handhold to another, one foothold to another, and the rock face is all you can see." You have to apply that to playing Hamlet. You have to be in the moment. The responsibility itself is inextricably linked with Hamlet's own journey and second nature. Hamlet himself says to the audience, in effect, "Why am I given this responsibility? Oh cursed spite, that ever I was born to set it right. Why me?" So the crushing responsibility that Hamlet feels in setting a rotten dynasty right is so massive, one thinks, compared to the act or struggle of getting through the performance—but they're parallel.

I discovered this parallel in great writing, and then I really learned to exploit it and explore it. It served me well playing Gandhi, because my journey through Gandhi, my relationship with the Indian crowds, and my acceptance of what it was to play him was a wonderful exercise in putting the ego in the right place. It was a challenge just to get through the film and to play another of the most intelligent people in the world— although Hamlet is fictional he is one of the most intelligent people who ever didn't live, and Gandhi is possibly the most intelligent person who ever did live. He's up there with Shakespeare. And my efforts to be the most intelligent man in the world, between action and cut, was a microcosm of Gandhi's effort to liberate India. It's all connected. If you choose the role or the role is chosen for you, either way it's blessed, since the state of grace that the actor's in is that his own state completely complements the journey of the character. It's no surprise to me, having played Hamlet, that Hamlet is carried off the stage at the end of the play by his fellow actors. He's exhausted. They bear him to the stage. He's carried off. I was carried off the stage by my fellow actors every night, lifted and carried. It was a wonderful moment, because you are high and you're completely exhausted, but you've done it. "Bear Hamlet, like a soldier, to the stage" (5.2.350) is what Fortinbras commands, and it should be done, as it was in my production—he should be lifted and carried.

What elevates the human being above other creatures on earth is that we are by nature expressive. We have to express. And Shakespeare gave himself expression. The intelligence, the questing, the unstoppable intellect was given expression through his plays. And I suppose that my journey as an actor is also expressive. Whether or not I'm expressing anything of any importance is not up to me to say, but I do *feel* it profoundly as an actor, through my craft, as fully expressed when I choose the right role, with the right director—and that covers every experience I've ever had with good directors and good material.

Just as, at the height of my adrenaline rush performing Hamlet there was a feeling of extraordinary public privacy, so, between action and cut—as for instance when I portrayed Feste in Sir Trevor Nunn's film of *Twelfth Night*—am I at my most sublimely private, even though the camera is there. The cousin to the soliloquy now is the close-up. And in a close-up of me under Martin Scorsese's direction—I've had the privilege of being in two of his films—I am secure in the knowledge that I am at my most private, and that Martin is getting it. It's a lovely feeling, and so in the same way is my dependence on the audience's participation to get me through *Hamlet* by sharing with them, "Should I commit suicide or should I carry on? What should I do?" And it's an absolutely honest, earnest question to the audience, in the middle of the play, when the actor doesn't know whether he has the strength to finish the play or not. Every night, I came to that point and I thought, "Well, of course, *of course* it makes sense to ask these questions" because

I didn't know whether I could finish the play. I was exhausted already. During the third soliloquy I even left the play, and then had to decide to come back. After that, of course, the rest of the play provides its own amazing, escalating energy.

The magic of bringing these characters to life, either on stage or in film, isn't as imprecise as you might imagine. I think it's a question of technique. In terms of the acting craft, what I can offer is a metaphor for what I was and what I now am: that I was a landscape painter, and that now I'm a portrait artist. However, my portrayal on screen is utterly dependent on the director understanding how I am exploring and sharing the character, and therefore putting the camera in exactly the right place to be a conspirator in the process of sharing with the audience—and it's absolutely crucial because, I promise you, if the camera is in the wrong place I am wasting my time. The connection will be lost.

Since acting is so essentially expressive, it's about getting close to other human beings, real or imagined. It's about overcoming the distances between us, and it's about exploring our affective and intellectual potential. In our world, however, technology is taking over and getting in the way. The antidote is not just Shakespeare; it's each other. It's the joy of that landscape which we mustn't allow to shrink—and yet it seems to be shrinking with every generation. So I find that my biggest hope for the future is that we don't sacrifice human contact. There's no substitute for it, either in life or in art.

Cicely Berry

KING LEAR IN RETROSPECT

CICELY BERRY, OBE, CBE, is Director of Voice at the Royal Shakespeare Company and an international dialogue coach who has taught in schools and theaters as well as in prisons and in the barrios of São Paulo, Brazil. Her workshop, *Working Shakespeare*, is available as a DVD series; her books include *Voice and the Actor*, *Your Voice and How to Use It*, *The Actor and the Text*, *Text in Action*, and *From Word to Play: A Handbook for Directors*.

I was truly delighted when, in 1988, I had the opportunity to direct *King Lear*. Tony Hill was Head of Education at the Royal Shakespeare Company at the time and I was Head of Voice, and he asked me if I would like to direct a Shakespeare play which would be performed in The Other Place, and around which we could arrange a number of open workshops. These workshops would focus on Shakespeare's language and would be practical, with those attending participating in the work. I agreed—a little nervously.

The idea was twofold: first, to see what would happen when a play was directed beginning from an awareness of the language of the text; second, to then perform such a piece specifically with a school's audience in mind. The project spoke to two sides of my love of the work I do: exploring and developing the use of the voice in communicating Shakespearean poetic thought, and sharing Shakespeare with both acting professionals and young people. I had got to know Tony Hill in the early 1980s when the Company had started their annual winter visits to Newcastle, and where I led workshops for schools and youth centres. One of these was Backworth Youth Centre, which was run by Tony: we worked together well and became close friends. Later, when the Company started up its education programme, Tony was asked to head the department, which he did—and our work was able to develop accordingly. The *King Lear* project was an important test of this—and I think it worked.

Because I feel so strongly that we cannot understand Shakespeare fully until we inhabit the language in our bodies as well as our minds, I looked on this as a great opportunity to test my beliefs in a full production of the play. It was a way of testing out the strategies and exercises I had developed doing such workshops in schools, colleges, and youth centres in order to enrich students' understanding of the text, and thus their understanding of the character. I was then also working with professional actors at the RSC and elsewhere who had not done this work in rehearsal before: the production was very successful, and I felt it proved my point. The work was thereafter taken seriously as part of the rehearsal process.

The production was to be staged in the old Other Place. I say old, because it had been a tin shed which housed theatre costumes and which was converted into a studio theatre by Buzz Goodbody in 1974. With both her vision and her strong political beliefs, Buzz created a space for both modern and classical work, which would change the actor/audience relationship, and create an environment in which the audience could feel a part of the work itself—it was affectionately known as the "Tin Hut." In 1989 it was deemed unsafe and so was pulled down. The new TOP (The Other Place) building was unveiled in 1991, but in spite of its facilities and its elegance, it does not have quite the ambience of that original "other" place.

Looking back, I realize that my choice of *King Lear* was an ambitious one, to say the least; but my reason at the time for choosing it was that the language offered such wonderful possibilities not only for the actors to work on and discover, but also to share with those coming to the workshops. I wanted to approach the play by speaking it first, and listening to the movement and texture of the language, before coming to conclusions about character, place, and relationships. I wanted them to hear where the language takes us.

Because this was primarily an education project, I needed, of course, to use actors who were working in the Company at the time, and this had to be on a voluntary basis. I was therefore very lucky in that the actors who volunteered for the work suited it perfectly. Richard Haddon Haines, a tremendous South African actor, seemed to be absolutely right for the part of Lear.

Having decided on the play, my next thought was to ring Edward Bond to find out his vision of the play. I believe that every play has a centre image, an idea, a feeling, around which the play revolves, and of course Edward came up with his unique vision; he said something like this: "It is a play where people are getting on and off trains with a lot of luggage." And that became my centre image.

At the same time as I was getting the cast together I approached the designer Chris Dyer, who had worked with the Company a good deal—including designing Buzz Goodbody's *Hamlet* at TOP—to see if he would be both free and willing to take on the job. Luckily for me he agreed. I knew he would be interested in working as simply as possible, and the result was brilliant—or perhaps I should say earthshaking, as we shall see.

Our rehearsal time was unbelievably short: the press night of *The Tempest*, which most of my cast were in, was delayed two weeks, and this badly cut into our rehearsal period, for very little work could be done during *The Tempest* understudy period as two of my main characters, Lear and the Fool, were understudying Prospero and Ariel, so it was hard for them; plus it limited the time at our disposal. But these difficulties were seen by the group as a challenge, and they responded to it with great enthusiasm.

I think *King Lear* is probably the greatest play ever written; I am sure I am not alone in this. But to me it is also a great Marxist play, for I do not believe it is a play about Lear getting old and losing his wits—that makes it sentimental. I believe Lear goes on a journey from first being ruler of a kingdom, then being rejected by his daughters, through madness on the heath, to finally realizing that he is but a man—like any other—and that he has not fulfilled his duty as a man.

Here are four key speeches which illustrate this. First, his opening speech as the King in Act 1, Scene 1:

Meantime we shall express our darker purpose.
Give me the map there.
(*Kent or an Attendant gives Lear a map*)
                              Know that we have divided
In three our kingdom, and 'tis our fast intent
To shake all cares and business from our age,
Conferring them on younger strengths while we
Unburdened crawl toward death.

(1.1.27–32)

Next, in Act 2, Scene 2, after Goneril and Regan have both disempowered him by denying him his followers, he knows he must take action in order to find himself again:

I will do such things—
What they are yet I know not, but they shall be
The terrors of the earth! You think I'll weep:
No, I'll not weep: I have full cause of weeping,
(*Storm and tempest*)
But this heart shall break into a hundred thousand flaws,
Or ere I'll weep. O fool, I shall go mad!

                                        (2.2.469–474)

Thirdly, on the heath with Kent and the Fool in Act 3, Scene 4, as he experiences the full force of the storm, he sends the Fool into the hovel:

In, boy, go first.—
                        You houseless poverty—
Nay, get thee in.— I'll pray, and then I'll sleep.
(*Exit the Fool*)
Poor naked wretches, whereso'er you are,
That bide the pelting of this pitiless storm,
How shall your houseless heads and unfed sides,
Your lopped and windowed raggedness, defend you
From seasons such as these? O, I have ta'en
Too little care of this! Take physic, pomp,
Expose thyself to feel what wretches feel,
That thou mayst shake the superflux to them
And show the heavens more just.

                                        (3.4.29–39)

Here, the realization of what poverty really means, and his own failure in attending to it, becomes apparent to him.

Lastly, a little later in the scene, after Edgar has entered disguised as Poor Tom, Lear says to him:

Is man no more than this? Consider him well. Thou ow'st the worm no silk, the beast no hide, the sheep no wool, the cat no perfume. Ha? Here's three on's are sophisticated. Thou art the thing itself: unaccommodated man is no more but such a poor bare, forked animal as thou art. Off, off, you lendings! Come, unbutton here. (*Tears off his clothes*)

(3.4.86–90)

And so he embraces his own nakedness, his own situation of having nothing.

There are two other lines which always remain with me: Lear's

Is there any cause in nature that makes these hard hearts?

(3.6.31–32)

and Edgar's

The worst is not
So long as we can say "This is the worst."

(4.1.31–32)

But the centre line of the play for me has to be Gloucester's words

So distribution should undo excess,
And each man have enough.

(4.1.72–73)

So how to make this huge play work in a small studio space, with limited resources and a very limited rehearsal time: that was my journey. We had to create the world through the language. I am just going to set out two instances of the work we did.

The first was this: at the end of the second week, after we had worked on each scene, and although the actors did not know their lines completely, I asked them to run the play through to clarify their own story line, and to work out their particular characters' journeys. But I asked them to do it in a very special way: with the help of our resourceful Stage Management, each actor had a lot of luggage, cases and boxes, etc., and I asked them to work through the play in the order of their own scenes. If scenes in the play were played simultaneously in time, then they were played simultaneously in the space, but at no time could they leave the building—they had to keep on the move carrying their luggage round the space. As you will obviously gather, this strategy was inspired by Edward Bond's words. At the same time I gave each actor a simple task to do at some time during the run: for instance, I asked the Fool to tell at least two jokes out to the audience while running the play.

The result was chaotic, but in a very positive way, for with it came a great sense of the urgency of the play. King Lear was thrown off centre stage, and scenes kept erupting all over the place. At one point Cordelia, played in Stratford by Maureen Beattie, drove off in her Fiat with the King of France, and when she returned she sent letters to Kent via the Stage Manager. This may seem absurd, but it most definitely made her aware of her distance from Lear and her need to make contact with him. I also wanted us all to get a sense of the land and the spaces they had to travel between castles, and also of the nameless inhabitants of that land. The actors became totally immersed in their own story through the play, and we were made aware of the

extraordinary dynamic of that journey and of the distance travelled. That awareness stayed with them throughout rehearsal.

Perhaps the key work was done on the storm, which evolved
through the whole rehearsal period. It started like this: as Lear
began his speech to the storm

Blow winds and crack your cheeks! Rage, blow . . .

(3.2.1)

the actors would surround him and throw the words back at
him. But as we got further into rehearsal it got rougher, for, as
well as bombarding him with words, perhaps sentences from
their own characters, they would also throw light objects at him
to represent twigs and leaves, etc., so that the story was palpable
to Lear, both by the noise around him, and by the words in his
own head. It became a storm both inside and outside himself.

Tim Oliver, who was our Sound Designer, recorded all
this: sometimes the words were whispered, sometimes shouted,
and he remembers that at one point when he was recording,
an actor sneezed, and this became the noise which accompanied the blinding of Gloucester. The recorded sounds were distorted, either by slowing them down or speeding them up. Tim
was extremely imaginative in the way he worked all this, and in
the subliminal way it was used throughout the play: he was also
able to give a "sound" presence to the hundred knights.

Now, for the design, Chris Dyer wrote at the time:

The design "idea" came after the main staging had been
decided on. What should the map be? Why not draw
it on the floor? Seems a good idea and a rough drawing was done. It then became obvious that what should

happen is for the pieces of the map to break and fall
apart, creating different layers and planes.

And that is exactly what happened. The cement stage floor broke
into three pieces, and it was quite literally an earth-shifting
moment, for it took us right into the world of the heath: it also
spoke vividly of the divided nation and the broken world of
Lear's mind. No image could have expressed this more potently.

Now to say something about Richard Haddon Haines: he
entered into the work in a most remarkable way. At the beginning he gave out a character with a great zest for life, who
bonded strongly with his knights: it was indeed a very masculine world, something which I think is interesting in terms of
his relationship with his daughters. His relationship with the
Fool, played by Patrick Miller, was particularly real and tender.
Throughout the play we felt his inner strength: he was never
made to feel comfortable, and was always fighting something
off in the storm, but he responded always in a very positive way.
It was particularly good because we were never conscious of
him playing an old man, rather someone who loved life, albeit
not in the prime of his life: and when it came to the storm, even
in his madness, he fought it. With his final reunion with Cordelia, it was never sentimental, but rather a very positive moment.

I learnt so much from this experience: the actors were all
totally responsive to the work, which was after all very different
from the usual rehearsal process, and because it was initially an
education project, the pressure was taken off them regarding
being ready for performance—though when the time did come
we were indeed ready. Also because nothing specific regarding
design or sound had been decided on before the Company got
together, it was an exceptionally creative experience collectively.

I also had strong support from Katie Mitchell, who was then one of the assistant directors in the Company, and who volunteered to work on the project. Katie threw in a lot of ideas and was very supportive to the whole work. Likewise I had support from Lesley Hutchison, the RSC's Movement teacher at the time, who worked alongside and who contributed a great deal to the end result.

It was a great journey for me, to bring this huge play into existence—and I think I can say successfully so, for it went on to play at the Almeida Theatre in London, with some change of cast. And here it was nominated for the Evening Standard Award for Best Director—alongside William Gaskill, Sir Peter Hall, Garry Hynes, Declan Donnellan, Adrian Noble, and Trevor Nunn. (In the end it was Nick Hytner who was preferred. But at least there was a nomination.)

The following pieces are taken from reviews that we had during the run at the Almeida Theatre. I am adding them, I stress, not out of vanity, but in order to underline the point that the language of a play can be as active and exciting as the movement or the set. It is up to theatre to excite people with language, to make them want to talk and exchange ideas: that surely is our mission.

> *The clarity of the whole production ensures that the words, simply spoken, explode like words in a combustion chamber.*   —John Peter

> *The major point to be made is that this production brings a great play alive with such immediacy that one feels nothing intervening between oneself and Shakespeare.*   —Charles Osborne

Richard Haddon Haines plays Lear as a vigorously genial aristocrat who responds to his early grievances by erupting into paroxysms of ineffectual wrath. The last of these outbursts coincides with the storm, after which he reverts to down-to-earth speech, as though the storm had been only a fantasy. Throughout the show, abrupt descents from sustained tone to conversational expression set the words on fire. And when Haines and Amanda Root's Cordelia link arms and set off for prison swapping cheerful matter-of-fact talk, the spectator supplies the tears.
—Irving Wardle

And Patrick Miller's Fool, with clownish white make-up superimposed on his black features, brings out not only the character's astringency but also his overwhelming pity. It is a stirring evening that proves several things: that great plays currently work best in small spaces, that truth to Shakespeare involves capturing precisely his antithetical mixture of harshness and hope and that understanding what you are saying is the key that unlocks Shakespearean word-music. "Was this well spoken?" enquires Lear. Indeed it was.
—Michael Billington

One last word: to everyone's great sorrow, Richard Haddon Haines died in 1990. I will always remember him for his truthful and haunting portrayal of King Lear.

Tobias Menzies

METHOD AND MADNESS

TOBIAS MENZIES is an English actor who has been in a number of modern and classical stage productions with theaters including the Royal National, the Young Vic, and the Donmar Warehouse. His stage performances range from *The History Boys*, *The Cherry Orchard*, *The Three Sisters*, *Arcadia*, and *The Recruiting Officer* to *Hamlet* and *King Lear*. His film credits feature *Casino Royale*, *Atonement*, *Anton Chekhov's The Duel*, *Persuasion*, and *Forget Me Not*, and his television credits include *Foyle's War*, *Midsomer Murders*, *Casualty*, *Rome*, *Eternal Law*, *Spooks*, and *Game of Thrones*.

My first professional production of Shakespeare was playing Hamlet, directed by Rupert Goold. I was quite young to be doing it, as I was thirty-one, and you rarely get the chance to play it around the age Hamlet is said to be. I look back with some compassion on that production. I think there was a roughness and a rawness that was great about it. It was imperfect, and I think I'd do it differently now. The Hamlets I've admired haven't been overly cerebral: they've all been very moving, and I think probably the best I've seen is that of Mark Rylance. When you're seeing someone explore what it is to be a human being as intensely as Hamlet does, then if it's done properly it can be incredibly affecting. They're so universal, those questions. "Who am I?" "What does it mean to be alive?"

"What is our purpose while we're here?" It's amazing for us to hear these questions asked, since they cut to the very heart of the human condition.

When you do a part like Hamlet, it comes with all the baggage and history of who's played it and what people have done with it, and that does haunt you—during rehearsal, at one in the morning, you begin to ask, "What am I doing?" and "Why am I even thinking I can take this on? Is it just sheer arrogance?" You have all those questioning thoughts (which is obviously quite Hamletian in itself). In performance there isn't much time to feel overwhelmed, but of course you feel fear. I remember, just before each show, feeling sick to my stomach at the prospect of doing that night's show, but of course you come to learn a lot about yourself at times like those. It's incredibly informative to pit yourself against such demanding material. Whatever comes out of it, if you're doing Hamlet then you will develop not just as an actor, but as a human being also.

One of the main reasons you do these plays when you get the opportunity is that you want to challenge yourself. There's probably an element of vanity about it too. And they're wonderful plays: there aren't that many texts where you get a chance to play that level of complexity, with such a large story journey, and to genuinely talk to an audience. In those soliloquies, in *Hamlet* for example, you get a chance to really commune with a group of people in a room and take them through a set of ideas. I've always found it incredibly exciting because the focus of that is so simple, and yet demanding: to piece a thought together, to take them through it, to make them feel and think and understand what you're wrestling with. It's also the challenge of bringing that language alive even though it's hundreds of years old, of making it seem that it's perfectly natural that it's being said now, of making it feel immediate and modern. And since it's so exciting when you feel all of that come alive in a room, you can't help but want more.

I worked with Rupert again as Edgar in his production of *King Lear*, which starred the late Pete Postlethwaite. It was certainly a type of production that's more in fashion in Germany, for instance, than it is in England. One of the most thrilling productions of *Hamlet* I've seen in recent years was a German production that came over from the Schaubühne in Berlin. While doing the play, they were also playing with the fact that there was an audience there, using us to illuminate the play, which is a play that is so much about what is true and what is not. There were moments which were completely naturalist—obeying the dramatic unities, if you like—but then they would flip that and comment on the fact that we were all in a theatre, participating in this make-believe. It felt incredibly modern. Seeing that, I thought that I'm not sure that we've quite got to that point of playfulness with Shakespeare in England. Maybe it's because it's our own language, and maybe because in German it's in translation and so they feel they have more license. The play felt dangerous. It was anarchic. You weren't quite sure what was going to happen next, and I think that in our production of *Lear*, Rupert was pushing at that door.

I think a potential pitfall of working on Shakespeare, certainly in our country, where he's our premier poet, is that one is too reverential. That attitude can affect the playing of it, and when I've watched Shakespeare I've always responded to something a little more visceral, a little more instinctual. When these industries grow up around Shakespeare they can entomb it in some way, and I'm not sure that it's helpful; for example, the academia that has built up around Shakespeare studies. That's not to deny that some of it is very interesting, but I think that if you're too slavish with the scholarship, it can get in the way when you're trying to perform Shakespeare, trying to bring it alive for our times. Sometimes you read notes on a play that make a statement on a character, but as an actor you know that whether or not the character is like that depends on how you say those lines. Shakespeare has been so enduring because he can be interpreted in so many different ways. You never tire of seeing *Hamlet*, for instance, because in a way each *Hamlet* is different depending on what each person brings to it, the different strands he draws out.

In *Lear*, for example, when Edgar is accused of intending to kill Gloucester, he flees the court and finds himself alone on the heath. He decides to pretend to be mad, and to become Poor Tom—and there are many ways of interpreting that decision. I felt that this choice was an instinctual, almost animal decision, not an intellectual one; that it would be through his body and through the physical reality of debasing himself that he would arrive at some sort of release, some sort of understanding. When Edgar heads onto the heath, it's an exploration of the wild, of the human being as creature: in the middle of that great storm, all the normal, civilizing accoutrements don't help you. For one of my physical models, I looked at a young Iggy Pop. I wanted Poor Tom to have that anarchic punkiness, to explore that wildness. One of the main challenges of playing Edgar was the very physicality of it. I was in the pouring rain every night, and I was cold, and got ill. So it was also about keeping fit, keeping healthy, not getting sick. There's a difference between theorizing about a play, and actually performing it.

I've played Hamlet and Edgar, both characters that assume madness and then, as a result of their experiments with madness, learn about themselves and those around them. The idea of madness meant different things in Shakespeare's time than it does in our own, for it had an existential dimension.

I explored these larger ideas of madness through wildness. That's how I accessed Edgar: through the expression of the wild, of freedom, of becoming a creature as Edgar debases himself to that animal place—a person who could say and do anything, a less medicalised, more existential idea of what it is to be mad.

One of the hardest movements in Edgar's journey is that first decision to turn himself into Poor Tom:

> Whiles I may scape,
> I will preserve myself, and am bethought
> To take the basest and most poorest shape
> That ever penury in contempt of man
> Brought near to beast: my face I'll grime with filth,
> Blanket my loins, elf all my hairs in knots,
> And with presented nakedness outface
> The winds and persecutions of the sky.
> ... Poor Turlygod, poor Tom!
> That's something yet: Edgar I nothing am.
> (2.2.161–168; 176–177)

It's a difficult pivot. It happens so quickly, and it's such a bizarre thing to do. Having seen it played a number of times before I did it, I had always disliked and struggled with Edgar being too wimpy. Poor Tom is usually portrayed as this weak, pitiful creature, and he is all those things—"Poor Tom's a-cold," he repeats again and again, stripped down to nothing and covered with mud. But he's not just that. What is his attitude toward it? I felt, in a paradoxical way, that to debase himself like that is an aggressive thing to do. It's kind of like saying, "You see what you've done?" It is a weirdly backward way of punishing the people who have done it to you. It's to outwardly demonstrate the fear and the anger and the hurt, and it's not a passive or feeble thing to do. It's actually violent.

The trope of madness allows Shakespeare to explore so much, in both *Lear* and *Hamlet*. When Hamlet "goes mad," suddenly the possibilities of what he can think and feel and talk about really widen. With Lear, the meeting between Poor Tom and Lear is pivotal to Lear's journey. "First let me talk with this philosopher" (3.4.128), he says, and then tears off all his clothes in imitation. You could argue that the meeting of Poor Tom on the heath is the moment Lear goes mad.

I had a similar approach toward the madness of both Hamlet and Edgar, which was that it was adopted, and they then slide into it further than they realize; it takes them over. For example, when Edgar comes up against real madness in King Lear, he recognizes it as the real thing. "My tears begin to take his part so much / They mar my counterfeiting" (3.6.16–17), he says in an aside. But they do lose their moorings, both Hamlet and Edgar. And I think it's partly because madness is seductive, it's liberating, and it releases you from the normal constraints.

In terms of ambition and power, I think both Edgar and Hamlet are naïve. They don't particularly care about either. Edmund sees the picture much more clearly than Edgar does. He's much more worldly. In *Hamlet*, Claudius is the politician, not Hamlet. What's beautiful in both Edgar and Hamlet is that there's an innocence about them. When Hamlet comes back after he's been exiled to England, he longs for death, like a lover. He goes to it lightly. It's almost spiritual, to have gotten to a place where the body is superfluous. I played it that Hamlet senses that his death is near when the fencing is proposed.

By contrast, at the end of *Lear*, Edgar is left behind, on the blasted heath, if you will. No bright light is being extinguished at the end of *Lear*, whereas a radiant light is being extinguished at the end of *Hamlet*. Hamlet is like a star, burning out. The texture of the tragedy at the end of *Lear* is very different from that at the end of *Hamlet*: there is nothing elegiac or redemptive about the end of *Lear*.

I wouldn't be at all surprised if Shakespeare was a real magpie in terms of stealing from personalities he knew in his life. Obviously he was a person who moved through different strata of society. Like a real Renaissance man, he seems to have had a handle on life from the tavern to the court and everything in between. For example, Polonius, in *Hamlet*, is a fantastic realization of a bumptious old man, and even if Shakespeare wasn't that himself, he certainly knew who that sort of person was and must have spent time around that sort of person to come up with such a loving portrayal. It's almost like he's looking through that set of eyes, and that's true of so many of his characters.

The idea of seeing as another sees, or trying to see where another can no longer see, is central to *Lear*. When Edgar meets his father, Gloucester, on the heath he responds in a very esoteric way. His father has been blinded, and he wants to die. Edgar then creates an imaginative and psychological journey for his father in which he will pass through death, in which he will believe that he has thrown himself from a cliff and that he has survived. Through that, Edgar hopes to lead his father to a more benign acceptance of his fate. It's incredibly strange. When we were doing it, Rupert was interested in sucking all the sentimentality from that scene, to have Edgar set up an existential laboratory in which he says, "I'm going to lead my father through this set of experiences, and see how he responds." Edgar is trying to lead his father out of despair, but rather than using kindness he uses a rigorous existentialism. Edgar does not comfort his father; he does not say, "Dad, don't worry, I'm here. I'm your son. Everything's going to be fine." Instead he says, "You want to die, and rightly so. Terrible things have happened to you." The proposition is that the only real cure is to actually look at what it is to die, and so Edgar creates this existential experiment.

Just before Edgar meets his father, he mocks the heavens:

> Welcome, then,
> Thou unsubstantial air that I embrace!
> The wretch that thou hast blown unto the worst
> Owes nothing to thy blasts.
>
> (4.1.6–9)

This is a brazen statement of self-realisation against the fates. And then he meets his blinded father, and he has that incredible line, "the worst is not / So long as we can say 'This is the worst'" (4.1.31–32).

What I get from that moment is that he realizes that you have to go through life: you never escape it. You have to go through experience: you can't go around it. In *Peer Gynt*, a voice cries, "Go roundabout, Peer!" and he responds, "No, through!" There's no getting out of pain and suffering. That idea goes to the very heart of Shakespeare's play. There's something in it that's quasi-religious, in a way. "Thy life's a miracle" (4.5.65), says Edgar. To live is to endure, to suffer, and at the same time it's also a blessing. You suffer, and you have to go through to the end of your suffering before you can turn the corner, or before you can shuffle off this mortal coil. As Edgar says, "Men must endure / Their going hence, even as their coming hither: / Ripeness is all" (5.2.10–12).

Rory Kinnear

CHARACTER AND CONUNDRUM

RORY KINNEAR has worked with the Royal Shakespeare Company and the Royal National Theatre. His performance in the Restoration comedy *The Man of Mode* was recognized with a Laurence Olivier Award and an Ian Charleson Award. He has been in *The Tempest*, *The Taming of the Shrew*, *Cymbeline*, two *Hamlet* productions, *Measure for Measure*, and the BBC adaptation of *Richard II*; he will shortly be appearing in *Othello* at the National. His film work includes *Quantum of Solace*, *Skyfall*, and *Mansfield Park*.

W hen I was very little I didn't want to be an actor. I wanted to be a butcher. Or a goalkeeper. Early in my adolescent years I took the risk of appearing as Sir Epicure Mammon in *The Alchemist* and Pandarus in *Troilus and Cressida* and then, finding to my young astonishment that I was getting attention and some praise for my performances, I began to think that acting might be a better fit. My father had been an actor, but he had died when I was ten, and so in lots of ways I had to discover it all for myself.

One of the things that I discovered, and which became clear especially when I was at university and working on Buckingham in *Richard III* and Petruchio in *The Taming of the Shrew*, was that what I got most excited by was the rehearsal process. It seemed to require identifying the particular conundrums that a play and character threw up, the various forks in the road

ahead, examining them thoroughly, and then making a decision. There wasn't necessarily a right decision—especially, as I
discovered to my delight, with Shakespeare—but there had to
be *a* decision. I tend to approach parts initially just by thinking
about them, and then afterwards I try to figure out what works
well in the doing—they're two different disciplines really, for
me—and then I try to marry them up to get a wholly successful and coherent performance, which then needs to fit in with
the design, direction, other actors, and all the other aspects of a
production which must combine so that everything is working
together and everyone is trying to tell the same story.

One of my first professional jobs was as Caliban in *The
Tempest*. I then worked at the RSC for a season, as Tranio in
The Taming of the Shrew and Caius Lucius in *Cymbeline*, and
then I did Laertes at the Old Vic in 2004 with Ben Whishaw in
the role of Hamlet. There followed a Shakespeare-less break of
six or seven years before I did Angelo in *Measure for Measure* at
the Almeida in 2010.

I had no idea how I was going to play that part—largely, I
guess, because I had a preconceived idea of what Angelo should
be like—and I didn't know if I could do it. Lucio says:

> Some report a sea-maid spawned him. Some, that he
> was begot between two stock-fishes. But it is certain
> that when he makes water his urine is congealed ice . . .
> (3.1.330–332)

Examining the text, however, I realized that Lucio doesn't actually know Angelo, and that he's just judging him from the new
laws he's introduced: harsh edicts against any premarital or
extraconjugal sex. There's actually a sense that no one knows
Angelo, and I thought that it would be more interesting, instead

of making him coolly self-important, or inherently demonic, to give him a genuine belief that the best thing for the society was abstinence. He reminded me of that kid we all know in school who is rather more geeky than threatening, and who, if he were ever put in a position of power, would be paddling furiously under the water. Angelo has presumably been chosen by the Duke because the city seems to have gotten out of control and the Duke believes that, since he is reputed "a man of stricture and firm abstinence" (1.4.13), Angelo is the best man for the job—but Angelo himself, I imagined, might well be absolutely unprepared. At the end of the first scene, Angelo having been installed as the Duke's temporary replacement, Escalus calls him "your honour" (1.1.89). The way we did it was to have me shush him, as if to say "Don't be silly," and then, almost instantly, realize what a shift in his life had just occurred—that everybody was going to be treating him with that sort of respect from then on. Shakespeare wrote his characters precisely, and yet there is room for each actor to find his own Angelo, and also—as I was then to discover—his own Hamlet and his own Bolingbroke too.

* * *

I had the opportunity to revisit *Hamlet* in the title role a little later that year at the National Theatre. Even before playing Laertes I had already been quite familiar with the play, having encountered it at school and having taken the opportunity to write on it during my English degree. Acting, though, requires a different skill set than academia. It was refreshing to be free from considering the various themes and refractions of those themes within the play. Rather, you just think about how a certain character reacts to a certain set of situations, and then focus on what that character says at any particular time. Shakespeare gives his actors quite a lot of open-endedness within which to work: you're not often given much backstory, and you're certainly never guided by him to any particular decision. You have to make your own. Consequently, there's a lot of thrashing about involved in figuring out how to create a character with a full life, including relationships that have already been formed and those parts of his life which have already been lived—and then connect that full life, largely of your creation, with Shakespeare's creation, the character's lines.

What surprised me most with *Hamlet* was that, having gone through that rehearsal process, it wasn't until the first time I performed it in front of an audience that I realized that it's only in relation to that body of witnesses that Hamlet discovers himself. If you're rehearsing in a white room, doing those soliloquies to a wall, even though it's quite self-reflective and leads to a number of important insights, you're not really getting anything back. To actually lead an audience of twelve hundred people through those soliloquies and to be openhearted in how you share them is incredibly moving, and I was surprised at the effect that had on me during the first week of performance. The rehearsal process had actually been quite isolating, since, as Hamlet, I'd spent seven weeks cut off from everyone: not only is Hamlet on stage most of the time and so excluded from the backstage experience, but the charting of the play is the deterioration of his relationships with everyone else (except for maybe Horatio, but even he gets it in the neck sometimes). So then, to finally find that "person" with whom you have the strongest relationship, at the latest possible moment in your creative process, provided answers to questions I was only dimly aware that I'd had: *this* is who I'm open to; *this* is who I can be myself with. And then you find that Hamlet's openness to the audience provides an important contrast to the artifice he uses with those around him. The solil-

oquies are supposed to be one-person events, but in my experience they can be the most collaborative moments in the plays.

*Rory Kinnear as Hamlet in the National Theatre production, 2011.
Photograph by Tristram Kenton.*

Since they know the play so well, the audience tends to
be ahead of him in terms of what he's thinking; as a result,
a lot of the time Hamlet seems to be playing catch-up with
what everybody else already knows. "O, that this too too solid
flesh would melt" (1.2.129). "Meet it is I set it down / That one
may smile and smile and be a villain" (1.5.113–114). "O, what a
rogue and peasant slave am I!" (2.2.481). "To be, or not to be,
that is the question" (3.1.62). " 'Tis now the very witching time
of night" (3.2.331). "Now might I do it pat, now he is praying"
(3.3.76). "How all occasions do inform against me" (4.4.105). If
you approach these well-known soliloquies as though you too
know what's about to be said, and you present them as though
Hamlet has just had a thought and now he's going to explain
it, then it's just not as dramatically interesting as having those

thoughts in the moment. "What's this? What's this? Is this her fault or mine?" (2.2.193) begins one of Angelo's soliloquies in *Measure for Measure*, and the fact that it's perhaps less well-known helps us to see how soliloquies are set up as unfolding self-questionings. If you actually work out your thoughts as you go along, then the soliloquies cease to seem like set pieces and retain their original impromptu quality. As a result, although at times I would hear contented sighs—and frequently people saying Hamlet's lines along with me—I also had people say to me afterwards that it was only after a while that they realized that I was doing such-and-such a speech. I suppose it can be surprising to discover these well-known words in the context of the narrative of a play, rather than as verbal set pieces. I suspect that secretly we might believe such great—and famous—outpourings of eloquence and wisdom should be heralded by a pause in the action and a suitable fanfare.

In his openness to the audience during the soliloquies, we get to witness the truth of who Hamlet is becoming. At other moments throughout the play, we get to glimpse a different sort of truth, which is the truth of who Hamlet was. The audience doesn't see Hamlet before tragedy strikes, and so part of our job is to hint as many times as possible what he was like before the start. In *Measure for Measure*, something happens to Angelo right at the start which changes his life; in *Hamlet*, that life-altering event has already happened. Therefore, as with every character you do, you have to build a character throughout his life so that you're not just focusing on the discrete bit that the play encapsulates, and so that the play feels like it is the continuation of a life. The play is a palimpsest of who Hamlet is and who he was. He used to be friends with Rosencrantz and Guildenstern, which is why it's so disappointing that they were there only because they were sent for. In the scene in which

Ophelia gives back his mementos, which she says he gave her with "words of so sweet breath composed / As made the things more rich" (3.1.105–106), you see that they had a shared history. Even in the final section of the Closet Scene with his mother, you get the sense that Hamlet and Queen Gertrude shared a dark sense of humour: he leaves with Polonius's body, saying, "Mother, goodnight. Indeed this counsellor / Is now most still, most secret and most grave, / Who was in life a foolish prating knave" (3.4.203–205).

I tried to hold on to the Hamlet whom everybody thought was so commendable, as in Ophelia's description of him:

> The courtier's, soldier's, scholar's, eye, tongue, sword,
> Th'expectancy and rose of the fair state,
> The glass of fashion and the mould of form,
> Th'observed of all observers . . .
>
> (3.1.149–152)

That description was true, and we don't get many opportunities to show that "noble mind" before it has been overthrown. Throughout, in our production, we tried to assume that if somebody says something, he or she means it, because you can hide a lot of Shakespeare with the archness of a raised eyebrow: but if you point with genuineness and openheartedness to the lines themselves, it tends to lead to a more emotional and rewarding experience for an audience.

It certainly did for me as an actor, since I felt the sense of his isolation growing stronger throughout. He had had a functional, happy, seemingly secure family life that he was able to rely on. Then everything is thrown up into the air; everything is now under the auspices of a king he is disgusted by, and yet everyone seems to accept it, unquestioningly. For the first time

Hamlet is seeing—as we all do at some point in our lives—
that no one really cares about the stuff he cares about. He's
strongly principled when it comes to how he thinks the world
should be, to such a point that anyone not with him is necessarily against him. And because of this vehemence he pushes
everyone he once loved and respected away from him further
and further.

Whom can Hamlet trust? Not only does he have to worry
about trusting those of his family members who are alive,
he also has to figure out if he can trust his dead father. If a
ghost—or what could very well be a hallucination—came to
you and told you to kill the king, what would you do? Would
you believe him without questioning and immediately go commit the murder? I wondered what it would be like to bring the
audience into that first scene by not showing the ghost until
Hamlet sees the ghost. That way, like Hamlet, the audience
would share that sense of instability, of not knowing whom to
believe, of wondering whether everyone was deluded—and yet
there would be enough light or sound to suggest that there was
definitely *something*.

Hamlet is haunted, not just by the ghost, but by the idea
of the ghost. Whom we believe on time is always difficult in
Shakespeare, but Ophelia seems to suggest that three months
pass between the first act and the second, and I think that
during that time Hamlet is constantly wrestling with what he
thinks he has *really* seen. Hamlet is often considered the dilet-
tante or the ditherer, but he's just being thorough. The ghost
with his revelation and command set the play up in the tradition of revenge tragedy, but Shakespeare subverts that tradition
entirely by presenting a psychologically plausible journey that
a person really would go on given the circumstances. It's this
new, extra narrative which makes us want to stick with Ham-

let, and the soliloquies are essential in taking us on this internal journey of doubts and decisions. If we don't follow him in those moments—the fear that the ghost might be real, for instance, and his hope that the play-within-the-play will reveal his uncle's guilt—then the play is at risk of flattening back into a failed revenge tragedy.

What's actually troubling Hamlet is the death of his father and the appearance of the ghost. At the same time, this has given rise to a continuing and sinking depression which he is later quite open about to Rosencrantz and Guildenstern:

> I have of late—but wherefore I know not—lost all my mirth, forgone all custom of exercise; and indeed it goes so heavily with my disposition that this goodly frame, the earth, seems to me a sterile promontory . . .
>
> (2.2.278–281)

But Hamlet doesn't want anyone to know what's actually troubling him, and so he assumes madness as a decoy. By the time we see him in Act 2, after those three months of confusion and of being utterly miserable, I thought about how bored he would have grown with performing the madness around Claudius and the court, and how he would be getting more and more dangerous with that performance, through boredom, and through the yearning for danger that you get when nothing seems to matter and the world has become a sterile promontory. Although the antic disposition appears as puerile, stupid nonsense, you see—especially with Polonius ("you're a fishmonger" [2.2.181], or pimp, Hamlet calls him, in reference to his trying to manipulate him with Ophelia), and in front of the King and Queen at the play scene ("look you how cheerfully my mother looks, and my father died within's two hours" [3.2.106])—that there is a very sharp, truthful edge to the humour. Hamlet could say whatever he wanted as long as he was thought to be mad, even if there was truth to it, and I thought of how freeing that must have been for him: they were things he had probably always wanted to say, and then under the cloak of clownishness he was able to be open with his opinions for the first time.

In our production, also in keeping with the principle of taking people at their word, Hamlet and Ophelia did once have a true relationship, and his words "I did love you once" (3.1.119–120) were entirely sincere. It's difficult to imagine, however, because just as we never see Hamlet himself before the events of the play take over, so we never see Hamlet and Ophelia together. Earlier, she had described Hamlet coming into her bedroom while she was sewing, but through so many prisms we cannot know what he was trying to do—whether he was trying to warn her, or whether he was sad, or whether he was using her to publicize his supposed madness to the others. It's a shame we can't play that scene, but in a sense the uncertainty of what really happened builds up a picture of Hamlet in that state of being not at ease—in disease. During the Nunnery Scene, which is right after "To be, or not to be," he's thinking about the evening's play, and about how terrifying it will be to know for certain what his uncle has done and what he himself must do. Ophelia arrives in the middle of those preoccupations, and then Hamlet discovers that she has been set up by Polonius to spy on him—and his feelings for her abruptly shift to something more paranoid, resentful, and accusatory:

If thou dost marry, I'll give thee this plague for thy dowry: be thou as chaste as ice, as pure as snow, thou shalt not escape calumny. Get thee to a nunnery: go,

farewell. Or, if thou wilt needs marry, marry a fool, for
wise men know well enough what monsters you make
of them. To a nunnery, go, and quickly too. Farewell.

(3.1.136–140)

Ophelia has this grief, the loss of her love, further compounded
by the grief occasioned by the loss of her father through murder at Hamlet's hands. The Ophelia in our production didn't
play her madness as weakness, but rather as anger responding
to those feelings of having been the victim of aggression.

Having been possessed for so long of a fear about having to
do the right thing—and of not knowing if it indeed is the right
thing given that his source could very well have been an evil
force—Hamlet is amazed, but not surprised, when the ghost's
story is confirmed by Claudius's reaction at the play. The doors
of his consciousness, which have been swinging by the hinges
since Act 1, get blown off: not only do ghosts exist, and not only
can they inform us of something, but he has spoken to the ghost
of his father and now he has to do the murderous act. To then
be sent away seems in many ways the most wonderful thing
that could have happened to him: to be away from all of that.
Before he leaves, however, he hears of Fortinbras's army fighting for land that's hardly worth it, spurred on by nothing more
than principle. "How all occasions do inform against me, /
And spur my dull revenge" (4.4.105–106)* he responds in a soliloquy
which charts the revelatory moments of his self-disgust and of
how he's going to put an end to it: "O, from this time forth, /
My thoughts be bloody, or be nothing worth!" (4.4.138–139). It's

---

* Editor's note: This is a passage from the second quarto which is not
included in the Folio, and therefore appears in the RSC edition at the end of
the text.

an important soliloquy for the play, since without that determination Hamlet really has no reason to come back. Perhaps, for him, it would have been better had he never met that Captain, never heard of Fortinbras's exploits, and sailed away with those pirates to warmer shores and a guileless death. We, however, would have been denied the *Hamlet* we know and love so well—and we're selfish enough to want to keep that heartrending, soul-revealing ending intact.

* * *

In contrast, Bolingbroke is the epitome of the joy of Shakespearean opacity.

When I started filming *Richard II* for the 2012 BBC series *The Hollow Crown*, I had just been performing *Hamlet* in twelve-hundred-seat theatres, on the Olivier Stage at the National as well as on tour. It was an abrupt switch: from engaging so directly with audiences that it sometimes felt as though they were making Hamlet ask those questions of himself, to doing a very different part straight in front of the camera. In the theatre, a glance to the left, for instance, is not going to read so much as a line of text, and so you use the lines as your only way of engaging with the story and with the audience. The camera captures details, however, and it captures them so minutely that I found it difficult to gauge the amount of thought and emotion that was necessary to have bubbling up inside to ensure that there was always something behind the eyes to support the text. Both on stage and in film, there's always an inner light, but it shines in very different ways.

Bolingbroke's light is particularly difficult to find the source of, since his lines are almost purely functional, with the two exceptions of his touching farewell to his father, John of Gaunt ("the apprehension of the good / Gives but the greater feeling to the worse" [1.3.264–265] he replies to his father's attempt to cheer him up), and his final speech ("my soul is full of woe / That blood should sprinkle me to make me grow" [5.6.45–46], he laments upon hearing that Richard has been murdered). Other than those two passages, there is nothing else that is emotion-based or that explains his narratives and desires. He's one of those characters where as an actor you can't help but notice how very little Shakespeare has given you to work with. Politically, Shakespeare probably had to err on the side of caution, but it's nevertheless surprising how Bolingbroke seems almost underwritten—but in a curiously good way.

Since there is so little to go on, there are many ways of playing him: I tried to play him as straight as possible. When he returns to England and claims he merely wants the lands that are rightly his—"I lay my claim / To my inheritance of free descent" (2.3.135–136)—there's a way of playing that where you think, "Yeah, right." If he's influenced by any motive larger than the restoration of his title and property, though, I believe it is to do with his feeling that the King is tearing up the natural, divine order of things. Even though Bolingbroke is willing to assume the throne, I don't think he came back to England for that purpose: things just fell into his path. He didn't think Richard was right for the job, everybody wanted him to do it instead, and so he concluded that maybe he should. Whereas Prince Hal gets to undergo a moment of change to become Henry V, Bolingbroke rather develops a sort of neurosis: it comes of being in a position that he genuinely doesn't feel he should be in, even if he thinks it's best for the people, and is then exacerbated when he discovers that there are plots against his life. Bolingbroke realizes the weight of what it means to be king, and it's an understanding that will lead into the plays whose name has become his, *Henry IV, Parts 1 and 2*; and that sense of unease at what he has done, and about what lies ahead, is then continued through *Henry V* as well.

Richard II presents two almost polar opposite attitudes toward being king. At the start of the play, Richard has been king for close to two decades and possesses a strong notion of his own entitlement. Not only was he cocooned as a spoiled child, but those around him found that it was in their best interests for him to stay that way. At the end of the play, just before he is murdered in his prison cell, he achieves a freedom which expresses itself in a long, lyrical speech. He reflects on the ups and downs of his life, then says:

> But whate'er I am,
> Nor I nor any man that but man is
> With nothing shall be pleased, till he be eased
> With being nothing.
>
> (5.5.38–41)

Despite the fact that Richard is no great intellect, and even seems to recognize it himself, there is an element of philosophical acceptance in his realization, "I wasted time, and now doth time waste me" (5.5.49).

Bolingbroke follows a contrary trajectory. He begins in relative freedom, and at the end he is just beginning to appreciate what kingship means, and comprehend that it's not who you are but how people react to you. Bolingbroke then realizes that he can do whatever he wants, and although there are moments of clarity and even charity—he spares the lives of Aumerle and the Bishop of Carlisle—he kills everyone else involved in the plot to have him assassinated. Consequently we suspect that, given another two decades, as long as Richard had been king when we first meet him, Bolingbroke too would grow self-interested, his neuroses would develop, and his sense of being able to use his power would get more and more corrupted. Richard II and Bolingbroke seem as different as can be, and yet in some ways they merely trade places. Because it is so intricate and balanced, *Richard II* is the ultimate meditation on kingship.

Try as they may, the Royal Family today seem fairly distant from the nature of kingship that Shakespeare is writing about: they feel decorative to us, whereas Shakespeare's kings and queens wield their power more sharply. *Richard II* relates less to actual royalty and more to a wide variety of power struggles, including political successions, business squabbles, and any area of life in which there is necessarily a leader. Why do people want to lead? What happens to those who are right for leadership but don't want to do it and are nevertheless pushed into it?

* * *

With each of Shakespeare's plays, the same cast and the same director could sit down again mere months after they've done a production and come up with a totally different production: the readiness is all. I'm sure that for each of these roles—Angelo, Hamlet, Bolingbroke—I would want to give a very different performance now. But however I did them, I would still want to focus on those moments when the characters become something they weren't before. I would want to try to hold on to who they were, with all the weight of their histories, and yet follow them in the successive moments of becoming who they are, as they are faced with those big questions. They are questions we all face in our own lives: questions about beliefs, and trust, and power, and how to do the best we can with whatever unexpected circumstances life throws at us.

Matt Sturges

I KNOW A HAWK FROM A HANDSAW REGARDLESS OF THE WEATHER, BUT THAT'S PRETTY MUCH IT

———————

MATT STURGES is an American comic book and graphic novel writer. His work includes *Jack of Fables,* for which he was an Eisner Award Finalist, as well as *Fables, House of Mystery, Justice Society of America,* and *Doctor Who.* He has also written the novels *Midwinter* and *The Office of Shadow.*

It's my junior year of college and I'm at a friend's house in Austin, Texas, for something called Shakespeare Night. There's mulled apple cider and guys with ponytails and girls with no makeup and Charlie Parker and intellectualism. Tonight's play is *Hamlet,* and we are seated in a circle in the friend's funky living room, doing a dramatic reading. I've been assigned the part of Horatio, and so I'm one of the first ones up to bat.

I'm excited, because I like attention, but also terrified because the truth is that I feel like an utter fraud. What the hell do I know about Shakespeare? What's *Hamlet* even *about*? Everyone else in the room looks way, way more intelligent and composed than I feel.

I realize that I'm thinking all this *as* I'm reading aloud, an unfortunate (though sometimes useful) habit I acquired

in public school; I have no idea what I'm saying. Have I been
inflecting my lines properly? Have I read them with any sensibility at all? I don't know, but I'm on track, so it's probably
okay. But now a problem looms: the name Fortinbras, which
I have no idea how to pronounce. Is the *s* silent? Which syllable has the accent? If I get this wrong, they're all going to
know that I'm a faker, even though I told the hostess that I'd
read the play *and* seen the Olivier movie, neither of which
is true.

I pronounce it (correctly, as it turns out) "FORT-in-bross,"
trailing off a bit on the *s* just in case. No eyebrows are raised. I
continue, breathing a sigh of relief.

When we get to Act 1, Scene 2, I get my first hit of Shakespeare dopamine. The guy with the scraggly beard (who can't
enunciate for crap, btw, and thus I was convinced he should
cede the part of Hamlet to me, who, whatever my other deficiencies, had some background in the theater) reads, "O, that
this too too solid flesh should melt . . . ," and I think, *I know this
part!* And then, a few lines later, "Frailty, thy name is woman."
It's like a Greatest Hits collection in one soliloquy!

That was twenty-some-odd years ago. As of today, I've read
Hamlet at least four times, seen the Kenneth Branagh film,
and written a comic book in which the play-within-the-play is
*Hamlet.** And if you put a gun to my head and told me to tell
you the plot of *Hamlet*, it would go something like this:

Some guards see the ghost of the dead king of Denmark. Hamlet sees his father's ghost, who tells Hamlet
that his brother, Hamlet's uncle, killed him. Hamlet

---

* *Midwinter* (Amherst, NY: Pyr, 2009).

wants to murder his uncle in revenge, but is scared to
do it. Polonius is there, and tells his son some stuff.
Hamlet stabs him at some point. Everyone thinks
Hamlet is nuts but he's just pretending. Actors show
up and Hamlet says the play is the thing. Ophelia goes
bonkers and kills herself. Rosencrantz and Guildenstern are dead. To be, or not to be. Some other stuff
happens. Hamlet talks to a skull. Everyone kills everyone else, and Fortinbras shows up. The end.

By contrast, I've seen *Fight Club* exactly once, and I could easily recount to you the whole plot, even without the gun to my
head.

Look. I'm no dummy. I'll put my brain up against just
about anyone's. I did *really* good on the SAT. I graduated college with a BA from the Honors English program. I read *Infinite Jest* twice, and I *totally* understood it (the second time). I
write stories for a living. So how is it that I'm so dumb when it
comes to Shakespeare? Why do my peers seem so much more
knowledgeable and conversant on the subject? Are they smarter
than me?

Or are they as full of crap as I am?

It's 1975 or thereabouts and my brother has been con-
scripted into playing Laertes in a second-grade production of
Hamlet. It's one of my earliest memories, watching him stand
on the stage of the cafetorium in a black cape, stiff as a board as
a stagestruck miniature Polonius mutters the old man's famous
advice to his son. It's excruciating to me, since I don't understand a word of what's being said, being five. Even had I been
able to hear the words (the young actor hadn't been taught to
project), I wouldn't have understood them. And had I under-

stood them, I most certainly wouldn't have understood them to be *comedy*.*

My earliest acquaintances with Shakespeare are all like this, whether it's my brother's class play, or the classic Bugs Bunny cartoon "A Witch's Tangled Hare," featuring Witch Hazel standing on a balcony, calling out, "Wherefore art thou, Romeo?"

That "wherefore" is one of my favorite literary misunderstandings, because it says so much about our culture's relationship with the Bard. In every childhood rendition of the balcony scene from *Romeo and Juliet*, whether it be that Bugs Bunny cartoon, or that episode of *The Brady Bunch* where Marcia is cast as Juliet and acts like such a pain, or wherever, the line is always given with Juliet scanning the horizon for Romeo, as if she is asking, "Where are you, Romeo?"

That's what I always thought she was saying too, of course, until I learned better. Not in *school*, of course, but in a 1986 episode of *Saturday Night Live*, in a sketch entitled "Shakespeare in the Slums," in which Danitra Vance plays Juliet's speech with explanatory asides to her audience. I'm watching the sketch and laughing, because, like everyone, I sort of know this speech because I'm fifteen and fresh out of ninth grade, which means I was forced to read the play. And then Vance says something that floors me. She says, "O Romeo, Romeo, wherefore art thou Romeo?" and then she breaks character and turns to the audience and says, " 'Wherefore' mean 'why.' She sayin' 'Why you gots to be Romeo?' "**

---

* I don't recall whether the much-abbreviated version of the play includes a seven-year-old prince stabbing my brother with a poisoned sword; it seems like something I would have remembered.

** Taken verbatim from a purloined video clip of the sketch. This is Shakespeare in the *slums*, remember?

"Wherefore" means "why"? I haul out the huge dictionary in the living room and there it is. As in "whys and wherefores." Meaning that all these people, all these years, from Mel Blanc to Marcia Brady, *had no idea what Shakespeare was talking about.* Juliet isn't *looking* for Romeo, she's asking why, of all the guys she could have fallen for, she had to fall for one of the Montagues. Pretty big difference. Once I figure that out, it is like I've unlocked a bit of hermetic, secret knowledge. I know something that actual adults didn't know. It's heady, and a bit frightening. What is going on here?

Flash back to ninth grade. We're watching a video of *Romeo and Juliet,* as some kind of backhanded reward for struggling through reading the damn thing aloud. The past two weeks have been a nightmare—but the opposite of the Shakespeare Night nightmare, which is still several years in my future—and so we've just finished reading *Romeo and Juliet* aloud, in the stultifying monotone that only a room full of bored teenagers can employ.*

But now that's over, and it's video time. Two things about it strike me immediately. The first is that Shakespeare is *funny.* In Act 2, Scene 3, we get Romeo and his friends Mercutio and Benvolio joking around, and I'm not really getting it. But then the fat nurse appears and they shout, "A sail, a sail!" (2.3.76)** and I realize that they're making fun of the fat lady, which is always funny, especially to a fourteen-year-old. And then a few lines later, Mercutio says, "the bawdy hand of the dial is now upon the prick of noon" (2.3.85). *Holy shit,* I think, *Mercutio just*

---

* I am no exception here. As much as I might want to show off my burgeoning theatrical panache, I'm not about to commit social suicide in order to do so.

** Editor's note: in the film they call out together. The RSC attributes the line to Romeo.

made a dick joke! I laugh out loud, and everyone in the room, including the teacher, stares at me. Am I the only one who got the joke? Or just the only one uncool enough to laugh out loud at it? My vanity desperately wants to believe the former but suspects the latter, as always.

The other thing I learn from this viewing is that our teacher wasn't paying attention when she rented the video. Because she rented the Zeffirelli version, not the BBC version. Which mistake she quickly realizes in Act 3, Scene 5, when we see Olivia Hussey's boobs and Leonard Whiting's bare ass. Everyone in the class notices this part.

So. Shakespeare isn't only funny, but lewd too? *William,* I wonder, *where have you been all my life?*

I decide then and there that I am going to become a Shakespeare expert. I'm going to read all the plays, and be able to quote lengthy swaths of dialogue upon request, like they did in that one episode of *The Cosby Show.* This feeling, heady and self-vindicating, lasts until about an hour after dinner, when I pull down my parents' huge leather-bound Shakespeare (whose spine is suspiciously stiff and pristine) and pry it open, and realize that Shakespeare is actually *utterly incomprehensible.*

Romeo and Juliet in school was one thing, because the text was glossed all to hell and back and we were reading slowly and not paying any attention anyway. But this, this is something else entirely. It's just words, words, words, spilling down the page with no footnotes or explanations. I flip to *A Midsummer Night's Dream,* which seems familiar because I watched Woody Allen's *A Midsummer Night's Sex Comedy* on HBO without my parents' permission.* I'm greeted with "Now, fair Hippolyta,

---

* A film that, to my fourteen-year-old sensibilities, contained neither sex nor comedy.

our nuptial hour / Draws on apace. Four happy days bring
in / Another moon: but O, methinks, how slow / This old moon
wanes" (1.1.1–4).

What the fuck does any of *that* mean? Nuptial hour? Apace?
Huh?

Worried, I flip back to *Romeo and Juliet*, thinking that I'll be
on firmer ground here. I already read this, and then I *watched*
it. So then it's "Two households, both alike in dignity, / In fair
Verona, where we lay our scene, / From ancient grudge break to
new mutiny" (Prologue 1–3). Mutiny? What?

Okay, third time's the charm. *Hamlet.* I know that's an
important one, not leastwise because of a Richard Scarry book
I had when I was little that had Hamlet as a kitten. But through
some other unspecified cultural osmosis, I know that this is
the "To be, or not to be" play. Which means it must be a very
important one. Because "To be, or not to be" is like the most
famous thing ever.

And for a little while, everything's fine. Just a couple of
guards talking. It makes sense. I'm reading Shakespeare! But
then I realize I'm not really, because I'm thinking this *while* I'm
reading, which is something I've recently learned to do. I giggle
at the word "Polack," but after that nothing really makes sense
and so I page through the thing, marveling at how long it is,
until I find "To be, or not to be" (3.1.62) and start reading again.
And oh my hell, this doesn't any sense at all! I slam the
book shut and back it goes on the shelf, very possibly never to
be disturbed again.

"To be, or not to be." Why *that*? For Shakespeare's most
famous and oft-quoted line, you'd think these words would
have some definitive meaning in and of themselves. You'd think
there would be some *there* there. But what does "To be, or not

to be" actually mean? And what does the soliloquy it so iconically introduces mean? Most college-educated people can eke out the first few lines of that soliloquy. We usually get to about "and by opposing end them," and maybe toss in "what dreams may come" and "this mortal coil" and "to sleep, perchance to dream," because those things are the names of rock bands and Richard Matheson novels and *Star Trek* episodes. We know that it has something to do with death, and the fear of what comes after death. And so the "To be, or not to be" is some kind of existential question about living and dying. Simple enough. But still—even weirder that *this* is the one everyone talks about. Similarly, Sammy Davis Jr.'s calling card was "The Candy Man."

My junior year of college (emboldened by Shakespeare Night, I guess), I decide I'm going to write a paper about The Soliloquy. So I read it over and over again, and I look at what other people have said about it, and I realize that there is nothing easy about this speech. It seems on the surface that Hamlet is considering suicide, right? That's what he's talking about, whether to go on living, or to die. But is that really it? It seems more like he's talking about futility, that you're literally damned if you do and damned if you don't. In other words, he's just bitching. He's not considering suicide at all. Is he? But then also, Claudius and Polonius are in the room with him. The text doesn't say whether or not Hamlet is aware of this or not, but we do know for a fact that Hamlet's explicit intent at this point of the play is to screw with everyone and make them think that he's crazy. So if he knows his uncle is in the room, it means one thing. If he thinks he's alone, it means another. Is he feigning madness? Or is he truly suicidal, only thinking he's feigning madness? Or is he not suicidal, but only putting off the inevitable by tying his mind in knots? Or some other thing, or recursive spiral of things.

We can go on like this for days, but long story short: I don't have a clue what any of this stuff really means. So in the end, I punt on the paper, and do what I always do, which is to write a faux-Jungian analysis of the speech, tossing in a bunch of references to "shadows" and "animas" and stuff. Like my dad says, if you can't dazzle them with brilliance, baffle them with bullshit. And this paper is five pages (with very wide margins) of grade A manure.

As it turns out, it's literally grade A, as in I get an A on the paper. A paper that is total nonsense. From a professor with a PhD in English literature. Specializing in Shakespeare.

What the hell is going on here? How did I get away with that? Am I smarter than I think I am? Did I somehow land on the right answer without knowing? Or is *Hamlet* so open to interpretation that you can say pretty much *anything* about it and no one will question you as long as you sound like you know what you're talking about?

Why is this obtuse phrase the most famous thing Shakespeare ever wrote?

I'm not saying that *nobody* understands *Hamlet*. But seriously, it's not even clear what it *means* to understand *Hamlet*. For instance, ask a dozen scholars one of the central questions of the plot: Why does Hamlet wait so long to take his revenge? You'll get a dozen answers. Some have argued that it was the difficulty of committing the crime and getting away with it. Others have argued that it's his conscience that stops him, or his lack of nerve. Goethe said it was because he is "a lovely, pure and most moral nature, without the strength of nerve which forms a hero." Or because he was overthinking it. Or because he was depressed. Or just procrastinating. Or all of the above. Or none of the above.

Is there truly that much richness of interpretation to be found in the text? Or does not one of us "get" it? Did *Shakespeare* even "get" Hamlet?

And what difference would it make if he did?

* * *

Talking about Americans in the nineteenth century, Kim Sturgess (no relation) says,

> I think there was a very wide consumption of Shakespeare. . . . It didn't necessarily mean that they thought very carefully about everything they consumed. It didn't mean they had developed a refined taste and they were able to actually separate the different types of words coming from the actors. They looked at it, they absorbed it as a whole. They saw the plays not unlike the way the seventeenth-century London Bankside audience did, who were also not necessarily the best educated population in the world.*

Not only is it not just me, it's not even *now*. Apparently, this is how it's always been. It's just that in the past, they didn't bother to pretend. When *you* see *Hamlet*, you go to a theater filled with clever people wearing glasses, sitting up straight, and paying

---

* This from the transcript of a talk that he gave that was then put on the web page www.shakespeareinamericanlife.org/transcripts/sturgess2.cfm. If you know how to cite that properly, let me know, because I graduated from college before the Internet. Or better yet, don't let me know, and just pencil it in here. I stopped learning new things a while back.

attention. You get a glass of chardonnay at intermission. When Elizabethans went to see *Hamlet*, they got a bearbaiting at intermission.*

Modern popular culture, though, doesn't like to admit that it's in the cheap seats. It likes to believe in its own canniness, whether deserved or not. In the 1980s, for instance, the British topless model Samantha Fox** released an album containing a song called "If Music Be the Food of Love." The chorus goes "If music be the food of love, then play on. Celebrate!" And a deep male voice intones, just in case we weren't sure: "That's Shakespeare."*** There's clearly a lowest-common-denominator vibe happening here, but at the same time, the lyric knows enough to know that Shakespeare matters somehow, and expects the listener to connect some dots here and there. There's some pretense of sophistication, even if the pretense is utterly devoid of content.

Here's the tricky thing about sophistication. We all know that some things must be "appreciated": fine wine, goose livers, cigars, and of course Shakespeare. But the trouble with things that must be appreciated is that people who crave respectability will pretend to appreciate them even if they don't. This has been demonstrated admirably by neuroeconomists (yes, it's a thing) at Caltech, who showed in a 2007 study that people

---

* Seriously, they brought a bear on stage and then they sicced dogs on the bear. And the dogs would attack the bear and the bear would fight back and everyone would have a gay old time until the bear was dead and then they'd drag him off, mop up the blood, and get back to Elsinore.

** Not the American porn actress, much to my present chagrin, having just now looked this up.

*** One of the verses goes, "To be, or not to be, / It doesn't matter much to me / Wherefore art thou, my Romeo, the only boy I want to know." I point this out only because it's so awe-inspiringly bad.

enjoy wine more if they're told it's expensive. At first blush (pun totally intended) it might seem to be just a poke in the eye of wine snobs, who patiently explain in response that *experience* is required to appreciate fine wine, and the immature palate simply can't tell the difference. Which I'll take as stipulated, and which you could certainly apply to Shakespeare appreciation as well.

But the takeaway from the experiment isn't that people are rubes who can't tell the difference between the wines. It's that people enjoy things more *if they're told that they're better*. Which is very different. It reminds me of the thrill I get when I come across a passage in Shakespeare whose words are familiar to me. It's not that's it's objectively *good*, because what does that even mean? It's the sense that we're part of something larger than ourselves. Something great. That dopamine hit that I got when I recognized "too too solid flesh" on Shakespeare Night. It's more than just recognition; it's a sense of belonging, of *mattering*. And that goes beyond appreciation into a different sphere entirely, a sphere in which anyone can reside. It's universal because we say it's so.

But not just anything can be universal. George Eliot isn't. James Joyce isn't. Molière isn't. They're all too hard or too dense or too specific, and nowhere near catchy enough. It takes lilt and panache to be universal.

Take Hamlet's catchy phrase "a custom / More honoured in the breach than the observance" (1.4.17–18). My daughter doesn't have any idea what that means, but she likes the sound and rhythm of it.* I've always loved the cadence, even though I

---

* She's eight. She likes to pick up my *Norton Shakespeare* and read aloud to anyone who'll listen. It sounds incredibly adorable, and it is. For about twenty minutes. And then it isn't.

just now realized that Shakespeare is punning on "breach" (he's talking about Danes shooting off cannons to celebrate their drinking). And many's the literate wag (including me) who has dropped the phrase into conversation, meaning "something given lip service to more often than actually performed." But here's the kicker—all of us wags are misunderstanding the quote. That's not what Hamlet means at all. Hamlet is saying that it's a custom that would be much more honorable if it were never performed at all, mainly because it makes other countries think they're a bunch of swinish drunks.*

So. If none of us even know what the hell Shakespeare is *talking* about a good deal of the time, who can truly say that they "appreciate" Shakespeare? And if it's only the obnoxious guy who starts all his sentences with the word "Actually . . ." and goes out of his way to correct more-honored-in-the-breach-than-the-observance failures like me, then what good is Shakespeare?

I guess the best answer is that, as with so many things, with Shakespeare you get out exactly what you put in. You can enjoy the pretty words, or you can smile at the Bugs Bunny cartoons, half-realizing that something deeper is at play. You can struggle through *Hamlet* and tell yourself you accomplished something, even if you're not quite sure what it was. You can put your mind to it and study hard, read aloud with your friends in a room that smells like mulled cider. You can devote your life to it and tease out every subtle pleasure (up to and including snarkily pointing out the cognoscenti's errors). And it doesn't matter, because ultimately there is no final arbiter, no judge. As Hamlet

---

* Nobody was more surprised to discover this than I was. But if you read the rest of the speech it's clear the line doesn't make sense otherwise.

himself says, "there is nothing either good or bad but thinking makes it so" (2.2.244–245).

Of course, he also says that he can tell a hawk from a hand-saw when the wind comes from the south, so, you know, grain of salt.

James Earl Jones

THE SUN GOD

JAMES EARL JONES has performed in both modern and classical theater, including *The Great White Hope, Fences, On Golden Pond, Driving Miss Daisy,* and *The Best Man.* His Shakespeare includes *Henry V, Measure for Measure, A Midsummer Night's Dream, Hamlet, Macbeth,* and *King Lear*; he has performed the title role in *Othello* seven times. His film credits include *Star Wars; Roots; The Hunt for Red October; Patriot Games; Cry, the Beloved Country;* and *The Lion King.* His work has earned him many distinctions, including three Emmy Awards and six nominations, two Tony Awards and two nominations, a Golden Globe Award and four nominations, a Screen Actors Guild Life Achievement Award and another nomination, a National Medal of Arts, and an Academy Award nomination as well as an Honorary Academy Award.

The first time I heard Shakespeare was in the cornfields of our subsistence farm in Michigan. We were hoeing the grass away from the precious seedlings that would feed our family and our livestock for the coming winter. My uncle Bob began reciting Antony's oration in *Julius Caesar*:

Friends, Romans, countrymen, lend me your ears . . .

(3.2.70)

That was my first impression: hearing a common person, not trained at all in theater and barely educated, recite something that he enjoyed, accurately and in such a way that we could all understand it.

At that time in my life, I was listening intently—and I was listening so intently because I wasn't speaking. I had been born in Mississippi, where the language was of the South and had a certain musicality and a certain rhythm. Then, when I was adopted by my grandparents and went to live in Michigan at the age of four and a half, my stuttering began. A young black man moving from the South to the North should have been jubilant, but I think it affected how I communicated with people. I had a difficult time talking to others, and it exhibited itself in the form of stuttering and stammering, and then for eight years I hardly spoke at all and was effectively mute.

What I experienced in the North was a different way of speaking: it was a clearer, if flatter, sound. There was a town in Michigan, a little further south from where we lived in Manistee, whose inhabitants were reputed to speak the most "medium" English of the entire country: the English with the clearest and most understandable accent. My spoken language of the South began to convert itself into the language of the North, even in my mind after my speech went dumb, although it was years before I began to speak it out loud. Similarly, during this time of incubation, those seeds my uncle had planted were taking root, and I was learning to appreciate a different kind of musical language in poetry. In high school, since the sound of poetic language is easier for a stutterer to learn to speak, I was encouraged to write my own poetry, and to recite it along with the verse of Edgar Allan Poe and Shakespeare. It was therefore by finding music in language again that I found my way back to voice.

* * *

I joined the New York Shakespeare Festival the year of *Measure for Measure* and *Henry V* (1960), and it was a season of notoriety for both myself and for the producer of the festival, Joseph Papp. Since I played Michael Williams, the only soldier who protests the war against the French directly to the King, critics wrote that Joe was reinterpreting *Henry V* to express his antiwar sentiments through a black man—as though Michael Williams was emblematic of the common man protesting the war in Vietnam.

The assertion was ridiculous, of course; what really happened was that I was walking on the street one day, and I ran into Joe Papp. He asked what I was doing, I replied that I wasn't doing anything because I was out of work, and he said I could come carry a spear. That's how it all started. I went and auditioned, and I got the role of Michael Williams, and I didn't think anything of it other than it was a good job. I loved the part, though, because I got to carry a longbow, which was even better than a spear, since in the hands of a strong man it could be used to pierce the French armor. It was an elite weapon, and similarly I found that I was playing a much more important role than I had expected. Furthermore, I got to mouth off at the king. Henry V, disguised, says that the war is just and his quarrel is honorable, to which Williams replies with the famous, "That's more than we know" (4.1.113); then, after the debate grows heated and they postpone their fight, he promises, "I will take thee a box on the ear" (4.1.174).

Then, too, I managed to persuade the director of *Measure for Measure*, Alan Schneider, that it didn't matter what color Abhorson was because, as the executioner, he wore a mask. At that time, I didn't know what a color integration that festival would turn out to be under the direction of Joe Papp. Even though we both denied that anything had been meant by casting me as Michael Williams other than giving an actor a role, Joe did have a broader mission, which was to make Shakespeare not only available free to audiences, but also available as roles to all cultural aspects of the American acting community. If you came from Brooklyn and spoke with a Brooklyn accent, the festival was a place where you could play Shakespeare, and Joe found a rationale to give you a part.

* * *

Since then, I've played Oberon in *A Midsummer Night's Dream*, Claudius in *Hamlet*, Macbeth, and King Lear, but it's Othello I keep coming back to: I've played him seven times, from the age of twenty-five, in 1955, to the age of fifty, in 1982. To be honest, my favorite character in *Othello* used to be Cassio; I was always baffled by the character of Othello, even after playing him so many times. I think I'm finally beginning to understand him, and the rest of this essay is a collection of my latest thoughts on how to reinstate him as a truly tragic figure. When Shakespeare writes "a *noble* Moor, in the service of Venice,"* that's not a joke. So the question for me has become: How can we sustain this sense of Othello's inherent nobility?

My feeling is that the play has to do with the delicate balance of an entire cosmos. Othello's life is fueled by violence and love, two contrary forces inhabiting the same body, and he is like a great fiery orb at the center, regulating and restraining other cosmic tensions. Shakespeare has placed around

---

* Editor's note: this is the description of the typical dramatis personae, but it is not present in either the First Quarto or the Folio. Perhaps Shakespeare penned the description; perhaps it was taken from Montano's "the noble Moor," Desdemona's "my noble Moor," and Lodovico's repetition of "the noble Moor." In any case, "noble" pairs with "Moor" as "honest" pairs with "Iago."

him other celestial entities, many of them already instable from internal confusion. Iago is a great force, but before the play even begins he has secretly spun out of his orbit. He recognizes his schizophrenia when he compares himself to the god Janus. Cassio has a split too, which reveals itself when he drinks. Desdemona is the only one who is whole. She has no demons, as Giraldi Cinthio wrote her name in the 1565 story on which the play was based; she is "Disdemona": without demons. She is a being of light, a light without violence, a lunar beauty, and her calm and steady presence is just as necessary to the cosmos Shakespeare has created. Iago conjures an alter Desdemona, however, and it is Othello's inability to reconcile the two Desdemonas which results in the tragedy. This is a deeply personal play: this is also a play that involves the greatest of all beings, and so the potential for greatness within each of us.

Just as the critical issue of the play seems to be about balance, so, I think, is its performance. In my experiences with the play, if the production doesn't allow Othello to fill out his stature as this celestial force and maintain it for as long as possible, and if the production allows Othello to succumb to self-pity, pathos, or any irrational petulance, then the play itself teeters in its orrery and can even become unhinged. I believe, however, that there is a production possible which avoids any farcical elements and allows the play to retain its tragedic balance. In what follows, I'd like to take a look at the characters of Othello, Iago, and Desdemona, referring not just to my own reflections but to the productions I have been a part of over the years, and I'd like to suggest a concept of one particular scene that has always troubled me. I'm not suggesting that anyone take on my interpretation; I'd simply like to explore what I take to be the problem and set out my attempt at a solution, in case my own journey of the play is useful to you with yours.

* * *

Othello's greatness is of a different model from those of Shakespeare's other tragic protagonists. Lear and Claudius are kings,
Macbeth murders his way to the throne, but Othello is a general, and I've always felt that Shakespeare seems more comfortable writing about royalty—probably because the possibility
of tragedy is inherent to royalty. A man is put in a position of
responsibility and control in which it's easy to fail, and then
he fails. Othello isn't royal, even though he can claim, "I fetch
my life and being / From men of royal siege" (1.2.23–24). In his
former life he was of royal lineage, which is why it's so ironic
that he then became a slave and a wanderer—but the fact of his
royalty is not a quality that plays dominantly in his nature. His
interest, rather, is in nobility: what matters to him is not what
he was born to, but what he has made of himself, how he positions himself within the rest of humanity, and how he exists in
relation to the cosmos.

At the same time, though, Othello is more than just a general: the director Gladys Vaughan and I once nicknamed him
the Sun God. He's more endowed with humanity than anyone
else in the realm of the play. In spite of, or rather because of, all
he has been through, Othello comes to that society standing a
head above anybody else, and possessed of the desire to be better than anybody else: to be kinder, to be more just, to be more
responsible than anybody else.* Desdemona sees this, and falls
in love with him, and marries him.

Brabantio, angry that his daughter has eloped, accuses

---

* Often, I've found that portraying royalty and nobility depends less on what
I do, or on how I act, and more on the counterpoint of how those on stage
treat me.

Othello of witchcraft. In Othello's testimony before the Senate, we can catch a glimpse of the source of his nobility:

> Most potent, grave and reverend signiors,
> My very noble and approved good masters:
> That I have ta'en away this old man's daughter,
> It is most true: true I have married her . . .
>
>   (1.3.86–89)

He then promises:

> I will a round unvarnished tale deliver
> Of my whole course of love: what drugs, what charms,
> What conjuration and what mighty magic—
> For such proceeding I am charged withal—
> I won his daughter.
>
>   (1.3.100–104)

In what follows, Othello reveals his nobility through both the account of what he has been through and the very way he tells it to us, and would have told it to her:

> Her father loved me, oft invited me,
> Still questioned me the story of my life
> From year to year: the battle, sieges, fortune,
> That I have passed.
> I ran it through, even from my boyish days
> To th'very moment that he bade me tell it,
> Wherein I spoke of most disastrous chances,
> Of moving accidents by flood and field,
> Or hair-breadth scapes i'th'imminent deadly breach,

Of being taken by the insolent foe
And sold to slavery, of my redemption thence ...

(1.3.142–152)

He further speaks of having seen "hills whose head touch
heaven" (1.3.155) and "the cannibals that each other eat" (1.3.157)
and "the Anthropophagi and men whose heads / Grew beneath
their shoulders" (1.3.158–159).

"And men whose heads / Grew beneath their shoulders":
James Earl Jones reciting Othello's speech to the Senate
at the White House, "An Evening of Poetry, Music,
and the Spoken Word," May 12, 2009.

I had the opportunity to recite that speech at the White
House in front of the Obama family.* It was an event that was
classified as a poetry jam, and given the title "An Evening of

* See www.youtube.com/watch?v=DJybA1emr_g.

Poetry, Music, and the Spoken Word" (May 12, 2009). Poets and musicians were to offer words and sounds, and I was asked to read something of poetry, such as Dr. Seuss or Shakespeare, and since I felt that I could not top Jesse Jackson's reading of *Green Eggs and Ham*, I chose Shakespeare in the form of Othello's oration. In front of me were the president's two little girls, and I tried to present that speech in the same spirit as Othello telling his stories to the much older girl Desdemona. Othello then relates Desdemona's response to his stories, and as I recited those lines I discovered exactly how outraged she was (in contrast to her father, who would have been thrilled by the stories), and I delivered my quotation of her reaction in an outraged voice, saying,

> . . . " 'twas strange, 'twas passing strange,
> 'Twas pitiful, 'twas wondrous pitiful!"
> She wished she had not heard it, yet she wished
> That heaven had made her such a man.
>
> (1.3.174–177)

In effect, she was saying, "That's *horrible*! No human being should have to go through such a life." And she means it: she is deeply troubled that anyone should have to endure slavery, and that anyone should have to go through such lonely wandering. I tried to make the speech simple, and as a result I found in it the very basis for nobility—that part that had impressed Desdemona, and that is behind her later assertion that she saw Othello's "visage in his mind" (1.3.267).

Othello's grandeur has a darker source, too, which is alluded to in the speech: it also comes from the fact that he has been a slave, and that he has been among the wretched, and that he has come out of all that misery and is on the other side of power and he is now a supreme warrior. He could kill everybody. He could become a tyrant. He could conquer the entire world—but he doesn't, because he can restrain himself in order to keep life in balance, and he knows that if he doesn't restrain himself then the entire world will fall to violence. It's his responsibility to keep this in check. Similarly, I believe that it's the actor's responsibility to make sure that Othello keep this in check for as long as possible, so that wherever there's a choice of meaning for a line, throughout, in performance we should choose the more positive version, the one that keeps Othello the most intact for the longest time. We should not anticipate his fall but rather, with him, resist it as much as possible, and be allies with him in his ambition to indulge his capacity to love and contain his capacity to kill.

Othello, Iago, and Cassio all possess a highly refined capacity to kill. It is suspected that Iago's name comes from Saint*iago* Matamoros: Saint James the Moor-Killer, a mercenary who specialized in killing Moors. Both Iago and Othello are mercenary killers of Moors, of Turks.* They are highly trained specialists who fight from ships, the ancestors of our marines and Navy SEALs, and perhaps every production should find a way to emphasize, through pageantry, how highly competent and very lethal they are—especially since Shakespeare doesn't give us the chance to see them in action, as he does other soldiers in the battle scenes of, say, *Henry V*. There is a scene in Laurence Olivier's film in which Olivier, as Othello, breaks somebody's neck in the Cyprian riot. I think he added that touch to give us a

---

* I would not want to suggest that either religion—Othello was born into the Islamic world, and he converted to the faith of the Catholic world of Venice—contributed to his character. If anything, Othello expresses an almost druidic awareness of the cosmos.

sense of how easy it is for Othello to take another life. Throughout the play, however, fighting itself is discouraged: after the
one true skirmish scene, Cassio loses his job. There's an uneasy
tension, for the warriors are needed—more than that: their status as soldiers outranks the status of the senators in dramatic
import—and yet off the battlefield they are felt to be a threat.
This is an odd play about warriors who don't war: the warring
is going on inside themselves.

Othello and Iago are supreme warriors, and their worth
as warriors is defined by what they're fighting for. Professionally, they're fighting for Venice; but in Othello's case, he's also
fighting for Desdemona—who is, in effect, the embodiment
of Venice to him.* When Othello thinks of Venice, he thinks
of Desdemona. She is that important, that beloved, that cherished. It's more than that, though: she is life itself, and she is
the continuation of life. Some scholars have written that the
couple didn't consummate their marriage before they're sent
to war because Othello is too old, or because there wouldn't
have been time for them to go to bed between their marriage
and the moment they leave—such arguments tend to come
from nothing more than an aversion to the idea of a black man
and a white woman sleeping together. In his torment, Othello
talks of "the fountain from the which my current runs" (4.2.65)
(referring to Desdemona), indicating that he expects to have
progeny with her. He fights, therefore, to protect Desdemona,
and so when Desdemona is on stage she must be fully formed, a
strong-willed creature who is full of vitality and love, and wor-

---

* Why Venice? Othello could find work as a mercenary anywhere. We never
find out why Othello abandoned Islam, but we can imagine that he finds
Venice to be worth fighting for because it is the most balanced state of all he
has known; it is the one that accepted him at last.

thy of adoration. She is the feminine to his masculine. They are the opposites of each other, and the complements to each other, and in that she gives his martial success reason. The play is a tragedy, and yet it must begin from a place of love.

*　*　*

After Shakespeare sets up the nobility of Othello and the love of the newlyweds, he takes the story on an intricate emotional journey which allows for a variety of interpretations on stage. The question then broadens for each actor, as well as for each production, and the results depend to a great extent on what each director is trying to achieve and who else is up there on stage with Othello.

There are examples from history to draw on. When you first see Sir Laurence Olivier appear with the black makeup on in his film, it's spectacular. He is an artistic creation. But as the film progresses, the more oh-woe-is-me he becomes, and then the eyes start rolling—a gesture which was highly effective on stage, but overwrought on film. As much as I admired that performance when I was younger, I knew that I wanted to explore a different kind of vulnerability and a different source of strength.

During the 1964 New York Shakespeare Festival production, the director, Gladys Vaughan, had a crisis with the producer, Joe Papp. He said that she was giving him an Othello that was an Eisenhower, and that he wanted an Othello that was a Malcolm X. She replied that she didn't want to go that way, no matter how tempting it might be given the social dynamics of the day, because Othello cannot be a negative person—and Malcolm X started out as a negative entity, caustic in his criticisms. As part of our response to Joe, Gladys and I first developed the concept of the Sun God, that creature of fire and light.

The sun is stable and still at the center of the busyness around it, but it is boiling and lethal.

For a 1971 production, the director John Berry introduced a contrary concept. He had had interesting experiences in cultural relativism: having traveled and worked with various groups all over the world, he had been surprised to find that treachery seemed to be a common, everyday occurrence in North Africa—it was culturally accepted, and even expected. John thought that such a darkly knowing attitude would work for Othello, and that we should feel even at the beginning the heavy undertow of negativity which eventually drags him under. I tried it, since I've also always found that Othello is just so savvy that I don't believe that anyone could slip anything over on him—but it didn't work, and perhaps it could never work. We were trying to add cynicism to the Sun God, and yet his knowledge is different from cunning. To give him that sly, defensive attitude is to take away from his vulnerability and the largeness of his understanding, and it's important that his nobility is maintained for as long as possible. We have to keep Othello's way of thinking distinct from Iago's, since although they are friends on the surface, they turn out to be mighty opposites in terms of their fundamental modes of thought.

The last production of *Othello* I participated in was in 1982. There are several reasons I will always remember that production, the most important being that I had just married my wife, Cecilia Hart. She came in after we opened on Broadway as a replacement for the Desdemona (we had already burnt out three actresses), and while we were still performing she was pregnant with our son, Flynn. The initial director was Peter Coe; through his decisions he allowed Christopher Plummer, who was playing Iago, to turn it into what one of the most caustic critics of the play, Thomas Rymer, called "a bloody farce" in

1693, and I think Peter's decisions leaned that way because he didn't understand the character of Desdemona, that essential third pillar, and so he wasn't getting what he needed out of the play. Instead, it seemed as if he figured that at least he'd turn it into a crowd pleaser. We were in a perfect storm for a farce. When we arrived in Minneapolis during the out-of-town try-outs, we were booked into a monster of a theater that was not conducive to subtlety, and where only the bold strokes of per-formance seemed to register: the tone was therefore set from the beginning. Then the audience surprisingly and rambunc-tiously responded to Iago's antics—so much so that I think it even embarrassed Chris, which wouldn't have been surprising since he is classically trained, and a fine actor. I remember quite vividly when he came off stage from a howl-fest, and said to me, echoing that unnerving line of Rymer, "Oh, darling, this is a bloody farce after all." At that moment, I knew I had a wonder-ful costar, but no ally.

Since Rymer, *Othello* has been described as a one-act com-edy followed by four acts of tragedy. However farcical or come-dic, Iago is a scary role (like Shylock), and it is a difficult role for any human being because it is so ugly. After all, Iago is the man who invents racism (in the context of the play). So, without the help of a good director the actor is tempted to take it to the jokes. The day I told Peter I couldn't work with him anymore, he responded, "You're just jealous because Iago's getting all the laughs." Well, I couldn't have stated my case more clearly, except that I wouldn't have used the word "jealous."

I've always felt that Iago encapsulates the hurt of the mod-ern man. He might be the most understandable character in this age, when all of us can, if we're not lucky, have the expe-rience of being passed over and of not having the chance to get ahead in society. Iago is sorely wanting, and the last straw was when he found out that he wasn't going to be chosen as Othello's lieutenant.

There's a reason Othello didn't choose Iago as his lieutenant. My suspicion is that Iago knew too much, and that he was the one who did the dirty work that allowed Othello to keep his hands clean. He was the Beria to Othello's Stalin—he was the head of their equivalent of a secret police, and he possessed information about Othello as well as about everyone he would have had to investigate, and in the text we can feel something of that in his valuing, search for, and manipulation of information. Whatever use the secret police can be, however, it eventually comes to an end—on the other side, the moral and emotional investment of he who operates as the secret police costs a great deal. Long before the relationship between the two men becomes completely destructive, it is perhaps already a subtly abusive relationship. That dark history is both why Iago isn't chosen, and why he thinks he ought to be. Othello has two liaisons in this culture—and he needs them both, for he is a stranger in a strange land. Iago is one; Cassio is the other—but Cassio has clean hands, and he is more socialized and less dangerous to be promoted to a position of power in this society.

As a result, Cassio is chosen and Iago is passed over, which must have hurt beyond anything I think Shakespeare was able to write about, but he indicated it, and he gave us the fruit of that hurt. "Revenge" is a small word when it comes to Iago, for he is motivated by a source much deeper; he's operating from the soul. He is not a motiveless villain in any way, for his motives are almost too common, and too real. Therefore, to play Iago as glib is to lose the essence of that hurt. Lucifer was God's most glorious angel until God asked something of him he couldn't do; Lucifer refused, and got kicked out of heaven. The disappointment drifted into bitterness, and that bitterness converted his nature and he became Satan. Iago's pain is that of Lucifer himself.

Zoe Caldwell was brought in as the rescue director, and she almost salvaged that production. She said that audiences were coming to see the classic Titans clash, both as actors on the stage, Chris and me, and as characters in the play, Iago and Othello. "You must take Chris on," she said. I didn't think that Shakespeare had written such a scene, and I said, "I don't know what you mean." Her response was simply, "I know you don't." I passed up the opportunity to explore something in that production, and now I'm coming to grips with it in this essay. But even though I do agree, and always did agree with Zoe that they are two great figures, I've never seen the play as a battle between them. In fact, it's the opposite: they are brothers, and the fact that there is a conflict between them is always a surprise to Othello. There can't be an out-and-out duel between them because they're fitted with different pistols. Iago is loaded with the prose with which he can counsel, charm, and diddle with the audience: this language is plain talk, close to everyday speech. Furthermore, Iago speaks directly to the audience in his soliloquies in what could even be called *The Confessions of Iago*. Othello, on the other hand, is loaded with iambic pentameter: this language, by contrast, is classical, poetic. He doesn't have the chance to speak directly to the audience in that familiar manner. Both Iago and Othello are great, but they are great in very different modes.

In character, in mode, in text, it sometimes seems to me that there are actually two tragedies intertwined in this one play. There is of course *The Tragedy of Othello*, but there is also the intercalated *Confessions of Iago*, and I want to give it its own title to emphasize that, just as Othello can be diminished as a tragic figure when he is made less noble, so can Iago be diminished as a tragic figure when he is denied his own journey. It is in these soliloquies especially that Iago can be seen most clearly, for indeed it is in them when, alone on stage, he unleashes his alter-Iago. This is when we see the Iago who hates people, who is tormented by his own jealousy, who is struggling with the pain of his own fall from grace. However the actor goes about it, Iago must deal with a tragedy of his own making, just as Othello must deal with his. In some ways, moreover, the tragedy of Iago is deeper and more modern than the tragedy of Othello, and the temptation for the actor playing Iago is to play Othello's story and dance around his own. But by avoiding looking into the source and development of Iago's hurt, the actor throws the play out of balance. There is a delicate fabric of credibility that exists in any play, and the responsibility of each actor is to face his own story head-on, and not be uncomfortable with the darkness of his character, and not transform those depths through cuteness into farce. Iago says that he will tell Othello all he knows, "Pricked to't by foolish honesty and love" (3.3.455). If you deliver that line with a wink, you destroy the suspension of disbelief and tear the delicate fabric of credibility. The wink is an apology for tragedy: Shakespeare's play needs no apology.

* * *

My father, who was an actor, was obsessed with Shakespeare, and he was obsessed with Othello. He never really achieved it, but it was his dream. He couldn't accept my Othello either. Gladys Vaughan, my director, warned me, "He can only try to get you to do his performance, and that would destroy yours." She was right, of course, but to this day I'm still haunted by my father's dream.

My father always spoke of Tommaso Salvini, the Italian

actor who traveled with Stanislavski's troupe. While everybody else spoke the language of their host countries, Salvini only spoke in Italian. Therefore, he spoke everything Othello said in Italian—but it didn't matter if the audience understood the language or not, since he was able to communicate the feeling. At the moment when he said that infamous line "be sure thou prove my love a whore" (3.3.397), he would throw Iago on the floor, and then he would stand over him and raise his foot as if to stamp his head in. Salvini was an operatic type, he was a big guy, and a stamp from his foot would have hurt—indeed, it would have killed the man lying there on the floor. At that moment, with his foot poised and about to come down, the audience would stand up en masse in protest.

Salvini's gesture won't work now, because the audience doesn't have that kind of connection to the stage anymore. In the age of television and movies, especially with special effects, all we see is brutality played out fully. In Trevor Nunn's 2004 film version featuring Sir Ian McKellen as Iago and Willard White as Othello, Othello charges Iago so that they both end up on the floor, Othello pinning Iago to the ground with his hands around his throat. It is a similarly threatening act—perhaps even more threatening than Salvini with his foot—but no matter how well executed, the context of theatrical convention has in part robbed such gestures of their effect. We know that the foot isn't going to come down; we know that the throat isn't going to be cut.

I've sought out different Othellos from my father's time over the years, but I've always been intrigued by his vision of that one, crucial moment. I'm now resolved that it has got to be something that the audience can't help but experience. We need to feel that Iago knows he is about to die—not that he may die, but that he is really and truly about to die. That Othello is going to kill him. That his next breath, his next heartbeat, will be his last. We, too, in the audience and perhaps even on the stage, need to feel that Iago is about to die—that the play has gone beyond mere fiction and is turning into a terrible reality.

* * *

My interest in this account of Salvini is not about pure shock value. It has to do with the fact that I have come to firmly believe that *the entire balance of the play depends on getting that one moment right*—one last chance to put Othello back in charge where he is not Iago's dupe and victim, but is responsible for his own fall from grace.

The long exchange between Othello and Iago in Act 3, Scene 3 is known as the Temptation Scene. Iago insinuates that Desdemona has been unfaithful. Taking Iago by surprise, Othello then commands:

> OTHELLO: Villain, be sure thou prove my love a whore;
> Be sure of it: give me the ocular proof,
> Or by the worth of mine eternal soul,
> Thou hadst been better have been born a dog
> Than answer my waked wrath!
> IAGO: Is't come to this?
> OTHELLO: Make me to see't, or at the least so prove it
> That the probation bear no hinge nor loop
> To hang a doubt on, or woe upon thy life!
>
> (3.3.397–405)

There's no way of knowing what actions Shakespeare had in mind to go with those words. Can I even speculate? In the source text, Cinthio's *Hecatommithi*, the character of the Moor threatens to cut out his ensign's tongue unless he can prove the allegations. We can be reasonably sure, I think, that Shakespeare took it for granted that his corresponding scene would be accompanied by a similar threat of torture.

To get the full effect of the scene today, though, the act of violence needs to be shocking even to what we think we know about savagery. There has to be something as impressive as Salvini standing with his foot raised over Iago's head, but it has to be more than simple violence. It has to be the violence of a certain mind game which has to do with the idea: *I take over your life.** The phrase "I take over your life" can mean different things to different people, but however you get there it should end with the victim not owning his life anymore.

* * *

I have an idea for how that could be staged and performed. I've never tried it, but I'm convinced that it's the only way to keep the scene, and the entire play, from turning to pathos. At the end of this essay, you'll find the detailed notes that I wrote into the margins of my Variorum edition, which show how I, as an actor, have found a way to make sense of this difficult transition. In the main body of this essay, I'd like to explain my reasoning. The only thing I can conceive of that would save the Temptation Scene, and so the play, is to employ an act of torture—and what is very present in the consciousness of the Western world is that thing we call "waterboarding."

---

* In the Sioux culture, as the movie *Little Big Man* shows, if you save a person's life then you own that person's spirit—but you also have to feed that person for the rest of his or her life. It's beyond slavery, for it's a possession of another spirit.

It's simple and believable; it's historical (the Spanish Inquisition used a version) and yet it's terrifyingly modern. Former Vice President Dick Cheney has called the use of waterboarding a "no-brainer" and encouraged it as part of a "robust interrogation system." I concluded, sitting there watching one of the first interviews in which he spoke of such "enhanced interrogation techniques," that anyone who condones such acts has joined the savagery.

If one were to do something of this sort in *Othello*, then the set designer would have to be prepared to provide some sort of fountain or tub of drain water in the Temptation Scene.* The actor's head would have to be under water for however long it would take until the audience started to become seriously disturbed. They would have to believe that they were unmistakably witnessing somebody being tortured, and water is the only thing that could do it—water and time. There would have to be many seemingly endless seconds when there would be no sound on stage except the splashing of Iago's hands flailing in the water. The average person can hold his breath for about a minute under water; after that, the body goes into stress. If, when he comes up, Iago tries to be cute again, Othello pushes him back under until he owns him completely. This is where the torturer says, "I hereby commit you to death," and then immediately says afterward, "I hereby own your life"—and that repetition should go on until there is a total submission of Iago's hubris. The rush of the verse would stop for these prolonged seconds of suspense; the iambic pentameter would be

---

* In Al Pacino's stage version of *The Merchant of Venice*, the people of Venice stick Shylock's head under water in a fountain to baptize him, but they really want to drown him—and then when Al comes up he looks like a wet rat, which is the kind of unresigned pathos that Al knows how to play gloriously. It was a great moment, I thought: a deeply disturbing moment.

suspended.* There are times when action is more important than poetry, and the savagery would disrupt those lines with an energy all its own. "Nay, stay: thou shouldst be honest" (3.3.421) could be a dunking of several seconds. The line suggests that Othello is wavering, and I don't think he should waver here. The submersions would continue until Othello says, "Now do I see 'tis true" (3.3.489). These vicious actions would transform a scene in which there is, I believe, too much talking between those two men into the dramatic turning point in both character and plot that it can be. It should be an ugly scene. Whatever hubris or fire that is left in Iago must be wrung out of him. Othello takes over Iago's life.

That play deserves that moment to be ugly, for it marks Othello's transition from a noble man to the alter-Othello, the man from chaos. He begins to sacrifice his larger, kinder, more magnanimous self for a much smaller and yet more violent self. The Sun God has chosen to no longer restrain himself, and his entire world is thereby thrown into peril. He has spun out of his own orbit; he has thrown the cosmology of that world off balance; he

---

* I also believe that some of Shakespeare's lines seem melodramatic today—and perhaps even seemed melodramatic in his day too. I would suggest cutting such lines. With playwrights coming to us in translation, it's more acceptable to alter lines, but Shakespeare wrote in English and so we feel more uneasy about making changes. Nevertheless, there are circumstances which allow us to reevaluate. In *Othello*, for instance, some lines are dispensable because they are purely melodramatic explosions that can only evoke titters of laughter in modern audiences, and my advice to all playwrights and directors is that a tittering audience is an audience that is rejecting your play, and that actors need not be subjected to lost audiences. I think some of Othello's expressions, such as "O monstrous! Monstrous!" (3.3.469), and "I'll tear her all to pieces" (3.3.475), as well as even Iago's line, mentioned previously, "Pricked to't by foolish honesty and love" (3.3.455), are risky lines in that they threaten to tear the fabric of credibility.

has fallen from grace. Just as you can't be the victim of that sort of savagery without being transformed, you can't commit that form of interrogation without giving up something of your own soul.

With such savagery surrounding it, that key line of the scene—indeed, of the entire play—wouldn't require additional force: "be sure thou prove my love a whore." It's all there in that one line. *Prove to me that she's a whore.* He doesn't say, "Prove to me she *isn't* a whore." I believe that Othello then terrorizes Iago into proving, and that Iago then has the license to tell all the lies he wants. We resort to torture to hear what we want to hear, and the irony is that if we want to hear lies then we'll hear lies. Iago offers the story of what he heard in Cassio's dream. Iago himself must be unprepared for the attack: "O grace! O heaven forgive me! / Are you a man? Have you a soul? Or sense?" (3.3.413–414). The lines cannot be Iago acting his part; they must come from a real place of fear. After the waterboarding, which is a sort of ghastly baptism, Iago would then return as a different man. I can't help but think of the photo of Khalid Sheikh Mohammed after he has been waterboarded, looking like he's practically dead. After Iago has gone through such an experience, his spirit would be more subdued even as his hatred would be empowered. His hubris is gone, replaced by animus; he is more lethal now, but he is strangely muted. Like Hamlet when he comes back from sea, having survived the attempt on his life, from that moment on Iago has nothing more to lose.

* * *

Othello is written with nobility and power, and so to diminish him, to make him the victim of Iago, is to lose out on one of the classic antagonistic relationships in all of literature. Othello is responsible for the loss of his nobility in the moment when he chooses to turn to revenge.

When you diffuse the responsibility of the hero and put it onto others, then you take away from his greatness, and from the tragedy. I believe that Shakespeare wrote his tragic characters as those who had great responsibilities and who failed in their responsibilities. There can be no pathos allowed in the lives of heroes, and there's only this one moment in *Othello* when that can be turned around. It makes Othello himself more of a monster, but that's better than a pathetic fool.

From that point on, it's Othello's fault. It has to be.

That's the essential question—whose fault is it?—not just for *Othello*, but for all the tragedies. It has to be the fault of Othello, and of Lear, and of all the other tragic protagonists, or the plays fall apart. The responsibility cannot be externalized. It cannot be the fault of the others, neither of Iago, nor of Goncril and Regan.

Tragedy happens when someone who has great potential does not live up to it and fails. I find that all the tragedies are the fault of the great men. When King Lear cries out, at one of his worst moments, "I am a man / More sinned against than sinning" (3.2.56–57), he must know deep down that he's lying, because he had all the power, and in particular he had all the power to sin, and he did, so he was more sinning than sinned against.

Similarly, Othello should know that it's not Iago's fault, and the audience too should know that the tragedy that will follow is entirely the fault of Othello.

* * *

Tragedy is about fault, I believe—not flaws. It should not be possible to ascribe the tragic outcome to some distinct, easily classifiable, and potentially extractable tragic flaw, such as jealousy or self-indulgence. The problem never gets to the point of a tragic flaw in either Othello or Lear. Instead they suffer from what I call "tragic confusion," which is confusion so deep that neither can escape it.

Othello never gets to jealousy, for instance, even though the traditional quick reading of the play has it that he is over-whelmed by that rancid emotion. Jealousy is when you only see one image: an image of a guilty woman. That's what Leon-tes sees in *The Winter's Tale*, and that's what Iago himself sees, since he believes that Othello slept with Emilia. But Othello himself is caught between two images: an image of Desdemona as an angel, and the alter-Desdemona as conjured by Iago. One moment he knows she's faithful; the next moment he hears something Iago says, and doubts: back and forth, back and forth, and then finally the savagery evinced during the Tempta-tion Scene resurges. Othello never quite makes it to jealousy, but on his way there approaches instead a form of madness—and in that madness, he kills Desdemona.

Lear starts out as an issue of King Lear's will and his reason. He has lost his reason to begin with, and he is just acting on his will: his will to be king, and his will to retire the way he wants to retire. He's like a grumpy old man who wants everything his way. Does he want to divide his kingdom equally? No, he wants to sponge off his daughters, one after the other. But without his reason, his will alone can defend him for only so long against the rise of his own tragic confusion.

Lear utters that chilling plea "O, let me not be mad" (1.5.34)—but how would that be worse than what's already hap-pening? He is already in the grip of his confusion, which is that he doesn't know where the fault lies, and that he doesn't want to accept the responsibility himself. Lear never goes mad; what he suffers from are severe exhaustion and exposure. He never loses his mind; he gains his awakening. This occurs on the heath, which is a moonscape devoid of all the comforts of humanity where nature hammers the characters out into what they really are and breaks them down into the elements, the bare essentials. He starts calling Edgar "philosopher" because he sees that in the simplicity of a man who has nothing, whose ass is hanging out of his clothes, there is wisdom. "Is man no more than this?" he asks. "Consider him well. Thou ow'st the worm no silk, the beast no hide, the sheep no wool, the cat no perfume" (3.4.86–87), and then determines, "Thou art the thing itself: unaccommodated man is no more but such a poor bare, forked animal as thou art" (3.4.88–89). Lear wants that wisdom, and then he starts gaining that wisdom—which is what he needed all along. Lear goes on to the wisdom he finds only by acknowledging that, in contrast with his previous indulgences as king, there are poor people out there in the storm who are freezing to death.

> Poor naked wretches, wheresoe'er you are,
> That bide the pelting of this pitiless storm,
> How shall your houseless heads and unfed sides,
> Your lopped and windowed raggedness, defend you
> From seasons such as these? O, I have ta'en
> Too little care of this! Take physic, pomp,
> Expose thyself to feel what wretches feel,
> That thou mayst shake the superflux to them
> And show the heavens more just.
>
> (3.4.31–39)

That recognition replaces him in society; it repositions him in humanity. A man is king when he finally learns to accept responsibility for his own actions, and his own life, and if there's any lesson Lear learns in his play it's what it means to rule, and to fail to rule, over himself.

Lear accepts his responsibility early enough to save his own character; but the tragedy must play out. Othello doesn't accept his responsibility until just after he has killed Desdemona:

> Methinks it should be now a huge eclipse
> Of sun and moon, and that th'affrighted globe
> Did yawn at alteration.
>
> (5.2.116–118)

He sees the cosmos out of balance and he's looking for the heavens to find an equilibrium after what he's done, and so he takes his own life. Othello accepts that life goes on beyond him, and around him.

* * *

I've always been interested by the issues that Hugh Quarshie has raised with regard to *Othello*. In "Second Thoughts About *Othello*" he writes (and Hugh Quarshie is a stunningly brilliant scholar):

> [I]f a black actor plays Othello does he not risk making racial stereotypes seem legitimate and even true? When a black actor plays a role written for a white actor in black make-up and for a predominantly white audience, does he not encourage the white way, or rather the wrong way, of looking at black men, namely that black men, or "Moors," are over-emotional, excitable

and unstable, thereby vindicating Iago's statement, "These Moors are changeable in their wills"?*

Hugh then concludes: "Of all the parts in the canon, perhaps Othello is the one which should most definitely not be played by a black actor."

Hugh gives us a lot of challenges, and I've thought a lot about them, but I'm coming to the conclusion that most of them are useless. At a certain point, you have to drop your personal sensitivity about race. Just like the problem of a black actor living in a racist society: you get on with it. And you get on with the play, too, in spite of what you might think was in Shakespeare's mind.** We mustn't throw the baby out with the wash, which is what we do when we discount *Othello* on the grounds of race.

On the contrary, the play is immensely valuable, given that Shakespeare deals with race in a way that's complex and even uncanny. The more I think about it, the more I think that the most interesting relationship between *Othello* and issues of race is that they're already woven into the fabric of the text itself. This play witnesses the birth of racism in its realm. Nobody cares about race at the beginning, least of all Othello. He's simply doing the job he can do. There is no consciousness of

---

* Hugh Quarshie, "Second Thoughts About *Othello*," Occasional Paper no. 7 (Chipping Campden: International Shakespeare Association 1999). Both quotations, page 5.
** Hugh is a brilliant Oxford scholar, and what I would suggest, rather cheekily, is that the best thing that he can do, after he has scared away all the other black actors who are crazy enough to listen to his theories about race in Shakespeare, is to pull up his socks and take on Othello himself—perhaps even along with an actor who doesn't mind getting his wig wet, and who can hold his breath for sixty seconds.

race, no mention of race, and certainly no disparagement. "Her father loved me" (1.3.132), says Othello of Desdemona's father, and we have no reason not to take him at his word. But Iago has begun to plant seeds, first by mocking him as "his Moorship" (1.1.33) to Roderigo, who responds by referring to him as "the thick-lips" (1.1.68), and then to Brabantio with the taunt, "Even now, now, very now, an old black ram / Is tupping your white ewe" (1.1.92–93)—and what we witness in those lines is the conjuring of racism.

I do believe, however, that if we take the fault away from Othello, then we make him a victim—which, in its own way, is a form of racism.

I think that if Shakespeare is read enough, or seen enough, or heard enough, then he has the power to change us. In general, though, I don't think that you can change anyone else's *mind* about anything: you can only change people's *feelings*. That's why I take exception to productions that are feelingless, and that's why I cheer when someone like Sir Derek Jacobi throws himself into every primal moment that Shakespeare offers— and Shakespeare offers you a bushel. I have a great respect for Derek's King Lear, because every time there was an opportunity he brought passion into it and it came alive. That's the only chance one has of creating any sort of changes. And they won't be changes up in the head: they will be changes about how you feel about Lear's life, about Othello's life—about old age, about racism.

If I've learned anything in the course of watching and playing Shakespeare over the years, it's that when Shakespeare's lines come from the head, they fall flat, and that when those same lines come from the heart, and when you feel them instead of think them, then they erupt, and they can be let loose in a fire and fury.

LINE NOTES

As an actor, I find my way into a text by looking closely at the lines themselves, and at how they follow one another. Here is how I see the movement of the Temptation Scene.

> OTHELLO: Excellent wretch! Perdition catch my soul,
> But I do love thee! And when I love thee not,
> Chaos is come again.
>
> (3.3.100–102)

"When" means the hypothetical "if," not the eventual "when," for the latter suggests too much premonition.

> IAGO: My noble lord—
> OTHELLO: What dost thou say, Iago?
> IAGO: Did Michael Cassio, when you wooed my lady,
> Know of your love?
> OTHELLO: He did, from first to last: why dost thou ask?
> IAGO: But for a satisfaction of my thought,
> No further harm.
>
> (3.3.103–109)

The temptation here is to have Othello busy with his papers, but he must give Iago his full attention throughout so that he hears all of Iago's insinuations. Othello knows that Iago has a cloud looming over him, and Othello wants to help him clarify his problems.

> OTHELLO: I prithee speak to me as to thy thinkings,
> As thou dost ruminate, and give thy worst of thoughts
> The worst of words.
>
> (3.3.149–151)

That is where Iago balks, and in balking he is disobeying his superior's orders. We must assume that, like any military officer, Othello assumes ownership of those who are subject to him, body and mind, and that he will not be denied a command.

> IAGO: . . . it is my nature's plague
> To spy into abuses, and oft my jealousy
> Shapes faults that are not . . .
>
> (3.3.166–168)

That Iago is plagued with jealousy and admits it should be common knowledge. Not only does Othello know all about it, but he must have tried to persuade Iago that neither he nor Cassio is guilty of cuckolding him—which cannot help a jealous man. Iago is caught between not being jealous and not being secure.

> OTHELLO: Ha?
> IAGO: O, beware, my lord, of jealousy:
> It is the green-eyed monster which doth mock
> The meat it feeds on.
>
> (3.3.186–189)

It is too early for that line to mean that Othello is exasperated, so instead of delivering that line with a sharp, *Ha!*, Othello cannot believe that this fellow is so stubborn, and the response is converted to ironic laughter, "Ha, ha, ha." In addition, that gives time to disassociate Iago's admonition, so it is clearer that Iago is talking about his own jealousy, not Othello's. It would be impertinent for Iago to imply, at this early stage, that Othello is jealous.

> OTHELLO: . . . No, Iago,
> I'll see before I doubt; when I doubt, prove;

And on the proof, there is no more but this:
Away at once with love or jealousy.
IAGO: I am glad of this, for now I shall have reason
To show the love and duty that I bear you
With franker spirit . . .

$$(3.3.212–218)$$

Now, the alter-Iago pounces, as if to say, "Good. Now I can test you. If you are so secure, take a drop of this poison."

IAGO: She that so young could give out such a
    seeming,
To seel her father's eyes up close as oak,
He thought 'twas witchcraft. But I am much to blame:
I humbly do beseech you of your pardon
For too much loving you.

$$(3.3.234–238)$$

At that word "witchcraft" Othello's whole body must convulse, so much so that it is obvious to the audience and Iago. Iago knows he has gone too far, as revealed in his next line, "but I am much to blame."

IAGO: I see this hath a little dashed your spirits.
OTHELLO: Not a jot, not a jot.

$$(3.3.240–241)$$

Iago's observation is certainly true. Othello's answer is true as well, however, because Othello still thinks he can handle it.

OTHELLO: And yet, how nature erring from itself—
IAGO: Ay, there's the point: as—to be bold with you—

Not to affect many proposèd matches
Of her own clime, complexion and degree,
Whereto we see in all things nature tends—
Foh, one may smell in such a will most rank,
Foul disproportions, thoughts unnatural.
But pardon me: I do not in position
Distinctly speak of her . . .

(3.3.256–264)

It's hard to tell what Othello means by that line, but Iago pounces again. He's defining Desdemona on a cultural level. Othello's response is reflexive: he strikes him across the face with his glove, or gauntlet. Iago says, "But pardon me," apologizing for painting Desdemona in evil colors. The same revulsion he had at the word "witchcraft" he now has at the phrase "thoughts unnatural."

OTHELLO: Why did I marry?

(3.3.272)

You can only read that line out of ironic laughter. He doesn't mean it, and it's not an expression of paranoia either.

OTHELLO: Ha, ha, false to me?

(3.3.370)

Let's try converting that "Ha, ha" to ironic laughter as well—it could be perceived as quite maniacal. More importantly, Othello has not resolved to rage yet. He's still trying to keep his rational self in charge. He's musing again. The opposite of self-pity, in plays, is that one is constantly in awe of things, not defeated by them. He's not amused, but he's constantly musing about what's happening and trying to understand it.

OTHELLO: What sense had I in her stol'n hours of lust?

(3.3.376)

No explosion should be attempted in this line and in the passages following. Rather, the attempt should be to hold on to rationality and reason. He's not only musing, but he has begun to challenge Iago: "Do you understand what's happened to me?" He goes through quite a confessional. He's not saying, "It's your fault."

OTHELLO: I had been happy, if the general camp,
Pioneers and all, had tasted her sweet body,
So I had nothing known. O, now, for ever
Farewell the tranquil mind; farewell content;
Farewell the plumèd troops, and the big wars
That makes ambition virtue! O, farewell!
Farewell the neighing steed and the shrill trump,
The spirit-stirring drum, th'ear-piercing fife,
The royal banner, and all quality,
Pride, pomp and circumstance of glorious war!
And, O, you mortal engines, whose rude throats
Th'immortal Jove's dread clamours counterfeit,
Farewell! Othello's occupation's gone.

(3.3.383–395)

This is a critical speech. Given that Othello believes his occupation to be a good one—that it is noble to save Venice—the conclusion "Othello's occupation's gone" is the pronouncement of the end of his nobility. If I were a director I would have Othello deliver the lines straight, without pathos, as they have a tendency to become mawkish and self-pitying. There's a quiet way of giving life to all those exclamation points, though, and I think it would be effective if this passage occurred as a moment of stillness, since what comes next is even greater in dramatic volume. There's another reason for a calm delivery, too. I'm reminded of a piece of acting advice I was once given, which was that an audience never likes to hear an actor complain. A character can raise his voice in rage, and he can express surprise and dismay at the state of things, but he should never raise his voice in self-pity because it's quite simply irrelevant and no one wants to hear it. A judge might have pity on you if you plead your case in this way, but the audience won't have pity on you. This is the end of Othello's previous life, his previous state of being, and this is where he begins to spin out of orbit and put that entire world in danger.

OTHELLO: Villain, be sure thou prove my love a whore.

(3.3.397)

At this point, the direct and rational man finally begins to convulse, but even then, his gambit is to demand proof. Since Iago has no way of anticipating that, it catches him off-guard.

OTHELLO: For nothing canst thou to damnation add
Greater than that.
IAGO: O grace! O heaven forgive me!
Are you a man? Have you a soul? Or sense?

(3.3.411–414)

This is where I imagine the first dunk. There would be nothing histrionic about it: these are professional soldiers. He's held under for a spell of time, and then when he's released he spouts out the lines which follow.

OTHELLO: Nay, stay: thou shouldst be honest.

(3.3.421)

This is the second dunking. It is not Othello wavering, or changing his mind, or letting Iago off the hook. He has given a command: prove she's a whore, and he has not backed off, and he will not back off.

OTHELLO: I'll not endure it. Would I were satisfied!

(3.3.431)

Othello is not pleading for Iago to give him satisfaction; he is not in the throes of pathos. If anything, this is the threat of more torture.

OTHELLO: Death and damnation! O!

(3.3.439)

The third dunking. After that, we're back to storytelling. No more dunking.

IAGO: In sleep I heard him say, "Sweet Desdemona,
Let us be wary, let us hide our loves" . . .

(3.3.461–462)

Iago is coming clean and confessing all he knows—only Cassio's dream did not happen. In his panic, he's giving Othello what he wants to hear, and so he makes up the story about the dream.

OTHELLO: Now do I see 'tis true.

(3.3.489)

That's when the alter-Othello takes over, and he begins to spiral downward.

> OTHELLO: . . . Like to the Pontic sea,
> . . . my bloody thoughts with violent pace
> Shall ne'er look back, ne'er ebb to humble love,
> Till that a capable and wide revenge
> Swallow them up. Now, by yond marble heaven,
> In the due reverence of a sacred vow
> I here engage my words.

(3.3.499; 503–508)

This is a battle vow; part of Othello's downward spiral is an alliance with Iago. Othello resorts to cosmology again in "by yond marble heaven," which is neither of the Christian nor of the Islamic faith, but of his own faith.

IAGO: Do not rise yet.

(3.3.509)

The line immediately follows Othello's vow. Iago is trying to gain footing to control Othello, but Othello must ignore the command. He must rise.

Eamonn Walker

OTHELLO IN LOVE

EAMONN WALKER is an English stage and screen actor. In addition to performing in *Julius Caesar* at the Belasco Theatre on Broadway, he was the first black actor to perform the role of Othello at the Globe Theatre; he played a different version of the role as John Othello in a modern film version of the play, for which he was honored with the BFM Film and Television Award. His film credits include *Cadillac Records*, *The Messenger*, *Legacy*, *A Lonely Place to Die*, and *The Company Men*; his TV credits include *ER*, *Kings*, *Lights Out*, *Chicago Fire*, and *Oz*, for which he was recognized with a CableACE Award.

The most powerful thing in the world is love. I come from that point of view, and I think that Shakespeare believed it too. Even though his works explore a great variety of emotions, it was finding the source of the love in the plays which finally helped me to understand them.

At school in North London, I hated Shakespeare. Everything about it seemed difficult, and it certainly wasn't my language. A friend of mine I've known since I was twelve years old, Vicky Lennox, used to encourage me to do Shakespeare, and over the years she wouldn't let it go even though I resisted. It wasn't until I was a working actor that I started picking up books and tapes. I started, almost grudgingly, to like it, and then at last I fell in love with it—but even though I ended up reading and watching everything I could find, I still had no intention of playing any

Shakespeare myself. There was still a certain amount of fear. I'm a self-taught actor, and other than going to Anna Scher's community-based after-school drama club, everything I've ever learnt I picked up by going to plays, attending seminars, signing up for classes, asking questions from all those actors and directors who knew more than me, and reading so much that my house is now full to the roof with books. When I had a production company, my partner and I would sit and read through as many plays as we could—new ones, mostly, but I also read and reread all of Shakespeare's, because I knew there was some magic in those plays and I was trying to touch it, even though I couldn't quite figure out what it was. Nevertheless, I always felt like I didn't quite own it, and so even though I was invited to work on Shakespeare a few times, I still didn't think it was for me. Fear is a funny thing, but once you've internalized your own limits it can take a miracle to overcome them.

*　*　*

For me, that miracle took the form of the chance to work with one of my heroes on stage. My first professional Shakespeare was as Mark Antony opposite Denzel Washington as Brutus in *Julius Caesar*. After a full day of rehearsals, I used to work on the text for another few hours every night because I was convinced that I needed to give it the extra time in order to try to make it fully mine. At first I worked with Vicky, and then after she left I learned as much as I could from Colm Feore, who played Cassius, and who is one of the real masters of acting Shakespeare. In our long conversations, he instilled in me an even greater appreciation of how the pictures Shakespeare draws in our imagination, through both his poetry and his prose, capture even the subtlest and most intricate of human experiences.

We all brought a huge intensity to the play which was thrilling to enact. When Mark Antony says "Cry havoc and let slip the dogs of war" (3.1.292), Denzel and I went to war with a real passion. For me, even though it's a political play, it's also a play about the strength of a certain kind of love: the love of Mark Antony for his mentor and father figure, Julius Caesar. Mark Antony has been a playboy, since under Caesar's protection he has benefitted from endless amounts of money, complete security, and the knowledge that there are no consequences to his actions. When Caesar is killed at the first pivot of the play, and Mark Antony is covered in the blood of this man who has been his father, he's wracked by a deep sorrow. This is the grounding for the revenge that ensues, and this is the birth of the political animal Mark Antony becomes in the second half of *Julius Caesar* and which he remains—with that love coming back and taking a different form—throughout *Antony and Cleopatra*. As an actor, you can viscerally feel this transformation during his speech after Caesar's death. It begins with those famous words:

> Friends, Romans, countrymen, lend me your ears:
> I come to bury Caesar, not to praise him.
>
> (3.2.70–71)

Towards the end, he says, echoing the words of the beginning,

> I come not, friends, to steal away your hearts:
> I am no orator, as Brutus is;
> But as you know me all a plain blunt man
> That love my friend ...
>
> (3.2.212–215)

We brought in the audience for that speech by turning up the house lights: I spoke to them, told them my plight, and tried to bring them around to my side. The speech works, both on stage and in the play, since Mark Antony comes to recognize—despite his modest protestations—that his rhetoric is powerful, that it is indeed effective, that he is someone to be listened to, and that he has a *voice*. And that political voice comes from the source within, which is grieving love of his friend, Caesar, his assassinated father.

We performed at the Belasco Theatre on Broadway, and Denzel's fans filled up all of Forty-fourth Street so that the traffic was at a standstill. Many of those who came to see the play were used to being in the cinema; they were taking the opportunity to see him live, on stage, and so some of them knew Shakespeare already and some of them did not. After the show, one of the wonderful things Denzel did was to sign everybody's program, with a smile, a personal word, and sometimes a picture—for hundreds of people, every night for each of our 128 performances. Sometimes I would sign too, and what I loved to hear was when those who had seen the show would tell me how much they had hated Shakespeare in school because it had seemed like it was not for them, or like it was beyond them, or outside of them. Then they would relate that when they had heard us saying the lines it had seemed like we were just talking to one another, and that they had felt like they were being woken up, and that they couldn't wait to go read and see all the plays to enter into an entirely new relationship with Shakespeare. I don't think I could ever have a prouder experience than to be a part of that—since I'd had to go through the same awakening. My job as an actor, which is, after all, as a kind of storyteller, is to awaken a different perspective in audiences than the one they already have, so they have a bigger, brighter, fuller picture of the world—and the subtlest and most spectacular picture of the world we have was gifted to us by Shakespeare.

The world of *Othello*, in particular, is on such a grand scale that it encompasses both an incredible sadness and a sublime beauty. I've had the great fortune to be in two versions of *Othello*: a modern version, with modern language, filmed for London Weekend Television and PBS in 2002, and a stage production at the Globe Theatre in 2007. *Othello* starts with a man who is at his highest point, and throughout the play we watch his downfall. The sad thing about playing Othello is that you're coming into this man's life at the top, at the very pinnacle of his achievement, and from there you're going downhill. That's the sadness, but if you get the love right then it's beautiful too, for tragedy is about more than just despair: it's the contrast between sadness and beauty, between what could be and what happens, between what happens to them and what, we hope, will happen to us.

"It's about love," begins the film version so masterfully scripted by Andrew Davies. We all enjoy a good love story, and we all see ourselves within such stories because we are all looking for love. Some of us are lucky enough to have had it, and to understand how unconditional love is a love that could be worth killing for. Mark Antony had unconditional love, since there was nothing he could have done that Julius Caesar wouldn't have forgiven. *Othello* is about many different kinds of love: it's about the light, beautiful side of love, and it's about the twisted, darker side of love, and it's about how, if you flip that emotional coin, love can make you do terrible things. Othello and Desdemona are deeply in love with each other, but the play is infused with more than just this romantic love for there's also the great love shared by the men. Whenever there's a friend and a woman, there is friction.

It gets sorted out eventually, one way or another, either by one person disappearing, or through compromise, but there's always an imbalance which must somehow be redressed. Iago admires Othello just as strongly as Desdemona does, but for different reasons: they have fought together side by side, and Iago knows that if he goes to war with Othello, he'll make it out alive. The martial side of Othello has been diminishing, however, since Desdemona brings out the gentle side of him, and Iago doesn't want their relationship to change—and not only are they no longer fighting together, but Othello even has him running errands for her. Iago can't help but react strongly. Since he can't turn around and ask, "Hey, what about us?" and since he doesn't even want to recognize he feels such strong love for a man, he tries to suppress it. Othello thinks that his love is returned in kind, but Iago's love has become twisted. The play is supposed to be about Othello's jealousy, but before the play even begins Iago has already been contaminated by what Shakespeare calls the "green-eyed monster"—and he then goes on to infect Cassio, Roderigo, Othello, and Desdemona. People are always trying to explain why Iago does what he does, and nobody can, and I don't believe Iago ever knows either—but I think that his own jealousy is one of the primary influences.

The Globe has an outdoor stage that juts out into the audience, and it can feel like you're in an arena about to face the lions. I'll never forget that the first time I walked out amongst the groundlings, I nearly turned around and walked right back in—but I resisted. It's a bit like when you're scared and you wish the earth would open up so you could disappear, but of course it never does, and so you've only got one option, and you have to step out and meet what's coming. Thanks to the educational staff at the Globe,* who had prepared me for the effect of that stage, I was able to turn on the technique of getting through it until the inspiration of the play took over and it didn't matter what stage I was on since I was so far in the story. When I walked out, I was Eamonn Walker, the actor, but then very quickly the character of Othello would start to crawl through my head because Brabantio, Desdemona's father, who is furious that they have eloped, immediately comes at Othello with insults and accusations of witchcraft:

> Damned as thou art, thou hast enchanted her,
> For I'll refer me to all things of sense—
> If she in chains of magic were not bound—
> Whether a maid so tender, fair and happy,
> So opposite to marriage that she shunned
> The wealthy curlèd dearling of our nation,
> Would ever have—t'incur a general mock—
> Run from her guardage to the sooty bosom
> Of such a thing as thou: to fear, not to delight.
>
> (1.2.76–84)

I am the father of a daughter, and so I understand Brabantio, and I understand his indignation and anger at the loss of his little girl. At the same time, though, the effect of those words is visceral. Those are the sorts of insults you latch onto as a human being, so that you respond as more than just an actor as you

---

* There's a person for movement, a person for voice, a person for the stage, a person you can go to with all the different questions you might have about the history, the folios, past performances—there isn't anything you could ask that the Globe wouldn't be able to supply you some information about so that you're then able to do the best you can do.

stand there, and you listen, and you see the hatred of somebody hating you because of the color of your skin. It is something I've seen several times in real life, and there's an unforgettable look in someone's eye. When I saw that same look mimicked on stage, it seemed as though there was no acting involved, and yet it was what jolted me into character.

Brabantio has the most robust racism in the whole piece, even though it's Iago's racist language which is so memorable. Iago calls Brabantio out of his house to give him the news of his daughter's elopement, and he uses phrases such as "making the beast with two backs" (1.1.123) and "old black ram / . . . tupping your white ewe" (1.1.92–93), but Iago is vivid in his description because he wants to get Brabantio out of the house and he knows that if he doesn't speak like that then Brabantio is not going to come. It's not clear whether Iago believes in his own racist comments, but he's a very clever individual and he knows how such racist comments will work on others because he's so adept at using people against themselves. Brabantio, on the other hand, is involved in all the pain and anger of losing his daughter, and when he calls the person to mind who's done him the wrong, the thing that's easiest to see is that he's black—but at first it's not about that. It's about how Brabantio has lost the love of his little girl to this other man. Every father goes through that; it's very painful, and it's not something that men talk about, but you see it in movies, you read it in books, and you can see that same look in any father's eye. It always occurs at some point as the little girl grows up, regardless of whether the father and daughter have a good relationship. Brabantio is in this particular state of shock, and so he's not beginning from a point of calm and conscious racism. It's not that he simply hates black people. It's that his daughter's abductor's color is conspicuous and right in front of him. When people want to hurt, they use whatever they can see, and Othello's blackness is immediately apparent to the eye.

Brabantio then gives the order to have Othello arrested: "Lay hold upon him: if he do resist, / Subdue him at his peril" (1.2.93–94), but Othello won't fight. "Hold your hands," he tells those who would fight for him. "Were it my cue to fight, I should have known it / Without a prompter" (1.2.95–98). When I was a youth, many times I went ahead into a fight, but I could have stopped it had I been armed with some good common sense, some good words, and the ability to hold my center. I am now bolstered, and I have as a comeback something I didn't have in real life: Shakespeare's words with which to answer whatever hatred I see before me. I wish I'd always known myself as well as Othello knows himself in the beginning, for even though he's a foreign mercenary and has had to learn the protocol of the Venetian culture, he never forgets who he is, and he speaks from the knowledge of his own extraordinary might and martial talent. Instead of engaging in arms, therefore, Othello and Brabantio exchange a look, and in that look they both realize that they were indeed friends, and at the same time they both realize that they will never be friends again.

The Senate hears Brabantio's problem, and they commiserate since no doubt each member of the Senate is glad that it's not his own daughter who has married a black man. The country is in danger and the Turks are attacking, however, and so the Senate couldn't care less that Othello is black: to them, he's the man who can get them out of a desperate situation. Shakespeare recognizes that we all put racism aside when something more important has to be played out. But it's more than that, though: Othello wins them over.

Othello relates to the Senate how, invited to Brabantio's

house, he would tell the story of his adventures while Desdemona listened. Then, he continues:

> My story being done,
> She gave me for my pains a world of kisses:
> She swore, "In faith 'twas strange, 'twas passing
>   strange,
> 'Twas pitiful, 'twas wondrous pitiful!"
> She wished she had not heard it, yet she wished
> That heaven had made her such a man. She thanked
>   me,
> And bade me, if I had a friend that loved her,
> I should but teach him how to tell my story,
> And that would woo her. Upon this hint I spake:
> She loved me for the dangers I had passed,
> And I loved her that she did pity them.
> This only is the witchcraft I have used.
>
> (1.3.172–183)

As his only defense, Othello is saying, "Yes, I have fallen in love
with this woman. Can I explain it? No, I can't really explain it,
but I can tell you how I'm feeling, and if after I tell you how I'm
feeling you can't turn around and say, 'I would feel the same,'
then kill me."

Othello is a warrior who has gone on long journeys, suffered grave things, and seen a lot of ugliness in the world; and
Desdemona, who has never seen any ugliness in the world,
opens up a door in him that he has forgotten, and after he walks
through that door and into the light he doesn't want to look
back to the darkness. He can be jaded, cynical, and angry—
but never with her, for she doesn't pull that out of him. She
wants his stories, she wants to go on those journeys with him,

she wants to use her imagination with him, and she's in awe that after undergoing such outrageous fortunes he has become a strong, balanced man rather than a brute animal. He still has the animal within, but he has it caged, and she has provided him with the key to lock the door. Desdemona doesn't know what she has given to him, but Othello understands what he's getting from her, which is why he's willing to stand up in front of the Senate and take whatever punishment they decree. In her young state she is more woman than he has ever seen, and she is a woman who, in her strength, will let him rest his head on her stomach and cry, while she strokes his head and sends him to sleep after the terrible nightmares that continue to haunt him. How could anyone not fall in love with that?

Through his honesty and openheartedness in this speech, Othello brings the Senate to his emotional place. That spirit of love is contagious, and they can't help but think, "I wish that would happen to me. I wish I could see life like that." The Duke even concedes, "I think this tale would win my daughter too" (1.3.185). When the Senate determines that no crime has been committed, the audience is in complete agreement—in fact, on stage, I used to hear them emit a great, collective sigh after the judgment was pronounced.

* * *

There are aspects of race in the play, including those previously mentioned, but it's not a story about race. It's a love story between two people who can't see each other's color, or, if they do, it's in the way that it should be seen: "Oh my God, look at that. How amazing is it when those two colors are next to each other?" Part of Othello and Desdemona coming together is when they hold hands, when they link arms, when her leg crosses his, and they see the blend of colors and they think it's a beautiful, fascinating thing, rather than an ugly, terrible thing. Some people get twisted out of shape about it, but the truth of the matter is that it happens every day, and it has been happening, and it will continue to happen no matter what anyone chooses to think about it. These two people have found each other in a world which has an issue with their colors, but they've made their own, private decision about it, as many people in Great Britain have done, especially since the immigration of West Indians. These modern-day descendants of Othello and Desdemona go through the same process of encountering others from different cultures who look completely different, of not being able to help but be attracted to them, of confronting their familiars who tell them to stay away and to stick with what they know, of trying to stay away, and then of realizing that the feelings are too strong because with their hearts and all the blood vessels in their bodies they are drawn to each other. These people don't see each other's color. Othello and Desdemona never mention each other's color once: everybody around them talks about it because they can see it, but the lovers themselves never do. They're just relating to each other as people. The play is quite right in its portrayal of a love which transcends color.

I've been lucky enough to perform opposite two excellent Desdemonas, Zoe Tapper at the Globe and Keeley Hawes in the film, and although each one's portrayal was unique, the fire within them made me love them both. The lines don't always give Desdemona a fight, which is something she has to have. I think that the character works less well when the attitude is desperate, as in, "Oh, please don't be angry with me"; and I think she works better when it's more determined, as in, "I love you, and I'm not just going to let you do this to us." It's a fight, just as every relationship is a fight: to be in it, to stay in it, and to keep it going.

There exists an exotic aspect to the fact that this young girl has been fascinated with—and turned on by—the stories and worldliness of this man who has traveled so far and fought so hard. In Shakespeare's text, there's a kiss and then they disappear upstairs, but that single kiss is important because that's the only time when the audience can belie what Brabantio and Iago are saying and come to feel the love between Othello and Desdemona. Above and beyond that kiss, though, Shakespeare is very sexy in his writing. Not everybody plays the sex, either because they don't see it in the lines or they're too shy to go there, but both Desdemonas I performed with let that side of them rise. I'm glad Andrew Davies picked up on that element and wrote it into the film script, because he found a way to tell more of the story, and to illustrate the different stages of their relationship, through a couple of scenes which followed the couple into the bedroom. Andrew also had the brilliant idea of exchanging the handkerchief for a majestic golden robe which Desdemona gives Othello. In one scene, Cassio tries on the robe and, speaking with a deep voice, tries to be as regal and imposing as Othello, who then walks in and finds Cassio wearing the robe. It's the beginning of the end; Desdemona sees that Othello is jealous, and she just wants to reach him and get him back in any way she can. Andrew wrote the scene so that Othello is confused and besotted, and in their angry sex you see that Desdemona is willing to give herself up to Othello completely to keep him from being jealous. Any woman who's been anywhere near that situation knows exactly what's going on. They're going to have full-blown sex, probably like they've never had it before. The act succeeds in calming him temporarily. When someone's reassuring you, either you listen and you believe, or you listen and you don't believe, but you're listening. It's not until you're by yourself afterwards that you listen to all your suspicions again: we are our own worst enemies. Therefore, although Desdemona believes they've come closer together, ironically she has proven herself as a sexual being and fed his suspicions of infidelity.

With the intensity of these middle scenes, both in the original text and in Andrew's version, you see that these two people are really in love and that they don't know that someone is telling lies to try to break them apart. As witness to the whole, you can't help but want to shout, "*Please*, Othello, wake up!" The effect is especially compelling in the theatre, where, just as the audience might want Othello to snap out of it, as an actor I always wanted to simply stop in the middle of a line and turn the play completely around. But no matter how much we want the end to turn out differently, Othello can't do anything other than what he does, because that green-eyed monster has taken him over.

"Love makes you blind": love makes you blind not because you can't see, but because you choose to see people in the light that they want to be seen in, which is their best light, even though your instinct may tell you that something isn't quite right. The doubt, in Othello, is coming from somebody else, and yet it ignites something in him that then takes him over. It's so easy to see Othello as a fool, but he's not. Even in the middle of his downfall, he's the best that he can be; if at any point he turns out of this dive, he wins. Othello isn't stupid; he's simply caught in a situation he only partly understands, and he's full of love for both his wife and his friend. He's a man who doesn't want any pain or hatred in his life anymore: he doesn't want to give any out, and he doesn't want to receive any. That doesn't make him simple. That makes him openhearted. That makes him, in my eyes, a good energy to be around. When the Iagos of the world treat those who have that good energy as though they are stupid, that reveals more about their proclivity to manipulate than it does about the gullibility of those who persevere in their optimism.

For a man, it takes a lot to understand what a man is. Most men, when they're young, are taught to be a man's man, but they aren't taught to take on board the side of them that's also a gentleman, a gentle man. Othello is both, at first. He is Desdemona's protector, and he can make her feel safe in the knowledge that no one can come at her while he's around—unfortunately, the person who comes at her turns out to be Othello himself. Some of the greatest moments of violence come from the attempt to overcompensate for vulnerability, which can feel like weakness: that's when men react in a way that's supposedly manly, and that's how domestic violence comes about.

Othello responds to Iago's insinuations about his wife by reminding him of that side of himself which is in some ways the opposite of weak, that pure animal violence. "Be sure thou prove my love a whore" (3.3.397), he says—and if you get the feeling right, it's scary how easily that line just rolls off the tip of the tongue. We played the scene as a warning to his friend: *If you're wrong, I'll kill you.* It's something more than a threat, for he knows that there's a whole brutal side of himself that can be unleashed. One of the most powerful moments of the film is the parallel scene which culminates with Othello's recognition as he turns around and says, "I'd kill them both." He doesn't have to shout it; the knowledge simply comes over him that he really would kill them. The position he holds in the film is that of the most powerful and most decorated policeman of British history, so it's huge to admit his murderous disposition, even to his best friend.

Andrew Davies wrote one scene which has no equivalent in the play. Othello, Desdemona, Iago, and Emilia are having dinner, and Othello begins to talk about what it's like to be black in that society, and how he wishes he were white for no other reason than that he wouldn't have to think about color. It's the only time he recognizes his wife as a white woman, and it comes from a deep-rooted identity crisis born of the fear mounting within him. Shakespeare's *Othello* witnesses the birth of racism, and now, four hundred years later, we're living in it—and that scene marks the difference. British society is a little better now than it was when we did the film, but one of the reasons it is better, I feel, is that Andrew wrote that scene. You can't change social perspectives by banging out your message, but if you represent other ways of seeing things, then you can indeed effect subtle, subliminal changes of attitude and perception.

* * *

The film made bigger changes to Shakespeare's original text of *Othello*, but there were changes in the play too. Even though it was the same words, depending on the mood and the energy, it took on different attitudes every single day, and so as a cast we were always surprised by each other.

The relationship between Tim McInnerny's Iago and my Othello would vary. Some nights Tim would just be cheeky, and he wouldn't even know why he was being cheeky. I remember one night, during the scene in which I have to come down to stop the noise because I want to be with my wife (2.3), when Tim obstinately wouldn't move from where he was on the stage.

I looked at him furiously, because if he didn't move then the play would come to a stop, and he was about to force me to take a different action to keep the play going: Iago's manipulative attitude was effectively taking over the playing of the play too. Since people have always identified me with Othello, I think it would be fascinating to feel the effects of playing Iago and therefore to see that play, and be in that world, on the other side.*

Likewise, the relationship with Zoe Tapper's Desdemona changed from performance to performance. Her Desdemona was completely in love with my Othello; I could look in her eyes and see it. Something had gotten in the way of our communication, and both of us were confused and lost. We were in a real relationship and so it was a real breakup, and it was hard to watch. If you take away the black-man slant to the story, then you just have these two people coming to an end in such a chilling way. Zoe had the frustration of not knowing how to talk to her man, and so, long after she should have been concerned for her own life, she was trying to reach inside of me with looks and touches. Some nights the death scene would take a soft approach, and some nights it would take a dark approach, and other nights it would take every color in between.

In the audience, during every performance I could hear men and women crying, even bawling, because they really didn't want that man to kill that woman—and for all sorts of different reasons. Some of them had been brought into the love affair, and some of them didn't want a huge black man to kill a

---

* The only black Iago I've ever heard about was played by Andre Braugher, and I know he would have been brilliant because he's an extremely talented man. Patrick Stewart did the mirror image of the play, with a black Iago played by Ron Canada.

tiny little white girl—so the suspense and disbelief and desire to stop the killing reverberated all around them, throughout the building, and it sat and hovered in the air.

When Desdemona briefly comes to and Emilia asks, "O, who hath done this deed?" (5.2.143), the look on Zoe's face as she replied, "Nobody" (5.2.144), crushed me every single night. I felt nothing but guilt. I had just strangled her, and yet she still loved me. There was one night when that look was still in me as I started to do my last speech, and I could hardly speak through the tears in my eyes, in my mouth, and in my voice. Emilia and Desdemona each, unseen by the audience, looked to see what was wrong with me. It was then that I learned another of Shakespeare's important lessons, which is that, unless you want to end up a blubbering idiot on the stage, as an actor you cannot let the emotion take you over.

The most challenging scene for me is the killing of Desdemona, and to make it work I've always begun from a place of: *Don't kill her*. In the period stage version, the killing was easier to comprehend since it was in a past age, he was in his soldier's mode, and he had decided on a course of action he was determined to see through to the end: *I'm going to kill her because what she did*—and he believes she did it—*was wrong*. But the modern man can't live by those rules, since he lives in a society in which therapy tells us we can fix things. In the film, he doesn't go into the room to kill her; he goes into the room to get the truth and then, when he thinks she's lying to him, he tries to stop her from talking to him and in the act of smothering those lies he ends up killing her. When she regains consciousness again, I finish killing her out of guilt and shame. Then, contrary to the stage version, when Keeley's Desdemona opened her eyes again she did *not* still love me—and that in itself would have given me something to play. And yet, all I can remember thinking was how, after all her kicking had raised her nightgown up about her legs, there was a bit of her knickers showing. I didn't want the world to see my woman's knickers when they found her dead, and so I pulled her nightgown down—it was me, it was Othello, it was confused. As an actor, I'd lost myself in that love which, the violence done, had turned to pure tenderness.

*   *   *

Othello's journey ends with the awakening of his self-consciousness—but it's a tragedy, and so it happens too late. In his last speech he says:

> I pray you, in your letters,
> When you shall these unlucky deeds relate,
> Speak of me as I am: nothing extenuate,
> Nor set down aught in malice. Then must you speak
> Of one that loved not wisely but too well:
> Of one not easily jealous, but being wrought,
> Perplexed in the extreme: of one whose hand,
> Like the base Judean, threw a pearl away
> Richer than all his tribe . . .
>
> (5.2.383–391)

He's saying, "Shit. I get it. I get that I was completely manipulated. I get that I've lost the love of my life. I get that I'm not worthy. And I know what you're going to do with this. You're going to turn around and say, 'It's because he was black.' And when you do, I don't want to be here." And so he kills himself.

I remember how tired I was after every performance at the Globe. I was mentally and emotionally exhausted, since it took every iota of my being to run that course. Most parts don't demand that people give that much of themselves. The play gets mistaken sometimes as being Iago's play, because Iago has more words to say than Othello, but Iago doesn't have the emotional journey to go on because he doesn't begin with the same emotional intelligence. I know he's a very clever character, I know it's a cerebral piece, and I know there are those who love it so well because Iago's words are excellent—but I believe that the essence of the play is the love story. It's the story of the love between Othello and Desdemona, and it's the love story between Iago and Othello.

Shakespeare is able to see through all the projected images and shields we put up in front of ourselves, and so we are able to see people as people. He takes these great, big, wonderful, huge situations, and then he makes them personal. His characters may be kings and queens. They may be leaders of men. At the same time, the reason we can experience this play over and over again is that we can feel attached to what Othello is feeling, or to what Desdemona is feeling, or to what Iago is feeling, depending on who we are at any given moment. So, in *Hamlet*, it's about the Prince's love for his mother and father. At various points, those around him try to urge him to put politics first, but he's in disbelief that anyone could be concerned with such issues when the personal is in such disorder. How can Gertrude go from her first husband's bed to her second husband's bed, Hamlet wonders, and say it's about the throne? When Shakespeare takes a big situation such as the royal succession of Denmark and makes it personal like that, we love the writing because we see and can identify ourselves in those characters.

When Shakespeare sticks a group of words together, it's for a reason. He gives you help as an actor, because he was one— and so he tells you when to start speaking quicker and louder, and he tells you when to start speaking slower and softer. These are things you have to learn as an actor, and once you do you want to thank Shakespeare for helping you find your way from outside the text to inside it. Nevertheless, there are still some great swathes of dialogue where I wonder, "What on earth is he talking about?" The only difference is that now I know that I'm not alone, and that scholars, directors, and actors have the same questions, whereas the schoolboy I used to be thought it was only him. It's not a matter of ignorance, I realize now: it's a matter of there being even more to discover and enjoy. We are not all born equal; we discover things at different times; we discover things when we are ready. But when we discover Shakespeare, then we can't help but see how the way we live now is connected to the way he lived then—same people, different faces. We're all still defined by our personal relationships, as Shakespeare knew so well, and we're all still searching for the love stories that are just right for each of us.

Barry John

OTHELLO:
A PLAY IN BLACK AND WHITE

BARRY JOHN is an India-based English actor, director, and instructor. He is the founder-director of the Theatre Action Group, the Imago Media Company, the Imago Theatre in Education Company, and the Barry John Acting Studio. He has received the Sangeet Natak Akademi Award for Theatre Direction by India's National Academy for Music, Dance, and Theatre, and the Sahitya Kala Parishad Award. He is the author of *Playing for Real*, a book of drama exercises for children. His film credits include *Gandhi*, *Massey Sahib*, *Thanks Maa*, *Tere Bin Laden*, *The Great Indian Butterfly*, *M Cream*, and *Chittagong*. He performed in the stage version of *Othello: A Play in Black and White*, and it was subsequently made into the film *In Othello*.

TO PLAY OR NOT TO PLAY

It began with a phone call.

"We're doing an *Othello*, and we want you to be Iago."

Images of Frank Finlay's portrayal in the Olivier film flew in and whetted my appetite. That appetite was swiftly assuaged, however, by further images of a recent, deadly dull Bombay production that had advertised itself as "a new Islamic interpretation": a film star sported Arab gear as Othello, and Bianca belly-danced in harem pants. Desdemona was played by an English actress—the only white face in a sea of brown.

In India, you learn to live with such anomalies. Sensitivity to colour is genetic, as it is elsewhere in the world, but on the stage anything goes. I have often been that single white face in a sea of brown. My King Lear had three Indian daughters, but nobody seemed to notice. Mrs. Lear presumably was an early settler in Southall.

So, back on the phone, it was not my white face that I was concerned about but my age.

"Am I not too old to play Iago?"

I was fifty-three at the time, and thought, "What kind of Venetian army is this?" Iago himself says, "I ha' looked upon the world for four times seven years. . . ."

"Are you going to be using prosthetic makeup?"

(*He laughs.*) "Ha-ha-ha! No, you're perfect for the Iago I have in mind. Come and read the script, and all will be revealed."

The caller was the director Roysten Abel—a burly, bearded, gentle man from Kerala, and a former student of mine from the National School of Drama in Delhi. After school and after marrying a classmate, he had stayed on in Delhi, and over the course of the preceding few years had tinkered with a few basement productions of Shakespeare. Then he teamed up with the actress Lushin Dubey, and the Indian Shakespeare Company was born.

There were a small number of people at the reading. Besides Roy (Roysten), the director, and Lushin, who was to play Desdemona, there was Adil Hussain (Othello), Dilip Shankar (Cassio), Vivek Mansukhani (Brabantio and Roderigo), and Daniella, an Italian lady, who was to play the role of the Director.

"The Director? What Director? Do you mean the Duke?"

"Yes, well, she plays the Duke, but in her capacity as Director."

"Roy, I thought you were the director."

"I am."

This Pinterful exchange was far from reassuring.

"I see. Does she play my wife too?"

"No, Emilia does not figure in our play. Some of her lines are used, but by Dilip and Vivek."

"I see. . . . So, who gives me Desdemona's handkerchief? The handkerchief spotted with strawberries that Othello gave her? The handkerchief that means so much to him, and that is the ultimate proof of her adultery because he believes that she has given it to Cassio and that Cassio has given it, in turn, to a whore?"

"Well, we don't really get into all that, though Iago does narrate the story to Othello in one scene, and at the end of it he gives Othello his own handkerchief."

"Why?"

"To wipe off his sweat. It's a long and strenuous scene."

"I see. Are we waiting for the rest of the cast?"

"No, this is the complete cast."

"Just the six of us?"

"Yes, any more and we could not afford to go to Edinburgh."

"Edinburgh?"

"Yes, the Fringe Festival in August. Are you game?"

I was noncommittal, because opening the script only added to my unease. It began as follows:

At first bell, the cast is already onstage rehearsing their Kathakali movements. They continue dancing as the audience enters. By the third bell, they are all visibly exhausted.

VIVEK: Why the fuck do we have to do this play in Kathakali?

As I am wont to do with a new script, I flipped to the last page next and was relieved to find some Shakespearean text. It was Act 5, Scene 2, in Desdemona and Othello's bedroom, but edited and concluded as follows:

> OTHELLO: It is too late. (*He stifles her as the light fades out.*)
> *It remains ambiguous as to whether it is the character killing Desdemona in the play or the actor killing Lushin in reality.*

Now I see! It's a play-within-a-play!

THE PLAY

It is proverbial to say that Shakespeare's plays are "universal," that their themes and issues resonate deeply within the human condition everywhere. Then why tamper with them? Why take *Othello*, the story of a black man in a white society, and transplant it into an Indian context?

Perhaps it is to do with the fact that some Indians are fair-skinned and others dark-skinned. Perhaps the traditional Indian issues of caste (untouchability) and class are still more sensitive than they should be in a postcolonial, modern, democratic state. Perhaps traditional patriarchal attitudes towards women cause those who have power to cling stubbornly to their rights of oppression. Perhaps all of this is further compounded by the coexistence of multiple regional languages, one of which (Hindi) has been appointed the "national language" but is in serious competition with a foreign language (English), the language of those who made slaves of Indians.

Roysten Abel might have written a treatise on these vexed issues, but he had the vision to dramatize them, to illustrate them through character and action. That he saw them through the prism of Shakespeare's play at once removed them from the harsh, direct light of "kitchen-sink" realism and placed them in an unexpected context. At the same time, the meaning of Shakespeare's *Othello* became enlarged as audiences saw it through the prism of contemporary Indian social conditions.

The play relates, in seamlessly joined fragments, the story of a Delhi theatre group going through the process of rehearsing Shakespeare's *Othello*. The group comprises an ex-pat Englishman, Barry, its director and lead actor; and the actors Vivek, Dilip, and Lushin, who are typical convent-educated, English-medium Anglophiles. With this new production of *Othello*, their ambition to be more experimental has led to their inviting an Italian, Daniella, to come on board as guest director. Following international trends, Daniella's vision encompasses the fusion of bare-stage Shakespeare and bare-stage Kathakali, a traditional dance-drama form of south India. Thus Adil, a young actor from Assam who has studied Kathakali, has been brought in to train the cast in its backbreaking movements and rhythms.

The first scene has Barry organising a rehearsal of his audition piece from Act 1, Scene 2, wherein he plays Othello and Vivek plays Iago, in anticipation of the expected casting. It also shows Adil being used as a silent proxy for other characters—silent because he does not know English. When he says in Hindi that he knows the text, they ignore him. By the end of the scene, the rehearsal has become the audition, and Daniella speaks from a seat amongst the audience. Dilip and Lushin, who seem to have a close relationship, come back on stage as Daniella announces the casting and turns their little world upside-down.

*The Director casts Adil as Othello, with (left to right) Barry John
as Iago, Vivek Mansukhani as Brabantio, Adil Hussain as Othello,
Roysten Abel as the Director, and Kristin Jain as Desdemona
in Roysten Abel's* Othello: A Play in Black and White, *1999.
Photograph courtesy Can & Abel Theatre.*

Barry is cast as Iago and not as Othello as everyone expected. He is visibly angry about this, but his professionalism bows before the director's prerogative. It plants the seeds of jealousy in the actor, however, and serves to fuel his portrayal of Iago's resentment in being passed over for promotion by Othello in favour of Cassio.

When Daniella casts Adil as Othello, it is because he is dark-skinned, tall, and handsome, but also because he is an "outsider," just as she is. When it is pointed out that Adil does not know English, she says that it does not matter, that he can speak in Assamese or Hindi, and that maybe Lushin can help him learn English. Lushin happily agrees.

In these opening sequences of the play, many of the major

issues and tensions that run through it have been set in motion. Adil, like any young actor, is ambitious and snatches at the opportunity to play Othello when it is offered to him. He knows that Barry and Vivek are aggrieved by this, but is determined to overcome his social inferiority and language problem to render their opposition unfounded. He has no inkling yet of the feelings for Lushin that will grow into a passion, into an obsession, into possessiveness, and into a violent madness. For all his ambition, it is borne by a mind and attitudes that grew in a remote and deeply conservative region of northeast India, where a woman is a man's possession.

Lushin will have none of that. She is the new, emancipated, urban Indian woman, who is educated and has both a mind and a will of her own. She shares a warm and caring relationship with Dilip, but sees nothing wrong in indulging her attraction towards Adil. As an actress, she is doing her homework by getting more intimate with him and helping him overcome his shyness. Although they have to represent a newly married couple in the play, in reality Lushin is married to neither Adil nor Dilip and will do what she likes.

Barry is set on a course of revenge. He schemes and he manipulates all the other actors and even Daniella in order to prove to her that she has made a big mistake. His duplicity engineers the falseness of wanting to help Adil so that he does not make an ass of himself as Othello, and at the same time he fertilizes Adil's growing suspicion and anger over Lushin's unfaithfulness and looseness. And, of course, Barry plays the same game with Dilip, who becomes genuinely concerned for Lushin's safety.

Things come to a head when Barry organises a party at his house. Vivek's unwitting complicity has been secured with the suggestion that he just might end up with the lead role, though he never really seems to understand what Barry is plotting. Having learned in rehearsal that Dilip has never touched a drop of liquor in his life, Barry and Vivek proceed to get him sloshed while haranguing him about his relationships with Adil and Lushin. "What is your friendship all about then? Are you just her flunkey, to fetch and carry, while she tutors this new guy?"

By the time Lushin arrives with Adil, Dilip can barely stand, and after throwing up he asks Adil, under the pretence of having a drink with him, "Have you ever tasted scotch before, you shit?" and spits into his face. In response, Adil hits him and they get into a fight, until separated by Vivek. At that moment, Daniella enters, learns what has transpired, and swiftly departs. So does Vivek.

Dilip has completely collapsed by now, and Barry carries him off into a guest room. Lushin makes to follow, but is called back by Adil, who attempts to hold her and kiss her. She resists and is saved by Barry returning and asking her to look after Dilip. She runs out.

Barry serves Adil more scotch while he comments on the funny relationship that Lushin and Dilip have, making fools of everyone. He tells Adil not to take things to heart and to concentrate on his role. He suggests that he too stay the night.

How Machiavellian is that? (Or is it more like Clausewitz?) In one fell swoop of a party, Barry has them all at each other's throat. Or, in the Indian context, is it an echo of the British imperialist tactic of "divide and rule"?

However you interpret it, post-party Adil is firmly on a downward curve of uncontrollable rage and insecurity. The rehearsals are charged with high-voltage tension. The stage becomes a battlefield on which a land mine can explode with any step, any word.

Daniella does not know how to cope, and with delicious

irony leans more and more on Barry for guidance and assistance. She leaves him alone with Adil in the hope that he can find out what his problem is. Adil sits simmering in a downstage corner, already physicalizing the metaphor of mocked meat that the green-eyed monster jealousy is feeding on. Barry approaches him, and lovingly tries to coax him out of his catatonic state into sharing what it is that is bothering him. Adil tries desperately to hold back his tears but is unable to as he speaks the English lines from Act 3, Scene 3, which begin, "What sense had I in her stol'n hours of lust?" (3.3.376). As Adil proceeds, Barry sits mesmerized by his command of the language and the depth of his feeling. He genuinely empathises with his situation and feels sorry for him, yet, at the same time, Adil is his willing victim. He wanted the role of Othello, so now he has taken it on, tortured soul and all. When Adil arrives at "O, now, for ever / Farewell the tranquil mind; farewell content" (3.3.385–386), he gets up and strides around the stage, working up a lather of bellowing rage. In these lines Othello is saying farewell to his glorious career as a soldier, and Adil is saying farewell to his dreams of success as an actor.

Suddenly he turns his attention on Barry: "Villain, be sure thou prove my love a whore . . . or woe upon thy life!" (3.3.397; 405). Barry is terrified as Adil pins him to the floor, attempts to stamp on him, picks him up and throttles him in an armlock, and then hurls him across the stage, where he crash-lands in a heap. He is stunned and pained, and takes a few moments to recover. As he struggles to his feet, he stares venomously at the dark-skinned savage before him and screams, "Are you a man? Have you a soul? Or sense?" (3.3.414). This is the first time since the casting that Barry has lost his composure, and he quickly turns it to his advantage. As an honest friend of Adil's, he resents the injustice of being treated so offensively and makes as if to leave. Adil takes the bait, tells him to stay, and expresses his desire for proof of Lushin's disloyalty. Barry is now of a mood to ram home his advantage up to the hilt and asks Adil if he means that he wants to see Lushin being fucked. He cooks up the story of Cassio's/Dilip's dream and relates how he saw Dilip in possession of the handkerchief spotted with strawberries. He has Adil threatening black vengeance and baying for blood. At the end of the scene, Barry hugs him and congratulates him for his good work. Adil touches Barry's feet (a sign of respect for elders in India), and Barry gives him his own handkerchief to wipe off his sweat.

As Adil kneels, staring at the handkerchief, Lushin enters to tell him that they should not see each other privately anymore. She says that their relationship is negatively impacting the play and everyone else. He does not respond at all and she leaves.

Left alone, Adil works himself up into a rambling, disjointed, psychotic fit. He rampages all over the space, creating a storm of sound and movement, as he tears apart Shakespeare's text of Act 4, Scene 1, reducing it to incoherent and agonized bits and pieces:

> Lie with her? Lie on her?—We say "Lie on her" when they belie her. Lie with her! . . . Handkerchief—confessions—handkerchief! . . . Is't possible? Confess? Handkerchief? O devil!
>
> (adapted from 4.1.42–47)

Daniella and the rest of the cast rush on to see what all the noise is about. Adil throws the handkerchief at Dilip, charges through them, and disappears into the wings.

There follows a discussion of the problem of Adil. Vivek bluntly says that he did not deserve the role of Othello in the first place, and that he should be thrown out. Dilip accuses Daniella of pampering him. Barry confesses to being guilty of pampering him too, but adds that he has just rehearsed with him and that he was fine.

Adil charges back in, still in manic mode, looking for Lushin to help him with his lines. "You need help," says Daniella, "not just with your lines but with your attitude! I did not give you the role for you to start an affair with Lushin!" When Adil says that it's a personal matter, Daniella yells, "It is *not* a personal matter! It is *my* play, and you are going to do it exactly as I want you to! Is that clear?"

Barry suggests that he apologise to Daniella so that they can continue with rehearsals, which happens. They get back into Act 4, Scene 1 from Adil's "How shall I murder him, Iago?" (4.1.169). With Lushin, Dilip, and Vivek waiting to enter on the edges of the space, both Adil and Barry become highly animated and shoot their lines like rapid machine-gun fire directly at the characters that they are referring to, namely Dilip and Lushin. The stage is flooded with the gruesome, violent images of revengeful murder that Shakespeare's text supplies.

They are interrupted by the arrival of Vivek as Lodovico, who bears the letter from the Duke ordering Othello to return to Venice and replacing him with Cassio. Adil's behaviour is that of a man deranged, and on his line, "Sweet Othello? Sweet Othello? Devil!" (adapted from 4.1.237–238), he brutally attempts to strangle Lushin/Desdemona. Dilip and Vivek leap to separate them as Daniella rushes onto the stage from the auditorium. She tells Dilip to take Lushin, still choking and now crying, off the stage. She turns to Adil and tells him that he's unbalanced, impossible to work with, and out of the play. He has to be replaced.

At this moment of triumph, Barry, having achieved what he set out to achieve, still wants to push things closer to a more complete calamity. Unbelievably, he defends Adil, suggesting that what happened was an accident. Adil himself is unsure whether it was accidental or deliberate, and so Daniella maintains that he cannot be trusted and must leave.

As Adil makes to do so, Barry stops him and tears into Daniella, reminding her that she is a guest director, that Adil was *her* choice, and that the performances are too close to replace anyone. Daniella says that she will not be responsible for what happens and leaves angrily, followed by a disgruntled Vivek.

In the next sequence, Dilip and Vivek sit on chairs placed right and left downstage. They face the audience and mime looking into mirrors, applying makeup. They are then replaced by Adil and Lushin, who rehearse the lines from Act 4, Scene 2, beginning at "Upon my knee, what doth your speech import?" (4.2.35). Adil is convinced of Lushin's disloyalty and dishonesty, and although the text mentions his weeping, both the actors deliver the lines coldly, eerily. When he reaches "I cry you mercy, then: / I took you for that cunning whore of Venice / That married with Othello" (4.2.97–99), he gets up and leaves quietly.

Barry enters and asks Lushin if everything is okay. She gets up, stares at him before saying, "You know, Barry, you are a real bastard," and leaves him alone. He turns to the audience, smiling, and says, "Fair is foul and foul is fair." He continues with a soliloquy that includes the following:

> It would have been better to have chosen the king with foresight. . . . We are all suckers for youth; but what about the willow that has weathered a thousand winters? Nay, we are not going to be cut down and cast

aside. These robes have not been earned cheaply. They are very dear to us, and they will not be handed over so easily. This worship of youth must end here.

The last scene of the play is a fragment of Act 5, Scene 2, performed with Kathakali movements and hand gestures. Following the conventions, Lushin sleeps sitting upright on a chair, and Adil enters behind a curtain held by Dilip and Vivek, who lower it to reveal the character of Othello before whisking it away. "It is the cause, it is the cause, my soul" (5.2.1) is the opening line, and the scene proceeds to the moment when he stifles Desdemona/Lushin.

THE PLAYING

As may be deduced, I did act in the play and it did go to the Edinburgh Fringe Festival in August 1999, where it won a Fringe First Award. Thereafter, it traveled to Cairo, Harare, Bonn, Lille, Amsterdam, Antwerp, and London, as well as to numerous cities in India. It was kept "alive" for almost ten years, of course demanding changes of cast periodically. Roysten himself took on the role of the Guest Director eventually.

The abridged description of the play that I have given is from memory, and purports to be the original version, when, in fact, it is likely to be an amalgamation of several versions. Each time an actor was replaced, the play had to be re-rehearsed, and each occasion was an opportunity to reevaluate it and refashion it. In this way, it was kept from becoming solidified and mechanical.

In 2000, Roysten was inspired to develop a sequel with Adil and me, called *Goodbye Desdemona*, and in 2002 a further version was shot on film and titled *In Othello*.

Shakespeare's *Othello* is reputedly the "tightest" of all his

*Barry and the Director watch Adil's rehearsal, with Barry
John as Iago and Roysten Abel as the Director in Abel's*
Othello: A Play in Black and White, *1999.*
Photograph courtesy Can & Abel Theatre.

tragedies, and the most "domestic." The way that Roy stripped
it down to its essentials, making it performable by six actors,
transformed it into a relentlessly electric and compelling experience for audiences. The average running time was in the
region of seventy-five minutes without break. Visually it was
stark: just three chairs and a trunk against black curtains. The
actors wore casual T-shirts and either tracksuit pants or skirts,
all in black and white. The props were minimal: a nondescript
gown in rags and tatters for Othello; a makeup kit and towel for
me to blacken my face for the audition sequence; a tray with an
empty scotch bottle and glasses for the party scene; a handkerchief; and a Kathakali curtain. Music was deployed briefly during the party only. The lighting was plotted simplistically and
without colour. It was "poor theatre" at its poorest and purest.

It meant that the actors and their skills became the uncluttered focus of attention and communication: bodies in an empty space, gesturing through the flames of their passions; voices, feelings and meanings resonating in and out of thunderous silences.

For me personally, it was the most intense, unusual, challenging, and fulfilling theatre experience I have ever been exposed to. I was aware of shifting between three layers of experience or identities while performing. The first was that of being the fictional Barry, the Director of the group in the story who nevertheless was willing to put the whole production into jeopardy because of his injured ego and his resentment of "young upstarts." He is representative of all senior people who are loath to abdicate power and position in favour of the younger generation and its new ideas.

The second layer of experience was that of being the Barry who is my own self, the lost soul who, thirty-odd years before, had migrated to India in search of himself and a meaningful life; the self that had forged a career in theatre and brought actual remembered experience, personal feelings and politics, gut reactions and impulses to invest in the performance.

The third layer, the darkest, was that of being Iago, the honest and trusted soldier whose ambition was thwarted when his due promotion was handed to Cassio instead; whose hurt at this unleashed a plan of revenge on both Othello and Cassio. In a sense, he "promoted" himself to a position of power over others; by his artfulness and opportunism he was able to exploit others' credulity so successfully that his plan began to run amok, and there was blood spilled that he never initially intended. He was for a while the master of destiny, but ended up among its victims.

If not an original concept, the idea of the play-within-a-play licensed the issues of race, colour, language, and class to be foregrounded in a contemporary Indian context. For some, it raised the contentious ethical issue of an artist's right to tamper with the classics.

To my mind, Roysten did to *Othello* precisely what Shakespeare himself had done to Cinthio's story in his *Hecatommithi* of 1566: he refashioned and revitalized it to make it relevant to his own times and concerns.

Jess Winfield

RE-REVISING SHAKESPEARE

JESS WINFIELD is a double Emmy Award–winning American author, actor, director, and producer, as well as the cofounder of the Reduced Shakespeare Company. The company's full-length show, *The Complete Works of William Shakespeare (abridged)*, which holds the distinction of having spent five years as the longest-running comedy in the West End, has been distinguished by an Olivier Award nomination and translated into a dozen languages. He is also the author of the work of nonfiction *What Would Shakespeare Do?* as well as the *New York Times Book Review* "Editor's Choice" *My Name Is Will: A Novel of Sex, Drugs, and Shakespeare*, and the non-Shakespearean (but positively Falstaffian) e-book *The Perfect Burrito*.

If you've ever uttered "Alas, poor Yorick, I totally knew that dude well!" in a roomful of Shakespeareans, you know that among certain parties it is considered distasteful to misquote, much less intentionally bowdlerize, the Word of the Bard.

I don't often get invited to those parties.

From my days as a founder of the Reduced Shakespeare Company to my recent book *My Name Is Will: A Novel of Sex, Drugs, and Shakespeare*, I've been ~~fucking with~~ revising Shakespeare my whole life: adapting, abridging, purloining, parsing, reframing, parodying. But until I sat down to write this essay about my own experiences with revising the Bard, I'd never much pondered an obvious question: Did he revise and adapt *his own works*, and if so, how much? I've always been the type to skim over the "About the Text" section of the front matter when reading a Shakespeare play, but after some deep digging in musty tomes, it has become clear to me that, if not the Bard himself, *someone* in the company in which Shakespeare was resident playwright, actor, and co-owner revised his work constantly. And that narrative both coincides with my own experience as a playwright, actor, and co-owner of a theater company, and highlights the unique potential of theater to maintain its relevance in a crowded contemporary market for arts and entertainment.

After a decade writing and performing in *The Complete Works of William Shakespeare (abridged)*, in 1995 I directed its first Off-Broadway production at the Westside Arts Theatre in New York.* In Christopher Duva, Peter Jacobson, and Jon Patrick Walker, I had a terrifically talented cast; they improvised and ad-libbed loads of new business and dialogue in rehearsal. Sitting with my assistant director, watching the comedy fly (or not fly), I'd give a thumbs-up or a thumbs-down to their new material. Any approved text went into the prompt-script and became part of the show. The weekend before the first preview, the production's general manager, Albert Poland, came to a rehearsal. "It's looking good," he said afterward. "So is the show *locked*?"

Now, in addition to the theater, I work in television and film, where a "locked" project has a very specific meaning: the editing of the video track of the episode or movie is completed,

---

* For those unfamiliar with the play, *Complete Works (abridged)* is a giant stupid human trick in tights, wherein three men attempt to perform all thirty-seven plays plus the Sonnets in less than two hours. It's one of the world's most popular plays for amateur and professional performance.

and it's ready to have musical score and sound effects added, to have the odd line rerecorded, and then finally to be printed and delivered to broadcasters or distributors, never to change (unless you're George Lucas and have the money to add new scenes to *Star Wars*). But Mr. Poland's question was one I had never heard in the theater before.

I instinctively responded, "The minute this play becomes 'locked,' it's dead."

He seemed taken aback.

"This show," I said, "depends on its ability to be flexible, to change jokes and topical references at a moment's notice, to swap out bits that may work in one place and time, but not another. In fact," I continued, clearly on a roll, "that's the single greatest advantage that live theater has over film and television: the ability to change, to live and breathe and grow in real time. Why would you give away that advantage by 'locking' a play?"

This was a cocky newbie director mouthing off to an experienced theater professional (the poor guy just wanted to know if we were ready to program light and sound cues during technical rehearsals), but I stand by the main point: that theater's most unique gift (along with the lack of a fourth wall—the subject of another essay) is its ability, in fact its *need*, to change. Certainly Shakespeare, the greatest dramatist of all time, didn't spurn that gift, but used it to its full advantage.

* * *

[*Warning to fellow academophobes: To illustrate my argument, I'm going to have to talk "About the Text" here. To keep us all as safe and comfortable as possible, I'll use* Hamlet *as an example, a play we're all familiar with, and one with a particularly interesting textual history. I promise that I shall not use the words "emendation," "provenance," or "ibid."*]

There are three primary sources for the text of *Hamlet*: the First Quarto (a quarto is about the size of a modern paperback) edition published in 1603; the Second Quarto, published a year later in 1604–1605; and the version in the First Folio, the large-format edition of thirty-six of the Bard's plays, compiled by Shakespeare's friends and fellow actors John Heminges and Henry Condell and published in 1623. One might think that, since *Hamlet* is *the* quintessential canonical text, there should be a single definitive version of it, but the three main texts that have come down to us are all different.

Not just slightly different, as in, this word is misspelled in this text, and that line is out of place in that text. Nor entirely different: the play is clearly *Hamlet*—its entire plot, its major soliloquies, most of its famous turns of phrase, and all of Shakespeare's themes of guilt and innocence, betrayal and usurpation, and thought versus action, are intact. But the texts are *notably* different—and in some places *radically* different—from the *Hamlet* we think we know, especially when it comes to the First Quarto. Reading the First Quarto is like a dream where you're back in high school except not exactly because the campus is on an asteroid with low gravity so you keep floating away and coming back to the ground uncontrollably, making it impossible to get to your algebra final on time. Scene after scene sails along much as we know it—although the exact words and their order are sometimes disorientingly varied—and then up pops a completely new line, or a differently named character (Polonius is "Corambis"; Rosencrantz and Guildenstern are "Rossencraft and Gilderstone"), or a scene that you recognize, but out of sequence, or, in one case, a new scene altogether. The most famous instance of a notable variation in the text is the beginning of Hamlet's famous soliloquy, which begins, in the version most of us are familiar with:

To be, or not to be: that is the question:
Whether 'tis nobler in the mind to suffer
The slings and arrows of outrageous fortune,
Or to take arms against a sea of troubles,
And by opposing end them? To die: to sleep:
No more; and by a sleep to say we end
The heart-ache and the thousand natural shocks
That flesh is heir to, 'tis a consummation
Devoutly to be wish'd. To die, to sleep;
To sleep: perchance to dream: ay, there's the rub.

(Arden, 3.1.62–71)

In the First Quarto, these oh-so-familiar lines are rendered thus:

To be, or not to be—ay, there's the point.
To die, to sleep—is that all? Ay, all.
No, to sleep, to dream—ay, marry, there it goes.

(Arden, 3.7.115–117)*

"To be, or not to be—that is the question" is so deeply ingrained in our collective lizard brain that when I saw this other version for the first time (at the Huntington Library in California, where one of the only two existing copies of the First Quarto is kept), my mind nearly froze. But there it is, an alternate version of the famous speech. The text of the First Folio is very close to that of the Second Quarto, but it's shorter; corrections have been made, speeches trimmed ("How all occasions do inform

---

* *Hamlet: The Texts of 1603 and 1623*, ed. Ann Thompson and Neil Taylor, Arden Shakespeare, Third Series (London: Arden, 2006).

against me" is notably absent), and scraps of new dialogue inserted.

So . . . of the three texts, which is Shakespeare's? Indeed, "That is the question." Or should I say, "Ay, there's the point"?

While most scholars agree that the Second Quarto or First Folio is closest to Shakespeare's "original" (if such a thing existed), theories on the curious First Quarto abound. Depending upon which scholar from which century you consult, it's: (a) a first draft that is all Shakespeare's work; (b) a "memorial reconstruction" of the text by an actor or actors who once played the play; (c) a collaboration between Shakespeare and another playwright; (d) all, or in part, the work of another, earlier playwright; (e) a version of Shakespeare's original and perfect manuscript that's been mangled by some combination of ad-libbing and forgetful actors, brutal censors, penurious playhouse owners, clueless provincial tour managers, unscrupulous publishers, half-deaf and harried stenographers, and incompetent editors and typesetters.

If pressed, I'd select (f) all of the above. Shakespeare might well have been brought in as a novice playwright to collaborate with another author on an adaptation of a previous version of the play for a tour, then later (presumably after someone said, "Your bits are good, that other guy's, not so much") written out his own complete version, which was then adapted by the company, workshopped in the suburbs, censored by the government, premiered in London, revised after so-so reviews, then later cut down for a touring company whose prompt-script was pirated and put out in an unauthorized edition.

That narrative certainly accords best with my own experience of how published play texts come about. Although there's obviously no reason to assume that Shakespeare's experience

was the same as mine (I am, I have been told, no Shakespeare),
such a fractious history absolutely accords with realities of the
theater that have not changed since Shakespeare's day. As anyone who's ever worked on a play—be it a second-grade holiday
pageant or a Broadway musical—knows, even the tightest theatrical production is a kind of barely controlled chaos, a mad-
house mix of playwright, director, performers, and technicians.
And what any given audience member experiences as a "play"
on a given night in a theater is an amorphous, untamed monster that grows and shrinks, thrives and starves, depending on
an infinite number of variables: time of day, flu in the company, a crying baby in the balcony, actors' drinking habits. But
those variables can be winnowed down to a handful of essentials that were just as fundamental and just as changeable in
Shakespeare's day as in ours: the cast, the venue, and, of course,
the audience. Or (with apologies to journalism's five W's),
Who, When, Where, and *for Whom?**

*   *   *

The *who* of the production—the play's casting—can subtly
or drastically change both the text and the tenor of a show.
For example, at the end of Act 1 of our *Complete Works,* the
skittish "Adam," with "Jess" hot on his tail, sprints out of the
theater in a blind terror at the prospect of having to perform
Hamlet, leaving "Daniel" alone on stage. The stage direction,
in our first published version of the script, reads simply: "*Daniel stalls.*" Now, Daniel Singer looks good in tights and has an

---

* I assume that the *why* of Shakespeare's motivation to write for the theater
was the same as mine: to meet girls (and/or boys—again, another essay), lob
a political grenade or two, bask in applause, and make enough money for
bangers and ale.

Ophelia interrupts "To be, or not to be," with Barbara
Reinertson as Ophelia and Jess Winfield as Hamlet in 1981.
Photograph by Marc Brody.

affable puppy-dog quality, so he just stood there for a minute
or two looking handsome and uncomfortable, got a couple of
pity laughs, and then said, "Why don't we take an intermission
here." But when Daniel left the Reduced Shakespeare Company
in 1989, we brought in Reed Martin, a former Ringling Bros. and

The moment took on a different flavor with Adam Long as
Ophelia and Jess Winfield as Hamlet in 1987. The entire scene
was eventually cut in The Complete Works *in favor of an*
extended audience participation sequence.
Photograph by Sa Winfield.

Barnum & Bailey clown. We expanded that section to showcase
Reed's somewhat dubious talents: he stalled by (among other
things) playing the accordion, swallowing fire, and playing
the "William Tell Overture" on his throat. That version of the
"stall" appears on the popular DVD of the play, recorded in

Vancouver. In the U.K. Acting Edition of the show, based on performances at London's Criterion Theatre, the actor "sings a lovely bit of opera." In New York, Peter Jacobson told several bad jokes ("A horse walks into a bar. The bartender says, 'Why the long face?'"), although the Off-Broadway Acting Edition of the show, published in 1995, simply suggests that future actors fill in with their own unique and slightly pathetic party tricks.*

Shakespeare, too, as playwright, co-owner, and player in the Chamberlain's Men and then the King's Men, would certainly have made, or consulted on, or at the very least been *aware* of adaptations to his own plays depending on who was performing them. Songs within at least two plays were reassigned or cut entirely, depending on the singing prowess of the actors in the roles, as Grace Ioppolo notes in her *Revising Shakespeare*: "The singing boy who originally played Viola in *Twelfth Night* may not have been available for a later revival, and the song before the Duke, as printed in the Folio, was transferred to Feste, played perhaps by Robert Armin"—a comedian known to have been an accomplished singer. In *As You Like It*, many scholars have noted an irresolvable discrepancy in the description of Rosalind's height in comparison to Celia's. The character Le Beau categorically calls Celia "the taller" (1.2.211) but in the next scene, when Celia suggests that the two friends flee in disguise as peasant girls to the Forest of Arden, Rosalind says she would be better disguised as a man, "Because that I am more than common tall" (1.3.111)—and presumably taller than Celia. Such a discrepancy may well have crept in when different actors

---

* I edited that text some weeks after the production closed, without referring to the prompt book. I wouldn't be surprised if a line or two of dialogue that I recalled from performing the show myself, but that had actually been altered for the New York production, crept into that edition.

played the roles. The Bard also demonstrably changed his portrayal of clown or fool characters when the more intellectual
comedian Armin took over from Will Kempe, who was prone
to long, improvised physical comedy and the pulling of "scurvy
faces." Where Kempe's early clowns are buffoons (Launcelot
Gobbo in *The Merchant of Venice*, Bottom in *A Midsummer
Night's Dream*, and Dogberry in *Much Ado About Nothing*), the
later fools, such as Feste and, most strikingly, the Fool in *King
Lear*, are fully drawn characters. One wonders if, for revivals of
Shakespeare's earlier plays, the clown roles were rewritten to
suit Armin in addition to giving him the odd song. If Shakespeare was half the dramatist we think him, then of course he
rewrote them.

✳　✳　✳

Beyond casting, another variable that can affect a play's text is
the *where*: the venue, or even the medium, in which the play
is to be performed. The Reduced Shakespeare Company's first
production was a half-hour version of *Hamlet*. Why a half
hour? Because that's how the slots were blocked out at the
Renaissance Pleasure Faire stages where we performed: we had
thirty minutes exactly to set up, gather a crowd, perform, gather
up props and costumes, and clear out for the next act. Later,
when we launched *The Complete Works (abridged)*, it clocked
in at an hour . . . because that was the length of time we could
afford to rent the cheapest available venue at the Edinburgh
Fringe Festival: a converted basement church. Still later, when
we expanded the show to a full evening of entertainment for
purposes of touring and extended runs in major cities, we
added introductory material to the beginning of the show and
augmented *Hamlet* with an audience participation segment, so

that *Hamlet* could serve as an Act 2—thus allowing us to sell merchandise at the intermission.

In Shakespeare's case, it's likely that the question of medium explains the very different versions of *Hamlet*. The text of the Second Quarto and Folio versions is at least four hours long in performance. But recall the half-length First Quarto version: many scholars believe, and I agree, that it was likely a version of the play specifically crafted to be acted in a theater. Elizabethan asses and seats were, after all, no larger or more comfortable than ours. In fact, unless you could afford double the "general admission" price of a penny for a seat on the shaded, hard wooden benches, or four pence for a cushioned seat, you were left standing, in the summer afternoon sun, in the notoriously smelly groundlings' pit. The First Quarto version can be performed in a merciful two hours, and although nearly all scholars quibble with the accuracy of the First Quarto's verbiage, most agree that it makes theatrical sense as a whole ("*Hamlet* with the brakes off," as Peter Guinness, who performed a stage version of the First Quarto in 1985, called it).* Some scholars suggest that the longer Second Quarto and Folio texts were intended for *publication*:** each a more poetic, "literary" text meant to be read, not performed—as Kenneth Branagh painfully demonstrated with his four-and-a-half-hour, "full-text" film of *Hamlet*.

Even within the context of performance for the stage, adjustments would have been made according to venue. Shakespeare's company was known to have given command performances at the Royal Court. *The Merry Wives of Windsor* was

---

* See *Hamlet: The Texts of 1603 and 1623*, p. 27.
** Including Gary Taylor and Lukas Erne, ibid. (sorry), pp. 82–84.

likely commissioned for such a performance, and that's reflected
in the Folio text. A speech in the Fairy Masque of Act 5 begins,
"Search Windsor Castle, elves, within and out." The Quarto
text of 1602, however, is clearly *not* designed for performance
at Windsor: the same speech begins, "You Fairies that do haunt
these shady groves, look round about the wood." Of course, the
Bard's works were also performed at various public theaters,
the most well-known being the Globe (outdoors), and, later,
Blackfriars (indoors). The change to an indoor venue allowed
the Bard to indulge in far more elaborate sets and staging. *Cymbeline*, a later play that would have been performed at Blackfriars, calls for Jupiter's entrance "in thunder and lightning, sitting
upon an eagle." That kind of rigging is unlikely to have been
attempted with the more Spartan outdoor technical capabili-
ties of the Globe. *The Tempest* shows clear signs of having had
an elaborate fairy masque—something that had become all the
rage halfway through Shakespeare's career—inserted into the
text sometime after its original composition, perhaps accompanying the move to Blackfriars. Prospero's unlikely statement,
after the extended interruption to the main story, that

> I had forgot that foul conspiracy
> Of the beast Caliban and his confederates
> Against my life.
>
> (4.1.151–153)

reminds me exactly of an ass-covering line we were obliged
to insert after adding a ten-to-fifteen-minute audience-
participation section to our tale of *Hamlet*:

> But we digress. Now back to Act Two, Scene Two: the
> famous play-within-a-play scene . . .

* * *

Early Reduced Shakespeare Company material also varied and evolved depending on *for whom* we were performing, and our relationship with them. For our first performances of *Hamlet*, we worked for the lofty sum of forty dollars per day each, paid by the Renaissance Pleasure Faire. The stage where we performed was in the middle of a noisy, boisterous, outdoor food-and-ale court; our first crowds were drunken, innuendo-loving partiers who had to be visually roped in to sitting and watching the show instead of wandering off for a turkey leg. We developed a loud, physical, slapstick style, our dialogue peppered with loads of goofy, bawdy, and marginally humorous ad-libs to spice up the Shakespeare. (Ophelia: "As I was sewing in my closet, lord Hamlet, his doublet all unbrac'd . . . *comes* before me." Polonius: "Ew, gross!"). The following season we shared a smaller, quieter stage with two jugglers, who told us how much cash they were raking in by passing the hat: hundreds, if not *thousands*, a day. So we began soliciting tips after our shows. We quickly learned that the harder we worked, the faster we moved, the more we sweated, and the more genuinely funny jokes we crammed into that half hour, the more money we made. That mad, joke-a-second energy became our signature style, and soon enough, we were performing not primarily to get laid, but to make a living and quit our day jobs. Inspired by Tom Stoppard's *15-Minute Hamlet*, we'd already been performing an "encore" version of the story to cap our play, but now we added two *more* encores, to help set up our pitch for money. By the time we reached the grand finale, where we performed *Hamlet* in forty-seven seconds—backwards—we had essentially established a contract between us and the audience: "We'll do it backwards, *if* you'll put money in our hats afterward."

Later, on tour, we discovered that our bawdy, mad-energy, buskers' version of the show played less well in the stuffy opera houses of England, where the atmosphere was more genteel. So in the United Kingdom we added more highbrow material, and took out some (but not all) of the pratfalls and dick jokes. After our first performance on a short tour of the American South, a local waited until after the show to warn us: "Y'all got filthy mouths." The *Deliverance*-like atmosphere inspired us to tone down our abundant left-coast political and sexual material for the rest of those dates—and to avoid further tours of the South. At least once, when we found ourselves performing for a particularly conservative, elderly, and unappreciative audience, we agreed backstage *in the middle of Act 1* to revert to the old, one-act, hour-long version of the play so we could get the hell outta Dodge. Pity our poor touring stage manager, who had to keep scribbling rewrites and new jokes and sometimes entire new bits into the promptbook, not to mention making lighting and sound changes on the fly. And that was when we *had* a stage manager . . . there's a reason why, in *The Complete Works (abridged)*, the characters often directly address the unseen lighting technician, "Bob," instructing him to bring up or down house lights, or to provide "a little mood lighting" for this or that scene: we often couldn't afford to travel with any crew of our own beyond the three actors and our backstage dresser and costumer (and fourth company member), Sa Thomson. Once or twice, we couldn't afford to travel with her, either—which led to several costume-snafu-related sight gags that became scripted parts of the show, as when Adam, having not-quite-completed a fast change, rushed onstage wearing Claudius's beard and crown . . . and Gertrude's dress and falsies. Responding to the audience's laughter, he ad-libbed: "Let's play *Guess What I Am Now*," and I, as Hamlet, responded with an accusatory "Here, thou incestuous, murd'rous, cross-dressing Dane!" Both lines have subsequently appeared in every version of the script. For one private performance only, however, we changed our onstage response to Adam's half-dressed state: "It's Schrödinger's costume change!" I said. The obscure quantum physics joke got a huge laugh from the invited audience: employees of the Fermilab particle physics research center.

Jess Winfield as Hamlet in The Complete Works of Shakespeare (abridged).

The Bard, too, must have altered text on occasions when the nature of the audience demanded it. The Folio text of the same speech from *Merry Wives* mentioned above contains numerous very specific references to the Knights of the Garter, including the instruction, "meadow-fairies, look you sing, / Like to the Garter's compass, in a ring" (5.5.54–55). There is scholarly controversy over whether this means that the text was taken from a performance at one of the Order's feasts; my personal experience with particle physicists tells me that there most likely were indeed garters in the house. Tellingly, in the Quarto version of 1602, which most scholars agree was probably taken from play-ers' scripts used in the venues of London and/or on tour, all references to the Garter are missing.

As another example, the Quarto version of *A Midsummer Night's Dream* features a closing speech, assigned to Oberon, that's unassigned in the Folio text: it's simply "The Song." The Quarto version is thought to capture a public performance in which the play ended with the Players dancing onstage and Oberon speaking or singing "Now until the break of day / Through this house each fairy stray" (5.1.371–372), and so on, followed by Puck's "Give me your hands, if we be friends" (5.1.405) epilogue. And the Folio version is thought to record a court performance that ended with the courtier audience joining the players in a final Fairy Masque as a segue to what presumably was to become one rager of a party. As an audi-ence you matter, whether you think you do or not, to such an extent that who you are and what you want out of a play can and *should* be reflected in the text of the play itself.

* * *

A final factor that can influence the text is *when*. Not what time of day the play is performed—although our show performed at ten in the morning in a high school auditorium had a very different flavor than a midnight gig in an after-hours Edin-burgh Fringe club filled with actors and comedians (dick jokes, back in!)—but when in *history*. Our 1980s version of the play, for example, featured loads of Ronald Reagan jokes and an extended gag about Adam believing *The Two Noble Kinsmen* was a cautionary tale about mutant televangelists created by nuclear disaster, entitled *The Chernobyl Kinsmen*. In 2007, Daniel Singer and I launched a twentieth-anniversary update of the script under the name *The Complete Works of William Shakespeare (abridged) [revised]*, an "official" author's revision with numerous tweaks and some all-out rewrites to sections of the show. The *[revised]* script replaced Reagan jokes with Facebook gags, while "Chernobyl Kinsmen" became a reference to cell phone market-share wars between Bill Gates and Steve Jobs: *The Two Mobile Kinsmen*. With Jobs's passing, that joke, which we expected would be good for decades, is (we hope!) already being revised by directors and actors around the globe. (Depressingly, as of this writing, "Newt Gingrich" and "Rush Limbaugh" are subjects as ripe for satiric skewering as they were in 1987.)

Shakespeare, too, would have had to tack the ship of his stagecraft to navigate the social and political currents of the day. Increased religious censorship under King James caused numerous "by God!" oaths in quarto texts to be changed to "by heaven!" in the Folio. Complaints by a certain Brooke family likely forced a change of character of the same name in *Merry Wives* to "Broome." And in the climate of Elizabeth I's later years, when assassination plots and the raising of armies to effect her deposition were rife, the extraordinary deposition scene in *Richard II* was apparently deemed too hot to handle, either by Shakespeare's company or by the Master of Revels, the Crown's official censor. The scene of Richard surrendering his crown to the usurping Bolingbroke is missing in the first three quarto editions of the play, finally appearing in print a respectful three years after Elizabeth's 1603 death. Its title page announces that it comes "With new additions of the Parliament scene, and the deposing of King Richard, as it hath been lately acted by the King's Majesties servants."

Like that text, the published editions of *The Complete Works of William Shakespeare (abridged)* have only ever been compiled after the fact, to capture the show as it "hath been lately acted." Further, to keep alive the play's spirit of experimentation and reinvention, the *Complete Works* scripts now available for licensees are, among all the major acting edition texts I'm aware of, the only ones that actively *encourage* actors to alter the play to suit their needs or whims. As a result, we've seen countless amateur productions with changes major and minor: an all-black cast, leading to a completely different take on our white-boy "Rap *Othello*"; a version where the "Reduced" cast of three was expanded to twenty-four; an all-female production that transformed our sketch of Shakespeare's history plays—a football game with the English crown as the "ball" being passed from generation to generation—to a catty beauty pageant, wherein the crown becomes the reigning beauty queen's tiara. Thus there are now, in addition to the three "official" editions of the play text by the authors* (four if you count the text used for the DVD), promptbooks for *hundreds* of stock and amateur productions, all out there somewhere, waiting to be discovered by scholars four hundred years hence, so that they might ask: "Which is the 'authoritative' text?"

The answer, of course, is that they all are, and that none is. A play exists in four dimensions; its documentation in text is merely a two-dimensional snapshot of it at a given moment in time and space.

* * *

At least, that *should* be the case. In contemporary practice, "the play" is too often a carven monolith contractually prevented

---

* The trade paperback edition, released in 1993 by Applause Books/Hal Leonard, now in its umpteenth printing; the U.S. Acting Edition of 1995; and the U.K. Acting Edition.

from alteration. To be honest, I rarely enjoy the theater, precisely because so many plays are "locked," performed without regard to who, where, when and for whom they are being performed. *Les Mis* is *Les Mis*. *Rent* is *Rent*. *God of Carnage* is *God of Carnage*. Costumes, sets, lighting, and blocking may change, but the text is usually sacrosanct.

Perhaps there's change in the air. The extracts from *Hamlet* above are taken from the extraordinary Arden Shakespeare editions of 2006. I say "editions" because the editors released *all three* major *Hamlet* texts—First Quarto, Second Quarto, and First Folio—concurrently, treating them as separate and valuable manifestations of the same play. It's my hope that this sort of treatment will bring more of a spirit of revision and experimentation to theatrical texts both classic and contemporary; that playwrights and theater companies will more often take advantage of theater's essential mutability to ~~dick around with~~ continually improve their texts.

Ironically, when tracking down our own scripts for this piece, I discovered that none of the coauthors of *Complete Works* had ever seen the U.K. Acting Edition. We each thought another had approved it, and no one can remember which of our many Microsoft Word files was the jumping off point for it. As it stands, it's a "bad quarto," rife with misspellings and poorly typeset. I've no idea what text we'll work from to fix it.

So I can easily imagine that if, even a mere ten years after their publication, some dedicated editor had shown Shakespeare the two then-extant texts of "To be, or not to be," and asked which bits were his, he'd shrug. "Well . . . I remember writing 'Ay there's the point,' here, but then Burbage came up with 'that is the question' in rehearsal—or was it Tom Pope? Anyway, we made a few changes, which the company scrivener scribbled in the promptbook in prose, and then I went

home and wrote it in verse in the margin of my own copy, and
I probably tweaked (yes, in my imagination Shakespeare says
"tweaked") the whole speech some more while I was looking at
it. We used 'that is the question' for a while, but then when we
were preparing the second, or maybe the third, revival, I came
across the original and I liked it better, so we tried 'there's the
point' for a week while Burbage was out with the clap. . . . Or was
it all the other way 'round? Truth is, I don't remember where we
landed on it. Did you ask Heminges or Condell? They're good
with that sort of thing."

Brian Cox

"I SAY IT IS THE MOON"

BRIAN COX, CBE, is a Scottish theater and film actor. His dozens of films include *Rob Roy, Braveheart, X-Men United, The Bourne Identity, Rushmore, Red*, and *Troy*; his television credits include *Deadwood, Frasier,* and *The Big C*. His performances, many at the Royal Shakespeare Company and the Royal National Theatre, include *Peer Gynt, Manhunter*, and *That Championship Season*, as well as the Shakespeare plays *The Merchant of Venice, A Midsummer Night's Dream, As You Like It, Titus Andronicus, The Taming of the Shrew, Macbeth*, and *Othello*. He played Burgundy in Sir Laurence Olivier's film of *King Lear*; his subsequent experiences in the title role are the subject of his book *The Lear Diaries*. He recently performed the role of Menenius in Ralph Fiennes's film version of *Coriolanus*. His work has been recognized with an Emmy Award, a BAFTA Scotland Award, a Gemini Award, a Satellite Award, and a Golden Globe nomination.

I first performed Shakespeare some fifty years ago: I walked on as Bassanio's servant in *The Merchant of Venice*. If Shakespeare lasts in anybody's life, it's because of the personal relationship one sets up with him. Just as our relationships with a common friend are never the same, so my relationship with Shakespeare won't be everybody's: it is simply and strongly my own relationship with Shakespeare. The whole premise of what I'm about to write is therefore based on a personal bond with this playwright which has lasted almost fifty long and rewarding years, during which I've grown to understand what that friendship is about, and what the product of that friendship is. With all friends, you have good days and bad days. You are friends for some time, and then you don't see each other for a while, and then you meet again, and the friendship moves to another level. It's always shifting, and although it starts with a common premise it develops into something much grander. When that familiarity is with a writer of the magnitude of Shakespeare, it cannot help but affect your life, since out of that friendship comes an appreciation of the values in your life, and the value of your life itself. And yes, I know it seems a bit mad, since this is a friend I've of course never met, but there are friendships in our lives which transcend distance as well. A good friend of mine died twenty-five years ago, and yet I still have conversations with him. "What would he do about this?" I ask. "What would he feel about this?" As with Shakespeare, I imagine the responses—and, in the process, I discover what I believe to be their true opinions.

What's missing in much theatre, film, and television today, I find, is the dimension of the human struggle: what it is to be alive, to live in a human society, and to obey or disobey the structure of that society. Since it is missing some kind of dimension—moral, philosophical, spiritual—I feel a lack. Then, when I come back to Shakespeare, I find that dimension again, and I can weave certain threads throughout his plays, tenuous though they may be. They're threads about existence, about how we become involved or detached, and about how we learn the value of something and then question it. As one gets older, one learns that life is not straightforward: it's paradoxical, it's yin and yang, it's black and white. As Ibsen's Peer Gynt says, "It's there—it's here—it's all about me! / I think I've got out, and I'm back in the midst of it." Shakespeare lives in the middle of it, and we live in the middle of it too; even though we may try to go to one extreme or the other, finding that contradictory area difficult, life is all about these contradictions. Character—on stage, just as much as in life—is itself a contradiction. As soon as someone does something that is "out of character," he or she is doing exactly what must be done to create character. Shakespeare is the best life dramatist there is, because he essentially lived in the middle of that paradox.

His own character was defined by paradox: the Shakespeare I know wasn't just a master craftsman and visionary poet, he was also a great pragmatist. He lived in a society whose hierarchies were all-pervasive and even ratified by the Church. The divine right of kings is about the pecking order: there is the peasant, and then there is the farmer, and then there is the baron who owns the farm, and then there is the king, and then there is God. The original kings were basically gangsters—the king, like the godfather, is the father nearest to God—who then ratified their brute conquests with a set of rules which then became the premise of an entire society. That order, which amounts to an internalized system of thinking, hasn't changed in the British DNA at all. The royals to this day still believe in the divine right of kings, and we groundlings tend to underestimate the continued power of that belief. It's still with us, and clearly it's what Shakespeare reflects—and that is one of the main reasons why Shakespeare continues to have such enduring dramatic power.

Even in our current, largely secular society, this need for some sort of order continues within us. Man hasn't found any other way to live except through the principle of freedom through constraint: we like a clear sense of how we can behave and how we can structure our lives. We find it very difficult to live without belief systems, and those who don't believe in a spiritual metaphysics create corresponding political and economic belief systems. These orders are manmade, no matter what higher powers we ascribe them to, for they have all been created and sustained by our sense of imagination to give us precepts to live by.

Shakespeare lives in the middle of various religious and social belief systems, and his plays are immensely allegorical because they're all about the displacement of the breakdown and reconstruction of those orders. His allegories are constantly portraying these hierarchies dressed up in other guises—in what is sometimes a romantic, and sometimes an historical or tragedic manner.

* * *

As You Like It contains numerous disguised hierarchies. It is very much a prose play, which suggests a temporary loosening of the traditional orders. After a political coup at court, mayhem follows the banished Duke and his followers into the Forest of Arden. Orlando, who is rather a beautiful character, has been deprived of his rights as a young lord. He's a noble savage, and when he falls in love with Rosalind he even recognizes that he must undergo training because he's too rough for her. Rosalind herself has had to throw off all pretence of being a princess and is in the forest pretending to be a boy, which, ironically, allows her to train Orlando in the traditions that are already set up: the traditions of courtly love which allow him to try to be her spiritual equal and to succeed in being her social better. To me, *As You Like It* is a great dramatic treatise. Even though there are extraordinary threads of humanist thought which Shakespeare wove into the play, essentially Rosalind is training Orlando in how to get his position back and then how to retain his position. She's giving him an education in order.

The other story in the play deals with the same theme even more clearly. It's the story involving Phoebe, a shepherdess, and Silvius, her simple shepherd suitor. Phoebe treats Silvius terribly and dismisses him because he's in love with her and therefore lowly. He has put himself in a supine position, and so she attacks him. Having witnessed their relationship, Rosalind steps in and argues for fairness and equanimity. She asks Phoebe who she thinks she is to be so high and mighty: "And why, I pray you? Who might be your mother, / That you insult, exult, and all at once, / Over the wretched?" (3.5.36–38). Then Rosalind gives her some hard advice:

> But mistress, know yourself: down on your knees,
> And thank heaven, fasting, for a good man's love;
> For I must tell you friendly in your ear,
> Sell when you can, you are not for all markets.
>
> (3.5.58–61)

In the exchange, the relationship between courtly love and social order becomes clear, since no matter how condescending the first system allows Phoebe to be, in the end Silvius is a man and therefore her social superior.

You see again and again how these themes reassert themselves in the other plays. In many ways *A Midsummer Night's Dream* is more allegorical than the others, probably because of the nature of that particular cosmos. In the play, we witness the breakdown of the natural world and the breakdown of the social order, and at the end we feel the urgency that the natural world be redone and the social order be reasserted. The play opens on the eve of the wedding between Theseus, Duke of Athens, and Hippolyta, Queen of the Amazons, and as they are old enemies—"I wooed thee with my sword" (1.1.17)—there is much uncertainty about it. Then Shakespeare pushes that uncertainty into the fairy world in which Titania has adopted a changeling boy, and Oberon is obsessed with taking the boy from her, believing that if he doesn't get that boy then there will be no balance in the world. Then, too, the lovers are unbalanced: Helena loves Demetrius; Demetrius loves Hermia; Hermia loves Lysander. They're thrown into even greater chaos in the forest, and we understand that all the intervening confusion is ultimately about restoring order. Everyone is paired up happily at the end, and so the society can continue. And everyone is in his or her place hierarchically as well, with the Duke and the Queen at the top, then the noble youths and their families, and then the mechanicals back at the bottom—and this is important, since Bottom has been the consort of Titania, Queen of the Fairies, the stand-in for Hippolyta. The happy mechanicals put on a play for the Duke in the last act, and they get celebrated for their play and for how it's done, but it's very patronising. Their play is a disaster, but of course it's meant well, and it's common, and it comes from the heart. At the end of *A Midsummer Night's Dream* you feel very complacent, and you think everything is fine and innocent, but at the same time that last, comic act is covering a multitude of sins.

The other play which is sharp on ideas of property and order and hierarchy is *The Taming of the Shrew*. Petruchio has been a fighter all his life. His father has died, and he arrives in Padua because he needs a woman in his life and a wife for his household—but he wants someone with spirit. He doesn't want a Bianca, who seems simple but who is actually quite subtle. She's the real shrew, it turns out, because she plays everybody against one another from her carefully chosen position in the middle. And then there is this rather bruised girl, Katherine, who is the eldest daughter and who understands only too well her position in terms of the world: she represents *property*. She is a cash cow, with her dowry and all the trappings of wealth and consequence, and because of the way the system is, since she's the firstborn, she must be the first one to go. Naturally she's angry, and she has every right to be angry.

The message in the play has its source in that anger, and it's an exceptionally keen message: that the world is not as we would like it to be, and so therefore we have to—especially in our relationships—turn the world on its head. We have to make the sun the moon and the moon the sun. Once you understand that, you do not become attached to how things are when they're unjust, and that's why Petruchio does what he does. The scene is the pivot of the play. They're travelling to her father's after the wedding, and she's hot, and tired, and Petruchio says, "Good Lord, how bright and goodly shines the moon!"

> KATE: The moon? The sun: it is not moonlight now.
> PETRUCHIO: I say it is the moon that shines so bright.
> KATE: I know it is the sun that shines so bright.
> PETRUCHIO: Now, by my mother's son, and that's myself,
> It shall be moon, or star, or what I list,
> Or ere I journey to your father's house.—
> Go on, and fetch our horses back again.—
> Evermore crossed and crossed, nothing but crossed!
> HORTENSIO: Say as he says, or we shall never go.
> KATE: Forward, I pray, since we have come so far,
> And be it moon, or sun, or what you please.
> An if you please to call it a rush-candle,
> Henceforth I vow it shall be so for me.
> PETRUCHIO: I say it is the moon.
> KATE: I know it is the moon.

PETRUCHIO: Nay, then you lie. It is the blessèd sun.
KATE: Then, God be blessed, it is the blessèd sun.
But sun it is not, when you say it is not,
And the moon changes even as your mind.
What you will have it named, even that it is,
And so it shall be so for Katherine.

(4.3.2–23)

The play is deeply spiritual and almost metaphysical, in a way, because it's about how not to become attached. "What goes on between us is one thing," Petruchio teaches her, "but we have to live in the world as it exists." That world is structured by a strict power pecking order, and to survive she's going to have to get with the program.

Of all the plays, the real problem play is *The Taming of the Shrew*. I don't think it's supposed to be a light romance with an awkward ending that Shakespeare didn't quite get right. It's a problem play, and I think it works as a problem play, and I think that those who say that it's a play which shouldn't be done because of how it treats women simply don't understand the reverberation of the play. The most controversial scene is at the very end, when Petruchio commands Katherine to "tell these headstrong women / What duty they do owe their lords and husbands" (5.1.142–143). She responds, "Thy husband is thy lord, thy life, thy keeper, / Thy head, thy sovereign: one that cares for thee" (5.1.158–159), and instructs the women, "place your hands below your husband's foot" (5.1.189)—for which she is rewarded by her husband with, "Why, there's a wench! Come on, and kiss me, Kate" (5.1.192). It could be that she has sold out, or it could be that she has found some method of peace, some way to deal with her pain, because her husband has given her the guarantee that the sun is the moon and the moon is the sun. Nothing is what it seems to be to anybody else. What it all means, Petruchio teaches her, is what it is between you and me.

Now, of course it's incredibly patronising, but then it's a patronising role. It was a patriarchal world. It was not a matriarchal world, even though Elizabeth I was the queen, but a patriarchal world which had been forged by going through the Age of Kings—and I think that's why the play makes a lot of sense and continues to have a certain resonance even though we wish it didn't. If you understand that aspect, then you begin to understand many of the aspects of the other plays. What Shakespeare is getting at in *The Taming of the Shrew* is a certain psychological state, and that same kind of psychological state, in various settings and inflections, can be found throughout his plays, and can still be found in all of us today.

* * *

The tragedies deal with the same sorts of psychological states, but they wear them with a difference.

Even *King Lear* deals with a psychological state similar to that in the high romances *As You Like It* and *A Midsummer Night's Dream*, because the order is out of whack. Lear makes bad decision after bad decision, beginning with dividing his kingdom and then giving it away, and for him the world turns upside-down. He has been thrust out of the patriarchal order he created, he sustained, and in which he was at the top. It was a bad decision, but it was a generous decision—and at the same time it was a self-indulgent decision, coming from the desire to retire in ease and revelry, with no cares of governance, and no responsibility for his people. Moreover, though, it was also an understandable decision, because he's a man who is coming

Brian Cox as King Lear at the
National's Lyttelton Theatre, 1990.
Photograph by Tristram Kenton.

to the end of his life. He can see his intimations of mortality, and the one thing that has been missing in his life and that he is desperate for is an affirmation of love. He knows that he has not been a great father and he is trying to make amends, and although his youngest daughter does love him despite his bad parenting, she doesn't say it. You can't ask people to say that they love you, since they either do or they don't, and you can't buy their love, either, since it's not a commodity—but those are the lessons he has to learn. His decision to divide his kingdom was therefore also made out of his need for love.

Cordelia sees what her father is doing, but it's not a conversation to be had at a formal gathering. She knows he's overturning the order, and making it unnatural, both in governance and in his family, and she can't agree—she can't bend to it. Katherine can, but she's in a comedy—hers is a problem play, yet at least it's one with a reasonably happy ending. Cordelia ends up dead, and Lear ends up dead, and it's because they can't survive the upending of power based on an unnatural bargain that results in a state of madness, both social and personal. Edgar can survive—he becomes king at the end—but the only way he can survive is by pretending to be even madder than the world itself. You have to make decisions, you have to think on your feet, you have to keep up with changes when changes are needed and there are tough times. Edgar becomes Poor Tom, Rosalind becomes Ganymede, the shrew Katherine becomes the good wife—and they make it out of the chaos they're in with a clearer understanding and better ability to live with the necessary orders of the world.

* * *

Every time I'm reintroduced to another Shakespeare play, I'm struck by how the theme of order comes up again and again.

Most recently, I was Menenius in the film version of *Coriolanus* directed by Ralph Fiennes. We filmed it in Belgrade, and the surrounding Serbian, Croatian, and Bosnian history helped to establish the strong military personalities of characters and allowed us to look at the questionable nature of political power. It's very timely, as a play, because of Coriolanus's position as

an outmoded figure: he holds on to values that are no longer
viable and so becomes obsolete. The order of the Roman world
is one in which Coriolanus no longer fits because the world
itself is moving on—and the fact that the world is moving on
is itself questionable, since it's not clear whether it's moving on
for the better or whether it's just moving on to another form of
corruption.

Titus Andronicus deals with the same theme. Titus also
believes in the myth of Rome, a myth he has doggedly served
his entire life; then he discovers that although he has served
Rome, Rome hasn't served him. He has believed in its structure, and he has lost most of his children—from twenty-six he's
down to just four, twenty-two sons having been killed in battle.
Then, when two more of his sons are about to be executed by
the state, he pleads,

> For pity of mine age, whose youth was spent
> In dangerous wars whilst you securely slept,
> For all my blood in Rome's great quarrel shed,
> For all the frosty nights that I have watched,
> And for these bitter tears which now you see
> Filling the agèd wrinkles in my cheeks,
> Be pitiful to my condemned sons . . .

> (3.1.2–8)

The Romans execute his sons anyway, and then he's only got
one son left and his daughter has been mutilated and raped,
and he asks: What's it all about? What have I been working for
all these years? What's the point? And that's what Shakespeare
always demands: What *is* the point? To what do I owe allegiance? To whom do I owe allegiance? And for what do I owe
allegiance? Rome has failed Titus, and so he goes mad. "When

will this fearful slumber have an end?" (3.1.253), he asks. His reality has become a dream, and so his world, too, has been turned upside-down.

No matter what happens, Titus is very much a soldier, as is Coriolanus. The difference is that Titus is at the end of his career, whereas Coriolanus is at the peak of his. Coriolanus can't shift to be that man in a suit, the political animal, and when he tries to be that man in a suit, he fails dramatically. Coriolanus is a hero, he has done his duty, he has been very popular, but he expresses nothing but contempt for the people who put him there. He doesn't think that they put him there: he thinks that he put himself there, which is the kind of mistake made recently by Qaddafi and Mubarak. Through Coriolanus, we see the similar breakdown of a society as mirrored by one man's slightly biased, almost reactionary vision.

America before the Civil War was essentially a hierarchical society, still very linked to its colonial past. Abraham Lincoln's assassin, John Wilkes Booth, grew up in Maryland, which was half South and half North. His father and his brother, Edwin Booth, embraced the northern perspective, but John went against the grain of his family and lived in a world of fantasy in which he decided that he was going to save the South. Lincoln was an apostate and a tyrant, he believed, but of course Lincoln was nothing of the kind: he was a man who was attempting to steer through a very difficult situation to try and appease all the various elements that grew out of slavery. But John Wilkes Booth saw it as the end of a way of life, and in that backwards belief he was a quintessential Coriolanian figure. The Civil War was the showdown between the progressive way of thinking and an archaic social stratification, and it marked the inevitable, classic shift between the old world and the new.

Titus, Coriolanus, and even John Wilkes Booth define

themselves as servants of an ideology and, because they are unable to keep up with their environmental structures, they become outmoded and ludicrous. The inability to move forward creates a loss of viability, and in turn that loss of viability leads towards great personal tragedy. It's their stubborn natures, their inability to see beyond what they think they know, which makes them unable to transcend the chaos and the confusion of structures that are being demolished.

* * *

Coriolanus has no interest in the structure of Rome, apart from his own extraordinary sense of entitlement; he is not interested in how Rome is reconstructing itself. That's what is always so difficult whenever soldiers such as Coriolanus and Titus turn to politics: they don't share the background, the interest, and the experience. Soldiers rarely know or even care to what end they operate, since their allegiances are to each other, rather than to any overarching cause; they tend to focus on strategy, not structure.

This is to do with how the imagination operates. The imagination is a creative force, but it's also a sublimating force which allows you to redirect things that you can't do in real life. To give a crude example, you can kiss someone on stage in a play, and you can enjoy every aspect of it even though it's not a real kiss. Or you can hit somebody on stage, and you can enjoy the rush that it gives you because it's in a sublimated form which fuels your own world of make-believe. The trouble about war and soldiers—and this is what I think all conflicts are about—is that the fantasy becomes a reality. You get it now with television and all the virtual games which involve blasting people with guns and bombs. Watching television and playing games are actually much more satisfying than shooting people for real—

and people get it wrong. They think that the pretending leads on to violence. No, it doesn't. Pretending leads on to more sublimation, and the problem is that it can lead to people in the army to sustain the cycle. But it actually never tells the truth of the situation, since the situation is always being formalized in some way.

Similarly, Coriolanus is one of the most fearsome warriors in Shakespeare's canon, but his motive isn't the sheer act of violence: he wants a structure to believe in that is already in place and that he doesn't have to question. The advantage of having an order to believe in is that it gives you a context of how to behave, so that you behave towards what you believe. When the Roman structure fails him, he switches fairly easily to the Volscian camp, since it's the fact of the structure rather than the basis for the structure which is most important to him. Even though Coriolanus and Tullus Aufidius are enemies, they share the same soldier's code of conduct; that explains why Coriolanus gets along better with his nemesis than he does with his own people.

What, then, is their war even about? It's about nation-building, and gathering bits of land and populace, and creating something greater out of them. It's about Tullus Aufidius shaking his sabre at everybody, and it's about the Romans shaking spears back at the Volscians—and it becomes a game.

* * *

What, then, are the rules of this particular game?

In *Coriolanus*, it's the Roman people themselves who define the rules. They want rid of the old order, and they want a new order, and because the power they wield is so astonishing, negotiating with them is the political challenge of the play. If the people say "grey," it's grey; if the people say "black," it's black;

if they say "white," it's white. The Tribunes reflect these sound
bites because it's in their interest to do so. They simply say
whatever the people want them to say, and Menenius calls them
on it: "I know you can do very little alone, for your helps are
many, or else your actions would grow wondrous single: your
abilities are too infant-like for doing much alone" (2.1.26–28).
The Tribunes merely reflect whatever is in fashion at the time.
"What I think, I utter" (2.1.39), says Menenius of himself, but
"You know neither me, yourselves nor anything" (2.1.49). I am
who I am, in other words, but you are not who you are because
you're basing yourselves on a constantly shifting society—but
then, of course that's the nature of society: citizens change. As
Coriolanus himself says to the Citizens,

> With every minute you do change a mind,
> And call him noble that was now your hate,
> Him vile that was your garland.
>
> (1.1.164–166)

Menenius, like Petruchio, understands the nature of the
confusion. In order to function, both have had to develop a
sense of detachment and the ability to rise above the chaos that
surrounds them. It's the salvation of pragmatism. You have to
just get on with it. Menenius understands, for instance, that
Coriolanus is very clean-limbed: "His nature is too noble for
the world" (3.1.300), as he describes him. Coriolanus doesn't
have any imagination, and in that he's like Lady Macbeth. She
functions best when she's pragmatic and efficient. Any imaginative awareness she has comes when she's unconscious, through
sleep. In her conscious life, she has no idea what she's doing to
Macbeth. It's Macbeth himself who has all the imagination. He
knows what the consequences are, but she can't see it through.

That's one of the great human dilemmas. The Macbeths function as a duo, and together they're a dream team, but when you
split them up, you split up imagination and pragmatism, and a
form of chaos ensues.

As it is in *Macbeth*, the drama of *Coriolanus* is also domestic. Menenius is very much like the benevolent uncle, for
instance, and the play is full of Coriolanus's relationship with
his mother, Volumnia. He's a mummy's boy: his mother calls
the shots, and when he doesn't quite go the way she wants she
has to steer him back on course. Coriolanus's *modus operandi*
and even his entire *modus vivendi* come from his mother and
the conservative, martial upbringing she gave him. His actions
are supposed to take him through a rite of passage, but he
fails because he has been overdetermined by his mother. He's
hopeless with his wife, he's hopeless with his children, he's a
martinet as far as being a soldier, but with his mummy it's,
"Oh yes, Mummy" and "No, Mummy," and when she exercises
her authority he cannot, somehow or other, extricate himself
from it.

That's why the play is so fascinating on both personal and
political levels. What if Coriolanus didn't listen to his mother?
What if he just went on his own way? He tries to, but he can't
shake off the sense of responsibility and all the excessive filial
devotion that has gunged up the works for years. Not only is
Coriolanus not pragmatic, in that he fails to keep up with the
changing times, but the little imagination he has, which allows
him to envisage a different future with Tullus Aufidius and the
Volscians, is outdone by his mother's even stronger vision of
how her son is a chick to her mother hen:

> Thou hast never in thy life
Showed thy dear mother any courtesy,

When she, poor hen, fond of no second brood,
Has clucked thee to the wars and safely home,
Loaden with honour.

(5.3.171–175)

If he had adopted some of his mother's imagination and his father-figure's pragmatism, Coriolanus would have been able to avoid his tragic fate.

* * *

No matter where and when they are set, of course, all of Shakespeare's plays are about Elizabethan England. The character flaw in Coriolanus involves his pride, his vanity, and his over-burdened sense of entitlement—which is absolutely the character flaw of the Earl of Southampton, or, even more so, the Earl of Essex. Essex reckoned that, because the Queen loved him and he was the most popular man in the kingdom, he could do what he liked, but he ended up on the chopping block because—also like Macbeth in this respect—he let his vaulting ambition o'erleap itself and fall on the other side. The Elizabethan Age was one of boundless possibilities, romantic optimism, and comfort in the conservative political and social hierarchies. Coriolanus represents this old, Elizabethan order, and *Coriolanus*, which was written in 1605–1608, reflects very strongly the move into the Jacobean Age, which was pragmatic without understanding the imaginative romanticism that had come before.

 Othello is another example of the changing times. Othello is like Coriolanus in his observance of the old vanities of the Elizabethan Age, and Iago represents the pragmatism of the Jacobean Age. The idea of reputation no longer meant anything. Iago is the archpragmatist; he is the fallen angel turned nihilist and anarchic—anything goes. He has no belief in any order at all because order has failed him: it has let him down, for he is still an ensign and hasn't been rewarded with a promotion. Dangerously, Iago is also endowed with a robust imagination. When pragmatism and imagination are united in someone with good intentions, as in the comedies, all of society benefits—but instead of using that knowledge for good, Iago uses it to destroy the society around him. He has no belief in anything, except in the random and arbitrary nature of things, for the arbitrary always raises its head in the godless society and becomes justified.

If there has ever been another Jacobean age since, there is one now: it's Jacobean in the sense that the virtue of heroes, which is the virtue of serving something above and beyond, is no longer fashionable. We've become more and more secular and efficient, and we're not interested in that service at all. There has been a loss of faith, and to a degree a loss of imagination. We live in a godless society. All our gods have failed us. The golden age of the Elizabethan time has passed, and we are now into the dark age of the Jacobean era.

* * *

The root of Shakespeare's plays is feudal, because the Renaissance was still deeply rooted in its medieval feudal past—but the measure of his greatness was his ability to rise above the structures of his time. The worlds and the themes he created were myriad because his narratives are poetic, allegorical, and metaphorical. He never writes in straight lines. As a result, the lessons in imaginative pragmatism we can learn from him apply equally to all social structures, whether they be Roman, medieval, Elizabethan, Jacobean, those of America before or after the Civil War, those of modern Britain, or those of any of the international structures struggling to gain preeminence today. Shakespeare teaches us how to live between one political paradigm and the next, in the middle of social contradictions, and right at the heart of all the emotional paradoxes of the human condition.

The ultimate paradox, of course, is that even though we're all going to die, we've all got to live in the meantime—and so all of Shakespeare's plays are, in some form, a debate about existence. Why? To what end? How do I create my life? And he asks these questions in all sorts of modes: theologically, romantically, spiritually, hedonistically, and politically. Shakespeare is such a great friend because he's constantly—with as much patience as insistence—throwing the important questions at us.

I think that Shakespeare wasn't a long liver because he had lived in the middle of those paradoxes for so long that he simply didn't have the endurance to keep it up. He got worn out by the endless debate, I believe, and his life became tragic. But that's what the artist does: he enacts that debate. Actors such as myself do it night after night in a form of ritual sacrifice that's performed on behalf of others. We pretend to be you, and we reflect back to you what it is to be human so that hopefully you come away with a slightly different perspective on your own life. It's energizing, but it's also exhausting, and I think that Shakespeare became overwhelmed because although he was a friend to everybody, nobody was his friend. Who could reflect Shakespeare back even greater than he was? He was isolated towards the end of his life because the theatre world had let him down. He had gone back to his family, but he had probably made too many mistakes throughout the years, much like Lear—and it's exactly that level of honesty that makes *Lear* such a depressing play to do. You can feel the difference between *Lear* and *Titus*, despite their shared nihilism, for *Titus* is by a young writer getting his rocks off, but *Lear* is written by someone who is extremely disappointed. Nobody can write like that, with that level of truthfulness and integrity, and not get worn out in the process.

And yet Shakespeare lives on, in those extraordinary plays, as our friend. Whether in the tragic form of *Titus, Coriolanus, Othello, Macbeth*, and *Lear*, or in the more comic tones of *As You Like It, A Midsummer Night's Dream*, and *The Taming of the Shrew*, Shakespeare is constantly searching, interrogating, and exploring, and his inability to be satisfied with any single answer seems to have led him on from one play to the next, as he is constantly reformulating the questions he asks us about the nature of both social reality and all our human cosmos. It's not the moon? Then God be blessed—we find ourselves agreeing—it is the blessèd sun.

Ralph Fiennes

THE QUESTION OF *CORIOLANUS*

———

Ralph Fiennes is an English actor and director whose performances, many of which have been at the Royal Shakespeare Company and Royal National Theatre, include *Twelfth Night*; *A Midsummer Night's Dream*; *Romeo and Juliet*; *Much Ado About Nothing*; *The Plantagenets: Henry VI, The Rise of Edward IV, Richard III, His Death*; *King John*; *Troilus and Cressida*; *King Lear*; *Love's Labour's Lost*; *Hamlet*; *Coriolanus*; *Richard II*; *Julius Caesar*; *The Tempest*; and *Hamlet* (which earned him a Tony Award). His many film appearances include *Schindler's List, The English Patient, Onegin, The End of the Affair, The Constant Gardener*, the *Harry Potter* films, *Skyfall, Great Expectations*, and *The Invisible Woman*; his work has earned him two Academy Award nominations, three Golden Globe nominations, one BAFTA and two nominations, as well as London Film Critics' Circle, New York Film Critics' Circle, and Chicago Film Critics' Circle awards. He directed and played the lead in the film *Coriolanus*, which was nominated for another BAFTA Film Award (for Outstanding Debut by a British Writer, Director, or Producer), as well as the Golden Berlin Bear for Best Director and a British Independent Film Award for Best Debut Director. He is the recipient of the James Joyce Award of the Literary and Historical Society.

*C*oriolanus is a terrifying play, though I've always found the part of Coriolanus himself to be curiously addictive.

———

This essay was compiled by the editor from an interview with Ralph Fiennes.

I haven't analyzed why, but I think I liked playing the part because of the anger in it. I *like* the outrageous anger and his contempt for the people. It's rather cathartic to express that extreme, obscene outrage. What Coriolanus says in his rage is fantastically politically incorrect, and I love playing that sense of his own certainty in his value system. And then, just dramatically, physically, vocally, there's a certain athleticism needed to play Coriolanus on stage, and that kind of challenge is like an adrenaline fix.

The play presents itself straightaway as hugely confrontational. Coriolanus talks to the people with such contempt—the people by implication being all of us—that audiences find it hard. But then Shakespeare reveals Coriolanus in stages: he's a man, he's a soldier, he's a man *and* he's a soldier. And it's uncomfortable for us to have to sit in the presence of this, since he's like a boy lost in a tunnel. He's stunted as a human being. I suppose a perverse part of me was drawn to the fact that with so many other of Shakespeare's tragic protagonists we're allowed to hear them delve into their confusion and their conscience, and we're not with Coriolanus. That hardness in him then spreads itself into the play itself—and the audience is struggling. I like that they're not given any lyrical interludes or "to be, or not to be's" where we can hear the pain of Coriolanus. We don't get any of that. We just get the man, in public, angry at everyone. Only at the end do we see him working through his issues, and then I find it very moving because he breaks. He's a boy inside and he weeps at his mother's feet, and we see his extreme vulnerability.

I think you can get closer to Coriolanus on film than you can on the stage. John Logan wrote the screenplay of the film I directed and we were both very aware that whereas on stage you just can't get in, film is often about getting into the eyes. That the eyes are the window to the soul is a cliché, but I think there's a truth in it, since if the camera goes in on someone's face, just simply the size of the close-up means I'm forced to confront what might be going on in that person's mind. As a director, I wanted to go in very close since I find the human face fascinating. When we meet people, we read their eyes as much as what they say. So although Coriolanus on stage is often a difficult part to get into, I think that on film you have a chance to at least try to glean what's going on inside—even though Coriolanus doesn't *want* to show the world much.

Ralph Fiennes directing Gerard Butler as
Tullus Aufidius in Coriolanus, *2012.*

There's an intensity, for instance, between Coriolanus and his nemesis, the Volscian leader, Tullus Aufidius, who was played in the film by Gerard Butler. The particular quality of that relationship isn't explicit, but it's there to be sensed—for instance when they're grappling, they're locked in the fight and they can't let go of each other. Later, there's also the scene with Aufidius's lines:

> I loved the maid I married: never man
> Sighed truer breath. But that I see thee here,
> Thou noble thing, more dances my rapt heart
> Than when I first my wedded mistress saw
> Bestride my threshold.
>
> (4.5.111–115)

That speech is the key acknowledgement of his romantic, erotic enthusiasm for Coriolanus. In the film, I also added a scene in which Coriolanus's head is being shaved after he arrives in the Volscian camp. A woman comes in to shave him, then it's Aufidius who is shaving him, and then it switches to Coriolanus's point of view, and it's all meant to be ambivalent because it could all be in Coriolanus's mind or not. I wanted to get across a sense of the intimacy of the act, of a man shaving another man's head in the shower. It's open to interpretation. Either it's ritual, or it's something else, or it's in the imagination, but in any case it feeds into the sense that there is this intimacy, or this potential for intimacy. The end of the film is the closest there is to a homoerotic expression, and I wanted to show it through the murder, the closeness of the death and the way Aufidius holds Coriolanus, the way the knife, which is the opening image of the film, finally penetrates Coriolanus.

The potential of this relationship is eventually destroyed by the other main relationship in the play, which is that between Coriolanus and his mother, Volumnia, played by Vanessa Redgrave. Vanessa is unquestionably one of the great actresses of our time. What excites me about Vanessa on film is her human-

Ralph Fiennes as Coriolanus, Gerard Butler as
Tullus Aufidius, and Vanessa Redgrave as Volumnia
in Fiennes's 2012 film.

ity. Nothing about her shouts her beliefs to the rooftops. It's always just a simple statement. She espouses humanitarian principles and beliefs very passionately, but expresses them with a sort of unnerving simplicity, and I found the idea thrilling that you'd get that simplicity in her Volumnia. It would not have been Vanessa's choice to play her as a commanding matriarch. One of the things I kept feeling was that if it's simple, it's more accessible, and especially with characters that are so high-definition in their extremeness: the warrior, the mother, the warrior's enemy. Volumnia's lines land all the more explosively, because you're lulled by a line like:

> Had I a dozen sons . . . I had rather eleven die nobly
> for their country than one voluptuously surfeit out of
> action.
>
> (1.3.15–17)

It's said so tenderly. I found it brilliant and scary and also slightly seductive to hear Vanessa, with her fantastic luminosity, saying those lines.

When I began working on the film, I didn't want Coriolanus to be so hard, aloof, and arrogant that there's no way in. But when I was editing the film, I found that you can't make him someone easy to empathize with. It actually weakens him as a character. He is what he is, so if you go soft it jars. Coriolanus is uncompromising, and I suppose I didn't want to compromise in the way I put the film together. That's the truth of who he is and I like him for that very reason. In the beginning I tried to come up with answers to the question, "How are we going to like someone like Coriolanus?" but finally I decided: This is who he is. This is what we're making. We're making *Coriolanus*.

I love those kinds of characters that are quite extreme. There's a great book by Lucy Hughes-Hallet called *Heroes*, and it goes from Achilles to Frances Drake to Garibaldi, who are all monstrously extreme men. They're heroic, but they exhibit huge narcissism, vanity, and courage. They're all so Coriolanian— and in that way, they are heroes. Generally I think those high-definition characters, men or women, are innately dramatic.

Shakespeare is always questioning order, especially the right to rule. There's the famous speech, Ulysses's speech in *Troilus and Cressida* (1.3.76–138), about the order of things and, if that order is disturbed—"Take but degree away, untune that string" (1.3.110)—then what chaos follows. My sense is that Shakespeare seems to be saying that there is a harmony where everyone has his place and that that hierarchy has a balance to it. If there's an imbalance to do with who's on the top and who's on the bottom, then it's up for grabs. So, for example, Richard II can't continue, even though there's a hierarchy. We need to have a king or ruler, but if he loses his humanitarian wisdom, then he must go. Richard II rules unwisely, with a sort of capricious arrogance and willfulness. He takes land when it's not his, and he takes peoples' possessions—and then he discovers himself in the necessary removal of him by Bolingbroke, who in turn starts to be compromised by the murder of Richard. Throughout the history plays you see the search for the good king. Henry V is the warrior king, but I think Shakespeare is completely aware of the tenuousness of Henry's claim on France, and he plays it up in the Archbishop's long legal speech of justification (1.2.35–97). And we see Henry questioning. We see his vulnerability on the battlefield: "What is it that makes me king? What is it?" So I think Shakespeare is always saying, "Well, here's this king, and look at how great and how brave he is, but actually he's going to war in a slightly dodgy situation—but here he is questioning." Again, there's this pattern of Shakespeare showing us different facets, which we then have to think about. I don't think he ever gives us a clear answer. He doesn't say, "This is how it should be." He's too smart for that.

Even more so than the British history plays, *Coriolanus* is about politics, but it doesn't tell you where to vote. It's also about war, but it doesn't tell you that war is pretty horrific. I'm not a soldier, but I've read and heard that for some people who go to war, it's addictive. To us, it's probably horrendous. We've seen pictures of what bombs, explosives, do to bodies, and to the bodies of soldiers and civilians and children, and yet there are people out there designing explosives that can be computerized to be so accurate they can take out whoever you want with the press of the button—and we're all supposed to be safe for it. And so, it never stops. The war in this film is all the wars that we can't stop having. Human beings can't stop fighting.

I think *Coriolanus* reveals to us how completely dysfunctional we are. It showed me that no one is right. Human beings kill each other and mess up. They manipulate each other, and even mothers manipulate their sons to get their own way. Then, when the son makes peace, he's knifed. I don't think *Coriolanus* has any resolution. I think it leaves audiences with a mass of questions. You diminish the play to give it any kind of fascist or socialist agenda. I think it's properly a tragedy, in which you witness the demise of the tragic protagonist, with all his flaws and his extreme nature, and the ambivalence of his heroism, and his pride, and you're asked to reflect on it. I wouldn't know how to say "Vote for Coriolanus" or "Kill Coriolanus." I think these are all human beings wrestling with their pride, their narcissism, their conditioning. Of course the people need to eat, but we don't like crowds on the streets when they run amuck. Some people want to bring out the water cannon or the rubber bullets, and then on the other side there's the liberal debate about whether or not to care for these poor people who are lost souls. If I understand Coriolanus, he's a man prepared to die, he goes to battle, he sees his men die around him, and of course he doesn't have any time for the guys walking on the streets who want to smash down the factory gates. I love the switch-back reaction. I think audiences don't know where to put their sympathies. They simply *don't know*. And I love their not knowing. I love how uncertain it should make you feel. Be uncertain. Have a lot of questions. There are no easy answers.

Richard Scholar

TRIAL BY THEATRE, OR
FREE-THINKING IN
JULIUS CAESAR

RICHARD SCHOLAR is Fellow and Tutor in French at Oriel College, University of Oxford, and a Director of the Oxford Amnesty Lectures. His many publications include the books *The* Je-Ne-Sais-Quoi *in Early Modern Europe: Encounters with a Certain Something* and *Montaigne and the Art of Free-Thinking*; he is the coeditor of *Thinking with Shakespeare: Comparative and Interdisciplinary Essays*. He was awarded a Philip Leverhulme Prize in 2007 for his "profoundly original" work on early modern European literature and thought and was made Chevalier dans l'Ordre des Palmes Académiques by the French government in 2008.

Can the bloody overthrow of a political leader be justified? If it can, then on what grounds and under what circumstances? And what fallout should we expect? The tide of events in the Arab world continues—as I write—to bring these questions to the fore. Qaddafi is dead. The internal uprising against the Syrian president, Bashar al-Assad, has entered its tenth month and is being met with brutal force: over five thousand Syrians are estimated to have been killed so far (though not the president

I would like to thank Ted Braun, Susannah Carson, Guillaume Pigeard de Gurbert, and Michael Scholar for reading this essay in draft and offering such helpful comments and suggestions.

himself). The Arab Spring has sprung. The questions with which
I started are, therefore, among the most pressing we all face today.

It was ever thus. Political killings are as old as politics itself.
The first audiences of Shakespeare's *Julius Caesar*, first performed in London's new Globe Theatre in the autumn of 1599,
needed only to look across the Channel to see France piecing
itself back together after a civil war marked, ten years previously, by the assassination of the country's king. Ancient history offered examples aplenty. The grammar school boys, of
whom Shakespeare had been one, had been taught to consider
the death of Julius Caesar in first-century-BCE Rome, under
the knives of Brutus, Cassius, and their associates, as the paradigm case of political assassination in the ancient world. Grammar schools in Elizabethan England expected their pupils, as
part of their core training in rhetoric (the art of persuasion), to
master the art of arguing "on either side" of a given question—
such as whether Brutus was right or wrong to kill Caesar in the
dying days of the Roman republic. I imagine a schoolteacher
setting that very question to young Will and his classmates in
Stratford-upon-Avon, one quiet day in the 1570s, unaware of the
indirect contribution he was making to world literature. *Julius
Caesar* is, after all, Shakespeare's answer to that very question.

But what kind of answer is it? Not the kind to satisfy those
who look to Shakespeare to teach us how to live. This is a playwright who offers anything but direct answers to our questions.
He has, instead, the unnerving capacity to transform those
questions by revealing and unsettling the hidden preferences
we bring to them. The Shakespearean stage is no lecture hall
in which the playwright transmits his opinions through the
voices of the actors; it is, rather, a controlled environment in
which he experiments with the stuff of human lives, and these
are experiments in which we audience members, as much as

his characters, have a part to play. We need to keep thinking with Shakespeare today because, as I have argued elsewhere, he continues to put, along with those of his characters, the most intimate sympathies and antipathies of his audiences and readers on trial.*

Allow me to insist for a moment on the trial as a way of understanding how Shakespeare makes theatre happen. His characters find themselves, time and again, caught up in some kind of trial or experiment. Consider the trials that take place in plays like *The Merchant of Venice* and *The Winter's Tale*, the false trials of *Macbeth* and *King Lear*,** the bed-trick in *All's Well That Ends Well*, and the Duke's experiment in *Measure for Measure*, to name but a few examples. Faced with the rigour of the law, the trickery of a deception, or another of life's great tests, the characters tend to halt the action of the play to reflect on what is happening to them in language that is suddenly, acutely, theatrical. It is as though they were trying to understand the experience they are living through by considering how it would look to them when seen, from a critical distance they cannot otherwise imagine, on a stage. The effect on the audience of these moments of theatrical language, meanwhile, is to draw our attention to the dramatic illusion that has held us in its grasp as we have laughed at, and wept for, the characters undergoing these trials. How are we to understand such sudden shifts

---

* See my essay "French Connections: The *Je-Ne-Sais-Quoi* in Montaigne and Shakespeare," in *How to Do Things with Shakespeare: New Approaches, New Essays*, ed. Laurie Maguire (Malden, MA, and Oxford: Blackwell, 2008), pp. 13–33.
** On false trials see Subha Mukherji, "False Trials and the Impulse to Try in Shakespeare and His Contemporaries," in *Thinking with Shakespeare: Comparative and Interdisciplinary Essays*, ed. William Poole and Richard Scholar (London: Legenda, 2007), pp. 53–74.

of attention? I see them as the playwright's way of signalling
that he has been performing another experiment, this time on
us, and of inviting us to consider what that experiment has
revealed to us of our own convictions and prejudices.

Julius Caesar is a powerful example of the Shakespearean
theatrical experiment. The play has lent itself to interpretations for and against assassination—on either side of the question—in the course of its stage history.* Productions in the new
United States of America, proud of its hard-won republican
independence from Britain, made Caesar a dictator and Brutus
a patriotic hero; productions in Victorian Britain, by contrast,
portrayed Caesar as a heroic leader cut off in his imperial prime
by Brutus and his fellow traitors. These productions all saw in
Roman history, as political theorists had long done, a test case
for the relative merits of republican and monarchic forms of
government; and they found in *Julius Caesar* an answer to the
question, not only of whether Brutus was right or wrong to kill
Caesar, but of which is the best state of a commonwealth.** It
is just that they found opposing answers. In twentieth-century
stagings, quick to draw modern parallels, Caesar appeared
in several guises: as Hitler, Mussolini, Castro, and Margaret
Thatcher, among others. Our contemporary political world is
not short of dictators, actual and aspiring. I see, as I put the fin-
ishing touches to this essay, that the RSC is about to contribute
to the 2012 World Shakespeare Festival a *Julius Caesar* set in an
unidentified African state sometime in the last fifty years. How

---

* I am indebted here to Robert S. Miola, *Shakespeare's Reading* (Oxford:
Oxford University Press, 2000), pp. 108–109.

** See Eric Nelson, "Shakespeare and the Best State of a Commonwealth," in
Shakespeare and Early Modern Political Thought, ed. David Armitage, Conal
Condren, and Andrew Fitzmaurice (Cambridge: Cambridge University
Press, 2009), pp. 253–270.

long will it be before we have an Arab Spring *Julius Caesar*? It
may have already happened.

The play accommodates such choices of interpretation. It
even anticipates them. Standing over the fresh corpse of Caesar,
in one of those self-referentially theatrical moments of which
I have already spoken, one of the chief conspirators exclaims:

> How many ages hence
> Shall this our lofty scene be acted over,
> In states unborn, and accents yet unknown?
>
> (3.1.111–113)*

This is surely encouragement to directors in countries all over
the world, where the play speaks with a sudden renewed urgency
of meaning, to stage it anew. Such encouragement does not
amount to a carte blanche, however, for, even as it anticipates and
accommodates future choices of interpretation, the play refuses
to be fixed by them in its politics. It reveals the choices to be just
that, and prepares silently to outwit them, remaining available
for contrary interpretations and alternative judgements.

What Shakespeare's great theatrical experiment in *Julius
Caesar* thus illustrates and exemplifies is neither this nor that
political position on the questions it explores—whether or
not Brutus was right to kill Caesar or what the best state of
a commonwealth should be—but, on the contrary, the perennial value to political and moral thinking of conflicting interpretations and alternative judgements made in the search for
that elusive thing called the truth. This is the process that I will
call, in the rest of this essay, "free-thinking." Free-thinking is a

---

* I refer here and throughout to the edition of T. S. Dorsch, Arden
Shakespeare, Second Series (London and New York: Routledge, 1955).

precious process because it offers us a potent antidote to the truth-economizing sound bites of our politicians as well as to the insidious pull of our own interests. But it is a fragile process, too, constantly threatened by the sheer power of those sound bites and interests. *Julius Caesar* has illustrated the process of free-thinking by attracting such differing interpretations in the course of its passage through history and evading each in turn. But any performance of the play worth the name offers, as we shall see, the same illustration. The surprise here is that it does so, not by dramatizing free-thinking at its ideal best, but by putting that very ideal on trial.

WHAT'S IN A NAME?

To appreciate the complexity of the situation Shakespeare chose to bring to life, you have only to read the names of the characters he put at the centre of his drama: the overreaching Julius Caesar; his huddling assassins, led by his erstwhile favourite, the noble Marcus Brutus, and by the envious Caius Cassius; and his thrusting supporters, chiefly his son Octavius Caesar and Mark Antony, who in avenging his death push the Roman republic over the edge and seize power for themselves. The list of dramatis personae is no catalogue of goodies and baddies. It is in itself a lesson in political and moral ambiguity.

But the contemporary fashion, at least in the Western world, is to view all the play's protagonists as we do politicians in general, as mad, bad, and on the make. It is hard for us, in our lofty postmodern indifference, to take any of them seriously. Perhaps that is why, in recent years, the play has appeared to wane in popularity in comparison with other parts of the canon: it so obviously takes its politician-protagonists seriously as complex beings caught up in a dire and ambiguous situation.

I now realize that my own reading of the play once drifted

along on the contemporary tide. I can see, too, how I let this happen: I put *Julius Caesar* to one side and stopped thinking about the play after reading it, as I first did, with all the knowing political indifference of a younger scholar.

Or of a younger Scholar, I should perhaps say, for I concede that my name—while being hard to live up to—nonetheless seems to have fitted me out for the life I lead in libraries and other places of learning. Various reviewers of my work have thought to point this out, just in case I hadn't noticed, and librarians occasionally chuckle on being presented with my reader's card. Family history has doubtless shaped my role in life as much as my name: the Scholar family contains other scholars and teachers (including my mother and younger brother) besides me.

But my father escaped both his name and the family history for a career in public service, working as a permanent civil servant under British governments of different political persuasions, and my older brother is now in the same line of work. Our father had a vision of rationality in government, of knowledge and analysis, and he felt that, to be a civil servant, to be required to offer independent advice, information, and help to those elected by the British people to govern them—without being any politician's stooge—was a high calling. He still does, and he admired personally some of the politicians for whom he worked at close quarters, including Margaret Thatcher (one of our erstwhile Caesars). But I know he has come to feel that there are increasingly intense forces at work—the chief of these being the unholy alliance between politicians desperate to get their "message" across to the people and those in the media and elsewhere hungry for influence—whose outcome is to demote rationality and to promote corruption within government.

Growing up in this family of two halves has left me both

fascinated by and suspicious of the world of politics. I find myself invariably bringing to political discussions a powerful sense (debilitating to my attempts at activism) of the inexorable wheel of public opinion, an abiding mistrust (currently fashionable in Britain) of journalists, and a residual conviction (currently unfashionable with my more radically minded friends and colleagues) that politicians are not merely surface effects of the clash of impersonal forces but are also possessed of individual histories and characteristics. To see politicians as I do makes them, of course, not less but more disappointing when they fall short of expectations. And how often they do! Politicians currently seem to me to exemplify the law that my mother's brother David (a scholar though not a Scholar) first formulated in respect of university administrators, and which says that however inadequate the last person in a particular post was, you can be sure that their successor will be even more so. I cling to the hope that this law, when applied to the political sphere, will one day be proven wrong. For now, though, I rarely escape its conclusions, and my righteous indignation then lasts only so long before it gives way to that knowing indifference I mentioned earlier, the dominant political temper of our age.

My impression of *Julius Caesar* had insensibly absorbed the temper of the age. Rereading the play reminded me of its very different temper. Seeing it again helped, too, particularly in Joseph L. Mankiewicz's classic—and still widely available—1953 film version. Mankiewicz's screenplay shows *Julius Caesar* to be a compact political thriller in three movements. The first portrays the huddled formation of the conspiracy and culminates in the assassination of Caesar in the Capitol. The second movement switches to the Forum to observe the public reception of the assassination, and pits Brutus against Antony, whose masterful and politically ruthless oration over Caesar's corpse turns the people decisively against the conspiracy. The third movement portrays the disintegration of the conspiracy, ending in the suicide on the battlefield at Philippi of Brutus, to whom the victors and rising stars of the Roman empire, Antony and Octavius, pay generous closing tributes.

Such is the compactness of *Julius Caesar* that each of its three movements contains, in concentrated form, an entire play. The first, which has Caesar at its centre, is a revenge tragedy, cast in the mould that Shakespeare had adopted in *Titus Andronicus* and was to adapt, brilliantly, in the play he wrote after *Julius Caesar*, namely *Hamlet*, by having his hero so unaccountably and perversely delay his revenge. The second is a history, akin to the first of the *Henry IV* plays, in which a future ruler, Antony, comes dramatically of age by rising to power (though the similarity conceals an important difference, for Antony's brand of Machiavellianism is altogether darker than Prince Hal's in *Henry IV*). The third is a classical tragedy, having as its focus Brutus, whose downfall and death provoke pity and fear alike. These three virtual plays run together in *Julius Caesar*.

Of the three, however, it is the story of Brutus that gives the play its beginning, middle, and end. In an important sense, then, *Julius Caesar* is misnamed: it should be called *The Tragedy of Marcus Brutus*. It is through Brutus that we observe the play's most intense engagement with the stuff of politics and morality and yet, at the same time, its political and moral ambiguity. Brutus is at once vestigially noble and incipiently decadent. In this respect, he embodies the spirit of Rome, or at least the Rome of his day as, with considerable historical specificity, Shakespeare portrays it.

But which Rome was that?

ROMAN MATTERS AND MANNERS

Rome was at a turning point. It was drifting from its republican past towards an imperial future under the authoritarian rule of the Caesars, and under the pressure of the moment, cracks were starting to appear in the political ideology and intellectual ideals of the Roman elite.

That elite looked back several centuries to the great democracies of ancient Greece for its political and intellectual origins. Athens in the time of Plato (427–347 BCE) and Aristotle (384–322 BCE) was the model.* While children, foreign workers, slaves, and women were all excluded from citizenship, all resident adult male Athenians were citizens of the polis, so the simplest baker and the smartest banker each had one vote. Their political freedom had its intellectual counterpart: philosophy in Athens flourished as its practitioners used their freedom to think against the grain. That spirit of free-thinking is encapsulated in a proverbial phrase attributed to Aristotle, "Plato is my friend but a greater friend is truth," which runs through a book I wrote recently about one particular chapter in the history of free-thinking.** Aristotle was a pupil of Plato, of course, so, in uttering that pithy phrase, he was claiming, above all, the freedom to disagree with his philosophy teacher. But, in making such a claim, he was appealing to an underlying principle of the Athenian polity.

The principle of freedom became a cornerstone of the Roman republic. Rome was not the democracy that Athens had been, but citizens had voting rights, and the philosophically

* See Robin Lane Fox, *The Classical World: An Epic History of Greece and Rome* (London: Penguin Books, 2006), for a comprehensive and accessible account of ancient Greek democracy and its Roman counterpart.
** Richard Scholar, *Montaigne and the Art of Free-Thinking* (Oxford: Peter Lang, 2010).

minded were free to ally themselves with a particular school of thought or to pick and mix ideas in an eclectic philosophy of their own making. Roman philosophy of the first century BCE bristles with "-isms" from the Greek world, most notably Stoicism, Epicureanism, and Scepticism, and each turns out, on closer scrutiny, to contain a spectrum of competing tendencies. You can see why scholars of this period have their work cut out!

The first of the "-isms" just mentioned, Stoicism, is the philosophy most visibly present in *Julius Caesar*. It came down to Shakespeare from this period in two differing versions, thanks to its most influential mediators, Cicero (106–43 BCE) and Seneca (ca. 4 BCE–65 CE). Cicero and Seneca both portray it as an ideal moral attitude of reasoned conduct in the service of the truth and of cultivated indifference towards life's turmoils.

That is the essence of Roman Stoicism as it pervades *Julius Caesar*. Nonetheless, there are significant differences of emphasis and attitude between Cicero and Seneca in their presentations of Stoicism, and these differences matter because they reveal Roman ways of thinking as Shakespeare dramatizes them in his play.* Cicero presents Stoicism as a framework for the civic virtues of consistency, honour, and public service: the Ciceronian Stoic faultlessly performs on the Roman stage the role in life that has been given to him. Seneca, writing after Cicero, emphasizes the more heroic virtues of constancy, steadfastness, and invulnerability: the Senecan Stoic, when faced with the worst, remains ever true to his own likeness. The two men also differ in the attitudes they strike towards Stoicism. Cicero writes from outside the tradition: he adopts the eclectic and quizzical perspective of the Academic Scepticism of his

---

* On this see Geoffrey Miles, *Shakespeare and the Constant Romans* (Oxford: Clarendon Press, 1996), ch. 7.

day, giving his provisional assent to ideas that seem plausible to him, while remaining certain only that the truth of no doctrine is certain. Seneca shows a greater allegiance to Stoic doctrine while stressing that the latitude for personal judgement Cicero sought outside Stoicism thrived *within* the school.

Note how keen both men are, in their differing attitudes towards Stoicism, to present themselves as free-thinkers. Cicero insists that, unlike their rival Stoics or Epicureans who cling limpet-like to the doctrines of their schools, Academic Sceptics such as he are "freer and more independent because their power to judge remains intact."* Seneca says in similar fashion that he will not look to the chief Stoic philosophers for authoritative pronouncements because, unlike the Epicureans, who submit themselves to the authority of the leader of their school, "we Stoics are the subjects of no king: each lays claim to his own."** Cicero and Seneca agree that, whatever else it may be, Roman thinking is and must always be free-thinking.

Shakespeare knew all this. He knew his Plutarch, studied Cicero at school, and may well have encountered Seneca directly or through attempts by writers on the Continent to revive his brand of Stoic constancy as a moral antidote to the ills of their own age. He also read his French near-contemporary Michel de Montaigne (1533–1592). An ardent admirer of Plutarch, Montaigne was fascinated by Rome's history and its philosophical traditions, not least the antiauthoritarian sensibility that he found in the selfsame traditions. He incorporates into his writing (among many others) the sentences of Cicero and Seneca I

---

* Cicero, *Academic Philosophy*, 2.8. Translation is mine. On this see A. A. Long, "Cicero's Plato and Aristotle," in *Cicero the Philosopher: Twelve Papers*, ed. J. G. F. Powell (Oxford: Clarendon Press, 1995), pp. 37–62 (especially 40–42).

** Seneca, *Epistles*, 33. Translation is mine.

have just quoted. In so doing, he not only inherits free-thinking from the ancients: he transforms it into the experimental and self-critical art of the *Essais*.

Shakespeare undertakes in *Julius Caesar* a similar experiment with the matter and manner of Rome. He does so, as Montaigne does in his own way, by establishing stereotypes and then unsettling them. Stoicism is a case in point. Shakespeare establishes this stereotype principally by making his Brutus a self-conscious Stoic. When James Mason first appears as Brutus in the Mankiewicz film version, he is seen wandering around the streets of Rome, Hamlet-like, with a book in his hand. I imagine this to be a Stoic manual. In Act 4, Scene 3 of the play, we watch Brutus react to his wife Portia's suicide with cultivated Stoic acceptance, and later Brutus goes on to die in the same unflinching manner: "Hold then my sword, and turn away thy face," he instructs one of his officers, "While I do run upon it" (5.5.52–53). And run upon it he does. By this late stage in the play, the Stoic manner is well and truly familiar to us, since we have already seen (in reverse order) Cassius's friend Titinius, Cassius himself, and Julius Caesar face death—that "necessary end," Caesar says, which "Will come when it will come" (2.2.36–37)—with the same equanimity. The moral attitudes of Stoicism are not exhibited in Brutus alone: they pervade the atmosphere of *Julius Caesar*.

How, then, does Shakespeare unsettle the stereotype of Stoicism he has so carefully constructed? By bringing it into collision with other, related, Roman stereotypes—starting with the very idea of Romanness.

ROMANNESS

Portia's horrible suicide prompts a repression of emotion in Brutus that is mortifying to behold, and we are shown this happening not once but *twice*, as if Shakespeare wanted to impress the discomfort of the episode upon us.* Brutus's repression of emotion on the death of his wife is, we surmise, not just an individual characteristic of Brutus but a deep-lying flaw within the Stoic performance of endurance. There is something to this flaw, however, that is also quintessentially Roman. Brutus first tells Cassius the news only at the end of their bitter row, and despite initially betraying his private grief, he is keen to show Cassius that he remains in control of his emotions: "No man bears sorrow better. Portia is dead" (4.3.146). Cassius is visibly upset until Brutus changes the subject: "No more, I pray you" (4.3.165). Then a messenger, Messala, enters and intimates that he brings Brutus bad news. Brutus challenges him to say what he has to say as befits a Roman. Messala replies in kind: "Then like a Roman bear the truth I tell" (4.3.187). With Cassius looking on, Brutus receives Messala's news *as if for the first time*, and in the high Roman style: "I have the patience to endure it now" (4.3.191). Messala and Cassius severally murmur their admiration. No wonder that the scholars insist on talking about *Roman* Stoicism: repression of emotion in the name of "strength" is intrinsic to being Roman as much as Stoic. It is a form of conduct that Rome's citizens (all men) agree upon as an ideal and support one another's attempts to emulate.

The women are not to be outdone. Portia herself—the daughter of one Roman Stoic and the wife of another—claims to possess the strength of the Roman male, asking Brutus, who is trying to protect her from his dilemma: "Think you I am no stronger than my sex, / Being so father'd, and so husbanded?" (2.1.296–297). The posturing is here more obvious, since it

---

* On this famous textual puzzle see Miles, *Shakespeare and the Constant Romans*, pp. 144–145.

requires Portia to deny her "sex," but it is equally to be observed in the performances of the men in *Julius Caesar*.

The play thereby exposes a contradiction deep within Roman Stoicism: this is a philosophy of introspection that nonetheless, even when it is confronting the inner world of private passions, sees itself as a performance on the public stage. There is to this brand of Stoicism a disquieting staginess: nothing is true, for Brutus and the rest, but what all Rome may perceive to be true.

FREE-THINKING

This fatally reduced view of truth suggests, in turn, how gaspingly little oxygen there is left in Rome for free-thinking. Shakespeare here once again establishes a stereotype only to unsettle it. The stereotype of the Roman free-thinker is embodied in one of his characters—none other than Cicero himself—who is, in *Julius Caesar*, a contrarian and unbiddable philosopher-statesman of the republic. Cicero looks with dissenting "fiery eyes" upon Rome's drift towards authoritarian rule (1.2.184–185). In a rare appearance on stage, he dissents from Casca's conspiratorial interpretation of the night storm shaking Rome as a portentous event, postulating that "men may construe things, after their fashion, / Clean from the purpose of the things themselves" (1.2.34–35). He remains aloof from the conspiracy but looms large in the minds of the conspirators. When one suggests inviting Cicero to join them, on the grounds that "his silver hairs / Will purchase us a good opinion" (2.1.144–145), an exasperated Brutus immediately rejects the idea as impracticable:

> O, name him not . . .
> For he will never follow any thing
> That other men begin.
>
> (2.1.150–152)

These lines will take on an explanatory force when we later learn that Antony, Octavius, and Lepidus have quietly liquidated Cicero along with other senators whose faces do not fit the new order (4.3.172–179). We infer then that the triumvirate shared Brutus's assessment of Cicero as the epitome of the Roman free-thinker, republican in his politics and independent of mind, and cut him down.

If there can be heard in Brutus's assessment of Cicero a note of admiration, as well as exasperation, this is because, while Brutus is less of a loner than Cicero, he sees himself as no less independent and honourable of mind. Brutus is, in fact, as much a self-conscious free-thinker as he is a Stoic. He considers Caesar a friend, as Aristotle did Plato, but truth—the truth about Rome—a greater friend. Brutus later uses these very terms to explain to the crowd why he resolved to assassinate Caesar:

> If there be any in this assembly, any dear friend of Caesar's, to him I say that Brutus's love to Caesar was no less than his. If then that friend demand why Brutus rose against Caesar, this is my answer: Not that I loved Caesar less, but that I loved Rome more.
>
> (3.2.18–23)

Brutus, too, connects intellectual sensibility with political principle: freedom from authoritarian rule is something to be fought for in the mind and the republic alike. "I was born free as Caesar," Cassius tells Brutus early in the play; "so were you" (1.2.96). This, for the insomniac Brutus, is the truth about Rome that slumbered while Caesar was stirring. The part Brutus must now play on the public stage is that of the watchful free-thinker who prevents the citizens of the Roman republic from sleepwalking into servitude. His illustrious ancestor Lucius Brutus, in driving the Tarquins out of Rome, helped to create the republic. It now falls to him to live up to his name and save it.

But Brutus does not act alone. *Julius Caesar* is the story of a free-thinker who walks into a faction. The result is disastrous for both the free-thinker and the faction. Brutus imposes his cherished independence of mind on every question the conspirators discuss, causing them to alter their course of action, and more than once this has dire consequences—not least when the faction decides, at his behest, to spare Antony from the bloodshed. The faction would have better prosecuted its interests unhampered by his scruples.

Brutus, meanwhile, would have better lived up to the ideal of free-thinking if, before joining the conspirators, he had turned his critical intelligence upon itself and thought against the grain of his own conditioning. The play, from the outset, pitilessly exposes all the forces limiting and vitiating Brutus's freedom of thought. We note that, while Brutus wants throughout to make up his own mind freely and to be seen to have done so, Cassius confides in the audience early on that Brutus's "mettle" may be "wrought" from its honourable disposition (1.2.306). We watch as the breach between the old Roman ideal of free-thinking and the reality of political manipulation opens ever wider.

The most revealing episode in this sequence sees Brutus alone in his orchard, thinking aloud about the assassination to come, and fixing on it as the best means of preventing Rome's probable slide into tyranny under Caesar:

> So Caesar may;
> Then lest he may, prevent. And since the quarrel

Will bear no colour for the thing he is,
Fashion it thus: that what he is, augmented,
Would run to these and these extremities;
And therefore think him as a serpent's egg,
Which, hatch'd, would, as his kind, grow mischievous,
And kill him in the shell.

(2.1.27–34)

How much room for ambiguity—and disagreement—there is in that phrase "Fashion it thus"! Does it encapsulate Brutus's fundamentally honourable admission in this speech that the situation permits of no more than probable conjecture? Or does it reveal the extent of his self-deception?*

I would suggest, for my part, that Brutus is trying—nobly—but failing to play the role of the free-thinker that he believes to be rightfully his. In the anguishingly difficult situation at hand, that role requires Brutus to acknowledge the impossibility of arriving at anything other than probable truth, but also—since the truth, while hard to fathom, remains nonetheless a greater friend than Caesar—to demonstrate his commitment to serving that truth by fabricating the most plausible account of the situation that he can muster. Which is that "Caesar may; / Then lest he may, prevent."

So far, so good and free of mind, but what Brutus ignores—

---

* I have in mind the exchange of views that took place between Will Poole and his former English tutor at Oxford and mine, Tony Nuttall, in the following publications: William Poole, "'Unpointed Words': Shakespearean Syntax in Action," *Cambridge Quarterly* 32 (2003), pp. 27–48; A. D. Nuttall, *Shakespeare the Thinker* (New Haven and London: Yale University Press, 2007), pp. 171–191. Poole's article took issue with the reading of Brutus's soliloquy given by Nuttall in his earlier study, *A New Mimesis: Shakespeare and the Representation of Reality* (London: Methuen, 1983), ch. 3.

disastrously—in "fashioning thus" his thinking is precisely how fashioned he is in that thinking. In this respect, the closing part of the soliloquy is crucial, for it reveals the forces at work in the fashioning of Brutus. Brutus's boy brings in the letters that Cassius earlier decided to counterfeit as the work of several citizens addressed to Brutus, "all tending to the great opinion / That Rome holds of his [Brutus's] name," and all hinting obscurely at Caesar's ambition (1.2.312–319). Brutus falls for the ruse, concluding tyrannical ambition in Caesar and recalling the anti-tyrannical glories that Brutus's ancestor conferred upon his name, and announces his resolution:

> O Rome, I make thee promise;
> If the redress will follow, thou receivest
> Thy full petition at the hand of Brutus.
>
> (2.1.56–58)

Brutus, by addressing Rome in this way, betrays his reliance on public opinion to decide for him, in his innermost private conscience, where the truth lies. He thereby embodies the disquieting staginess of Roman Stoicism that Shakespeare observes in this play. The public has engulfed the private. It is in that sense that Brutus represents, to borrow William Poole's phrase, "the logical extreme of Stoicism."* But Stoicism alone cannot account for Brutus's incoherence. Two further forces—Brutus's unquestioning commitment to the city's republican past and his family's role therein, to which he clings for a sense of identity, and the rhetoric of Cassius's letter in its flattering appeal to that same commitment and sense of identity—combine here to limit and vitiate Brutus's capacity to think freely even as, with a

---

* Poole, " 'Unpointed Words,' " p. 47.

certain residual nobility, he clings to a simulacrum of that freedom. The would-be free-thinker, as duped as he is self-duped,
has walked into the trap that the faction laid for him. Caesar is
doomed. So is Brutus.

Once Caesar is dead, Brutus walks again, this time into
the Forum. Does the aftermath of the assassination not offer
the perfect opportunity for all to judge whether Brutus the
would-be free-thinker was right or wrong to kill Caesar? Brutus certainly thinks it will: "I will myself into the pulpit first, /
And show the reason of our Caesar's death" (3.1.236–237). In
the scene that follows, Shakespeare works theatrical magic with
his main source, the *Lives* of Caesar, Brutus, and Antony which
Plutarch wrote in Greek around the end of the first century CE
and Shakespeare read in the 1579 English translation of Thomas
North. Shakespeare takes from Plutarch the main events of his
drama—Brutus's speeches justifying the assassination and Antony's oration at Caesar's funeral—but these events, which days
separate in Plutarch, Shakespeare compresses to form a single
scene in which Brutus and Antony address, in turn, the same
crowd of people.

This scene resembles nothing more closely than a trial,
containing speeches for the defence and prosecution, with the
people acting as judge and jury. Brutus speaks first, from a position of power, since he is at the head of the faction that has just
assassinated Caesar. He urges the crowd to exercise its judgement with the old Roman freedom: "Censure me in your wisdom, and awake your senses, so that you may the better judge"
(3.2.16–18). He explains, as we have already seen, that he slew
Caesar to save Rome from Caesar's ambition. He puts his case
with compelling force. The people, who had first demanded
satisfaction, now acclaim Brutus as Rome's saviour. In a chilling moment, and, as many have observed, the play's single most

politically telling line, a member of the crowd shouts, of Brutus, "Let him be Caesar!" The crowd has responded to the rhetoric of Brutus and not the reasoning: the Forum is no arena for free-thinking. That shout from the crowd suggests that Brutus has misjudged a political mood that is turning away from republican freedom towards voluntary servitude. It seems that the people of Rome really want, and deserve, a Caesar after all.

RHETORIC

Mark Antony then steps forward. Closely associated with the dead "tyrant," as people are now calling Caesar, and permitted to speak only on the whim of the new darling of the crowd, Brutus, Antony starts from a dangerously weak position. He does not take long triumphantly to transform it. The words he utters over Caesar's corpse amount to, in A. D. Nuttall's words, "the greatest oration in the English language."* Look at how quickly he turns the tables on Brutus and his associates. Only some one hundred and thirty lines into this most powerful and ruthless of political speeches, Antony has the entire crowd screaming to his tune, as one: "Revenge!—About!—Seek!—Burn!—Fire!—Kill!—Slay!—Let not a traitor live" (3.2.206–207). Antony's job is done, and when left alone on stage, he reveals, Iago-like, his satisfaction at the turn of events: "Mischief, thou art afoot, / Take thou what course thou wilt!" (3.2.262–263). The wheel of opinion in the Forum has turned once again, and the credulous mob proceeds to dispense rough justice, putting an innocent man to death in the following scene merely because he shares his name with one of the conspirators. The dogs of civil war are afoot.

---

* Nuttall, *Shakespeare the Thinker*, p. 186.

Antony's triumph in the Forum is not exactly that of rhetoric over free-thinking philosophy, not least because free-thinking has a rhetoric of its own and has in any case already veered into incoherence, as we have seen in the central case of Brutus. But Antony's speech is certainly a triumph for rhetoric. In countering Brutus's claim to have detected signs of tyranni-cal ambition in Caesar, Antony offers arguments that immedi-ately appear threadbare, when coldly enumerated. That Caesar did not pocket the ransoms extracted from prisoners of war but put them in the general coffers, sympathized with the plight of the poor, refused three times the kingly crown that Antony publicly offered him, and in his will left seventy-five drachmas to each Roman citizen and his gardens to the state: this is, on the face of it, unpromising material for the defence. And Shake-speare has in fact already dismantled one of these arguments by having Casca report earlier to Brutus and Cassius that, while Caesar did indeed refuse the crown three times, he appeared increasingly loath to do so (1.2.232–247). Casca describes a mot-ley scene in which the streets of Rome suddenly seemed for all the world a stage, and all the men and women merely players: "If the tag-rag people did not clap him [Caesar] and hiss him, according as he pleas'd and displeas'd them, as they use to do the players in the theatre, I am no true man" (1.2.255–258). An-tony transforms the story in his telling of it. "You all did see," he says to the whole crowd with the air of a man clinching an argument,

> that on the Lupercal
> I thrice presented him a kingly crown,
> Which thrice he did refuse. Was this ambition?
>
> (3.2.97–99)

Antony's question immediately obtains the answer it invites. "No!" the tag-rag people roar on stage, and—whenever I see this scene in the theatre—the same wave of conviction runs like an electric current through the watching public. We inwardly urge Antony on in his demolition of Brutus without so much as pausing for thought.

The thought, when it finally comes, is that the credulous mob listening to Antony on the steps of the Forum resembles nothing more closely than the audience in the theatre. We, too, are the tag-rag people. Once again, Shakespeare has chosen to draw our attention to the dramatic illusion that has held us in its grasp, and reminded us that he is conducting a theatrical experiment. This time he has put our own capacity for free-thinking on trial.

Stanley Cavell

SAYING IN
THE MERCHANT OF VENICE

———

STANLEY CAVELL is Professor Emeritus of Philosophy at Harvard University. His many books include *Disowning Knowledge: In Seven Plays of Shakespeare, The Claim of Reason, Pursuits of Happiness, Must We Mean What We Say?*, and *Little Did I Know.* He is a Past President of the American Philosophical Association and the recipient of a MacArthur Fellowship, as well as a Junior Fellowship in Harvard's Society of Fellows, the Morton Dauwen Zabel Award in Criticism from the American Academy and Institute of Arts and Letters, the Centennial Medal from Harvard's Graduate School, and the Romanell–Phi Beta Kappa Professorship.

Can Shakespeare's judgment ever be wrong? I have never satisfied myself about the ending of *The Merchant of Venice*, reading it or attending it. Shylock's defeat has kept seeming to me to be abruptly pat and his thwarting and grief to go insufficiently expressed. I seem to recall, or recall the description of, a performance of Laurence Olivier's in which, after Shylock's expulsion at the end of Act 4, he is heard to utter a long scream. But I am sufficiently convinced by Shylock's taking his departure on saying that he is sick—"I pray you give me leave to go from hence, / I am not well" (4.1.403–404)—that I do not imagine him to have enough available energy to scream. I perceive him, with his penultimate words—"I am content"—as spiritually disabled, without recognizable emotion or comprehension, not even angry or contemptuous. I do not regard this as a particularly contentious observation, but I am concerned to understand what causes this perception and to ask how it might plausibly be played.

How do we get from endlessly expressed murderousness to a virtually immediate acceptance of a quibbling, at best, interpretation of the taking of "a pound of flesh"? Even if a law existed in Venice using words such as "taking" or "spilling" or "wishing to spill Christian blood" (since Portia doesn't tell the unvarnished truth about almost anything else, why believe her implicitly here?), there is room for interpreting them as *not* being descriptions equivalent to killing or seeking to kill. And so, Shylock ought to be able to deny murder as his motive for demanding his "bond."

What then suddenly, as if physically, deprives him of all protest or contest and reduces him, as it were, essentially to an all-suffering Jew, a creature without the right to speak? It was my impression of Shylock's over-swift reduction and acquiescence to silence and ruin and departure as suggesting a fatal sense of the loss of the right, hence of the power, of speech, that set me thinking about this play as taking up the uniquely human fate, explicit since Aristotle, of being the animal possessed of language. We are fated to speak, that is to converse, but we are more controlled by words and their (other) speakers than we are controlling of them. And if we are responsible for speech, then we are responsible for silence—that is, for the refusal to speak, whose consequences equally famously interest Shakespeare (as illustrated by Cordelia and Lady Macbeth).

This was not the first time that the right to speak had come up in my work. I have, for example, recurrently been moved to recognize, as I put the thought, that philosophy does not speak first. (This is, I suppose, my version of Wittgenstein's percep-

tion that philosophy does not advance theses. Or, as I sometimes have urged the point, that philosophy knows only what
everyone knows.) Perhaps once more in my experience, reading a play of Shakespeare's will help arrive at fresh tuitions for
intuitions. My first impulse was simply to check my impression that the word "say" occurs an unusually large number of
times in *The Merchant of Venice*. My Shakespeare Concordance
shows the number to be large, but not uniquely so. Then I considered further that my impression could have been formed
by the occurrence in the play of other terms calling attention
to the fact of speech. A not particularly rigorous search produces, beyond the words "say" and "speak," the following terms:
"talk," "bid," "exclaim," "utter," "presage," "pray," "tell," "swear,"
"promise," "call," "whisper," "cite," "praise," "question," "answer,"
"inquire," "urge," "gossip," "report," "voice," "pronounce," "eloquence." I shall not undertake to compare this array of human
possibilities of articulation with their notation in the rest of the
Shakespearean corpus. I am immediately moved to express my
surprised sense that the play precisely presents the fate of the
human and its capacity for speech as incessantly demanding
attention and calling for pertinent response from one another.

A perfectly decisive emphasis on word and sentence in the
play concerns its climactic, mortal point turning on an interpretation of words, namely of the now too-familiar "pound
of flesh." Or, it is rather more accurate to say that it turns not
on interpreting the words but on literalizing or stressing them
past the possibility of reference and verification. (This result,
uncannily to my mind, resembles the philosopher's denial that
we see a material object on considering that we do not really,
or strictly, or literally see *all* of it.) "Pound" is said by Portia to
mean one pound determined within the difference of a hair or
a grain:

> If thou tak'st more
> Or less than a just pound, be it but so much
> As makes it light or heavy in the substance,
> Or the division of the twentieth part
> Of one poor scruple, nay, if the scale do turn
> But in the estimation of a hair,
> Thou diest and all thy goods are confiscate.
>
> (4.1.332–338)

And this quantity of "flesh," more famously, is taken explicitly to require cutting into a piece of living flesh without shedding blood—as likely as running without standing:

> This bond doth give thee here no jot of blood,
> The words expressly are "a pound of flesh."
> Then take thy bond, take thou thy pound of flesh,
> But in the cutting it, if thou dost shed
> One drop of Christian blood, thy lands and goods
> Are by the laws of Venice confiscate
> Unto the state of Venice.
>
> (4.1.310–316)

Shylock's response is to accept without argument Portia's interpretations as faithful representations of what he calls "the law" and to proceed at once to commence bargaining—increasingly weakly—for the former, more normal, return on his loan: "Pay the bond thrice / And let the Christian go" (4.1.323–324). And then: "Give me my principal, and let me go" (4.1.342).

This instant collapse is what I have had recurrent trouble in understanding. Are we seriously to understand this as Shylock believing Portia's testimony and reasoning? And is this because he is so foreign to, or alienated from, his surrounding culture that nothing a gentile says makes much sense in any case? But where has the daring gone that proposed his surrealistic bond of the notarized pound of flesh? I find I can only assume that he is not convinced by Portia's mock talmudism, but is at a stroke spiritually overborne and thereby rendered helpless or hopeless to expect mere tolerance of his existence, let alone whatever is to be called justice. He has become incapable of so much as questioning the forced, dubious meaningfulness of Portia's equally surrealistic interpretations. But if this is the case, then what, exactly, has rendered him helpless and overborne?

I note first the possibility of envisioning and performing this reading. The concluding, retreating protests on Shylock's part against his destruction can all be imagined as being voiced by him in an increasing state of bewilderment or a dream. Coming to earth in the everyday realm of principal and bond and forfeiture invokes his previous form of life as having become unreal in comparison with the fantasy of disfiguring a voluptuously hated enemy. And then, when he arrives at Portia's demand to acknowledge his stripped state, he uses the words "I am content," which are repeated from Antonio's previous speech—

> So please my lord the duke and all the court
> To quit the fine for one half of his goods,
> I am content . . .

(4.1.387–389)

—as if manifesting that even the possibility of originating words is past his invention. If nothing matters, there is no cause for speech.

But the sense of my claim is that the voiding of Shylock's hold on an entitlement to speech and existence is not gradual—only his manifestations of dissociation from the world are comparatively gradual—but is in calamitous effect with his first response to Portia's interpretation or dictation of the laws of Venice. He responds to her merely by forming the question "Is that the law?" (4.1.318). (Call this the essential Jewish question—but now voiced not as the route to divine acceptance but as the edict of the rejection of other men.) If this sense of sudden inner collapse is accurate, it must be something in Portia's interpretation that has caused it. What she has announced is that "This bond doth give thee here no jot of blood" (4.1.310) and that "if thou dost shed / One drop of Christian blood, thy lands and goods / Are by the laws of Venice confiscate" (4.1.313–315). Am I alone in wondering why apparently it is not given to Shylock to contest this reading? Why does he not insist, for example, that everyone knows that blood must be implied in the bond, and is not to be understood as a separate element meant to make the bond effectively unachievable?

I find my answer to be that this was not known and understood, or rather its imagination was unavailable to Shylock, so that confronted with it, or opened to it, he is, let us say, appalled. How could he not have known and imagined this inevitable consequence of his demand, as if for the first time awakened to the horror of his wish? When Portia cautioned Shylock to have a surgeon in attendance to prevent the possibility of Antonio's bleeding to death, Shylock asks whether the possibility is named in the bond, and discovers that it is not. This may be taken as drawing Shylock's attention to blood, but may also be taken as showing his obliviousness to its existence unless it is officially "nominated." Portia agrees that it is not named "expressly," but adds, " 'Twere good you do so much for charity" (4.1.265). That charity here is implied to be Christian (as moments earlier "the quality of mercy" was so taken, in explicit opposition to how the Jew thinks of justice) is an implication as clear as that blood is implied in cutting living flesh.

I propose, then, that with the knife in hand before Antonio's bosom laid bare, implying blood, Shylock perceives the madness in his fantastic fury. He has no quarrel with *this* man; disfiguring him, or perhaps anyone, is no recompense for the injustices Jews learn to live with and perhaps become disfigured by. I imagine the knife to fall, as Shylock's mind and body fall slack, going through now irrelevant and diminishing memories of motion and interest. He cannot, even if he had thought to say it, claim that blood was irrelevant to his invented bond, because he now sees that Christian blood is what he wanted.

*   *   *

It seems familiar by now to take up the question whether the play *is* anti-Semitic or whether it is *about what it is to be* anti-Semitic. The problem for me in understanding the play's conversation along this line is that it seems to take it too much for granted that we are deft in recognizing expressions of anti-Semitism and in feeling confident in the justice, or perhaps the mercy, in our responding to it, or in resisting response to it, in its conventional or in its novel forms. In writing my autobiography, recently brought to an end and published, I included a range of such uneasy encounters over my eight decades of memory.* (I had begun the record imagining that I did not want to be alive when it came out. This thought pretty thoroughly vanished as I grew more and more interested in, fascinated by,

---

* *Little Did I Know: Excerpts from Memory* (Stanford: Stanford University Press, 2010).

the sheer facts of what survives in a life, and in what forms.) For a certain minimal concrete orientation here, I abbreviate from the autobiography two trivial but lucid expressions of the attitude coming my way from my high school years.

The immediate background is that my father and mother, during the Great Depression, had moved back and forth several times from Atlanta, Georgia, to Sacramento, California. My father had lost his reputedly swanky jewelry store, and the large and, for me, boisterously happy household of my mother's musical family was broken apart. An adventurous brother of my father who had sought his fortune out West had established, of all things given this present exposition, the largest and busiest pawnshop in Sacramento. He offered my father a job, which was gratefully, if humiliatingly, accepted. When I was fifteen years old, roughly two miserable years younger than my classmates because of the "reward" of being what was called "skipped" two grades (a more accurate description would have been "sent into exile"), I still bore the obviously Jewish name Goldstein, given to my father's family—when my father was himself something like fifteen years old—by immigration officers upon their arriving in New York from Bialystok, on the ground that the officers could not spell the family's actual name Kavelierusky (or Kavelierisky—I have seen it both ways). The following year, turned sixteen, I in effect took back the stolen name by legally changing it to an Anglicization of the opening two syllables of the Russian name, whereupon I went down the road ninety miles to the university in Berkeley, as it were, anonymously. To understand why my family acceded to this drastic early self-transformation (because of my age, they were legally required to approve it) requires, at a bare minimum, that I recount a couple of incidents from my youth.

The first of the encounters I have in mind is as follows.

Friends of mine who played in the Sacramento high school dance band, of which I was the first and last student to become the leader (the faculty sponsor of the band had without warning to us been drafted into the army), proposed to nominate me for membership in their high school fraternity. This was, at this point in my life, perfectly irrelevant to me, but trying not to offend my companions I asked them not to go ahead with this, on the ground that while they might not think so, some one or other among the members of their group would in a secret vote cast a blackball against me, and that this would cause embarrassment and unpredictable difficulty for us. They protested that this could not happen, and that I was oversensitive and unjust to their comrades. I relented, and the blackball promptly came, along with embarrassments that proved to be permanent because, sometimes it seemed, we did not have, and did not know how to acquire, the language in which to modify them.

The second contretemps, rather more imaginative, concerns the moment when, as I was walking with a member of the band on a path across the large high school playing field, we approached and were about to pass not far from a student I did not know. My companion called out to him not to fail to get tickets for the senior ball, where the Goldstein band would be playing. The boy's response was to touch together the five fingertips of one hand to form a kind of claw, and with it pull on his nose to lengthen it. My companion's baffled response was to baffle all three of us by introducing me to the fellow.

Of course, I count such incidents to be common as dirt—certainly not lethal, hardly even consequential—yet they occur to me after some sixty-five summers. It is equally common, I believe, to take it that Shylock's extremities of response, and his unforgiving giving of offense, form a caricature of being a Jew. One can hardly fail to see that his behavior is extreme, but I do

not think of the violent passions his behavior encases as themselves caricatures. The clearest evidence I perceive as caricatur-
ing and discounting his passions can be found in the inevitably
quoted speeches (credited as fact, or remembered as dramatic
fact) in which Salerio and Solanio are pleased to elaborate a
report of Shylock hysterically juxtaposing the disappearance of
his daughter and the theft of his ducats, always interpreted, so
far as I know, as suggesting that Shylock vulgarly equates these
losses.

> SOLANIO: I never heard a passion so confused,
> So strange, outrageous, and so variable,
> As the dog Jew did utter in the streets:
> "My daughter! O my ducats! O my daughter!
> Fled with a Christian! O my Christian ducats!
> Justice, the law, my ducats, and my daughter!
> . . .
> She hath the stones upon her, and the ducats."
> SALERIO: Why, all the boys in Venice follow him,
> Crying, his stones, his daughter, and his ducats.
>
> (2.8.12–17; 22–24)

But the caricature here, while no doubt intended by those
amused and engaged reporters, seems to me an imposition. For
Shylock, the relation of his daughter to his ducats is that she
has *stolen* his ducats (as it were her eventual dowry), thereby
marking that he has lost not only his daughter but his trust in
his daughter's feeling for him.

The inability to recognize and acknowledge (which means,
as I have elsewhere argued, to avoid) the unpleasant Shylock's
incoherent grief is something I understand the play to offer as
an image of the perpetual failure to recognize the unfathom-

able reach and spread of lethal radiation in racial distortion and fumbling. Shakespeare's play has struck me as unique in the fullness of this perception. This is how I answer my opening question about Shakespeare's judgment in his calibration of Shylock's swift decline in the scene of his exclusion or expulsion. I take it that we are to perceive Shylock's ending, his continued mere repetition of words he once upon a time could mean and could use to effect in confronting others, as showing him now working to cover the vanishing powers, or the increasing consciousness of the emptiness and the suffocation of his possibility of speech. Put otherwise, his ending shows him becoming drained of the effort to continue assuming, to the extent he has ever assumed, participation in the human.

F. Murray Abraham

SEARCHING FOR SHYLOCK

F. MURRAY ABRAHAM is an American actor who has appeared in both modern and classic plays, including *Othello, Richard III, King Lear, Much Ado About Nothing,* and *Twelfth Night.* His experiences as Bottom are recounted in his book *A Midsummer Night's Dream,* in Faber & Faber's Actors on Shakespeare series. His performance as Shylock in *The Merchant of Venice* earned him an Obie Award. He has also appeared in dozens of films, including *The Name of the Rose, Scarface,* and *Finding Forrester;* for the role of Antonio Salieri in *Amadeus* he was awarded a Golden Globe and an Academy Award. In 2010, he was honored with the Sir John Gielgud Award for Theatre.

The concept of Justice is an inherent sense that can be seen in any playground. Children spend as much time making up the rules for a game as they do playing the game, and are furious when the rules are broken. The American people are still suffering from the manipulation of the financial system by a bunch of crooks who not only got away with it, but are richer than ever. This is only the latest example of a justice system that is anything but blind; the public knows it, and in the 2011 touring production of the Theatre for a New Audience I strove with Shylock to embody their frustration.

The demand for Justice dominated my Shylock; I imagined myself as a Palestinian in an Israeli court, or a Chinese–Italian–Irish–Japanese–Black–Arab–Native American on trial. I wanted my audience to identify with Shylock in a deeply personal way, so much so that they would involuntarily nod and think, "Yes, I understand, I have been there."

For me, the connection with his daughter was always the key to Shylock. Jessica runs off with her Christian suitor, Lorenzo, and takes with her all the money and jewels she can carry; her thefts include a turquoise ring which was given to Shylock by his late wife, Leah, when they were courting. His last connection with his great love Leah was important to him, of course, but the pain he goes through, the epiphany he experiences, is caused by his daughter's disregard for the ring that she must have known was so dear to him. When Tubal tells him that a Genoan "showed me a ring that he had of your daughter for a monkey" (3.1.78), Shylock replies, "I would not have given it for a wilderness of monkeys" (3.1.80–81). The great line leapt out at me the first time I read it, and I believe that this is the moment Shylock becomes another person, a lesser but very dangerous man. His greatness had been in his ability to rise above the crap that he had had to go through as a Jew each day, to remain aloof for the sake of his community, his daughter, and his faith; but the turn to actually consider claiming his pound of flesh—the mere thought of which is anathema, and which had perhaps initially been proposed as mere melodrama on his part—instantly damns him. Shylock, the smartest, most reverent person in the play, is completely aware of his damnation, as well as of the terrible violence it will bring to the Ghetto. Were he to carry out the penalty in his bond, there undoubtedly would be a pogrom and many would suffer, many would die. Yet he is unable to stop himself.

There is a distraction in the play when Shylock gets the news that Jessica has traded the ring away, which is this: How, amid all the stolen jewelry, when Tubal has simply called it "a ring," can he know it is that particular turquoise ring? It's an assumption that denigrates Shylock, and indicates a cynicism that is not characteristic of this superior man. In our modern production, the problem was solved with cell phones. We placed Tubal in Genoa, and had him send a photo of the ring to me; this provided me with the opportunity to be alone in my misery and to make that connection with the audience I so desperately wanted. There is only one moment in the play when Shakespeare gives Shylock a chance to address the house. In Act 1, Antonio comes on stage, and before Shylock speaks to him he says in an aside,

> How like a fawning publican he looks!
> I hate him for he is a Christian,
> But more, for that in low simplicity
> He lends out money gratis and brings down
> The rate of usance here with us in Venice.
> If I can catch him once upon the hip,
> I will feed fat the ancient grudge I bear him.
> He hates our sacred nation, and he rails—
> Even there where merchants most do congregate—
> On me, my bargains and my well-won thrift,
> Which he calls interest. Cursèd be my tribe,
> If I forgive him!
>
> (1.3.28–39)

That aside established a certain complicity, and I stretched it to the moment when Tubal texted the picture of the ring to me. Some actors do not like to engage the audience; I believe it is my long suit. After a shocked pause, I shared the picture of the ring with them, explaining, "It was my turquoise"—show it, show it, look at it, pause, look at them—"I had it of Leah; I would not have given it for a wilderness of monkeys." At this point I would be weeping, and then, clutching myself in pain, I would stumble toward a place to sit; once seated I began keening and dovening until Tubal got my attention once more on the cell phone. This description may sound ordered and cold, but in fact it affected me deeply each time. It was an extension of my explosive interpretation of the "Hath not a Jew eyes" speech, full of years of frustration and abuse culminating in the abduction, elopement, and betrayal of my daughter.

At this point Tubal says, "But Antonio is certainly undone," to which Shylock answers, "Nay, that's true, that's very true" (3.1.82; 83). Those two lines should chill the audience as Shylock changes before their eyes; the expression "a weeping man is a dangerous man" becomes vividly clear. It is his pain that is his salvation, because no matter how far his vengeance carries him, if his anguish has been sincere the audience will continue to sympathize with him, up to the moment when he nearly kills Antonio. They may even wish I would go ahead and do it.

Antonio is one of the most difficult parts in the play, and ours, Tom Nelis, was stellar. I had never liked that character, never had any respect for him, until Tom said he had the impulse to do something when he was tied to the chair during the trial scene, right before Shylock is to cut out his pound of flesh. I told him not to tell me what it was, just to do it; he said it might be a good idea to let me know, but I insisted. That night while I was poised over him with murder in my eyes, he spat in my face. It was electrifying. And at that moment I suddenly had enormous respect for this Antonio, and he became deserving of my respect—my possible equal in the gentile world. I think it must be the first time in history that that has ever happened.

I had a connection with the role of Shylock that served me each time I did it. There's no way to explain the phenomenon of an actor's identifying with a character. This role is about much more than anti-Semitism—do we have to say that prejudice is everywhere? My objective was to make Shylock a human being, someone who continued to live long after the curtain went down. But that's what I try to do with all my work. It's what every artist tries to do, isn't it? Create life.

* * *

Over the years I've become increasingly fascinated by the fact that the magical way in which figures such as Shylock come to life in theaters depends so strongly on elements as concrete as wood and plaster.

The Merchant of Venice has been dated to 1596–1598; it would have opened at the Theatre in Shoreditch. The Theatre was torn down in 1598, and in 1599 its timbers were moved across the Thames to the south bank and repurposed to construct the Globe. *The Merchant* was a favorite play in the repertoire, and although there's a gap in the Globe's archives, there's every reason to believe it was performed there too. These two three-story, open-air, polygonal amphitheaters with thrust stages welcomed different classes of people, from aristocrats to members of the bourgeoisie to those who paid a penny to stand in the round pit before the stage. There is also a record of *The Merchant* being performed twice at court for King James in the years 1604–1605. With a ceiling, smaller dimensions, and an audience consisting of the king and his noblemen, the setting would have encouraged a very distinct performance. Before Shakespeare's very eyes, *The Merchant* would have already been transforming itself in response to the forces of different theaters and different audiences.

A few years ago, I performed Shylock for the Royal Shakespeare Company's "Complete Works." The production opened in New York, and then went to the octagonal Swan Theatre in Stratford-upon-Avon. That is the greatest theater for Shakespeare I have ever performed on, and if you could interview the other actors in our show who played it they would tell you the same. The first time I stepped on that stage, I froze; not only at the history, but at the sudden confrontation with a stage unlike any I had ever played. The balconies are stacked one above the other, and you have to really take the audience members up there into consideration, because those in the back rows of the balconies are on high stools and must lean forward in order to see. It was one of the biggest jolts I ever had when I looked up and saw rows of people straining over the rails so as not to miss a thing. It's only fair that you include them, that you take your time and really look, because you will see a bunch of people who are at this performance for one reason only: to see you do this play. And that lifted our performances beyond our expectations.

I had arrived a week before the company and had been working alone there with complete freedom of the stage all by myself. When the company got there, I watched their responses when they walked in and found that my first impression was not an illusion: they felt the same way. As good and as successful as our show had been in New York, it went to another level, truly, at the Swan. You may choose whatever descriptives you wish—"elevating," "humbling," "thrilling," and so forth—they are not enough.

We also were suddenly burdened with the responsibility of proving our American worth in Shakespeare's backyard. We needn't have worried, however, for the audience stood and cheered on our opening night, and wouldn't stop till we came out for a second company call. We sold out quickly and there was a queue at the cancellation window that went out the door to the street. It was the greatest affirmation not only of our work, but of the influence that a theater can exert.

That first tour of *The Merchant* visited only the two theaters, but the changes the setting made to the play were considerable, and it was then that I became keenly interested in this subtle, almost inarticulable, but very visceral relationship between a theater and a production. I had the chance to explore this relationship further with the Theatre for a New Audience when we took our performance of the play on a tour that comprised two coasts, four cities, eight weeks, and sixty-four performances.

The performances in this remarkable company have always been good, but the pressure of having to adjust to four very different theaters, after a cramped rehearsal space, refined us into a tough, tightly knit, self-assured Shakespearean troupe. We still feel we own this particular production of the play, and I believe that reshaping our performances to fit each house had a great deal to do with this exhilarating feeling.

To begin with, a rehearsal space never relates to a theater apart from tape marks on the floor indicating the deck, entrances, steps, et cetera. None of this matters at first because at that point we are feeling each other out, testing rhythms and sounds, and learning how we fit together with this four-hundred-year-old language. We were basically off book in a little over two weeks and anxious to get into the theater, because it's always a surprise when you first walk out on stage after the security of a little room with your fellow actors as your only audience. Suddenly you're facing a back wall that's quite a bit further back than the five feet you've grown used to. The beautiful words you've shaped into meaningful expressions sound weak, tentative, and not at all like what you had in mind, simply because the chore now is to fill the house—to expand everything you've worked on to fill the needs of that particular space.

Our first theater, the Schimmel Center for the Arts at Pace University in New York City, is a 750-seat "letter box." It's very wide, for it was designed primarily as a lecture hall, with pull-up desks on the seats. There is quite a gulf between the apron and the audience, and we had to overcome this separation while opening up from a 110-degree span to 180 degrees.

Each physical adjustment affects the actor's interpretation accordingly. The Schimmel forced us to open up laterally and to physically broaden ourselves. The performances expanded into wider gestures and larger steps, and of course that affects breathing and voice production. The lines take on a different quality and we need some time to hear ourselves as we speak to find out if it's working; as we listen, we learn from our instinctual selves some secrets about the character that have nothing to do with control. The subtleties that simply can't be seen over there on the sides are instantly rejected by the next performance. The line that was so charmingly snappy seems too quick for a stage this wide, so you take a few extra steps before you start the line, and you find that the pause is very good for the line—or it's very bad for the line, so you rethink the line for the next show.

Our preparation was such that the show started previews at the Schimmel Center on March 1, two days earlier than scheduled—still, though, it was hard. The particular demands of that space forced us to shift our focus from ourselves to the tasks at hand: namely, how do we slightly change the blocking so as to be seen by all the people way the hell over there on the sides, yet stay in the light and act our pants off at the same time? How do I play a favorite intimate speech to the front row when it's twenty feet away? And how do we stay focused in spite of all this while the *New York Times* is deciding our fate?

How is what a company discovers, and it either happens or it doesn't.

The first house was full of that kind of discovery, and we were learning a great deal in a very short time—with one of the hippest audiences in the world. The New York Jewish audience came to see why anyone would do this anti-Semitic play, and when they left they were glad they came because this Shylock was a man of great dignity, a man who was terribly wronged, a man who stood up to the system and demanded his hour in court. The play had its most critical audience in New York, where there are more Jews than in Tel Aviv; the laughs and the groans were aimed at the stuff that we knew was sensitive, but we were not prepared for the vocal response, which indicated to us that they were pulling for us, agreeing with us, letting us know that we were on the right track—and sometimes the wrong track.

The Schimmel Center happened to be our first hurdle and it served to gather us, to shape us. The box office treasurers welcomed us into their community with homemade cookies from time to time. Cold New Yorkers? I don't think so. I should add that some of the company liked the Schimmel best; it was very good to us. To top it off, we got some of the finest reviews for American Shakespeare ever.

The show moved to Chicago and opened in the Bank of America (Majestic) Theatre on March 17. It was the biggest house we played, and the sight of those 2,200 seats and three balconies took my breath away. It was like looking at the bleachers from home plate. It's daunting, because after successfully adjusting to the Schimmel with a back row several feet above your eye line, you now had to tilt your head considerably: first of all so they could hear you, but also, and equally importantly, so they could see your eyes. In warm-ups before each performance we were continually reminded to keep our chins up, which is a dandy note when you're trying to do Shakespeare as naturally as breathing.

There were a few other elements of the Chicago stint that contributed to the success of that run. First of all, it had horsehair-plaster walls, which are excellent for acoustics; and second, it had one of the best crews I've ever worked with. The crews in all the theaters were fine, but Chicago is a union town and so everything was smooth as silk, from the treasurers to the house staff to the running crew. It was a terrific organization and contributed much to our performance.

The Chicagoans in the audience changed the flavor of the show as well. I'm from the Mexican border; most of my school-mates were Chicanos, and Spanish is my second language. I spent a great deal of time in Juárez with the families of friends who lived there, and I believe that I have a Mexican soul, so the presence of a large Chicano population in Chicago reminded me of their second-class status in the 1950s. It was rotten, and there are still echos of it now. So when I played Shylock in that big theater, I was playing that time of my life when the cops kicked us around and made jokes about our accents. Chicago also injected an American energy into the show, a bustling, big energy that shored up our American interpretation. It was the time of the Japanese tsunami, and after each performance we made an appeal for donations to the American Red Cross Japa-nese Relief Fund. I thought about how we were helping those people who not many years ago we had thrown out of their houses and interned, imprisoned, and ghettoed.

Chicago was great because we learned not only that we could play a house that size, but that we could play it well. By the end of two weeks there, we were really cooking.

We opened on March 29 in Boston's Cutler Majestic, a

gorgeous, beautifully renovated Beaux Arts theater at Emerson College. When it opened in 1903, it was dubbed "The Gold Room": gilt decorations are everywhere, from the huge roses on the gently curving proscenium to the angels with outspread wings that hold up the balconies. It is glorious to play this house. And voluptuous. The dominant color is a dark rose-pink, and from the actor's point of view it feels like you're standing in an open mouth, the back of the throat being the stage, with the roof of the mouth mounting in ornate, flower-decked trellises to enclose two cantilevered balconies. There are no chandeliers or support columns, so the sound is unobstructed. Horsehair-plaster walls help make it a 1,200-seat acoustic gem.

This was the third of the four theaters on our tour, and I feel it's the one where our *Merchant of Venice* came into its own; we gave a solid, assured, freewheeling performance every time. No one said a thing about this sudden state of grace for fear of jinxing it, I guess, but by Saturday's matinee we were grinning at each other.

Boston had a vigorous college atmosphere, full of eager anticipation and excitement. The house was so welcoming that the performances seemed to soar. I don't know how the history of that town affected the performances. I'd like to be romantic and suggest that we were touched by the proximity to its early American inhabitants, but mostly I remember feeling completely at home in that great theater. The show fit there perfectly, and the town made us feel like it had taken us in. I don't know how else to describe it except to say that some of the actors came into themselves in that place—partly because we had begun replacement rehearsals and were forced to reexamine the work rather than rest on our substantial laurels.

We closed in Boston in the rain, which pretty much describes the weather we had had for those first four weeks on the road, and then when we got to Santa Monica we moved into our sunny digs on the beach. Really, *on the beach*, and let me tell you what it's like to play *The Merchant* in the bright sunlight. It's *tough*. Because you just don't want to work. It takes a different sort of concentration, a disconnection from that mesmerizing beach and the lazy bodies lying on it. So Santa Monica was the perfect place to close the play; it was a little present after all the rain.

But also, because we had to replace the actors in two major roles, it was like starting all over again, exploring our new relationships in this theater. The show didn't suffer for that, but we simply couldn't accomplish in two weeks with the new ensemble what had taken us two months to build.

We spent those last two weeks of our tour, from April 13 through April 24, in the Broad, the most actor-friendly theater I've ever seen. At 499 seats, it's an intimate space, inviting and warm, with great acoustics. And they do something there I'd never seen before: they provide food and snacks for every performance. That's unheard of—at least I'd never heard of it. What a terrific idea, and I imagine it has something to do with the fact that the director, Dale Franzen, was an opera singer, and that Dustin Hoffman had so much to do with the theater being built. No matter the reason, it was a real treat. It's surprising how the little backstage details affect the energy of a production.

As for performing there, it was a relief not to have to push to be heard. After playing to some big houses it felt like we were on holiday, but no one got lazy—as always, we warmed up on the stage before each performance, and no one slacked off.

My "ring" speech was fairly consistent throughout the tour, and the audiences seemed to be touched by it in each of the theaters, but as the Broad in Santa Monica was the most intimate theater, it was the one in which the speech affected the audience most deeply. It was possibly that effective in the other theaters, but at the Broad I could see the audience much more clearly than in any of the others, and their response hit me every time. I felt as though they were going through that pain with me.

The difference in the performances at the Broad was our focus—we were concerned with moving on and with saying good-bye to this experience, which we were all aware was uncommon. I found myself curiously emotional the last week; tears would fill my eyes at the damnedest times. Naturally it affected the work, though by now we were so solid that, whatever our wanderings, the performance of the play was completely satisfying—and that is what bound us together so tightly. We knew what we had and we were justly proud, but we were never arrogant. There was a genuine humility about this company, a gratitude to have been part of such a good show. Our company pulled so closely together partly because of the vast differences between one house and the next. Doing the show on the road proved that our work was not limited to a so-called New York audience; it reached people all across the country just as deeply each time. I wish the custom of touring the original Broadway cast would return: the country deserves to see the people who create the events.

The experience of each performance—whether it be *The Merchant of Venice* or any other play—cannot be dissociated from the theater it's played in. And I believe that the memory of each play remains in that theater, making up its soul. Every house has certain demands, and when you serve them the house will open to you. And of course if you are playing Shakespeare then there is always Will himself, ready to lend a hand whenever you let him.

Jessie Austrian, Noah Brody, and Ben Steinfeld
(Fiasco Theater)

BOLDNESS BE MY FRIEND

REPRESENTING FIASCO THEATER are its three founding members, Jessie Austrian, Noah Brody, and Ben Steinfeld. They have presented *Cymbeline* five times, including twice off-Broadway: first by Theatre for a New Audience and then by the Barrow Street Theatre, where it won the 2012 Off-Broadway Alliance Award for best revival. Other Fiasco productions include *Twelfth Night* and, in the spring of 2013, *Into the Woods* for the McCarter Theater. Fiasco is currently developing productions of the new play *The Vexed Question* and Shakespeare's *Measure for Measure*. The company has served as artists-in-residence at New York University, Duke University, and Marquette University.

C*ymbeline* is often thought of as a problematic play. Or a bad play. Or a just plain silly piece of theatrical meringue. It shifts rapidly between tragic and comedic tones; the plot is epic and involved, convoluted and often ridiculous. And yet when it came time for us, as the new Fiasco Theater company, to produce what was our first full production,* we chose *Cymbeline*. Why? Well, in addition to its complexities, *Cymbeline* offers the chance to take on an utterly transporting text, sing a song, dance

---

* We went all-in on *Cymbeline*, committing the totality of our resources, $18,000, rehearsing nights and weekends for a total of sixty hours. That's about one and a half weeks of rehearsal on a standard contract.

a jig, have a sword fight, play lovers, villains, and fools, and have another sword fight, all before the intermission. Then, of course, we love Shakespeare for expressing the fullness of humanity through language and for the fullness of experience an actor gets linguistically, physically, musically, and emotionally when playing his characters. *Cymbeline* had roles we wanted to play, wonderful and daunting language, and a seemingly impossible challenge of making it all hang together. Yet we weren't scared of producing it, because we were sure that no one was going to see it anyway. After all, we had never done a full production and few people knew us. We figured that, at best, we might convince two hundred people to come over the course of eleven performances.

We were, very happily, quite wrong about that. To date, *Cymbeline* has gone on to be presented four more times, running for over two hundred performances to thousands of audience members, including 159 continuous performances Off-Broadway at the Barrow Street Theatre—the first time Shakespeare has run commercially Off-Broadway in over twenty years.

So what made Fiasco's production of the play such an improbable success? Here's our attempt at an answer.

* * *

Cymbeline's plot is so full that its summary is nearly as long as the play itself. In Augustan England, the princess Imogen has married beneath her. Alone after the banishment of her husband, Imogen is beset by the angered King, her wicked stepmother, and the stepmother's dolt of a son, as well as a blackguard of a Roman who has bet his fortune against her fidelity. Escaping to rugged Wales dressed as a boy, Imogen meets a group of rustics whose fates are locked with hers. And all the while, a Roman invasion draws near. She takes a healing draught that temporarily poisons her while her tormentor is beheaded by her long-lost brother. Her husband is captured by the invading Italian forces shortly before their own defeat and, in his slumbers, is visited in turn by the ghosts of his ancestors and by Jupiter from on high. The final scene of the play uncoils a host of character and plot revelations wound up by the first four acts and usually demands a cast numerous enough to populate a Cecil B. DeMille epic.

The play is categorized as a "romance." If you had asked us to define that genre prior to our work on *Cymbeline*, we probably would have waived our arms in the air and said something like, "Romances are those late plays that scholars can't neatly define as comedy, tragedy, or history." But we learned that the plot-driven, epic nature of *Cymbeline* was hewing precisely to the form of romance, replete with wicked stepmothers, mistaken identities, and poisonous potions. Examples of the romance abound: *Don Quixote* and *Le Morte d'Arthur* in Shakespeare's time, *Harry Potter*, *The Princess Bride*, *Raiders of the Lost Ark*, and *The Lord of the Rings* in our own. In *Cymbeline*, as in all of those stories, wild action and broad characters rule the form. When we looked at the play through this lens, it was clear that there was no "problem" to solve. We don't think of the above titles as "problem" stories; we take joy in the sweeping, sometimes ridiculous plot elements and action-driven nature of these adventure tales.

So we decided to trust that old Will knew what he was doing and hoped that if we stayed true to the tone and rhythms he had written in each scene, and in each moment of each scene, we could put comedy right next to tragedy, and prop two-dimensional stock characters next to deeply introspective and multidimensional ones, as he had written, and that they would work, eclectically, to create a whole which was more than the sum of its parts. It's also a philosophy of acting that, incidentally, reflects the motley assembly of types and temperaments that make up our company.

As with all of Shakespeare's plays, there are many different themes at work in *Cymbeline*. But the ones we latched onto at the beginning were the ideas of belief and illusion: over and over again in *Cymbeline* things are not what they *seem* to be. The characters all *believe* things to be true based on seemingly irrefutable evidence that is actually false (e.g., Cloten's dead body that seems to be Posthumus's, a girl who seems to be a boy, the Doctor giving the Queen what seems like deadly poison but is actually not). True seems to be false, and vice versa. And so the characters believe they are at rock bottom when, in actuality, the tragic events they suffer are the pivot points on which their ultimate triumphs *necessarily* turn. Posthumus's banishment and his belief that Imogen is false are required to set in motion the plot that will restore a fractured court to order and, in turn, allow Posthumus and Imogen to be reconciled. But, of course, none of the characters can know this in any given moment. Nor do many of us recognize it in our own lives; it is only at the end of a journey that we can clearly see where we were in the middle of it. We lack perspective on the ground—as Belarius says, "Consider, / When you above perceive me like a crow, / That it is place which lessens and sets off" (3.3.13–15). We can never know where we are in our own story.

Okay, so "things aren't what they seem to be" is essential to both plot and theme? Eureka! We've got a production aesthetic engendered by the play. It was these two driving ideas— honoring the wild form of the romance, and the thematic content of illusion and belief—that guided our approach to cutting and adapting the script, and to creating a physical and musical life for the show.

* * *

At the outset of any Fiasco production we ask ourselves: "What do we absolutely have to have to tell the story?"* This is a question which proves very effective for focusing a production, and very prudent when you've little more than pocket change and the goodwill of others to create it. How that question is answered will define most of the production's textual, casting, design, physical, and musical parameters.

When we asked that primary question of *Cymbeline*, we kept coming back to one answer: a trunk. And that's really about it. "Send your trunk to me, it shall safe be kept" (1.6.238), says Imogen to the scheming Iachimo, who plans to hide inside the trunk himself and so gain access to her bedchamber. We then asked ourselves what would happen if we *only* had a trunk. And what if

Ben Steinfeld as Iachimo and Jessie Austrian as Imogen in Fiasco Theater's Cymbeline, *2011.*
Photograph by Ari Mintz.

---

* Hint: If your answer is "a rotating stage with a hydraulic lift and twenty-five tap-dancing Ziegfeld girls," you may not really be asking the question.

that trunk had some surprise elements and could seemingly become other things? Could the audience have a parallel experience to the characters' in which they believe they are seeing one thing but it turns out to be something else? We conceived of a fabulous, deceptive, "magic" trunk that became Imogen's bed, but contained a secret panel that allowed Iachimo to emerge from its side. It was passage into the cave home of Belaria (Belarius in Shakespeare's text), Guiderius, and Arviragus. It became a throne, a billiard table, and the ship carrying Posthumus to Italy. Arrows shot through its top during the war between Britain and Rome. The world of our production metaphorically (and often literally) revolved around that trunk. Moreover, its rough magic and surprising qualities complemented the tone and content of what is at times a preposterous and crazed play.

Our "magic" trunk also allowed us to bring one of the most notorious events in *Cymbeline* from off stage to on stage: the decapitation of Cloten. In some of the plays, all the action of a fight takes place on stage, as with Mercutio and Tybalt in *Romeo and Juliet*. "*Exeunt, fighting,*" however, often signals that one of the characters is about to get skewered or decapitated off stage. This is what Shakespeare does in Act 4, Scene 2 of *Cymbeline* when Guiderius and Cloten exit fighting, and Guiderius reenters holding Cloten's severed head. Soon after, the headless body is brought on for burial. Knowing that we weren't going to be able to credibly produce either a headless body or a disembodied head, we simply asked: What if we made this entire event happen on stage? Decapitation—*on stage*. Headless body—*on stage*.

In essence, we designed one of the side panels of our trunk to be made of foam with a slit down it, but to be indistinguishable from the rest of its wood-and-steel construction. During the

fight between Cloten and Guiderius, the trunk, which had previously served as the gateway into the cave home of Guiderius,
was "discovered" by Cloten as a possible escape route. Facing
upstage, the trunk and its open lid provided just enough cover
to mask the blow that severs Cloten's head. At that moment the
actor playing Cloten would collapse into the trunk. As his neck
slid down through the foam slit his severed head appeared to
be falling to the ground outside of the trunk. Voila! Decapitation. A few lines later Guiderius says he'll toss the head into
the stream behind their cave, at which point the actor kicked
Cloten's severed head back into the trunk. Voila! Disappearing
head. The boys then discover the supposedly dead body of their
new friend Fidele (who is really Imogen cross-dressed as a boy),
drag it on stage, sing a beautiful eulogy, and decide to "lay him
down." Now, the audience knows that Imogen/Fidele has in fact
taken a potion that will only make her/him seem dead temporarily. They've also just finished howling in laughter at the
world's stupidest magic trick in the form of our decapitation.
Yet without fail they would sit rapt and deeply moved by the
sorrow expressed in the funeral song: Shakespeare's magnificent lament for the dead, "Fear no more the heat o'th'sun . . ."
(4.2.323–346).* Despite the fact that the audience knew Imogen
wasn't really dead,** the song always created a moment of deep
pathos. Every time the song concluded, there was a holy silence
in the theater (broken only by an occasional sniffle). This ten-

---

* We chose to set the song to the tune of the traditional dirge "Long Time
Traveler." As we had already established the Appalachian musical world of
the rustics, the bleak and haunting sound of "Long Time Traveler" proved
a perfect complement to the pastorally stark imagery of the "Fear no more"
lyrics.
** This is the power of art, that we can feel deeply for something without
actually "believing" it is real.

sion was then released comically when, in the next moment, the actors would drag the body toward the trunk and open the lid in time for Belaria to exclaim, "Great Gods! Cloten is quite forgot! . . . Come, let us bury him" (adapted from 4.2.304–305). They would then drag Cloten's body outside the trunk while leaving his head inside the trunk. Voila! Headless body.

Neither the moment of decapitation nor the reveal of the headless body ever failed to meet with huge peals of laughter and appreciation from our audience. We hadn't succeeded in providing a realistic decapitation; but that wasn't possible. Shakespeare knew that. What we had managed was a way to keep a huge and otherwise offstage event before the audience, and to do it in a way so that their reaction to it was both thematically resonant and consonant with the production's aesthetic.

It struck us, night after night, how the audience responded to the events in this sequence. One could scarcely imagine an eight-minute piece of theater with more wild mood shifts than this scene, yet the audience transitioned through each of them effortlessly and completely; they were willing and able to laugh with us and cry with us and laugh with us again. It was an object lesson to us of the value of maintaining the peaks and valleys of Shakespeare's writing, the dramatic topography that is so often flattened by a production's desire for tonal consistency.

* * *

Once we decided we only needed a trunk, the next question was: How many actors do we need? Let's see . . . there are about twenty named roles and thirty-five or forty characters, so . . . six. Six actors (four men and two women) are needed in order to play every scene without having to switch roles internally.

Until you reach the final scene. Then you're screwed. But we figured we'd solve that in rehearsal.

But *why* do *Cymbeline* with only six actors? The saying goes, "There are no small roles, only small actors." That may be true, but there sure seem to be a lot of roles that demand spending most of the show backstage filling in crossword puzzles. We're a company of actors. We love to act. Shakespeare was an actor too; he understood how thrilling it is to say this shit out loud. So it was important to us that each member of the ensemble have a good amount to work on, which would mean doubling up many of the roles in the play. This also nicely mirrored and resonated with the play's themes of mistaken identity and illusion.* The magic of theater is in asking the audience to *believe* we are someone else, to become transformed and transported with us; we wanted to celebrate this and so never sought to hide the actors or their transformations. When the actors weren't acting in a scene they would sit upstage of the action in full view of the audience and watch the play. (Basically: I'm sitting on this bench, so I'm the actor; I stand up, step forward, and now I'm the character.) This allowed us to flow in and out of the action fairly seamlessly and to contribute musically even when we weren't acting, so all six of us were always responsible for the entire play regardless of who happened to be in each scene. It also told the audience that the magic of our produc-

---

* We ended up with some happy accidental resonances in the doubling: we changed the character Belarius to a woman (Belaria) and thus got to see the same actress embody the wicked stepmother, as the Queen, and the loving, philosophical mother trying to keep her boys from experiencing pain in the world, as Belaria; the actor who played Pisanio and took a verbal (and sometimes physical) beating from Cloten in the first three acts also played Guiderius, who gets to cut off Cloten's head in Act 4.

tion wasn't based upon realistic set pieces or fancy spectacle: the magic lay in conjuring Shakespeare's story practically out of thin air.

Noah Brody as Posthumus and Ben Steinfeld as Iachimo in Fiasco Theater's Cymbeline, *2011.*
Photograph by Ari Mintz.

As we've already mentioned, we love to act. It also turns out that all six of us love to make music. So we asked ourselves how we could use our vocal and instrumental skills to make the music in the show as surprising, satisfying, and versatile as the trunk. *Cymbeline* has a few songs in it that we needed to set, but we also wanted to use additional music to create atmosphere and place, to help with the storytelling, and to expand the emotional scope of important moments in the story.

Early in our process we happily decided that since Shakespeare makes the rustic family in Wales a musical one, we would follow through on that by making them a sort of family band in the American folk and bluegrass tradition. This allowed us to show that Belaria, Guiderius, and Arviragus are a genuinely loving family, and that they express their love through making music together.* We introduced the audience to Belaria and her boys at the top of our second act by having them sing the Carter Stanley tune "Think of What You've Done." Despite the jaunty tempo and exuberant feel of the song, the content is about a lover's betrayal, and specifically a lover asking if what he believes is true. Thus we got to experience the rustics as a joyous, music-making family while simultaneously echoing the play's thematic content.

Because the genre of romance is purposely eclectic, we felt we had license to use varied genres of music, and delighted in singing bluegrass in the same production in which we sang Italian madrigals and folk tunes. We even began the production with an old sea-shanty with rewritten lyrics to ask the audience to turn off their cell phones. From the first moment of the production we were acknowledging that the actors and audience could experience the live music in the same way, as opposed to in a movie, where underscoring is meant for the audience, but the actors in the movie don't hear it. In our production, the actors and audience are in the same room together, bringing the world of the play to life through shared imagination.

*   *   *

Before rehearsal began the three of us set out to cut and adapt the script for six actors. We left much of Acts 1 through 4 largely uncut, particularly the longer two-person scenes as well as the

---

* Not only did this present a huge contrast to the broken family dynamics of Cymbeline's court, but it also created a way for the rustics to welcome Imogen when they find her in the cave dressed as Fidele—they can teach her/him to sing.

monologues and soliloquies—they are so deft and so well-structured that for us to "help" the text would be to risk hubris. The major adaptations we made were in combining multiple characters and in reassigning text from one character to another. For example, in Cloten's first two scenes he is accompanied by two Lords, one a sycophant, and one who reports on Cloten's foolishness in asides to the audience. We decided to combine these two Lords into one voice, and to make it that of Pisanio. This meant the audience could spend a little more time with Pisanio, and could see how his job as a servant meant bearing the brunt of Cloten's brutishness. Thus, by the time we got to Cloten's actual scene with Pisanio in Act 3, when he threatens him and extorts information about Imogen's flight, the audience understood their relationship and its arc. We also adapted the play's opening expository scene between two unnamed Lords into a prologue spoken directly to the audience. This allowed us to give the audience the information they needed to follow the story, but also gave us a chance to establish how we would be including and engaging them in the performance throughout the evening.

We cut the text with a scalpel for Acts 1 through 4, but in Shakespeare's Act 5 we used an axe, cutting whole scenes and characters (deploying hubris now). The major sequence that we cut in Act 5 follows the capture of Posthumus. He falls asleep and is surrounded by the ghosts of his ancestors, who implore Jupiter to explain why he has brought so much sorrow upon Posthumus; then Jupiter descends from above on a golden eagle* and tells the ancestors to pipe down and quit worrying,

---

* *Cymbeline* was one of the late plays written to be performed in Blackfriars, an indoor space with a winch system, giving Will the ability to fly things in. Who doesn't like a new toy?

and that the gods have got everything under control, thank you very much.

Because we were less interested in the thematic content of the gods and our noble ancestors guiding our fate, and because we wanted to highlight the theme of lacking perspective within one's own story, we decided to cut this event. We felt secure in doing this because the events of the jail and Jupiter are not actually required to move the plot forward toward resolution.*

One of the reasons *Cymbeline* is notoriously difficult to pull off is the number of events and revelations that occur in its final scene. It is five hundred lines of revelation upon revelation—*seventeen revelations*, in fact—in which each character recapitulates his entire story. At first glance we thought it all seemed superfluous because the audience already knows the information that is revealed. What was Shakespeare after? Perhaps Will had set himself a challenge within the genre of the romance: How many plot threads could he spin throughout the play and then neatly tie together in one final scene at the last possible moment? The production had set itself a similar challenge: How can multiple characters be on stage for all of these revelations with only six actors to play them? Thus the audience had the experience of watching so many plot pieces be spun into existence and wondering how they would come together, while simultaneously wondering how the hell these six actors could ever pull it off. In other words, the story and the

---

* We took some of Jupiter's language that was thematically resonant and used it at the end of the play as a sort of epilogue, delivered by the actor who played Cymbeline: "Be not with mortal accidents oppressed, / No care of *ours* it is, *it is the Gods'*. / Whom best *they* love, *they* cross, to make *their* gift / The more delayed, delighted" (italicized changes ours; adapted from 5.3.202–205).

production were reaching their climax at the same time—form and content working hand in hand.

We signified each change of character with one loud drum-beat, while the actor who was changing roles moved or shifted physically to become another person. While earlier in the play we had avoided switching roles within scenes, here it worked beautifully because it turned out the content of this scene was about *that*: the scene is about revelations of identity and information, and the event of the scene is watching Cymbeline receive all of this information and put it together. We made internal cuts so that each recapitulation wasn't quite so long, and reassigned a bit of language (so that the actor playing the Doctor and Cymbeline didn't have to talk to himself, for example), but otherwise we just did the scene using the simple convention of a drumbeat to signify that someone was becoming a different character. We solved the problem of *How do you pull off a series of seventeen revelations in a row?* by embracing the problem as the solution: *Let's attempt to make seventeen revelations in a row happen with only six people.* We discovered to our amazement that there was no solution necessary; the thing that seemed like a problem with the scene actually turned out to be its intent, and what the audience didn't even realize they were waiting for. In performance the response to the final scene was often uproarious laughter of appreciation for the feat.

Perhaps our production was successful precisely because we didn't attempt to "solve" this "problematic" play. Maybe productions of this play go wrong when one tries to even out its tone, or make it into just one thing. Perhaps trusting that Shakespeare was consciously putting eclectic elements next to each other and delighting in their juxtaposition, consciously setting a challenge and attempting to meet it, is more effective. We continually asked ourselves what Shakespeare was trying to

do and how we could make it happen in ways that would gal-
vanize our audience and ourselves. While many who saw the
show thought the specific answers and choices we came up with
seemed a perfect fit for *Cymbeline*, we have found that it is asking the right questions that matters most.

And we further believe that it is only in risking a fiasco—as
Shakespeare himself did in writing *Cymbeline*—that one takes
the leaps that may lead to the creation of something wonderful.

Karin CoonroᎠ

KILLING SHAKESPEARE AND
MAKING MY PLAY

———————

KARIN COONROD is an American theater maker and founder of the
Arden Party Theater Company and the Compagnia de' Colombari.
She has directed numerous productions internationally, as well
as at the American Repertory Theater, the New York Shakespeare
Festival/Public Theater, Theatre for a New Audience, and the New
York Theatre Workshop. She teaches at the Yale School of Drama,
and has been a guest artist and teacher at Stanford, Harvard,
Columbia, New York University, the University of Iowa, Fordham
University, and the California University of the Arts. In addition
to recently written works, her productions include *A Midsummer Night's Dream*, *Hamlet*, *As You Like It*, *The Taming of
the Shrew*, *Love's Labor's Lost*, *Othello*, *Twelfth Night*, *All's
Well That Ends Well*, *Romeo and Juliet*, *King Lear*, *King John*,
Henry IV, *Henry VI*, *Coriolanus*, and *Julius Caesar*; she is currently working on *The Tempest*.

Shakespeare is my deer and I need to kill him to make the
blood flow. So I'm aiming for the heart.

Love's Labor's Lost (spelled this way in the first printed
quarto) is known for its arch wit and wordy one-upmanship,
and yet it is often forgotten because of the wild turn it takes
when the messenger of death crashes through the spirited verbal hijinks in the final moments of the play. I, however, love this
juxtaposition: Shakespeare brings death to comedy, which for

me translates into catharsis. It's not worth making a play and inviting a huge group of people to attend if catharsis is not in the plan. So when I was asked to direct one of Shakespeare's plays for the Public Theater in 2011, I chose this early but challenging comedy.

Love's Labor's Lost has a simple plot: the King of Navarre and his royal cohorts set up an academy for men only with strict precepts—to which all in the small court must abide. The Princess of France and her three royal ladies-in-waiting appear on a diplomatic mission from Paris. Inside their hearts, the oaths the men have taken are smashed apart by the mere appearance of the women. The undoing of their oaths is the main concern of the men, and the observing of this dissolution is the main action of the women. Clowns are interwoven throughout the play and bring all together in the Pageant of the Nine Worthies, the occasion for the sudden announcement, by the messenger from Paris, of the death of the Princess's father, the King of France. In desperate hope, the young men propose to the women, but the women decline to marry them for at least a year, setting each suitor a task of service and spiritual reflection. At the end, the King and the clowns are brought together through the words of the final song.

Whenever I've directed Shakespeare—*Henry VI, Parts 1, 2, 3*; *King John*; *Romeo and Juliet*; *King Lear*—I've never wanted simply to do another Shakespeare play; rather, I've always wanted to identify what, for me, is the essential line or scene that distinguishes each one. In *Love's Labor's Lost*, there is a moment late in the play when Rosaline, close friend to the Princess, says to her suitor Berowne, "A jest's prosperity lies in the ear / Of him that hears it, never in the tongue / Of him that makes it" (5.2.860–862). The play has been a battle of wits and quibbles, but one which usually leads to a final, often viciously funny send-off. But this line opens it up, moves it from monologue to dialogue, to a conversation, not a battle. It is fundamental to the arc of the play, this trajectory from monologue to dialogue; it is the secret movement of the play that I wanted to track.

The King begins the play with his edict to ban women from his kingdom in order to enforce extreme study—accompanied by little sleep and little food—in his new academy. However, the King has revealed his underlying goal in the play's first line, "Let fame, that all hunt after in their lives, / Live registered upon our brazen tombs" (1.1.1–2). He wants fame, a very modern conceit, because he reckons that he can—by very finite means—triumph in an infinite game. He also assumes everyone is after fame, but perhaps his assumption says more about himself. Yet this fame he blithely mentions in the opening line is in some way likened to honor, the subject of the pageant the clowns perform for the royals at the end. The men are clouded by their own narcissistic mockery, and they are observed carefully by the women who say next to nothing, with the exception of the Princess who offers words of encouragement to the performers. Her monologue is left in the dust when the messenger of death comes. The Princess then turns her perspicacious gaze on the King and begins the conversation. It is the first moment he listens.

There is an interlude earlier on in Act 4, Scene 1 when the women take a hunting trip. To prepare for this scene, I took the four actors to an archery lane in Brooklyn for some bow-and-arrow work—probably not a bad thing for the girls to know anyway. They were competitive about hitting the bull's-eye. Who hit it the most? I discovered their fierceness and loved them for that. In the scene of the killing of the deer, there is the play's first direct confrontation with mortality. The Princess is conflicted; she struggles with the morality of this act of killing a fellow creature. But she looks within and fires the arrow. It is a foreshadowing: she is the one, ultimately, who must shoot the arrow. Later, she is the one whom fate has determined will be the queen.

The women lead the characters to the major transformations in the play, so it is important to figure out what they are telling us. At first they are excluded from the kingdom. Classic, isn't it? But Shakespeare doesn't stop there. The women are sly, and they are even wittier than the men. The men are after fame and sex; the women, even from the first, know more. But it would be too simple to limit this just to girls turning around a one-night stand, a tired cliché. We discover there is far more at hand with the Princess killing the deer, the anticipation of death, and the Princess's contemplation of mortality within life. We see the men make self-serving oaths and then easily drop them. The women take us to universal truths. If the men really want marriage, then they will have to pay with their souls. Like the clowns, the women are outsiders who see more than those at the center of the mainstream culture.

The clowns also play an important role, counterpoint to the King and his men. They are the ones under the radar, the despised, the mocked; yet they are the very ones who expose the falsity of the King's edict. In the first scene, after the King's men have set up the new academy, the lowly Costard is dragged into the arena of their attention as a transgressor against the new edict. The scene ends with him saying, "I suffer for the truth, sir" (1.1.272). Costard is jabbing us all. Costard, the slacker, has an ally in Berowne in terms of their gut responses to the edict. Berowne, the King's man, would never hang out with the knave, but theatrically they are rivals for the attention of the audience.

*   *   *

The journey of the play takes place entirely on one acre of humanity's green carpet, outside the King's castle. I set the actual stage on a large square of green grass to bring out the role of nature in the play. The theater space used to be a library, and so the audience could imagine the shelves of books on the walls around them. The juxtaposition of indoors and out-doors, scholarly study and natural impulse, was intended to be a bit disorienting. My designer, John Conklin, and I loved this idea of a universal field on which the play is played. Of course this grass is Whitmanic in the sense that nature's carpet for all humankind is the grass. And it is fitting, funny, and duly sur-prising (and so like Shakespeare) that this play known for its linguistic wit is played out on a field of grass. Grass is the great leveler, covering the graves on which we all tread daily, and as such even anticipates the wild turn at play's end. The King and the clown meet not on a Persian carpet or a roughly woven mat, but on the common carpet.

But is *Love's Labor's Lost* truly universal? This play is about young lovers, and it is by a young Shakespeare, so the question I kept asking was: Does it speak to a young audience? When I read the play I found a remarkable mirroring between the repartee of the new generation and that of Shakespeare's dialogue. I see a lot of wit in today's texting—a lot of sharp, direct, back-and-forth. *Love's Labor's Lost* seemed very in tune with that. One of my actors, Francis Jue, arrived to rehearsal one day with a story fresh from the subway. Some young kids were en route to band practice. One said to another: "If you don't *listen*, I'm going to *left-hook* you, so you better *lighten up*—and that's three *l*'s." A line worthy of Shakespeare on the subway in American idiom!

To capture this I wanted a young cast of lovers, hormones on steroids, more raucous and less studied. That naturally led to the play becoming more physical. When the King, for instance, is revealed to have violated his own prohibition on love, he literally bolts from the stage and is tackled as he returns down the stairs. The audience loved the King's instinctual lizard brain response: flee.

The clowns are also physical. Holofernes and Nathaniel, the comedic scholars, should not be talking heads. In a way they are a reminder of what the King and his men might have become had they zealously followed their academy rules. Holofernes's language is so monologous, so isolated and nearly insane, that it needs to be accompanied by the landscape of his body. They

Karin Coonrod directing Steven Skybell as Holofernes (with the cuckoo on his hat) and Francis Jue as Nathaniel (with the owl on his hat) in the Public Theater's Love's Labor's Lost, *2011. Photograph by Raphaele Shirley.*

are hilarious and terrifying, like in an Ionesco play, yet all the characterization began from a real human place. I was fortunate to work with Steven Skybell, who took on "The preyful princess pierced and pricked a pretty pleasing pricket" (4.2.45) as a performance (art) piece, playing all the parts. The clowns are a varied group, some with boots on the ground (Costard, Jaquenetta, Dull) and some with boots in the air (Holofernes, Nathaniel, Armado, Moth). I wanted Jaquenetta to be played by a smart, fierce, no-nonsense Fellini-type actor, and Stephanie DiMaggio was perfect in her grounded truth. With the fewest lines in the play, Jaquenetta, unobserved, observed the action from the edges of the stage world and thereby had the opportunity to expose Berowne's hypocrisy when he holds out against his fellows, mocking them for having fallen in love and pretending that he hasn't likewise succumbed. In that way she could also get the eye of the audience—not just to be gazed at, but for the fire of her silent wit. Our shared secret—arrived at independently—was that she is the smartest character in the play.

The clowns are often seen as a distraction from the play's theme, but I saw them as honing the message of the play. Shakespeare throws a devastating twist on the hollow fame sought by the King. When deciding on a play to bring to the King and his court, Holofernes ignites the interest of his fellow clowns with the Pageant of the Nine Worthies. But watching this play-within-a-play, the King and his men mock and humiliate the clowns during their performances. The clowns, pushing the edge of their capacity, speak from their hearts and souls by honoring the great historical and legendary figures they are playing. After much cruel heckling, Armado, playing Hector, says to the courtiers: "beat not the bones of the buried. When we breathed he was a man" (5.2.673–674). With Reg E. Cathey, who played Armado, we discussed the action inherent in this line: to shame the entitled men, to remember what it was to be a man. This line needed to be heard above all the other lines in the scene, a warning to all present.

Harold Bloom, in his chapter on *Love's Labor's Lost* in *The Invention of the Human*, says in the final line: "Shakespeare's most elaborately artificial comedy, his great feast of language, antithetically subsides in natural simplicities and in country phrases." For me the pith of the play's meaning lies in this radical antithesis. Death has cut the space in two and in the ensuing suffering the Princess-turned-Queen and her women challenge the men to experience silence. We do not know what will happen in a year's time—and it is not our business in the birth of this performance—but what is apparent is a newfound kindness (*caritas*) on the part of the King to the clowns when they enter with their request to sing an epilogue. I imagine the King looking to the Queen for approval of the clowns' entrance, since it is she who has just received the news of her father's death. In our production, Tony Geballe's haunting music allowed the clowns to sing sensitively and poignantly in the beginning . . . and as the music's rhythm takes over, the characters slowly morph back into the actors of a company dancing and singing in the space of the audience, a space they have freely inhabited throughout the performance. The song begins with a consideration of spring and moves on to winter, with its characters the essential persons of life, the Jaquenettas of the world. It concludes:

When all aloud the wind doth blow
And coughing drowns the parson's saw
And birds sit brooding in the snow
And Marian's nose looks red and raw,
When roasted crabs hiss in the bowl,
Then nightly sings the staring owl:

"Tu-whit, tu-whoo."
A merry note,
While greasy Joan doth keel the pot.

(5.2.918–926)

The play does not end in exclusive weddings (with the business
of marriage); rather, the whole community is embraced . . . all
shine with wondrous equality. This is a play about love, and
love takes no prisoners.

Dominic Dromgoole

PLAYING SHAKESPEARE
AT THE GLOBE

DOMINIC DROMGOOLE is an English director and author. He is currently serving as Artistic Director of Shakespeare's Globe Theatre; he was previously Artistic Director of the Bush Theatre and the Oxford Stage (now Headlong) Company. In addition to modern and classic works such as *The Three Sisters, Easter,* and *Someone Who'll Watch Over Me*, he has directed *Troilus and Cressida, Coriolanus, Antony and Cleopatra, Hamlet, Love's Labour's Lost, King Lear,* and *Henry V*. He is also the author of *The Full Room: An A–Z of Contemporary Playwriting* and the memoir *Will and Me: How Shakespeare Took Over My Life*, winner of the inaugural Sheridan Morley Award.

There has been a great transformation in how Shakespeare is taught in schools in the United Kingdom in recent years, and it has largely been led by the creation of the Globe Theatre in 1997—not only by its outreach education department, but also by the simple fact of the Globe's presence. The sea change has taken Shakespeare away from the page and towards the stage, and as a result students are more frequently encouraged to speak it aloud, to act it, and to understand its playfulness and performative nature. Rather than being seen as imagistic poetry, as discreet philosophy, or as political statement, it's being seen much more as something that is there to be made and acted, and that is only fully realized in performance. Shakespeare, as a consequence, becomes an experience that is available and enjoyable, rather than distant and difficult.

At the Globe, we don't try to modernize Shakespeare and make him something other than he is. We use Renaissance costumes rather than jeans and motorcycle jackets; we don't need elaborate sets or lighting because the reconstructed Globe, with its wood beams, its pit, its thrust stage, and its sky canopy, is already both minimalist and complex; and we don't rewrite Shakespeare's original language to supposedly make it more accessible to modern listeners. If one tries to bring Shakespeare by the hand towards the modern day, what one is really doing is shaving off all the marvelous exoticism and everything that was different about the spirit of that time. We need difference so that we can understand that the world hasn't always been the same, that not everyone's viewpoint has always been the same as ours, and that society did dance to an entirely different beat at one time. Modernizing Shakespeare also seems to me to be reducing him, and I don't think we do any artists a service by reducing them. If Shakespeare is looked at through his own time instead, then (a) the audience is taken to a different world where they can come to appreciate that the human is capable of doing things in different ways, and (b) we just get closer to what Shakespeare himself was attempting to do. Of a recent RSC production of *As You Like It*, an English critic wrote that thank goodness they had gotten rid of all that hey-nonny-no stuff. But Shakespeare wrote that hey-nonny-no stuff, and he wrote that hey-nonny-no stuff because he liked it, since for him it was exciting and fun and full of flavour. So if you cut that flavour out, you're cutting some of Shakespeare out—and why should we be saving Shakespeare from himself?

Love's Labour's Lost, which I directed not too long ago, is woven full of linguistically sophisticated wordplay and rhetoric—so much so, in fact, that it's notoriously difficult to stage for modern audiences. When we did it at the Globe, we used two different keys to try to unlock it. *Love's Labour's Lost* was a very popular play in Shakespeare's day, and the reason it was so popular was because it's absolutely filthy. An enormous amount of the humour in it is staggeringly dirty, with outrageous puns and code-speak throughout. Even though it's also very witty, tickets aren't sold to people who appreciate the wit: tickets are sold to a broad mass of people who find that kind of bawdy humour uproariously funny. The way those jokes and allusions are brought out today is through the simple sexuality of them. We tried to understand that—to play it a bit, but really just to understand it, to know that it was in the air. Rather than performing with winks and nudges all the time, we just wanted to be conscious of all that dirt because it tickles the audience's imagination in a certain way and helps them elucidate the meaning. Also, of course, if an audience is listening for filthy jokes, it tends to be listening harder—and if the audience is listening harder, it means we can unpick some of the more knotty thoughts. That's one way to unlock such a linguistically difficult play; the other way is to share the problem with the audience, rather than being ostentatious and pretending to be terribly clever. With your attitude, you try and say, "We love doing this complicated and weird language. Come with us on it and see how much of it you get, and let's try and work it out together." It thereby becomes a generous act, rather than the mean act of being pretentious with it.

Although both in directing my own plays and in overseeing the productions of the Globe I have my own ideas about how to best do service to the writing, I also adamantly believe that every production of Shakespeare is good in some way. All of God's children have wings: it's very hard to have something so definitively wrong that you can't give it some credit. Some Shakespeare is very lifeless, but when it is dead it's usually a byproduct of institutional deadness. If the institution behind the production has no heart or imagination, then they can produce work that's very cynical and hasn't got a spark of life or a reason to exist—and if it hasn't got a reason to exist, then it can be very dull to watch. There is no easy solution, though, since one can put together productions with great, good intentions which then come out a bit turgid. And then, too, a show can be absolutely festive, wild, and brilliant one night, and then on another night it can be flat on the floor. The success of any Shakespearean performative venture is very hard to understand or predict.

Similarly, I believe that Shakespeare-related versions and variations have their value too. Any great—I always tend to want to term it a religious movement, and I don't quite mean that—but any great cultural happening is going to spin out of the world in a whole variety of ways. If you then believe that the happening in itself, Shakespeare, is a virtuous, useful, beautiful, and generous thing—which I think it is—then you'll want to deem anything that can lead us back to Shakespeare to be good too. If kids love finger puppets and if those, in some way, introduce them to Shakespeare, then so much the better; or if you see a condensation of the play, or you read a comic based on the play, or you see a film that's drawn to the play, and if in some way those experiences lead you back to the source, then, likewise, so much the better.

* * *

In something of this same spirit—this spirit of broadening horizons and yet bringing us all back to the source—our contribution to the 2012 World Shakespeare Festival was the Globe to Globe Festival, in which thirty-seven plays were done by thirty-seven international companies in thirty-seven different languages over the course of six weeks. For example, a New Zealand company brought over a production of *Troilus and Cressida*, the Belarus Free Theatre did *King Lear* in Belarusian, and the national theatres of Albania, Macedonia, and Serbia performed a Balkan trilogy of the *Henry VI* plays. *Henry V* was the Globe's own contribution to the festival, for it seemed that our contribution—which would be the only play done in the original—should be a play that's very much about how you use and abuse not just the English language, but any language. In this version that I directed, consequently, I tried to be aware myself and to bring out that awareness in audiences of all the ways that Shakespeare shows us how language can be played with and employed.

Throughout *Henry V*, language is used for exultation, seduction, manipulation, and inspiration; language is used to summon up the imaginary stage, and it is used to tell stories about people and their relationships. It also has a very real force: the French Governor of Harfleur, for example, is actually defeated by language. The final reason why the English get into Harfleur isn't the endless bombardment or the endless tactical charging of the breach: those military attempts all fail. The way that Henry gets in is by giving a terrifying rhetorical speech in which he says that his soldiers are going to do unspeakable things:

> . . . why, in a moment look to see
> The blind and bloody soldier with foul hand
> Defile the locks of your shrill-shrieking daughters,
> Your fathers taken by the silver beards,
> And their most reverend heads dashed to the walls,

Your naked infants spitted upon pikes,
Whiles the mad mothers with their howls confused
Do break the clouds, as did the wives of Jewry
At Herod's bloody-hunting slaughtermen.
What say you? Will you yield, and this avoid?
Or, guilty in defence, be thus destroyed?

(3.3.33–43)

The French open their gates.

The scenes featuring combinations of the Scotsman, Welshman, Englishman, and Irishman are very much about how languages collide. In one scene, the Welshman, Fluellen, begins to make a comment to the Irishman, whom he can't stand: "Captain MacMorris, I think, look you, under your correction, there is not many of your nation—" (3.2.88–89), and MacMorris interrupts him with, "Of my nation? What ish my nation? Ish a villain and a bastard and a knave and a rascal. What ish my nation? Who talks of my nation?" (3.2.90–91).

We then see the French Princess, Katherine, learning English from her lady's maid—"de hand, de fingres, de nails, de arm, d'elbow, de nick, de sin, de foot, de coun" (3.4.43–44). The last two inspire the Princess's blushing laughter, as they have a dirty double entendre in French which would be right at home in *Love's Labour's Lost*. This comedy, however, distracts us from the fact that the Princess isn't learning English purely for pleasure, but because she must deal with an invading force. Then, at the end, in the wonderful scene between Henry and Katherine, we see the power of language to seduce:

. . . a good heart, Kate, is the sun and the moon—or rather the sun and not the moon, for it shines bright and never changes, but keeps his course truly. If thou

would have such a one, take me: and take me, take a
soldier: take a soldier, take a king.

(5.2.143–146)

Although it is genuinely charming, in that last scene you see
Henry's ability to bring other people into his own corner, into
his own imaginative place.

* * *

When I began working on *Henry V*, I was surprised by how
much broader a landscape the characters all traveled through
than the one I had in my imagination connected to the play.
The films by Laurence Olivier and Kenneth Branagh, which
I think are both terrific in different ways, give an impression
of a very streamlined, linear, purposeful beast that's marching
steadily forwards towards a collection of questions and a collection of images, and it was on rereading it and working closely
with the text that I realized that it's telling a very big story about
lots of people other than Henry V: Pistol, Fluellen, MacMorris,
the soldier Williams, the Princess, and all of those characters
at the French court. All of those relationships and all of those
textures are part of the landscape of that whole world, and they
should be respected equally. Together, they all throw up a much
more anarchic, irreverent, and confused landscape than I'd previously thought the play occupied.

In his own mind, Shakespeare probably intended the play
to be more rectilinear, but I think he was always subverted by
his own enthusiasms and humours. At the outset, I think, he
thought he was really going to write a proper play about a king,
with lots of kingy stuff in it reminiscent of Marlowe's great
kingy play, *Tamburlaine the Great*. But then he started writing
and he couldn't resist hearing other noises, and latching onto

different tunes, and then exploring that different music and growing it in much the same way that a jazz musician follows a motif. Shakespeare killed off Falstaff because he had decided that Falstaff couldn't be in a play that was going to be all about the King, but then he found that Pistol was rather a nice noise, and he thought that he might just extend that noise a bit and explore it; and then he created Fluellen and found that to be a fascinating noise, and realized that Fluellen could say something rich about war, and that he could then say something rich about the relationships of men at war, and that he could also cheek the King a bit. . . . And so Shakespeare is always being subverted by himself. He has far more schematic intentions than he can realize, for they are continually being derailed by life, humour, and enthusiasm.

The characters which result are not merely incidental; there are deep resonances in them. A very emotional encounter occurs between Henry and Fluellen after the battle of Agincourt. Henry has just asked the name of the castle near the field of battle and, upon learning its name, he has solemnly declared, "Then call we this the field of Agincourt, / Fought on the day of Crispin Crispianus" (4.7.75–76). There follows a moment of stillness, and then there's a ridiculous response from Fluellen:

> Your majesty says very true: if your majesties is remembered of it, the Welshmen did good service in a garden where leeks did grow, wearing leeks in their Monmouth caps, which, your majesty know, to this hour is an honourable badge of the service . . .
>
> (4.7.81–84)

They then combine over saying that they are countrymen of each other—Henry V was born in the Welsh city of Monmouth—

but at the end of the exchange Fluellen very toughly says, "I need not to be ashamed of your majesty, praised be God, so long as your majesty is an honest man" (4.7.93–94). There's a caution in it which gives it a deeper resonance and provides more depth to Fluellen, who is fanatical about a certain sort of honesty and honour. His words leave something unresolved, because he says "so long as," not "since you're an honest man," indicating that the process of looking for approval is continuous. It's a very testing question for Henry.

Some people say the play is a celebration of bringing together the various countries to create a Great Britain, but in the scene in which the Scotsman, Irishman, Welshman, and Englishman are all together, they end up hating each other and are about to have a massive scrap—"So Chrish save me, I will cut off your head" (3.2.97–98), MacMorris threatens Fluellen. The question of nationalities remains thereby unresolved. There's the additional myth that Henry in some way settles class issues by bestowing his munificence on the people of the working class, as he promises in the famous St. Crispin's Day speech:

> We few, we happy few, we band of brothers.
> For he today that sheds his blood with me
> Shall be my brother, be he ne'er so vile,
> This day shall gentle his condition.
>
> (4.3.62–65)

The only scene in which Henry does hang out with the people of the working class, however, is a disaster, and it, too, almost ends up with a fight. After an unresolved philosophical argument about the responsibility of the King for the souls of the men who die in battle for him, Henry and the soldier Williams almost come to blows when Williams calls into question the King's word. "Let it be a quarrel between us, if you live" (4.1.166), challenges Williams. Although it raises those issues, the play does not knit together the perfect Britain, and it does not knit together the perfect marriage of all the classes; rather, it seems to call up those issues for no other reason than to leave them wide open.

Henry V is a play about war, valor, and just causes, but perhaps the most interesting aspect of those debates is that they call out a more important set of questions concerning how to live. The St. Crispin's Day speech begins, for instance,

> If we are marked to die, we are enough
> To do our country loss, and if to live,
> The fewer men, the greater share of honour.
>
> (4.3.22–24)

When there's a high probability of dying, it adjusts one's attitude to the present moment, to posterity, and to the idea of reputation. In general, it's something that's very hard for us to comprehend. A company from South Sudan came here with *Cymbeline* for the Globe to Globe Festival. Four of the company were going to go back to fight in the war, in which there is only a 50 percent chance of survival. Those odds didn't make them miserable—they were a wild, jolly, and weeping company— but there was the sense that they were appreciating the present moment in a way that we do not, and also that they were conscious of being involved in the festival as something they might be remembered for in a way that doesn't matter in the same way for us. When you have the threat of death very close to you, you can't help but think, "What am I going to leave behind?" Reputation and the notion of a legacy become much more quick and important—but of course there, too, Shakespeare doesn't have any answers for us. He merely picks up on and follows the music of these characters and questions, and leaves us to decide how we're going to incorporate those tunes into our own lives.

* * *

In the process of preparing *Henry V*, I became intrigued by the question implicit in the very opening line, the famous "O! For a muse of fire." I spent a long time thinking about that invocation, because usually it's played by a bullying, older male actor who comes out and commands, *"O! for a muse of fire,"* in a way that sounds like the order "Come here immediately, muse"—as though the muse hasn't got a choice. Then I started to play with the idea that, on the contrary, perhaps it could be somebody asking, saying, "Please, I need a muse. I'm in trouble." If *Henry V* was the first play in the 1599 Globe, as people think, then it's possible that Shakespeare was considering, "I need a special inspiration," and then wondering, "How do I get that special inspiration?" and then hitting on the answer: "It's you, the audience. You can do it for me. We can do this together. If you can use your imagination, if you can will these strange things into existence, if you can come with me on this journey, then we can do remarkable things together." That idea helped me to understand the imaginative framework of the play, in that it's not masculine and beefy, it's actually quite modest and questioning. Rather than "We're going to do this," the line—and so the entire play—becomes "Can we make this happen?" It's much more tentative than it appears to be.

The reason that speech works so well that way at the Globe, and the reason why it can't work in quite the same way anywhere else, is that the reality in the Globe is a communal, collaborative, willed reality. It's not a given reality. The speeches of the Chorus are prescriptions for how to make the Globe work:

"And let us, ciphers to this great accompt, / On your imaginary forces work" (1.1.17–18); "Piece out our imperfections with your thoughts" (1.1.23). Even though they work best at the Globe, they're also prescriptions for how avant-garde theatre has worked for the last four hundred years, which involves the whole idea of using the imagination, and the complicity and collaboration between the audience and the stage.

When the audience fully enters into that imaginative game, then they become full participants in the experience. They become characters themselves, which Shakespeare calls into form as listeners to his Chorus in *Henry V* and then explicitly brings into his dramatis personae as Citizens in *Julius Caesar* and *Coriolanus*. Doing *Coriolanus* at the Globe is exciting, because you can play with all those different conceptions of the crowd: you can set up the crowd against itself by opening up divisions and arguments within it. When Coriolanus has to go show his wounds in the marketplace, the actor can go down into the yard and walk amongst the audience, showing them the wounds and thereby inspiring a very complex set of reactions. At one moment the crowd adored Coriolanus, and then at another they despised him because he was insulting them and even spitting at them. The fact that the crowd is so erratic feeds back into the play: it's very disorienting for Coriolanus, who is on this side and then that side, in love and then exiled from love. Actors and audience combine to create a turbulent experience, illustrating how that sort of emotional participation can be astonishingly powerful.

I think that Shakespeare was anxious of the real power of crowds. He understood the attraction of being part of a crowd and of giving oneself up to a communal sense of purpose, but he seems to have been suspicious of mass enthusiasms. A crowd can be fantastically intelligent as a group: the reason that we go to the theatre is to be in a body of people who communally are more intelligent than we are sitting on our own at our computers. When we participate in a heightened sense of communal perception, then we get taken to areas of quickness of wit in responding to language and imagery that we don't get alone. On the other hand, crowds can be sentimental, manipulable, and very easily riled into a state of rage. I think Shakespeare was suspicious of that volatility and that in his plays he was constantly subverting, twisting, challenging, and demeaning that element.

The greatest act of martial rhetoric ever committed to a play is the speech Henry gives to his troops at the battle of Harfleur:

> Once more unto the breach, dear friends, once more,
> Or close the wall up with our English dead.
> In peace there's nothing so becomes a man
> As modest stillness and humility,
> But when the blast of war blows in our ears,
> Then imitate the action of the tiger:
> Stiffen the sinews, conjure up the blood,
> Disguise fair nature with hard-favoured rage . . .
>
> (3.1.1–8)

And so on, all the way until the rousing,

> The game's afoot:
> Follow your spirit, and upon this charge
> Cry "God for Harry, England, and Saint George!"
>
> (3.1.32–34)

Then, immediately after everyone runs off once more unto the breach, Bardolph, Nym, and Pistol come on to take the piss out of it all. "On, on, on, on, on! To the breach, to the breach!" (3.2.1), cries Bardolph, but Nym holds him back with, "Pray thee, corporal, stay: the knocks are too hot, and for mine own part, I have not a case of lives. The humour of it is too hot" (3.2.2–3).

Shakespeare had an in-built sense of humor and irreverence that made him careful to puncture any moment that was about to become too clear of purpose. Henry speaks with enormous conviction, but Shakespeare as an artist is capable of being wholly sympathetic to entirely different points of view. He can be sympathetic to the heroism of Henry, and he can believe passionately in the necessity of exalting that hero and of having him do extraordinarily heroic things; then, at the same time, he can also believe passionately in the right of Pistol and his friends to come on and puncture that balloon and make what just preceded look extremely silly.

* * *

The nineteenth-century critic William Hazlitt, who felt "little love or admiration" for Henry, wrote that we nevertheless "like him in the play," where he is "a very amiable monster, a very splendid pageant." I don't think we're supposed to like Henry or dislike him: I think we're supposed to watch him improvising and learning how to do things as he does them. I think that Jamie Parker, who was Henry in this production, is particularly good at getting across the idea that the events of the play do not take place following a collection of choices made prior to the beginning of the play which are then executed and carried through on a determined pattern. Rather, Henry discovers how to take those monumental decisions, how to invent that battle rhetoric, how to come up with that personalized language, and how to meet those challenges as they happen, moment by moment.

Sometimes he is even in a profound state of disrepair, as he is before the battle of Agincourt when, in a curious episode of slumming, he wanders through camp and meets people in the middle of the night. It's a continuous process of intellectual discovery for Henry, and so when he talks about the purpose and justification of going to war with the soldiers Williams and Bates, he's not teaching, but learning. "Methinks I could not die anywhere so contented as in the king's company; his cause being just and his quarrel honourable" (4.1.110–112), offers Henry. "That's more than we know" (4.1.113), replies Williams, and Bates continues,

> Ay, or more than we should seek after; for we know enough, if we know we are the king's subjects. If his cause be wrong, our obedience to the king wipes the crime of it out of us.
>
> (4.1.114–116)

In the conversation that follows, Henry is in part learning from himself, and in part, as always, he is learning from the people around him. The clarity and the simplicity that he finds on the morning of the battle of Agincourt, in the rousing St. Crispin's Day speech, is not easily arrived at: it is the result of having passed through all the preceding turbulence, difficulty, and discord.

One of the exhilarating things about the play is that we get to witness somebody discover who he is in the moment, and the fact that he's never settled draws us from one scene to the next. It can be a fantastically boring play if an actor comes on pretending to know exactly who Henry is already, since then there's nowhere to go. If we watch someone inching his way towards becoming a man, however, then we can go on the journey with him. Even at the very end, when Henry has emerged victorious after all the battles and we might expect him to be all-powerful and complete, there's his glorious confusion, modesty, and incompetence when he's faced with a woman. It's very beguiling. We have watched someone become a man, not just a king, and whether or not you choose to like him is irrelevant in comparison with the visceral pleasure of that watching. Hamlet, by way of contrast, is somebody you feel desperate for at the beginning because you see that he would have been your best friend in the world had the roof not fallen on his head. His journey is not that of him becoming a man: it's a journey from being a man in a state of great turbulence to being a man in a state of grace. Hamlet ends up in an exquisite, extra-human space which is a place of clarity, a state of insight, a position of understanding, a marriage of thought and action, a lack of worry for the self, and an awakened sense of care for others. No matter how much he has learned, Henry never quite arrives at such a state of grace, but with both characters the pleasure of getting to know them resides in their continuous, never-resting development as human beings.

It's a development we get to read about, we get to witness, and—if we have the chance to enter into a communal reality— it's also a development we get to participate in intimately. The ability to experience theatre in that way is not a dying ability; it's a returning ability. It's still very viable, and not only do I see it happening night after night at the Globe, but I see how potent it is in other shows, too, where there's the stripping away of a certain sort of cinematic realism, the rediscovery of simplicity in storytelling, and the invocation of the imaginative participation of the audience. If we offer ourselves up as part of the experience of the Muse that Shakespeare was invoking, then we get to go on the journeys with these characters, whether they be in the romance world of *Love's Labour's Lost*, the historical pageant of *Henry V*, or the transcendental tragedy of *Hamlet*. Even in this very image-saturated age, the idea that you can task people to see nothing and yet to create is just as powerful as ever.

Angus Fletcher

TOLSTOY AND THE
SHAKESPEAREAN GESTURE

———————

ANGUS FLETCHER is Distinguished Emeritus Professor of English and Comparative Literature at the Graduate School of the City University of New York. He is the author of several works of literary criticism, including *Colors of the Mind: Conjectures on Thinking in Literature, Evolving Hamlet: Seventeenth-Century English Tragedy and the Ethics of Natural Selection*, and *Time, Space, and Motion in the Age of Shakespeare*. He is the recipient of the Truman Capote Prize in Literary Criticism, a Guggenheim Fellowship, a Getty Fellowship, and a Senior Fellowship from the Endowment for the Humanities.

Every imaginative art has identifying poetic practices and skills, but few of these are more difficult to describe than the art of the drama. In this curious art form, action on a stage implies a psychological austerity of probable causes, supported by a suggestive, if never quite determining, rhetorical style of utterance. The system of causation remains, for good or ill, a theatrical illusion.

While in the West we can trace this illusion in many variant dramatic forms all the way back to ancient Greece, there is even today no artist more available and yet more mysterious than William Shakespeare, and if I have chosen what might appear a strange approach to his genius, its oblique view of verbal music is simply intended to illuminate meanings lying below the surface of the drama, that action hidden in plain sight, when immediately presented by the players. My sense is that although ethical themes and allegorical icons may legitimately occupy critical space, a rather deeper ethos resonates in the cryptic gestures and stray broken hints of what the poet once called "sweet silent thought."

The scholar's tradition of exact appreciation accompanies whatever stance we take toward any classic author, and the present case is hardly an exception. I once heard the late Professor Hyder Rollins, editor of the Variorum Edition of the Sonnets, quietly announce to us, his students—and we believed him—"Ladies and gentlemen, I have read everything ever written about these poems," as if the aim of critical judgment were to assimilate every single available prior response to the text, not solely to impose an authoritative collector's opinion, but more critically to bring to literature the wisdom of time itself. When the classic does survive, the critic is placed in the position of knowing or learning how just assessments of value may best be made.

The elite roll call of great Shakespearean critics—before our time one might instance Johnson, Hazlitt, Coleridge, and Bradley—along with hosts of lesser shining lights, may suggest that our values are mainly won from the perusal of essentially *positive* critical judgment. Suppose then, on the other hand, that we entertain a *negative* critical judgment instead; suppose that we question the economy of Shakespearean form; suppose that we entertain the familiar French judgment that the Elizabethan drama is fundamentally too chaotic in shape to provide any great aesthetic harmony—"too English," like the so-called English garden—would it follow that we had lost all aesthetic and linguistic citizenship? Suppose we agreed with Doctor Johnson's view that some late romances, like *Cymbeline*, are carelessly and irresponsibly improvised from start to finish. Or suppose we adopted meticulous editing with Ben Jonson, the poet's friend, critic, and colleague—would this mean rejecting the basic Shakespearean conception of drama? Doubtless not wholeheartedly, for all these critical voices and their countercurrents are united in a general chorus of praise and virtually universal approval of the poet's manner, since he speaks with the Voice of Nature, however the second term is defined, a chorus easily documented from virtually all the most powerful critical accounts, right up to the twentieth century.*

When we learn to differentiate values by critically studying those whose views are not absolutely at odds with our own, those values comprise our legacy, as we argue within, not radically against, that tradition.

By contrast, the approach I am taking in this brief foray is deliberately antinomian, much as if I were to argue (which I find an appealing project) that Thomas Rymer was not really so wrong when he said that *Othello* is "nothing but a bloody farce." The Shakespeare-hater I wish to agree with here (if only for the sake of argument) is a much greater man, Count Leo Tolstoy, whose celebrated attack on the poet's reputation will be my main critical exhibit.

This essay, entitled *Shakespeare and the Drama* (written around 1903; translated into English and published in America in 1906), is an angry, indeed enraged, manifesto, not only emotionally inflamed by moralistic fanaticism, but also in a de Manian sense paradoxically possessed of a blindness betokening profound insight. Along with other aspects of his genius, as Isaiah Berlin showed in *The Hedgehog and the Fox*, Tolstoy

---

* For example, even T. S. Eliot's neoclassic "objective correlative" makes an appeal to nature.

seems to have been unaware that such an attack could actually amount to a brilliant defense of that which is itself attacked. Choosing Tolstoy's essay on Shakespeare as a hinge for criticism, although I shall note only a small portion of its considerable length, is thus not so perverse as at first sight it might appear.

Yet even when we have adapted our critical perspective to assimilate the violently antithetical Tolstoy, we have yet another adjustment to make, before returning to the unwitting Tolstoyan insights.

Simultaneously we must recall the sudden transformation of Elizabethan dramatic technique wrought by the verse of Christopher Marlowe's two-part tragedy *Tamburlaine* (1587–1588). Marlowe was born in 1564, the same year as Shakespeare and Galileo, but his story ends untimely on May 5, 1593. Victim of a brutal assault, he is murdered at Deptford, some three miles below the center of Elizabethan London. As the tidal waters of the River Thames flood past Mistress Bull's Deptford tavern—like dark brown ale, one said—the poet's life as a secret agent for Sir Francis Walsingham takes its toll. There is a disagreement over some unknown decision—or is it about love?—with fatal consequences for our literature. Stabbed through the left eye, the first great master of Elizabethan dramatic verse falls down, his heart pumping streams of blood. Where his story of love and espionage ends we cannot say, where his poetry ends, we cannot say—like spying, the poem carries us always to another country, where we are forced to make our own critical judgments. This is of course a matter of vastly varying genres and styles in literature, for as Susannah Carson has reminded me, "Our representations of the human condition in our literature define how we see ourselves (we are what we read, at least to a certain extent) and determine who we will become, as individuals, as cultures, and as a species (for the imagination broadens the horizons of the human spirit)."

Before turning to the encrypted Tolstoyan defense of Shakespeare, let us recall the part played in all this by Christopher Marlowe, the doomed poet. All students of the English Renaissance are familiar with his short-lived Faustian poetic eminence. There is none to match him for titanic sonority; his blank verse lifts *Tamburlaine, Parts 1 and 2* (1587–1588) to a "translunary" height, as a contemporary said, virtually revolutionizing the poetic art of English drama in the Elizabethan and Jacobean periods. It is as if he taught the leaden-footed older Senecan tragedies how to sing.

Perhaps the most mesmerizing effect in *Tamburlaine* is the cadenced use of resounding proper names, as in the echoing line "And ride in triumph through Persepolis," or those repeated magical lines ending with the name of the beauteous queen, Zenocrate: "Ah fair Zenocrate! . . . — Divine Zenocrate!" In such lines, Marlowe achieved irresistible cadences whose transcendently powerful ritual rhythms declaim an elemental language. Nobility in tone is pushed almost beyond what language will permit, fearlessly risking monotony, as if the poet were a magically agile weight lifter, possessed by a ravenous *libido dominandi*. As Ben Jonson epitomized the effect in his marvelous elegy written for the First Folio (1623), what thereafter became known as Marlowe's "mighty line" established a standard for rhetorical panache, such that scholars like Harry Levin and David Daiches debated whether this driving, majestic iambic pentameter line was intended to substitute mentally for physical action occurring on the field of battle, or whether perhaps the rhetorical persuasion is itself a kind of interiorized physical force. Certainly on the Elizabethan public stage speaking the speech with sufficient brio and declamatory power to

launch language into a large open-air space was the most critical of all acting skills.

Along with these projecting vocal powers went a mode of
declaiming gesture. We would never associate these rhythmic
blank verse dramas with the subtle interruptive mannerisms of
modern naturalistic acting, which are influenced by the art of
cinematic close-ups—or so it seems at first appearances. The
great Elizabethan actor Edward Alleyn, declaiming speeches of
an unrelenting world-conqueror, could never have used a tic-
driven "Method acting" style, but instead thundered his way
forward, using expansive gestures and irresistible vocal grandeur.

If, however, rhetoric alone could seem to win the field of
battle in *Tamburlaine*, it remained for Marlowe's followers,
and Marlowe himself in his *Jew of Malta* (ca. 1589) and *Doctor
Faustus* (ca. 1589, or ca. 1593), to move in the opposite direction
toward a more naturalistic style, often intermingling satire and
comedy into the more ponderous Senecan tones of tragedy—-
exactly what Hamlet's players satirize. This evolution took place
not only in Marlowe's increasing subtlety of poetic line, but
even further in the plays Shakespeare was to write in the years
following Marlowe's sudden death. The chief Marlovian effect
remains one of monumentality, of dramatic utterance approxi-
mating an elemental material force, and precisely this grand
warrior code needed soon to be undercut by a more intimate
expressive practice. But how exactly was ruthless Marlovian
rant and eloquence to be tamed, if never quite overthrown?

My proposed antinomian angle of vision should illuminate
the Shakespearean response to this task, namely his delicate
treatment of dramatic presence, which underlies the invention
of what is called "character." Recall that we are looking for clues
to a denied, unacknowledged virtue in the poet. Tolstoy's savage

assault is a most curious performance, but it reveals a critical inversion of aesthetic judgment. A scornfully privileged aristocratic novelist of worldwide fame, Tolstoy states violently that Shakespeare's even more universal fame completely baffles and outrages him, claiming that only by contagious magical influence could such a renown be manufactured and promulgated by a crew of German Romantic critics, such that the poet's fame had never honestly earned its place on its own merits.

His dislike of Shakespeare, the great Russian maintained, "is not the result of an accidental frame of mind, nor of a light-minded attitude toward the matter, but is the outcome of many years' repeated and insistent endeavors to harmonize my own views of Shakespeare with those established amongst all civilized men of the Christian world." Nothing if not serious, Tolstoy now tells us he has recently reread the entire body of the playwright's work, and further acknowledges that his uneasy relation to Shakespeare has for many years troubled him in its radical opposition to the universal flood of an idolatrous, beatifying judgment—with his whole soul Tolstoy cannot believe in the supreme power and genius of his rival.

In our time, Tolstoy's critique of Shakespeare has been made famous by George Orwell's own essay "Lear, Tolstoy, and the Fool." Arguing that Tolstoy unconsciously identified his own aging despair with that of the tragic Lear, Orwell exposed, analyzed, and finally rejected Tolstoy's would-be "disagreement with the established opinion about Shakespeare." Tolstoy might have claimed he did not like Shakespeare, according to Orwell, but he was living, breathing, and thinking—intimately, inextricably—like a Shakespearean character. He had already lost himself in the world of Shakespeare, or as Borges's parable put it, the poet had become "everything and nothing," and since Tolstoy did not realize this, he of course would never be able to find his way out of his own pathological identification. The realistic novelist had created his own Elizabethan maze.

With literal accuracy Orwell gives us a clear sense of the novelist's savage polemic: Tolstoy finds the plot of *King Lear* "at every step to be stupid, verbose, unnatural, unintelligible, bombastic, vulgar, tedious and full of incredible events, 'wild ravings,' 'mirthless jokes,' anachronisms, irrelevancies, obscenities, worn-out stage conventions and other faults both moral and aesthetic." Tolstoy much prefers the "older and much better play, *King Leir*, by an unknown author, which Shakespeare stole and then ruined." The aging count could not tolerate seeing his own plight in the mirror the tragedy held up to his infuriated, glittering eyes.

With such pronounced denial or Negation (the Freudian *Verneinung*) at work, we may well ask what it is that is so bad about Shakespeare that we may say it shows us why he is in fact so good at his trade. The critical blindness is complex, to be sure, but it centers upon the task of representing or creating "character." In thinking about this and partly contradicting his own novelistic practice, Tolstoy virtually defines two antagonistic worldviews as expressed by the nineteenth-century novel in prose and the much earlier Renaissance verse drama. The following excerpt from *Shakespeare and the Drama* catches Tolstoy's general view, and from it we may follow his train of thought:

> However unnatural the positions may be in which he places his characters, however improper to them the language which he makes them speak, however featureless they are, the very play of emotion, its increase, and alteration, and the combination of many contrary feelings, as expressed correctly and powerfully in some

of Shakespeare's scenes, and in the play of good actors, evokes even, if only for a time, sympathy with the persons represented.

Shakespeare, himself an actor, and an intelligent man, knew how to express by the means not only of speech, but of exclamation, gesture, and the repetition of words, states of mind and developments or changes of feeling taking place in the persons represented. So that, in many instances, *Shakespeare's characters, instead of speaking, merely make an exclamation, or weep, or in the middle of a monolog, by means of gestures, demonstrate the pain of their position (just as Lear asks someone to unbutton him), or, in moments of great agitation, repeat a question several times, or several times demand the repetition of a word which has particularly struck them, as do Othello, Macduff, Cleopatra, and others. Such clever methods of expressing the development of feeling, giving good actors the possibility of demonstrating their powers, were, and are, often mistaken by many critics for the expression of character.*

The italics are mine, intended to accentuate Tolstoy's account of how Shakespeare creates character through technique. So far the methods are dismissively taken to be "clever," as indeed they are. But then Tolstoy continues, and here is the direct line of attack:

But however strongly the play of feeling may be expressed in one scene, a single scene can not give the character of a figure when this figure, after a correct exclamation or gesture, begins in a language not its own, at the author's arbitrary will, to volubly utter

words which are neither necessary nor in harmony
with its character.

A whole aesthetic attitude, not to mention a moral persuasion,
underlies this passage. There is a refusal of the actor's ironic
truth, according to which an actor must perfect his artifice in
order to seem as natural as possible. There is a desire to smooth
out, to sand down the surface, to deny ellipses, to regulate the
passions that in the nature of things will always break through
any formal conventions of polite or noble speech.

Tolstoy seems to be terrified by the magical lyric power of
Elizabethan dramatic verse, and even more seriously, he seems
to lack patience with poetic drama as a presentation and representation of real life in a real world (albeit sometimes belonging
to archaic periods of human history). In mocking the poet for
his celebrated "great talent for depicting character," paradoxically Tolstoy reveals a hidden reason for praising him! Naturalistic notions of storytelling do not easily tolerate that all
human acting is make-believe, that history is fiction of a kind,
as if we could never finally establish a test for honesty of heart
and accuracy of perception. In this domain Tolstoy strives to
maintain a puritan worldview, being unable to tolerate his own
willful, aristocratic position, where he must pretend to love
the peasantry. His puritanism extends to formal preferences,
so that he cannot make much of the cinematic fragments and
skipping jumps that make *Antony and Cleopatra* so wondrously
prophetic in form. Above all, he cannot stand the inmixing of
heightened poetic eloquence and realistic expression.

Let me put this simply: Tolstoy mocks Shakespeare and
condemns him to critical obloquy by instancing the very things
that made the playwright the master that he is: the play of
emotion, the play of fragmentary natural language, the play of

half-hidden human consciousness. In this light Shakespeare's mastery stems from a resolute refusal of puritan pinching, and therefore, like other puritanical aspirants to sainthood, Tolstoy cannot handle the doctrinaire artistic consequences of his own late-in-life asceticism, which he had already expressed in his lengthy treatise *What Is Art?* Above all, absolutely unlike Sir Toby Belch in *Twelfth Night*, he wants no more "cakes and ale."

The question of Shakespeare's genius nevertheless continues to haunt Tolstoy, and we cannot too frequently repeat the clinching sentence: *"Shakespeare, himself an actor, and an intelligent man, knew how to express by the means not only of speech, but of exclamation, gesture, and the repetition of words, states of mind and developments or changes of feeling taking place in the persons represented"*—again, the italics are mine, and by them I mean to suggest that, contra Tolstoy, life in its final meanings, not just in its passing throb of action, is ambiguous and vague.

"Changes of feeling" provide the key to the essential dramatistic question, for they always imply a gestural fragmentation of reason, a measure, as modern critics have at times argued, of turbulent breakdown in the evenness of declamatory texture. That is where the problem lies for Tolstoy: the fragmentation defines this human mobility of feeling that allows the artwork to approach closer and closer to an actual flux of experienced life—and not necessarily a cheerful flux. He wants dramatic causality to make too much sense, speaking a potentially dangerous music. "However unnatural the positions may be in which [Shakespeare] places his characters, however improper to them the language which he makes them speak, however featureless they are, the very play of emotion, its increase, and alteration, and the combination of many contrary feelings, as expressed correctly and powerfully in some of Shakespeare's scenes, and in the play of good actors, evokes even, if only for a time, sympathy with the persons represented." Yet to reject such sympathy was the novelist's main aim, as we learn from stories of living death, like "The Death of Ivan Ilyich" or "The Kreutzer Sonata," the latter a particularly critical instance of aesthetic terror, the fear of music and its contagious hallucinations.

Something very deep is blocking Tolstoy from savoring poetic freedom, a resistance so strong that he has no willing ear for the magical lyrical force of Elizabethan dramatic verse, when with its music it sets a character's emotions free upon the imagined stage of life, a life both inwardly felt and outwardly masked, as Hamlet tells his mother. His "inky cloak" (1.2.77),

> Together with all forms, moods, shows of grief,
> That can denote me truly: these indeed seem,
> For they are actions that a man might play,
> But I have that within which passeth show;
> These but the trappings and the suits of woe.
>
> (1.2.82–86)

Such unstable changes of feeling and stance are in their nature the counterpoint to Marlovian monumentality, and it was and remains the actor's task to articulate a fundamental gestural fragmentation or interruption of reason, without which interruption literature lives in the denial, as modern critics have at times argued, of human nature as it resists the evenness of declamatory texture.

In the interest of this resistance, prose passages of notable wit and weight abound in the tragedies as well as the histories and comedies, while throughout the canon the speaker's breaking of standard Marlovian pattern leads to an increase in "defective meters," where great lines of verse simply refuse a full pentameter accentuation. A two- or three-stress iambic

pentameter verse is almost a poetic contradiction, yet it raises
energy and forward motion; it permits many virtually inarticu-
late touches of verbal truth-telling. Such subversions of rigid
ritual consistency are the new Shakespearean ingredient that
makes mature Elizabethan drama so rich with broader human
truth, but they will trouble any author wishing to deny or disin-
herit an excessive identification with so many different persons.
Tolstoy is at home with his own hysteria, though when he finds
that in others he panics. Ivan Turgenev once observed of Tolstoy's "Kholstomer: The Story of a Horse" that one would have
had *to be* a horse in order to write it, yet exactly that intrusive
hysterical gift is what does *not* disturb Shakespeare, who finds a
way to express it cryptically, through the almost hidden verbal
particles and torn phrases of the actor's seemingly incoherent,
orally drifting gestures.

Few are the American actors who can hear, let alone enunciate, the Shakespearean mixture of blank verse and the fragmentary prose asides of broken feeling. We lose the roundness
of noble speech, that "English accent" so often mocked in earlier, less global days, but we know that in the original London
performances the spectators were also audiences listening for
the silent intonation, the cultural resonance whose effect is to
create what we call character.

Since, like an Elizabethan performance at the Globe Theatre, a break in the monotony of empty time seems essential
to our experiencing the life process, perhaps Tolstoy still may
have the last word, if only by perverse denial. What frightens
him in the spoken music thrills the groundlings and nobility alike, and while their theatrical history is socially complex,
individual character remains the issue. Ever since Clytemnestra
or Oedipus the King, this was always our destination in Western drama (though no longer in Brechtian epic theater), and

we now can see that character resides less in the grand Marlo-vian declamation than in the voicing of seemingly lesser truths and thrown-away half thoughts. Tamburlaine's rant gives him power, but these lesser private thoughts make us what we are, and Shakespeare knows how simultaneously to get them across. He knows how to let them flow alongside the scripted public speech, as if we single persons were at all times at least two people. It is our task as thoughtful readers and performers to learn how he achieves this duplicitous intimacy.

J. D. McClatchy

THE RED SCARF

J. D. McClatchy has published six volumes of poetry and three of prose, and edited dozens of other books as well. His most recent book is *Seven Mozart Librettos: A Verse Translation*, published by W. W. Norton in 2010. He has also written the libretti for operas performed at the Metropolitan Opera, Covent Garden, La Scala, and other leading houses. He teaches at Yale, where he edits *The Yale Review*. He is President of the American Academy of Arts and Letters and has previously received their Award in Literature, as well as fellowships from the Guggenheim Foundation, the National Endowment for the Arts, and the Academy of American Poets. He is also a New York Public Library Literary Lion.

I like a traditional calculus. A few books ago, I named one *Ten Commandments* and arranged it into sections of poems that broke against the Mosaic cliffs of "Shalt Not." Elsewhere, I have used the Four Seasons or the Four Temperaments. It has always seemed an advantage to edge up to the way the world for centuries has been fractioned. The ways we have portioned experience—the better to pause, focus, and compare its parts— are not merely a convenience, but a challenge. How does a late modern use the ancient viewfinder to make sense of today's accelerated time and emotional muddles?

So when, a decade ago, I had fixed on writing up a sequence of poems called "The Seven Deadly Sins," I approached it as I had other projects in the past—what had writers thought about it all before? Undertaking some research, I visited a religious bookshop and asked to see their "Sin" section. "No such thing," the clerk quickly and brightly responded. The idea of a moral absolute that deserves punishment—rather than an emotional glitch that requires understanding or therapy—apparently no longer exists, or sells. And later, as I went down the list of Seven, certainly *lust* was the quaintest to modern ears. In an age when everything is allowed, and has long since been quantified or theorized away as mere "compulsion" by the psychopatholo-gists, *lust* has come to seem the dinosaur of sins. In fact, the only references that came immediately to mind were the Bible and that notorious interview with Jimmy Carter . . . oh, and Shakespeare.

Which sin would describe what I did next? Pride? Envy? Sloth? I returned to the great Sonnet 129.

Th'expense of spirit in a waste of shame
Is lust in action, and till action, lust
Is perjured, murd'rous, bloody, full of blame,
Savage, extreme, rude, cruel, not to trust,
Enjoyed no sooner but despisèd straight,
Past reason hunted and, no sooner had,
Past reason hated as a swallowed bait
On purpose laid to make the taker mad,
Mad in pursuit and in possession so,
Had, having and in quest to have, extreme,
A bliss in proof and proved a very woe,
Before, a joy proposed—behind, a dream.
All this the world well knows, yet none knows well
To shun the heaven that leads men to this hell.

I took the last word of each line and used the words in a pastiche on the same subject—one that allowed my diction to jump from "Aristotle" to "fuck"; one that I wanted to sound tough but that probably comes off as dainty or squeamish; one that stressed the pathetic or maniacal aspect of things.

> The hallway's trail of clothes leads to that shame
> Compulsive indifference better names than lust.
> When Phyllis saddled Aristotle, who'd blame
> Philosophy for what wisdom should not trust?
> Dogged voluptuaries usually make straight
> For the very thing they have over and over had,
> Then vomit up the greedily swallowed bait.
> The stalker and nympho would drive each other mad.
> They want to be wanted yet be in control, so
> Each follows a mirrored logic to its extreme.
> That they cannot fuck the world is all their woe,
> To watch the pain and pleasure they cause, their dream.
> > Who can't be stopped or satisfied knows well
> > The little death whose legacy is hell.

In retrospect, of course, my poor squib only points to Shakespeare's mighty monument. The literary decorum of mine only highlights how *dramatic* his is—a lost monologue of Hamlet's, say—the very *voice* of repulsion and helplessness. It was foolish to have, mothlike, approached the flame. But doing so brought back to me the time I first immersed myself in Shakespeare.

It was 1966. I was a junior in college. For the two previous years, I had been besotted with Elizabethan England. The walls of my dorm room were covered with cheap posters of paintings by Nicholas Hilliard—languid young men in velvet doublets and ruffs leaning on trees. Renaissance lute music plucked by Julian Bream was endlessly on the turntable. Marlowe and Dowland and Hooker were touchstones. It took me two years to edge up to Shakespeare, and that summer I fell headlong over the cliff. I had signed up to attend courses at the Shakespeare Institute in Stratford-upon-Avon. There were daily lectures by the likes of Dame Helen Gardner and sessions with a graybeard tutor. But the headiest part of the experience was the chance to go, night after night, to performances by the Royal Shakespeare Company at their Stratford theater.

Peter Hall's riveting 1965 production of *Hamlet* was being revived, with David Warner's Hamlet and Glenda Jackson's Ophelia. I must have gone a dozen times, drawn to Hall's haunted, vaguely absurdist take on the play. It was less the philosophical slant than the dazzling melodrama that held me. When Hamlet and Laertes come to their duel in the last act, each stamped his feet in a box of—was it chalk? Something to steady his feet. As the fighting proceeded, intricate white footsteps crisscrossed the black marble floor . . . until Gertrude suddenly rose, staggered forward, and vomited violently across the pattern of confrontation.

But it was David Warner whom one's eyes never left. Dressed in a ratty black gown, he looked like what I was: a morose undergraduate. And around his neck, he wore a long red woolen scarf. What was meant to protect only seemed further to expose his vulnerability. Perhaps that is why I thought of that red scarf after I'd written the aping sonnet. When I wrapped Shakespeare around my neck—thinking it an act of homage when it may well have been merely parody—it led me to think of how infrequently that happens.

There have been poets—from Keats to Stevens, from Ted Hughes to Anthony Hecht—in whose lines you can hear Shakespearean echoes and ambitions. But it seems odd that Shakespeare, the language's premier poet, should have had almost no direct influence on his poetic progeny. It cannot be merely that his work no longer has a literary existence but has come also to have a scriptural one. After all, the King James Bible itself has been a decisive stylistic influence on writers since it first appeared, and Milton's influence can be sensed in the very fabric of subsequent poetic rhetoric. But Shakespeare—so rich and abundant, so confoundingly brilliant as stylist and seer—why is he the most conspicuous *silence* in the history of poetry in English? My own fool's errand aside—and of course it is merely words I stole, not the animating spirit of his indictment—perhaps most poets have felt that Shakespeare as an "influence" would devour anyone's attempt to appropriate him. Besides, who would know where to begin, or how? He stands by himself, and has not become his admirers.

Germaine Greer

SPRING IMAGERY IN
WARWICKSHIRE

———

GERMAINE GREER is an Australian author, academic, and social activist. She is Professor Emerita of English Literature and Comparative Studies at the University of Warwick. Her many works of literary, art, and feminist criticism include *The Female Eunuch*; *Sex and Destiny: The Politics of Human Fertility*; *The Change: Women, Ageing, and the Menopause*; *The Madwoman's Under-clothes: Essays and Occasional Writings*; *Slip-Shod Sibyls: Recognition, Rejection, and the Woman Poet*; *Shakespeare's Wife*; *The Whole Woman*; *The Beautiful Boy*; and *Shakespeare*.

The Australian household I grew up in had very few books. Most of them were special offers from the newspaper publishers who employed my father: *Fifty Famous Australians*, *The Complete Speeches of Sir Keith Murdoch*, *The Wit and Wisdom of Sir Robert Menzies*, that sort of thing. Being a nominally Catholic household we didn't have a Bible, but we did have a Shakespeare. It was a fat, red, cloth-covered, cheapo Victorian edition, printed in double columns and minute characters, enlivened by the occasional steel engraving. I began reading it when I was about nine, simply because I was bored and lonely and had read everything else in the house. At first I understood very little, though enough to ask my father in a spirit of pure mischief what a "whore" was. "What are you reading?" he shouted. "Shakespeare," said I demurely.

I went on reading the family Shakespeare for years, until the cadence of Shakespeare's lines had worn its way into my synapses and I spoke in iambic pentameter. When I got to the end of the last play I simply started again. By the time we were doing "Scenes from Shakespeare" at school I knew whole plays almost by heart, which endeared me to neither my fellow students nor my teachers. It never occurred to me to read *about* Shakespeare. If I was curious about something, about how Shakespeare felt about war, say, I simply read the plays again. The time came, however, when I had no choice but to read about Shakespeare because I had to draw up reading lists for my students.

I was appalled. Appalled by the sheer perversity of what my distinguished colleagues chose to believe about Shakespeare. Part of what they believed was that Shakespeare abandoned his wife and children in 1585 or thereabouts and then moved back into the marital home after twenty-six years or so of bachelor living in London. Odysseus was away from home for twenty years and when he got back only his dog could recognise him. Poor old Enoch Arden was unrecognisable by man or beast after ten. Only an academic could believe that Shakespeare slid seamlessly back into a household he had pretended he didn't have for more than a quarter of a century.

John Aubrey, who began compiling material for his "Lives" in the 1660s and continued doing so throughout his life, is one of the earliest observers to write about Shakespeare. "He was wont to go to his native country once a year," Aubrey reports. Aubrey is an unreliable witness to be sure, but when what he says is less remarkable than what is commonly believed, and not in the least titillating, we might perhaps entertain it as a possibility, rather than insisting on an impossibility. We know that Shakespeare had no permanent lodging in London, but moved from one rented address to another. We have disconnected documentary evidence of his residence in Shoreditch, Bishopsgate, Southwark, and Cripplegate. The one detailed account of his accommodation shows it to have been more like a student's room in college than the apartment of a successful theatrical entrepreneur.

Every year the theatres were required to close for the entire penitential season of Lent. This was forty days, nearly six weeks, when no play could be performed. Why pay rent in London when you are paying to keep up a big house in Warwickshire? The journey from London to Stratford took three days, so quick visits were out of the question, but a six-week break made worthwhile the six-days' journey there and back. Lent can begin as early as 10 February and end as late as 25 April; for the most part it coincides with early spring. Was Shakespeare usually in Warwickshire in the early spring?

The Winter's Tale is set in late summer, but when Perdita, decked like Flora peering "in April's front," laments that she has no flowers for her boy lover, she lists flowers of early spring:

> Daffodils,
> That come before the swallow dares, and take
> The winds of March with beauty: violets, dim,
> But sweeter than the lids of Juno's eyes
> Or Cytherea's breath: pale primroses
> That die unmarried, ere they can behold
> Bright Phoebus in his strength—a malady
> Most incident to maids: bold oxlips and
> The crown imperial: lilies of all kinds,
> The flower-de-luce being one.
>
> (4.4.136–145)

The exactness of this compressed account is wonderful. Daffodils do come before the swallows arrive, and take their chances with the often-cruel winds of March. Violets, primroses, oxlips, and fritillaries are all flowers of early spring. The name "flower-de-luce" was used for all kinds of irises including the native *Iris pseudacorus*, another flower of early spring.

Again, though the play is called *A Midsummer Night's Dream*, the action seems to take place in early spring. Oxlips and violets are in bloom on the bank where Titania sleeps, along with woodbine, musk roses, and eglantine (2.1.256–257). Puck would find it hard to "hang a pearl in every cowslip's ear" (2.1.15) in any other season.

> The cowslips tall [Titania's] pensioners be,
> In their gold coats spots you see,
> Those be rubies, fairy favours,
> In those freckles live their savours.
>
> (2.1.10–13)

The freckles on a cowslip are not so conspicuous that they can be seen by a casual passerby, but Shakespeare and his characters know them well.

In *Cymbeline*, the wicked Iachimo can describe the mole on Imogen's breast as "cinque-spotted: like the crimson drops / I'th'bottom of a cowslip" (2.2.40–41). Once again the play seems set in early spring, as the wicked Queen orders "the violets, cowslips and the primroses" she has gathered to make her potions to be carried to her closet (1.5.92). Arviragus thinks he will deck Imogen's grave as long as summer lasts, but his mind is turning on the flowers of the spring:

> . . . thou shalt not lack
> The flower that's like thy face, pale primrose, nor

The azured harebell, like thy veins: no, nor
The leaf of eglantine . . .

(4.2.277–280)

In *The Tempest*, Ariel's favourite resting place is a cowslip's bell
(5.1.94). Even butch Henry V thinks with nostalgia of the "even
mead, that erst brought sweetly forth / The freckled cowslip,
burnet and green clover" (*Henry V*, 5.2.48–49).

Shakespeare's favourite month would seem to be April,
when "wheat is green, when hawthorn buds appear" (*A Midsummer Night's Dream*, 1.1.188). No other month is mentioned
half as often in his works as showery, windy, sometimes unforgettably exquisite April.

O, how this spring of love resembleth
The uncertain glory of an April day,
Which now shows all the beauty of the sun,
And by and by a cloud takes all away.

(*The Two Gentlemen of Verona*, 1.3.85–88)

It takes no great leap of imagination to see Shakespeare in Warwickshire in April, because there is so much of Warwickshire in
April in Shakespeare.

There is yet another obvious fact about Shakespeare that
Shakespeare scholars refuse to accept. He wrote his plays alone.
He was not a collaborator. More ink has been expended on
laborious proofs that he collaborated on bits of *The Two Noble
Kinsmen*, and of *Henry VIII*, and that somebody else wrote
some of *Pericles*, than has ever been devoted to explaining the
singularity of his sole authorship of all thirty-six plays in the
First Folio. The writing of plays in the 1590s and the early sev-

enteenth century was like the writing of scripts for TV soap
operas and situation comedies today, though very much worse
paid. Shakespeare was not part of that system, but outside it. To
find space outside it, he needed to leave London.

At home in Stratford he would have been far from the distractions of the fastest-growing and already the largest metrop-
olis in Europe. He would have had peace and quiet, as well as
three good meals a day and his washing done. And when he
needed to stretch his legs he could regale his imagination with
the countryside, with Ceres's

> ... rich leas
> Of wheat, rye, barley, vetches, oats and peas;
> Thy turfy mountains, where live nibbling sheep,
> And flat meads thatched with stover, them to keep:
> Thy banks with pionèd and twillèd brims,
> Which spongy April at thy hest betrims
> To make cold nymphs chaste crowns; and thy broom-
>   groves,
> Whose shadow the dismissèd bachelor loves,
> Being lass-lorn: thy poll-clipped vineyard ...
> *(The Tempest,* 4.1.66–74)

Nothing about this evidence is conclusive. A poet may recol-
lect the early spring of his native countryside when he is far
away. For him to do so as vividly as Shakespeare does, however,
suggests that for him rural Warwickshire was not a place of irksome exile in the custody of an aging and unloved wife, but a
place his soul longed after, and where it eventually found peace.

James Proꝫek

WHAT'S IN A NAME? OR UNNAMED IN THE FOREST

JAMES PROSEK is an American artist, author, naturalist, conserva-
tionist, documentary filmmaker, and curatorial affiliate of the Peabody Museum of Natural History at Yale. His art has appeared in
galleries and museums all over the world, including the National
Museum, Monaco, and the National Academy of Sciences, Washington, D.C. His articles have appeared in the *New York Times* and
National Geographic, and his many books include *Trout: An
Illustrated History; Trout of the World; The Day My Mother
Left; Bird, Butterfly, Eel; Eels: An Exploration from New Zealand to the Sargasso of the World's Most Mysterious Fish;* and
Ocean Fishes. His film *The Complete Angler* won the George
Foster Peabody Award. He is currently filming a documentary
called *Secrets of the Eel* for the PBS series *Nature* and writing a
book about naming nature.

I have lately been obsessed by our legacy of naming nature,
which started with Adam's task to name all the creatures in
the garden (as the story goes), but is really as old as language
itself. Whenever I read Shakespeare, I'm struck by what seems
to be a deep preoccupation with the names of his own creation,
their beauty but also their failures. He uses names not just to
label, describe, and pin down, but to call them and their reso-

---

Special thanks to Harold Bloom and Kate Cummings.

nant power into question—and in doing so, to call into question the slipperiness of *all* language. Although he is universally
hailed as the master craftsman of this English language, part of
his possession of the language is illustrated by his recognition
of and very exploitation of its deficiencies.

Language is arguably our single most powerful invention.
Among human innovations—harnessing fire, domesticating
animals, agriculture—which have shaped the way our bodies have evolved (our dentition and loss of gorilla-like body
hair, for example), language has done more than any to actually shape the evolution of the human brain. As our language
became more complex, our brains adapted to accommodate
that complexity. John Hawks, a paleoanthropologist at the University of Wisconsin, has found that a host of hearing-related
genes evolved very quickly, over the last forty thousand years,
to receive and understand our increasingly complex language.
More than simply being useful, however, language can be beautiful, as it is in Shakespeare, for it can evoke emotions beyond
words or names themselves. Shakespeare knew, however, that
as with any tool, language can be used to create beauty or to
bludgeon and wound. Names can be helpful, allowing us to dis-
tinguish what is harmful from what is not, but they can also be
destructive.

* * *

Romeo and Juliet revolves almost entirely around the damaging
weight that a family name can carry, for the two lovers cannot shed the feuding that their surnames, Capulet and Montague, represent. If the essence of Shakespeare is in the lines
we remember most, Juliet's question is second only to Hamlet's when she laments, "O Romeo, Romeo, wherefore art thou
Romeo?" (2.1.80). She then famously elaborates,

'Tis but thy name that is my enemy,
Thou art thyself, though not a Montague.
What's Montague? It is nor hand, nor foot,
Nor arm, nor face, nor any other part
Belonging to a man. O, be some other name.
What's in a name? That which we call a rose
By any other word would smell as sweet,
So Romeo would, were he not Romeo called,
Retain that dear perfection which he owes
Without that title. Romeo, doff thy name,
And for thy name, which is no part of thee,
Take all myself.

(2.1.85–96)

This passage always puts me in mind of the lines in Wallace Stevens's poem "Man with a Blue Guitar," passionately wrought:

Throw away the lights, the definitions,
And say of what you see in the dark

That it is this or that it is that,
But do not use the rotted names.

Is it possible to go beyond our attachments to what something is called and see it for what it is? Is it possible to get to the essence of experience? Using a number or a symbol for a name is no answer. Are humans capable of shedding our attachments to language and stepping closer to pure nature, and pure emotion, or are our brains too much a product of what has been created by names?

The system we use to classify and order the natural world, created by the Swedish botanist Carl Linnaeus in the eighteenth century, is hierarchical, much like the feudal hierarchies that Shakespeare knew in his time. It puts creatures into categories with names like "kingdom," "phylum," "class," "order," "family," down to "genus" and "species." It is not so much a reflection of biological reality, but we still use it today, largely, as E. O. Wilson has said, "because it conforms to the manner in which the human mind works." We must name, we must put things into boxes, to file, to understand, because we are prisoners of our own invention.

In the course of my personal inquiry into how we name nature, I decided that I should start at the beginning and try to observe the process firsthand (I promise to return to Shakespeare). I learned skills of the biological investigator—shooting a gun, setting a net, skinning and preparing specimens—and found my way on a collecting trip, during which new species are discovered and named, with the Peabody Museum of Natural History at Yale University.

In the spring of 2010, I joined an expedition to Suriname (a former Dutch colony north of Brazil) led by Kristof Zyskowski, the ornithology collections manager at the Peabody. Our goal was to extend the known geographical ranges of tropical bird species; moreover, it was to look for new species of birds, record their vocalizations, collect (i.e., kill) them, skin them and stuff them with cotton, and preserve tissue samples for DNA analysis. We succeeded in this mission. During our three weeks in the mountains we found one new (previously undescribed) species of bird. The responsibility of naming the bird fell to Kristof, our resident Adam. The bird which he decided to call by the common name "Tepui antvireo," or *Dysithamnus surinamensis* (the males are a beautiful slate gray, the females a rusty brown) is the first endemic bird species known in Suriname. Naming a bird that didn't have a name before allows the bird to enter human reality;

it permits us to pile characteristics into that label, and to mount a conservation campaign to protect it (if necessary). But in observing the process of naming, I could not help but be struck by the fact that naming, even in this age of the eco-friendly, is largely about possession and control. We cannot name a creature unless we take possession of it, kill it, bring it home, and put it on a shelf in a museum as proof of its own existence.

I remember when I was a child my father taught me the names of the trees in our local woods. Before he did, the forest was like a beautiful green blob. Learning the names helped me compartmentalize the world and see things more clearly. Each name was like a file folder into which I could store the tree's characteristics: those of leaf size, color, and shape, or texture of the bark. As soon as I learned the word "sugar maple," whenever I spoke it, or heard it spoken, I saw the tree's shaggy bark, the shape of its leaves, the twisted branches of a particularly beautiful specimen that had gnarled itself over a stone wall by my favorite trout stream. The world was altered now, with the names—no less beautiful perhaps, but different.

As an unexpected aside of the Suriname trip, I was able to witness the colloquial process of taking possession of a forest through naming in camp. Our first task after being dropped off by helicopter on an unnamed mountaintop was to clear a space for our living area. The following day we began clearing trails to the river below us and the peak above us. Inevitably, without even intending to, we named the trails. The names highlighted the tasks and observations of daily existence—there was "the water trail," because it was the path to our water source, and "the bellbird trail," where we caught our first glimpse of the mystical white bellbird (one of our main target species). But cutting paths, like naming, limits our view, and our ability to make personal discoveries.

One way to shed the burden of a name and all that it represents is to keep renaming. The renaming of a character happens often in Shakespeare's plays; it is usually self-imposed and it usually happens in a remote place away from town, like a forest, or in the wilderness, or in a cave. Night can also be the occasion—more temporal than spatial—for characters to attain freedom from names and the structure of their world.

To rename oneself is a powerful action, as Romeo suggests when he answers Juliet:

> I take thee at thy word:
> Call me but love, and I'll be new baptized,
> Henceforth I never will be Romeo.*
>
> (1.2.97–99)

Wallace Stevens writes in "The Auroras of Autumn":

> This is nothing until in a single man contained
> Nothing until this named thing nameless is
> And is destroyed.

Throughout Shakespeare, men rename themselves to at least temporarily live other lives. Florizel assumes the name Doricles in *The Winter's Tale*, for example, to woo the shepherdess Perdita. At the beginning of *Measure for Measure*, the duke goes into disguise (on the pretense of travel) and leaves

---

* Marjorie Garber, in her critical volume *Shakespeare After All*, highlights the role of family names in the play. "Names in this play are, it seems, deliberately symmetrical [MON-ta-gue, CAP-u-let/RO-me-o, JU-li-et]. . . . In terms of prosody there is indeed no difference between 'Montague' and 'Capulet,' yet both are restrictive terms that, in the stubborn and recalcitrant feuding, cry out to be abandoned, superseded, or lost."

the governance of Vienna to his deputy. Throughout the play he is "undercover" as Friar Lodowick. Unlike Romeo, the Duke is powerful enough to effectuate his own makeover; naming is, essentially, a matter of power.

In her short story "She Unnames Them," Ursula Le Guin cleverly reverses Adam's dominion over the creatures in the garden. Eve unnames all the creatures that Adam has been asked by God to name.

> None were left now to be unnamed. . . . They seemed far closer than when their names had stood between myself and them like a clear barrier: so close that my fear of them and their fear of me became one same fear. And the attraction that many of us felt, the desire to feel or rub or caress one another's scales or skin or feathers or fur, taste one another's blood or flesh, keep one another warm; that attraction was now all one with the fear, and the hunter could not be told from the hunted, nor the eater from the food.

After unnaming all the animals, Eve hands her name back to Adam in protest and walks out of the garden. "Thank you," she says politely, "but I won't be needing this anymore."

Shedding the control of nature that men in particular imposed with language seemed to become a kind of subtheme of the feminist movement of the 1970s and '80s, as in Le Guin's story, but as usual Shakespeare got there first. How Shakespeare often provides new names and alternate identities to his women merits consideration. As part of naming is about possession and control, I often think that what Shakespeare's women find in a new name and identity is freedom from the constraints of the societies in which they exist.

My favorite instance of name change in Shakespeare is in *As You Like It*, in which Rosalind enters the Forest of Arden and masquerades as a young man: "I'll have no worse a name than Jove's own page, / And therefore look you call me Ganymede" (1.3.120–121). In *Twelfth Night*, shipwrecked on the shore of an unfriendly land, Viola says, "Conceal me what I am" (1.2.55), and undertakes the name and identity of a young man, Cesario. In *Cymbeline*, Imogen listens to Pisanio's advice—"I see into thy end, and am almost / A man already" (3.4.184–185)—and disguises herself as Fidele to survive in the wilderness and evade her jealous husband's order that she should be killed (and meets three nobles who have similarly assumed names to conceal their identities). In *The Two Gentlemen of Verona*, Julia disguises herself as a page, Sebastian, to follow her wayward lover, Proteus, to Milan. The heroine of *The Merchant of Venice*, Portia, disguises herself as a barrister named Balthasar to intervene in court and clear her lover's debt.

* * *

With new names come new opportunities and near-limitless potential. Juliet can be with Romeo if they both "doff their names"; Rosalind finds her way through banishment; Imogen survives the fatal censure of a male-dominated society. In most of the instances in which women take on a new name and identity (usually male) in Shakespeare's plays, they seem to do so to gain some control over their own lives and to evade possession. Alternatively, these gender and name changes could just have been practical devices for Shakespeare, used to build complexity and confusion. As boys played the parts of the women when his plays were first performed, perhaps it was easier and more theatrically convincing to have the boys masquerade as women playing boys for most of the play. Whatever his reasons, the results are moving.

Shakespeare usually chose the forest as the transitional place where this kind of transformation could happen. Contrasting the forest with the court would also have been an opportunity for major shifts in sets, and shifts in the minds of the audience. Sometimes the magic is real, as it is in the wilderness of Prospero's island; sometimes it is the magic of sheer glittering personality, such as that which Rosalind brings to the Forest of Arden; and sometimes the true source of the magic is dark and unknowable. One could even argue that in *Macbeth*, the forest (men disguised with branches) comes to Macbeth to take away his title and his name.

*   *   *

I have lately been in love with English author John Fowles's essay "The Tree," in which Fowles chastises language for its destructiveness in standing between ourselves and nature, causing a deleterious pattern that has in part led to our destruction of the planet. The forest is where his revelation takes place. It is where he can be stripped down and become nameless himself, doff his own name, all the while hoping not for the end to names and language but for an evolution to the point where language can achieve a description of something closer to reality.

> It is the silence, the waitingness of the place, that is so haunting; a quality all woods will have on occasion, but which is overwhelming here—a drama, but of a time span humanity cannot conceive. A pastness, a presentness, a skill with tenses the writer in me knows he will never know; partly out of his own inadequacies, partly

because there are tenses human language has yet to
invent.

This brings to mind one of my favorite passages from all of
Shakespeare, the words of the banished Duke in *As You Like It*,

> And this our life exempt from public haunt
> Finds tongues in trees, books in the running brooks,
> Sermons in stones and good in everything.
>
> (2.1.15–17)*

In the Duke's lines, Shakespeare may be making fun of the
romantic pastoral conceit that a life in nature is more free from
stress, but whether or not he intended this to be tongue-in-
cheek, for me the sentiment is real. Where in our modern world
can we achieve a place that has not been named, a forest interior
where the sound of the brook is the language we absorb? To this
end Aldo Leopold wrote in *A Sand County Almanac*, "Of what
avail are forty freedoms without a blank spot on the map?"

When we form that connection to nature, then it is very
true that language is eroded, at least partially, and that we can
hear the music of the earth directly and drink from the spring,
the source. With the journey to the forest, the girls' given names
are eroded too, a practical device, but their renaming of themselves is symbolic of the control they are taking back from their
fathers, their Adams.

---

* To me, these lines presage Izaak Walton's work of thinly veiled banishment
to the countryside, *The Compleat Angler* (in part, code for "the Complete
Anglican," in which he encourages Anglicans pushed out of their places of
work and worship by Cromwell in the seventeenth-century English civil
wars to practice Christianity as the early Christians, who were fishermen,
did by the shores of Galilee).

There is a place in all our lives where we can live beyond names, whether it be fishing, or listening to music, or running, or meditating. Perhaps Shakespeare (whose own name and identity, ironically, are still an enigma) is encouraging us all to find that place and to remember that we are just players coming and going in the great continuum of life.

David Farr

THE SEA CHANGE

DAVID FARR is an English playwright and screenwriter. He is Associate Director at the Royal Shakespeare Company, and he previously served as Artistic Director at the Lyric Hammersmith, Bristol Old Vic, and Gate theatres. The Shakespeare plays he has directed include *Coriolanus*, *Julius Caesar*, *The Winter's Tale*, *King Lear*, *Twelfth Night*, *The Tempest*, and *A Midsummer Night's Dream*, for which he won the Theatrical Management Association Award for Best Director. His plays include *The Queen Must Die*, *Night of the Soul*, and *Metamorphosis*; he has written for the television show *Spooks* and is coauthor of the film *Hanna*.

"I shall have share in this most happy wreck."
So says the reawakened Duke Orsino at the denouement of *Twelfth Night*. In this comedy of shipwrecked souls and lost hopes, the magical ending of reunion and love turns the sea from destructive terror into redeeming angel.

Perhaps no other natural force has this double edge. It rips you up, shatters you, spews you onto foreign lands without care or compunction. But nothing is so beautiful, so serene. Nothing but the sea reflects the mystery of our soul.

You can't be born in the United Kingdom much further from the sea than Stratford-upon-Avon. It seems unlikely that the young Shakespeare would even have seen it. How astonishing this is. The forests of Arden on which he based his forest comedies were just round the corner. But the ocean?

Shakespeare wrote at least six plays in which shipwreck is the cause of the comic chaos that leads ultimately to joyful or semi-joyful reunion. From one of his very first plays, *The Comedy of Errors*, to *The Tempest*, his last, a ship smashing on a shore is what causes all the drama to happen.

In *The Comedy of Errors*, two sets of twins are separated by a huge storm that severs the boat they are traveling on in two.

In *Twelfth Night*, twins again, this time male and female, are shipwrecked on the coast of Illyria, each believing the other dead.

In *The Winter's Tale*, a storm hurls the boat on which the baby Perdita is being carried onto the coast of Bohemia, and all the sailors are "sea-swallowed."

In *Pericles*, the Prince of Tyre is shipwrecked on the shore of Pentapolis, loses his daughter Marina (she of the sea), and searches the oceans to find her again.

And in *The Tempest*, a whole political family is shipwrecked on Prospero's isle so he can enact his project of revenge and reconciliation.

I have directed four of these plays, and am constantly drawn back to my favourite metaphor in Shakespeare—the sea storm as redemptive force.

> O, if it prove,
> Tempests are kind and salt waves fresh in love.
>
> (Viola, *Twelfth Night*, 3.4.304–305)

What these plays all need, in production, is that sensitivity to the sea. They need a strange, elusive poetry that renders fortune, fate, chance (all words constantly used in these plays) as agents of a greater power. That makes the sea both God and Devil, and that makes man tiny and vulnerable. In the *Twelfth*

Night I directed for the Royal Shakespeare Company, the world of Illyria was a hotel, its furniture seemingly drifting on an endless wave, the flotsam of human disappointment. What one learns in working on *Twelfth Night* is that the truly shipwrecked souls of this play are not Viola and Sebastian but the wretched inhabitants of Illyria, clinging to the driftwood of their dashed hopes as their world goes under.

But we are not just overwhelmed by the ocean, we also contain it. Orsino in *Twelfth Night* describes his passion as "all as hungry as the sea" (2.4.101). The human soul is an ocean tossed by storms of passion, deep and bottomless in its need for succour and nourishment. Storm is a metaphor for our own desires.

And then again we are just a drop of water. Lonely, lost, bereft. In *The Comedy of Errors*, Antipholus of Syracuse, searching for his lost twin, remarks:

> I to the world am like a drop of water
> That in the ocean seeks another drop,
> Who, falling there to find his fellow forth—
> Unseen, inquisitive—confounds himself.

(1.2.35–38)

This wistfully fluid elasticity of self is a great challenge for an actor. To contain at one moment oceans of passion, at the next to feel as tiny as a single drop, to sense the hugeness of fate and destiny, to be both agent and nothingness, this is at heart the challenge of Shakespearean comic acting. The comedy comes from these contrasts and conflicts. No one in Shakespearean comedy knows who the hell they are. All are in a constant state of becoming. And the performances need this liquid lightness, this unknowability, this strange magic.

As a director I always try to find a world that allows the space for this search, this poetic lostness and this strange mystery. No stage set can be as beautiful as the ocean. But that feeling is what must inspire the director of these plays. It's worth looking at the video of the great Italian director Giorgio Strehler's remarkable production of *The Tempest* to see the most heroic literal attempt to create the illusion of ocean on stage, without one drop of real water. It's something special indeed. Valiant and light.

In my production of *The Tempest*, I created an austere world of imprisonment, but with a magical "cell" of reflective glass, which like the sea contained and revealed its magic. In *The Comedy of Errors*, I was also drawn towards the use of reflective glass both to reflect the mysterious doubleness in the play and also to remind one of the reflectivity of water.

Only once in *Twelfth Night* did I use water itself. Somehow, water is not always the best metaphor for itself.

In the end, the literal is not what's important. You just need to find a world that justifies the internal poetic journey of loss and renewal as sung unforgettably by Ariel in *The Tempest*:

> Full fathom five thy father lies,
> Of his bones are coral made:
> Those are pearls that were his eyes:
> Nothing of him that doth fade,
> But doth suffer a sea-change
> Into something rich and strange.

> (1.2.460–465)

Say those last two lines slowly and you can hear the ocean. Can one seriously imagine that the man who wrote so stunningly of the sea never truly saw it?

Alan Gordon

LOOKING FOR ILLYRIA

———

ALAN GORDON is an American novelist and musical librettist. He
is the author of the popular Fools' Guild mystery series, which
includes *Thirteenth Night, Jester Leaps In, A Death in the
Venetian Quarter, The Widow of Jerusalem, An Antic Disposition, The Lark's Lament, The Moneylender of Toulouse,*
and *The Parisian Prodigal.* He is also a defense attorney with the
Legal Aid Society of New York.

For the last eighteen years, I have been writing a series of
mystery novels and stories with central characters borrowed from Shakespeare. No, not borrowed—unlike Huck
Finn, I never intended to give them back. Stolen? Too harsh,
and is it wrong to steal from a thief? Appropriated. I'll go with
that. It's a much nicer way of saying I stole them.

The principal characters are Feste the Fool and the Duchess Viola from *Twelfth Night,* put through many changes and
frequently renamed as they pass from one thirteenth-century
setting to the next, performing on stages high and low while
involved in espionage, intrigue, and murder. You might suspect
that, to write these tales, I must have come from a background
in medieval history which somehow incorporated a vast knowledge of Shakespeare and all things jesterial. The truth of the
matter is that I studied the Bard for one semester in college
as an English minor and had no courses in European history,
much less in medieval history. So, how did I get here?

* * *

It started with Mister Magoo.

Yes, I refer to the dangerously nearsighted little denizen of animation who blithely wreaked havoc wherever he went. In 1964, he appeared in a series of long-form cartoons, including an adaptation of *A Midsummer Night's Dream* in which he played Puck. Despite the presence of such notable Shakespearean actors as Morey Amsterdam and June Foray, I remember little of this depiction. But with every production I have seen since (twice on stage, twice on television, three movies), I invariably hear Jim Backus's voice gleefully saying, "Lord, what fools these mortals be! (*Pause.*) Hee, hee, hee!"

The "Hee, hee, hee" was Magoo's own interpolation. But I think Shakespeare would have liked it. I certainly did. I was five.

My first exposure to jesters? Danny Kaye, of course, in *The Court Jester*. "A jester unemployed is nobody's fool." And "The vessel with the pestle has the pellet with the poison, but the flagon with the dragon has the brew that is true." Say the last one fast. I can say it faster.

What was it about jesters that appealed to me? Not only to me—to enough of the world to keep them going throughout history? If you look back far enough, you'll find them popping up in every culture in every period in some form or another. (See Beatrice K. Otto's *Fools Are Everywhere* for a good compendium, although I knew about a couple that she didn't, proving how very pervasive they have been.) During their peaks of popularity, they were found entertaining Byzantine emperors, Catholic cardinals, English kings (and queens—Eleanor of Aquitaine had one), and the lowest of the low in the grungiest of taverns. They were both men and women—Linda M. Paterson in *The World of the Troubadours* notes that a 1204 Toulousan ordinance banned fools of both sexes from entering houses uninvited unless there was a wedding in progress. Apparently, there were enough of them there to be a problem worth regulating.

The European foolish tradition traces its origins to, among other things, the Rites of Dionysus in the Roman Empire and the pre-Christian celebration of Fasnacht in the region of Swabia near the Black Forest. The latter is of particular interest: a select group of villagers would gather to don masks and costumes in the middle of February, the coldest part of the year, and they would dance and lead revels to drive away the winter. And the winter would always go away, so we can see how important the revels were in facilitating that process. The group in each town responsible for this vital task was called the Narrenzunft, or Fools' Guild.

Christianity, as it so often did, took the "if you can't beat them, co-opt them" approach to Fasnacht. The celebration became Fat Tuesday, Mardi Gras, Carnival. But when the Church let the fools into the building, something unexpected happened. No, something *completely expected* happened if the Church had been paying attention and thinking about what they were doing. The fools started making fun of the Church.

The end result was the topsy-turvy Yuletime celebration known as the Feast of Fools. For centuries, the beginning of the Twelve Days marked an inversion of the ceremonies, as a boy was invested with an oversized miter, paraded down the aisle on an ass and called a bishop, while the sanctuaries were invaded by lewd dancing, ribald song, ridicule, and the occasional heaving of ordure. (That's a polite word. Look it up.)

Even when Pope Innocent III banned the feast, it persisted in one form or another for a couple of centuries. Ridicule has that kind of power. And its modern-day exemplars led me back to the Shakespearean fools. Starting with Mr. Magoo, as I mentioned. But others would come.

* * *

What liberated me during the deformative years of my youth were those foolish siblings the Marx Brothers, whom I discovered in fourth grade in my quest for Jewish hero-figures. Anarchy, anti-institutionalism, improvisation—heady things for this bookish, bespectacled, bumbling boy with low self-esteem. Attack authority! Skewer pomposity! Nothing is sacrosanct, not plot, not logic, not language. Especially not language, whether played with by Groucho with the skill of a juggling alchemist, mangled by Chico with unjustified confidence, or most profoundly abandoned by Harpo with puffed cheeks and a deranged glint in his eyes. "I know, you're a girl whose gotten nothing but dirty breaks. Well, we can clean and tighten those brakes, but you'll have to stay in the garage overnight." "I'da do anything for money. I'da kill for money. I'da kill *you* for money. Hey, what am I talking about, you're my friend. I kill you for nothing." *HONK!*

I needed comedy. I needed it to break through the barriers that kept me shy and nerdy. I needed structures to topple, meanings to stretch, bullies to deflect and deflate. One revelation after another—Chaplin, Keaton, *Laugh-In*, Woody Allen, Mel Brooks, the National Lampoon Radio Hour, Monty Python, Richard Pryor. And then came Stoppard.

Rosencrantz and Guildenstern Are Dead. I mean, Jesus, those guys didn't even make it into the Olivier movie, did they? Here was another thing you could do with an institution—you could turn it inside-out, transform major to minor and vice to versa. "Every exit is an entrance somewhere else." You could find comedy in the cracks, in the interstices, yet still make it tragic—the rational man trying to rationalize his way through an incomprehensible and uncontrollable situation. Yeah, that appealed to my adolescent self, the one that slapped on the greasepaint mustache and tailcoat for Halloween. And when I saw *Travesties*, that compounding of Joyce, Wilde, Dada, and senile reminiscence, I was a goner.

I needed to be Tom Stoppard. I needed to be a writer.

Shakespeare was at the heart of writing. The institution, the father of the Mother Tongue, the one that Czech-born Stoppard assailed while loving, whether by having two minor characters from *Hamlet* play at questions, or by having Tristan Tzara cut a sonnet into its individual words, pull them out of a hat, and read them as a fractured love scene.

I wanted to have fun like that too.

Swarthmore College, junior year, spring semester. At long last, Shakespeare: The Seminar! All of the plays in thirteen weeks. Seven of us sat in the living room of Professor Susan Snyder once a week for four hours plus. No dry academic, she, Professor Snyder treated Shakespeare as something to be staged, not just read. Between the papers presented and the snacks consumed, she would regale us with tales of productions seen—the Jonathan Pryce *Hamlet*, the Sir Antony Sher *Richard III*. She listened as well as she spoke, and took our proposals seriously.

I studied all of it, but the fools more than anything. They fascinated me. Lear's unnamed Fool: Why did he stay? And then why did he leave? Touchstone: Why did he stoop to marrying a shepherdess? Feste, Feste, Feste—what did he know about everyone else that allowed him to push their buttons so well?

Marian Bock sat next to me in that living room. She was a year ahead of me, and had directed the first *Twelfth Night* I had ever seen, in Bond Hall in 1978. They put on the play with a budget of maybe fifty bucks. This was a production that made virtues of necessity, where the "identical" twins were played by a blonde and a brunette. Marian introduced them before the performance began and said, "I just want you to know that when these two dress alike, they look so much like each other that you can't tell them apart, okay?" And we happily assented. When they appeared wearing matching red T-shirts, disbelief was willingly suspended. Illyria was now reduced to a fifteen-by-ten-foot space. The grated fireplace became Malvolio's jail; the overstuffed couch was just long enough to hide the three conspirators; and gallumphing through it all was a tall, lanky, mustachioed young man named Fred Daly playing Feste, sending quips out of both sides of his mouth in a manner that was Grouchoesque and Shakespearean simultaneously.

For me, that production began a love affair with the play and with jesters that has lasted to this day. A licensed fool! The power to mock freely, because power needed to be freely mocked to remain legitimate. I got it at last.

* * *

Marian and I were the most theatrically oriented of the group in the seminar, I having directed my first play (by Stoppard!) a semester after her *Twelfth Night*. We would toss out production ideas, and continue the discussions as we walked back to campus afterward. It was during one of these walks, while we were tossing silly scenarios back and forth at each other, that I came up with the notion that the three jesters were one and the same, a master fool who kept moving from gig to gig while changing his name, who then died in Elsinore and left his jester's scepter to be passed on to Portia, where it turned up in the silver casket in *The Merchant of Venice*.

A silly idea, yet it left me with an image of Feste, sitting at the end of the bar in a tavern—and then a man walks in and says, "Orsino is dead."

I could not shake that image. I wanted to write that story. But I was twenty, and not ready to write it yet. I didn't have the skills, the tools, the knowledge. I thought about making it a fantasy, a battle across a vast Shakespearean landscape, with my name-changing jester pursuing a villain who would also shape-shift, becoming Edmund, Jacques, Malvolio.

After thinking about that idea, I decided that I really hated it. It was too cutesy, too precious. Fantasy was not where I wanted to be, so I put it aside. In fact, I put writing aside in a burst of pragmatism and became a lawyer. But a public defender. Anti-institutionalism! Improvisation! A jester in a different kind of court.

The writing began in earnest ten years later, following my premature midlife-crisis-precipitating thirtieth birthday. Some short stories sold. The first completed novel did not, will not, don't ask to see it, it's terrible. It was 1993. I was thirty-four, walking across the footbridge over the railroad tracks and wondering what to write next when that old image, which had been hibernating patiently at the bottom of the sludge in my subconscious, floated up and attached itself to the forefront of my brain with an industrial-strength nail gun.

Feste sits at the end of a bar. A man walks in and says, "Orsino is dead."

A mystery. It had to be a mystery. Realistically set. A historical mystery. A medieval mystery!

Which, given my aforementioned complete lack of European history, let alone medieval history, meant that I was going to have to learn it just to write the book. This was going to be fun.

I studied medieval history, and I studied fools. Precious vacation days were spent in the Main Reading Room of the New York Public Library, notebook filled with—well, notes, with inspirations jotted down into the margins. My first general history of the period was *The Age of Faith*, by Will Durant, a thousand years in a thousand pages. Then I got specific.

I was looking for Illyria.

Illyria, the country in which *Twelfth Night* takes place, was originally Illyricum, the old Roman province where they pensioned out the soldiers lucky enough to survive to that age. It would become Dalmatia. What happened in Dalmatia that could give me an overall frame for my story? I trolled through the histories and learned about the invasion of the city of Zara in the beginning of the thirteenth century. Zara was a trading rival of Venice which was leveled by the armies of the Fourth Crusade, who had been carried by a Venetian fleet en route to besieging Constantinople, another Venetian rival and a Christian city itself. All of this was a deadly diversion from the original purpose of the Crusade—to retake Jerusalem from the Muslims.

A cynical, powerful enterprise, ripe for mockery. Only this would be mockery in service to a higher purpose. I made Feste part of a Fools' Guild, a group who worked behind the scenes to secure peace while using their status as entertainers to gain access to every level of society. This was also during the reign of Pope Innocent III, the man who banned the popular festival that mocked the Church: the Feast of Fools, which culminated on—all together now!—Twelfth Night.

I had found my way into Illyria. I took *Twelfth Night* and inverted it so that it became a tale told by a fool, but a wily, brilliant fool. I made Feste the detective, the master manipulator, the juggler of events. I killed off Orsino fifteen years after the end of the play, brought Feste in to investigate, and lo and behold, *Thirteenth Night* was born. Between the research and the writing, it only took me three and a half years, and then it took another two to sell it. But sell it I did.

I had finally become a published novelist, thanks to Shakespeare and all those other people. And one cartoon character.

During the rewriting process, my editor at St. Martin's Press asked me, "So, what's the next book about?"

Immediate panic. I had written *Thirteenth Night* without thinking "series," although I left the ending with some possibilities of moving on. But I had not become an improvisor in my life for nothing. I quickly responded, "Feste goes to Constantinople to investigate the disappearance of all of the city's jesters."

Based upon that, I received a contract for two more books.

I remember thinking, "What a wonderful scam! They're giving money for things that do not exist." Then the reality sank in. I was going to have to actually write them, because I did not want to give the money back. So, back to the history I went.

Now, the next three books were not drawn from Shakespeare, but from where the history was leading me. I had a terrific central character and a fascinating, terrible time for him to play in. I decided to have Viola join him as his partner and apprentice fool, and off to Constantinople we went, staying just ahead of the Venetian fleet. But before I began, I laid out one-sentence premises all the way through Book Five—and I knew that the fifth one would have to involve *Hamlet*.

I wasn't quite sure who Feste would be in *Hamlet*, but I started seeding clues throughout the earlier books. As of the second, *Jester Leaps In* (and jazz aficionados will appreciate the pun in the title), we learn that he was of Danish birth. The series marched on. In the third, *A Death in the Venetian Quarter*, the fleets and armies of the Fourth Crusade arrived to besiege Constantinople. The fourth, *The Widow of Jerusalem*, took Feste back to a story from the Third Crusade, found in a footnote to history involving the death of a dwarf.

And then I took a deep breath and started researching *Hamlet*, its source material, and twelfth-century Danish history. This was to become Feste's origin story.

An Antic Disposition remains the most challenging thing that I have ever written, and maybe that I will ever write. It takes a look at the *Hamlet* story based upon its first written form, as found in the *Gesta Danorum* by the thirteenth-century Danish cleric Saxo Grammaticus, then transplanted for my purposes to the tumultuous, turbulent times of the Danish civil wars of the mid-twelfth century. A fool, Terrence of York, is sent by the Fools' Guild to the southern border city of Slesvig to work his way into the wooden fortress of the local ruling family. He ends up befriending a two-year-old boy named Amleth, who mispronounces "York" as "Yorick."

What's in a name, right?

*   *   *

Now that I have eight books and four short stories devoted to these characters, it is not surprising that I have taken a proprietary interest in all things foolish, particularly of the Shakespearean kind. *Twelfth Night* cannot pass through New York without my checking out the production. Including that heady Swarthmore opening, I have seen six live productions; the brilliant 1980 BBC production with Felicity Kendal, the greatest of all Violas, and Alec McCowen, the greatest of all Malvolios; and Trevor Nunn's 1996 film. Add in a handful of Touchstones and a passel of Lear's Fools, and we have a dozen or so portrayals of these witty pranksters.

And speaking on behalf of Shakespeare's fools, I would like to register a complaint.

Why aren't they funnier?

So many of these productions take the fool and make him a melancholy man. Yes, that is one way to play it. Two of the three Shakespearean fools find themselves in melancholy circumstances, accompanying their masters into exile. Look! The clown is weeping! O paradox! O tragedy! O despair!

It has become a cliché. It seems as though each director during the rehearsal process said, "Darlings, I've had an interesting idea. Why not make the fool be, you know, that thing that's the opposite of funny? Wouldn't that be interesting?"

Maybe once. But it would be more interesting to take centuries-old humor and make it live and laugh again. Not the easiest thing—comedy from different eras doesn't always travel well. There was a brilliant sketch by the Canadian troupe from *Second City Television* with a pair of over-earnest actors offering a collection of Shakespeare's greatest jokes, all of which depended upon Elizabethan wordplay that failed to tickle the modern funny bone in any way, shape, or form. The Flying Karamazov Brothers, in their all-juggling circus production of *The Comedy of Errors* which featured Shakespeare himself as a mute character, offered similar commentary in the Syracusans' "dry basting" bit, failing so miserably to amuse that they had to point to the author and complain, "Well, *he* thought it was funny."

As the famous and probably apocryphal story goes, the fill-in-whichever-notable-nineteenth-century actor upon his deathbed said, "Dying is easy. Comedy is hard." But it is well worth the effort. When the going gets tough, the fools should get funny. The play and the audience need some comic relief, and if the fool is just as glum as everyone else, then we've lost all hope. Yet the melancholiness of the fool persists in modern Shakespeare.

I think the problem lies with the casting. They keep casting actors, people with serious Shakespearean training, with some Method thrown in. Many of these actors are fine in comedies, but they aren't fools. We need clowns—people who can tumble and extemporize, mug and do funny voices. There are people who have done both—Robin Williams studied at Juilliard with John Houseman while street-miming on the steps of the Metropolitan Museum of Art. In his early stand-up, he would improvise mock-Shakespearean scenes, complete with iambic pentameter. Why has no one ever cast him as Feste? David Strathairn trained at the Ringling Bros. and Barnum & Bailey Clown College, yet has only played Shakespearean kings. Another missed opportunity.

Bill Irwin, who finally played his first Shakespearean fool in 2011, once observed, "A comedian says funny things; a comic says things funny. I'm a clown." A fool should be all of these, while singing, juggling, and playing instruments. Normal acting training doesn't encompass this. I am not saying that the fools cast in Shakespeare are never funny—no doubt there are productions all over the world where actual funny people play them. But in my experience, I can only name two Festes that filled the bill—although Sir Ben Kingsley's sly, omniscient, PTSD war vet resonated with what I was trying to do with Feste in my novels.

The 1989 New York Shakespeare Festival production of *Twelfth Night* in Central Park featured a cast of stars who seemed to be acting in different plays at the same time. Mary Elizabeth Mastrantonio was a workmanlike Viola; Michelle Pfeiffer a luminous Olivia; Jeff Goldblum a disastrous Malvolio. The most surprising bit of casting was Gregory Hines as Feste. Hines was the greatest tap dancer of his generation, having come up with his father and brother in an act called "Hines,

Hines, and Dad." I first saw him in the musical *Eubie*, where his solo number elicited applause so many times that he could confidently yell out, "Not yet!" when it first happened, followed by "Soon!" and, finally, "Now!" He showed decent comedy chops in Mel Brooks's *History of the World: Part I*, but I never expected the range he showed in *Twelfth Night*.

His Feste could sing, no question. But he brought to the role a show-business savvy and the timing of a comic dancer. His encounter with Viola (in the guise of Cesario) in Act 3, Scene 1 was accompanied by a snare drum, which he played expertly (Viola: "Dost thou live by thy tabor?") while playing *her* expertly ("No, sir, I live by the church" [3.1.1–2]). I have never seen that scene performed so clearly with the implication that Feste knows full well what she really is—a woman disguised as a page, in love with her master. "Who you are and what you would are out of my welkin" (3.1.40–41), he said as his drumsticks headed toward her crotch. Hines and Pfeiffer redeemed what otherwise was a mishmash of a production.

The single greatest and funniest Feste of my life was David Patrick Kelly in the 1998 Lincoln Center Theater production. A diminutive man, he scampered about the vast stage, and sat in with the band playing the mandolin and a large bodhran drum. Scampering was his signature pace—never have I seen someone scamper so much. He played every scene as if he was improvising the dialogue on the spot, taking what was given to him by both words and situation. You saw why this man would become a fool—he delighted in making something out of nothing, and yet he was possessed of an apartness from the mere mortals who stumbled blindly through a folly that only he saw fully. His fool was indeed everywhere, and it was fitting that he would have the last word, and that the last word be sung.

So, I wait for more productions, hoping for the perfect

one that is better than the one that plays in my head. It may never happen. It may not even be possible. We are imperfect, and Shakespeare captured us in our imperfections as well as anybody ever has.

* * *

I continue to write. Touchstone made a cameo appearance. I hope to get to the *Lear* book someday, and Feste has had a daughter with Viola whom they have named Portia. I have interesting plans for when she grows up, if time, opportunity, and inspiration permit me the privilege to keep writing about them.

Here's hoping, and, as Feste would say, "Wit, an't be thy will, put me into good fooling!" (1.5.25).

Hee, hee, hee!

Eleanor Brown

SHAKESPEARE'S SIBLINGS

ELEANOR BROWN is an American author. Her debut novel, *The Weird Sisters*, is a *New York Times* and international bestseller.

The fact of our families is this: for better or for worse, they have formed who we are. Whether we are best friends with our relatives or we do not speak at all, we are who we are because our families helped to make us that way.

I am the youngest of three sisters, which means that by the time I came along I didn't have much choice in which role I would take on in our family. In siblinghood, in friendships, in *Charlie's Angels*, roles are distributed carefully, one to a customer: the smart one, the funny one, the quiet one, the beautiful one. Both of my sisters are beautiful and smart, and because they had already divided those roles between them, I had only a few obvious options left. I began defining myself immediately by who my sisters were.

Maybe because I was first introduced to *The Taming of the Shrew* when my eldest sister played Bianca in her sixth-grade class production, it is Kate and Bianca Minola I think of most often as examples of the curious way siblings battle out their places in a family. I wonder how they worked out their not-so-peaceful détente—whether Kate had been, well, so *Kate* from the start, leaving Bianca to cast about for who she was going to become until she settled on being beautiful and compliant. Or was Kate at one point a pretty peacemaker, until Bianca came along and proved herself better at the role?

I spent a great deal of time when I was growing up looking at the deals my sisters and I seemed to have made in the roles we chose. But at the time, I didn't understand it in terms of Kate and Bianca, or in terms of Shakespeare at all. I came to Shakespeare late in life. I read *Romeo and Juliet* when I was in ninth grade, as you do, and I thought it was a snooze. (It's still among my least favorite plays.) I read *Macbeth* in tenth grade, and that was a bit better: an aspiring actress at the time, I couldn't think of anything more fun than playing Lady Macbeth. And then I didn't read or see any Shakespeare at all until graduate school.

Studying abroad in Oxford, I was determined to take advantage of everything England had to offer. And so I saw *The Tempest* at the reconstructed Shakespeare's Globe in London, Caliban leaping off the stage and running among the groundlings. The Royal Shakespeare Company in Stratford-upon-Avon staged a production of *As You Like It* that began in black and white—costumes, set, props—and ended in vibrant, glorious color so happy I could hardly breathe for the joy. An open-air production of *A Midsummer Night's Dream* on the campus of one of the colleges in Oxford featured Titania and Oberon arriving by boat, skimming down a stream that wound past the seats and the stage, until they alit beneath the trees.

I was in love.

The difference was clear, and I finally understood. These were *plays*. That seems an incredibly silly epiphany to have, and yet it was an incredibly important one. I was introduced to Shakespeare, as most people are, as literature to be read. And now, having seen tremendous actors performing Shakespeare (not only in England but also in the United States, for instance at the Folger Theatre), I know that in the hands—well, the mouths—of the right actors, the thing that keeps Shake-speare at arm's length for most people, the language that, at first glance, is so dense and archaic, blooms into precise, beautiful clarity.

It was that love of the language that drew me to Shake-speare when I wrote *The Weird Sisters*, though I did not ini-tially intend to write a book that incorporated his work at all. I wrote the book because I was trying to answer questions that I was struggling with, like what it means to be an adult, and why it is so difficult to move away from the roles that our families give us. But as I wrote, the more I thought about families, the more I found related topics I wanted to explore—the seismic shift as children become caregivers, the way our parents' mar-riages (both happy and sad) affect us, the uncomfortable code-switching that can happen when we are one person outside of our family and another inside it, and the curious diversity in the ways families communicate.

It was this last issue, family communication, which first led me to introduce Shakespeare into the novel. Families have their own languages, consisting of nicknames, mispronunciations based on a child's adorable sayings, and references to family history. They also have their own ways of communicating—some families share too much, others too little. Some families are serious in the face of crises or pain, others have to laugh their way through.

So as I created the Andreas family, I introduced a father whose academic expertise in Shakespeare has shaped the way this fictional family communicates. The father in particular, but each of them, will, especially when things become emo-tionally difficult, quote Shakespeare rather than speak for him-self or herself. In telling his daughters that their mother has been diagnosed with cancer, Dr. Andreas uses lines from *Titus*

Andronicus: "Come, let us go; and pray to all the gods / For our belovèd mother in her pains" (4.2.46–47). When one of the sisters somewhat enviously admires another's engagement ring, she quotes *The Merchant of Venice*: "I gave my love a ring and made him swear / Never to part with it" (5.1.180–181). Like any other family, the Andreas family has a private language, but their vernacular consists largely of someone else's words.

Shakespeare seemed to be the right choice for a number of reasons. In addition to the breadth of topics covered in his writing, he has a cultural currency that no other writer enjoys. Though most readers immediately seize on the "weird" portion of the title—who, after all, doesn't have a weird family?—and miss the Shakespearean allusion, the moment I refer to *Macbeth*'s witches, the three sisters of Fate, there is an instant recollection. Even if you had never read or seen *Macbeth*, if I said "Double, double, toil and trouble," you would likely recognize that as Shakespeare. His works seep in via cultural osmosis.

Once I introduced the father and decided he would be a Shakespearean scholar who spoke through quotations, the rest of the Bard's impact fell into place. I knew I wanted to have three siblings in the family, since that would allow me to explore the three major birth order roles: the oldest/only, middle, and youngest. I thought of Kate and Bianca again, and realized that the beautiful second daughter in my fictional family would, of course, have to be named Bianca. The favorite third, the "baby" in this family of three daughters, had to be Cordelia, from *King Lear*. The oldest daughter's name eluded me for a long time, but I thought of the heroine in *As You Like It*, and the lengths she went to in order to make absolutely sure that Orlando loved her, and I knew that Rosalind would be her name.

The stories of the Andreas sisters in my novel are not the stories of the women in those plays, but those women did help

me form the sisters' templates. In the same way that Shakespeare's language has seeped in to our culture, so have his
characters—Hamlet's existential angst, Beatrice and Benedick's
verbal sparring, Romeo and Juliet's starry-eyed, star-crossed
love. I built each sister's personality on her birth order's ste-
reotypical traits—the controlling, driven eldest; the social,
attention-seeking middle; and the charming, irresponsible
youngest—and then added a dash of her namesake's personality: Rosalind's love of love, Bianca's identity-driving beauty,
and Cordelia's devotion to her father.

As I wrote, I also came to realize how very much Shakespeare had to show us about sibling relationships. The process
of searching for quotes for this family so steeped in Shakespeare
had me constantly stumbling across siblings, or siblinglike relationships, in the plays: Ophelia and Laertes in *Hamlet*, Prospero
and Antonio in *The Tempest*, Hermia and Helena in *A Midsummer Night's Dream*, Richard and Edward in *Richard III*, the two
sets of twin brothers in *The Comedy of Errors*, Beatrice and Hero
in *Much Ado About Nothing*, Henry and the Dukes of Gloucester and Bedford in *Henry V*—the list seemed to have no end.

In particular, the rivalries between Kate and Bianca, and
between Cordelia and her sisters, Goneril and Regan, were on
my mind as I wrote *The Weird Sisters*, because they are such
excellent examples of the complexities of sibling rivalry. As a
woman I cheer Kate's stubbornness, but as a younger sibling
I resent the way she selfishly blocks her younger sister's way,
while at the same time I appreciate that Kate seems to believe
that she is actually protecting Bianca. The immature, knee-jerk
little sister in me loves that Cordelia is the favorite, but objectively I feel sympathy for her older sisters. What would it have
been like to grow up in a family where you were, so clearly, *not*
the favorite?

There's a curious saying to describe close friends: "They're as close as sisters!" or "They're just like brothers!" This strikes me as not just curious, but ridiculous. For as many sets of siblings as I know who get along famously, I know three sets who can barely stand each other. It might be more accurate to look at siblings who are close and cry, "Why, they're just like friends!" I think of Rosalind and Celia in the Forest of Arden in *As You Like It*, and their proclamations of sisterly love . . . but they are *cousins*. If they were sisters, Shakespeare could have had them at each other's throats, like *Lear*'s Cordelia and company. In fact, Rosalind and Celia's fathers, the brothers Frederick and Duke Senior, *are* at each other's throats, given that Frederick has stolen Duke Senior's title and lands, and then additionally banishes Rosalind, Duke Senior's daughter.

The point is, siblinghood is contentious. We siblings war for attention, for objects, for family roles and recognition. The adults in our lives do not make it any easier—a younger sibling walking into a classroom with a teacher who taught his or her predecessor is highly likely to be greeted by a set of expectations more appropriate to that older sibling than to the younger. And if in any way our parents set us up against each other, they are dooming us to fail. I would like to think that Signor Baptista Minola had nothing but the best of intentions to protect both daughters when he decreed that Bianca could not marry until Kate did, but the end result is one sister's standing in the way of the other's happiness, and we siblings are capable of setting that situation up all on our own. From the moment we enter onto our family's stage, looking for the part we will play, we are defining ourselves in terms of our relations.

I speak to a lot of book groups and often someone will mention how little they know about Shakespeare, or their anxiety when they first realized the novel contained allusions to the plays. And when I ask, they tell me, with relief, that it wasn't difficult at all. Nothing makes me happier than this, in hoping that I was part of breaking down the wall that so many of us have built against Shakespeare. It helps, I think, that I am not an expert, but a fan, who saw in Shakespeare's plays what people have been seeing for centuries: ourselves, reflected back. I saw our family conflicts, the burdens of our names, the way we communicate—all the themes I wanted to explore in *The Weird Sisters*, threaded through the plays.

Though I didn't find the answers to all the questions I wrote the novel to address, I did make peace with a number of them, and incorporating Shakespeare played a part in that. Seeing Goneril and Regan's jealousy of Cordelia, the way Kate and Bianca play with their family roles, Rosalind and Celia's devotion, and Frederick and Duke Senior's conflict led me to realize that even if the ways our families influence and shape us can be uncomfortable, finding the same moments of discomfort in these stories lets us know we are not alone.

Eve Best

"A STAR DANCED"

EVE BEST is an English actor. She was awarded an Olivier for the title role in *Hedda Gabler* and a London Critics Circle Award and Evening Standard Best Newcomer Award for *'Tis a Pity She's a Whore*; she received Tony Award nominations for *The Homecoming* and *A Moon for the Misbegotten*. In addition to performing in the Sheffield Crucible Theatre's *As You Like It*, she has performed in the Globe Theatre's *Macbeth* and *Much Ado About Nothing*. Her TV appearances include *The Shadow Line*, *Vital Signs*, and Dr. O'Hara in *Nurse Jackie*. She played Wallis Simpson in the film *The King's Speech*.

At the beginning of last year I was in India. Sitting at breakfast in a B and B in Delhi, waiting to catch my plane home, I found myself in conversation with a seventy-five-year-old Indian farmer. On the surface we seemed worlds apart—he had a farm a little to the north of Delhi, and he had come to the city to sell grain that was in a large sack which he then used as a sleeping bag on his way back to his village. I was a foreigner, British no less, and, horror of horrors, a lone woman. I think he thought I was an idiot. I certainly felt like one, and conversation was a bit of a struggle—until for some reason I mentioned Shakespeare. The effect was miraculous. All of a sudden his eyes lit up. "Oh, *Shakespeare!*" he cried. "I have loved it all of my life!"And he told me how he had learned it as a schoolboy, how he had once been in the United Kingdom for only two days

and had made a special pilgrimage to Stratford-upon-Avon to
see *The Merchant of Venice*, and then he started to quote huge
chunks of the plays. I asked which play he loved the most, and
after a moment's thought he said, "Well . . . *Twelfth Night* is a
very nice play . . . *Merchant of Venice* . . . also very good . . . but
the play that speaks most to the heart of the Indian people is . . .
KING LEAR." We parted firm friends, with a plan to bring a
troupe of actors to perform *King Lear* in his village, with him
as their interpreter.

It was the first time I'd been back to India in twenty years,
and I didn't go with the intention of talking about Shakespeare,
but I found that everywhere I went, it kept coming up—almost
everyone I encountered seemed to have a knowledge and thirst
and love for these plays. It's something you feel in your gut,
but it is still amazing to witness firsthand the extent to which
Shakespeare transcends every historical, political, and cultural
division and connects with people—and so connects people.
He connects on some much deeper level: he connects straight
to the heart.

* * *

That sort of magical, alchemical connection happens nowhere
in London with greater or more intense immediacy than at the
Globe Theatre. Performing Shakespeare in that space feels like
how it's supposed to be: less like doing a play, and more like
having an enormous party in which everybody is involved, even
though some people are doing more talking than others. Unlike
in a conventional theatre in which usually a small group of
people "performs" before a larger group of people, who are set
behind a dividing line and kept in the dark, at the Globe it feels
as though there is very little distinction between audience and
actor. There is no imaginary fourth wall. There is no pretence

that the audience doesn't exist. The play is a conversation that happens between characters via the audience. It is as though the words travel *through* the audience, around the whole circle of the Globe, and back to you. When you're on stage and you look out, you're engaging right with people. You can see the play happening in their faces.

I've done two seasons at the Globe, first as Lady Macbeth in 2001, and then as Beatrice in *Much Ado About Nothing* in 2011. As plays, and characters, they are possibly polar opposites: Beatrice is so much light and laughter and love, whereas Lady Macbeth literally invites the dark, dissolving into isolation and madness. And yet perhaps at core they are not so very different as women. Insofar as all Shakespearean characters, like all people, have "infinite variety," they, as we, all contain everything.

When I'm preparing roles, one of the things I sometimes find helpful as a way in is to write down words for my character. In the case of Shakespeare, I end up with a completely contradictory collection: *strong, vulnerable, soft, fiery, passionate, lazy, vengeful, shy, intelligent, misguided, sentimental, willful, still, dancing.* Although the weight given to each quality might be different moment by moment, the characters do each seem to contain everything, just as if in the same way you were to try to describe yourself you would probably include every possible description: it's immensely hard to create a defined black line around anybody. To say, beyond all reasonable doubt, *that* is that person. If I were asked to describe myself, I would be a whole mass of contradictions—and I think Beatrice and Lady Macbeth would feel the same. They encompass, as we all do, an abundance of contrary qualities, for they are as infinite as people as we are. They have no end point. They, as we, defy definition.

It is already impossible, then, to generalise these characters on the page, and it is even more so when bringing them to life on stage. You just try to play each moment as fully and truly as you can.

Kenneth Tynan (the great London theatre critic of the 1950s) famously described Lady Macbeth as "sexless," presumably responding to her invocation

> Come, you spirits
> That tend on mortal thoughts, unsex me here
> And fill me from the crown to the toe top-full
> Of direst cruelty.

(1.5.38–41)

Do these words, as Tynan seems to imply, literally work? Thereafter, does Lady Macbeth become sexless? Or does she become a different sex, i.e., "masculine"? What does "more masculine" mean for us anyway? More courageous? Less pitying? Stronger? Crueller? More brain, less heart? More yang, less yin? And does the "feminine" resurge? Does she become a monster of coldness and cruelty? Or does she conversely become more truly "feminine" as the play goes on? I'm not sure it's possible to be black and white. There are infinite possibilities for her as a character because there are infinite possible choices for the actors who play her.

Moreover, there are infinite numbers of people to view her. And each person's opinion is, must be, entirely valid, for each according to his own life experience will respond to her in a different way. It always amazes me how people's individual responses to the same performance on the same night can vary so radically: more proof, it seems to me, that these characters can never be put in any kind of box, that they live and flow and change and grow as much as we do.

Looking back, I feel that with that line, "unsex me here," in some unexpected way Lady Macbeth actually becomes an entirely *sexual* being, insofar as what she is specifically doing with that plea is becoming visceral: she is switching off her mind. It is the mind that is the instrument of sense; it is the mind that would have introduced logic, caution, and the conscience which would have questioned the murderous plan and brought it to a stop.

In that moment she becomes the fundamental opposite of Hamlet, who is blocked from taking action by his overactive mind. She becomes all about doing. Traditionally, the mind is considered a "masculine" drive, whereas the "feminine" is more closely linked to intuition. And whereas Hamlet is all talk, no action, Lady Macbeth is quite the opposite. It's as if in order to go through with this plan, she needs to function on some deep, nonintellectual level, to allow herself to be driven by passion, hunger, and instinct, to be driven solely by her intuition. As an actor, embodying a part on stage night after night, you get a physical feeling of where the source of your action comes from—and I had the sense that Lady Macbeth's hopes, fears, and other emotional energies were all coming from deep within her belly. If Beatrice is operating from the head, Lady Macbeth, in contrast, seems to be working more from the groin. It feels sexual. And in her passionate persuasion of Macbeth to man up, "When you durst do it, then you were a man" (1.7.53), her unquestioning drive completely overrides the cautious logic of his (and possibly her) mind. Then, as the play goes on, far from being "sexless," which suggests to me someone cold, machinelike, she seems to me to become more and more "womanly": increasingly soft, increasingly humane, increasingly vulnerable—until she unravels completely. She literally "loses her mind."

The moment of killing King Duncan is the moment at which the power between the couple shifts completely and irrevocably. In the act of murder, Macbeth crosses a line. And he leaves Lady Macbeth standing on the other side. They're separated by that act, detached from one another by that experience—and they can never meet again. For Lady Macbeth, it's this separation which is the real tragedy, for it felt to me at the time that even though the spur for the murder is on the surface to do with ambition, with power, for her, at root, it is about their relationship. It is about love. And, very possibly, it is about finding a replacement for their child. For her, I think, the point, the irrepressible need to accomplish this project, is that it is a shared experience: one that will bring them together in the same way that a child might, or that their lost child perhaps did. Tragically, that which she thought was going to bind them in fact drives them forever apart because they didn't do it together. Perhaps it might have been a very different story if they had both stood over Duncan with the knife and plunged it in as one.

* * *

That desire for true partnership is played out in a very different way in *Much Ado About Nothing*. Beatrice's wit is not only most explosive and sparkling with Benedick, it needs him for it truly to work. There are people who can, to an extent, appreciate Beatrice's cleverness and laugh at her jokes when he's not there—Leonato, Antonio, Hero—but it's not the same thing as having a perfectly matched tennis partner. Beatrice at the top of the play feels a bit like Borg waiting for McEnroe to show up: she's practising brilliant serves, but there's no one to lob the ball back. It's only when her partner arrives that she can start

Eve Best as Beatrice and Charles Edwards as Benedick in the Globe Theatre's Much Ado About Nothing, *2011. Photograph by Tristram Kenton.*

playing a really exhilarating game—and that's what brings her mind truly alive.

It can be quite lonely being the court jester, which is a role I feel Beatrice seems rather to take on, given her place in that family, and in that society. She is an orphan, living in her uncle's house, in part chaperone/sister/companion to her cousin Hero, but without any clearly defined role, and to an extent there is the feeling that she must sing for her supper—much in the same way that, when you're a guest in somebody's house, you feel like you've got to do the washing up or tell a funny story at lunch to validate your presence in the household. She's an outsider, and perhaps to satisfy the need to feel defined she takes on the role of the fool. It's a special role—as seen brilliantly in *King Lear*—since the fool is given the license to deliver a certain slant of truth, but at the same time it's an alienating role, since the very definition of the fool is to be on the outside looking in.

Furthermore, when Beatrice, as a female fool, offers up her truths they mark her as intelligent—and intelligence was, at the time, a threatening quality for a woman to possess. When we were doing the play, I remember feeling annoyed, on Beatrice's behalf, and on my own behalf, that a lot of this sentiment hasn't changed: that an intelligent woman like Beatrice who speaks her mind and who happens not to be married finds that she has criticisms leveled at her, is constantly being told that she's too much, or that she's over-the-top, or that she's "difficult"— and that moreover she should get married. The lone female was viewed with the same sort of suspicion as the lone wolf. Moreover, she was expected to be a "carer," a teacher or a chaperone, certainly not the life and soul of any party. A woman was expected to be silent, obedient, and chaste, and to get married to the person she has been told to marry (not too different from many societies still today). Hero is the archetype of this in the play: in public, and certainly in the presence of men, she hardly opens her mouth. Beatrice, however, is a wild card: she does not conform to the model of the ideal woman, and so although she's tolerated and loved by the rest of the household, I think deep down they're wary of her; she's a bit like the cuckoo in their nest. Although I'm sure that their hopes for her come from a place of love, at the same time I'm intrigued by the possibility that they want to see her paired up partly for her own sake, and partly just for the sake of having her paired up.

I'm sure on some subliminal level she must sense this. It must contribute in part to her consistent declarations of independence, her insistence on never marrying, her fervent eschewal of marriage and men: she thanks God he has sent her "no husband, for the which blessing I am at him upon my knees every morning and evening" (2.1.19–20). There's also an element in there perhaps of self-preservation: if her heart has indeed been broken by Benedick as she hints it was—"indeed, my lord, he lent it me awhile, and I gave him use for it, a double heart for his single one" (2.1.192–193)—it doesn't surprise me that she should want to protect it, nor that she should want to protest very loudly to anyone who'll listen that she considers him, and the idea of marriage in general, a nonsense: "Thus goes everyone to the world but I, and I am sunburnt. I may sit in a corner and cry 'Hey-ho for a husband!'" (1.2.220–221).

Then we come to one of the most difficult moments in the play—and also, potentially, the most beautiful. It's the moment when Beatrice, after the gulling scene in which she hears about Benedick's love for her, must, in one short speech of ten lines, *completely* cave, retract everything she has said up until now, and open her heart. It's a moment of total transformation. And it is the heart of the play, occurring almost exactly halfway through: a single character left alone on stage to speak with the audience, and furthermore, speaking in verse. It's almost the first time the play has done that, and it is certainly the first time Beatrice has used verse. That seemed important when I went to recite those lines, for where prose feels like the language of the head—of wit, banter, and intellect—verse is very much the language of the heart. It's like she's opening the curtains, and becomes for the first time vulnerable:

> What fire is in mine ears? Can this be true?
> Stand I condemned for pride and scorn so much?
> Contempt farewell, and maiden pride adieu!
> No glory lives behind the back of such.
> And, Benedick, love on, I will requite thee,
> Taming my wild heart to thy loving hand.

If thou dost love, my kindness shall incite thee
To bind our loves up in a holy band.
For others say thou dost deserve, and I
Believe it better than reportingly.

(3.1.109–118)

It's the greatest moment of transformation in the entire play.
And yet it's so short. Beatrice (along with the actor, and, of
course, the audience) has to travel very far and very fast in the
space of only ten lines. Her heart explodes, and she is given very
little language to express the most enormous feelings.

I could sense the significance of the moment: I knew that
by the end of those few words, Beatrice and I needed to have
emerged as a butterfly from a chrysalis, yet because the speech
is so condensed, it was incredibly difficult to do. (Ellen Terry
had apparently despaired of it as a "dreadful little speech" that
she "never got right.")

It was not until one rain-sodden matinee that I looked out
into the yard and saw in the eyes of the girl standing opposite me that she was going through everything that I was going
through—so much so that I found myself grabbing her hand.
And in that moment, suddenly, the scene unlocked. From then
on I connected with someone every night in the same way.

Is it difficult, Beatrice's total abandonment of her principles? It's a question that's sometimes asked: Why should the
happy ending of a comedy necessarily be that people get married? It's certainly a question that Beatrice herself might be
asking. You can almost hear her head shouting, "Hang on a
minute! What happened to all that stuff you said before about
marriage being rubbish? What about that? What's got into you,
girl? What about your independence?" In that moment, it feels
that Beatrice's decision to encourage Benedick to "love on" is

more than Shakespeare following a generic convention, more than society wanting to pair up a single intelligent woman, and more than their friends plotting to put together two slightly awkward, outsider court jesters. That total reversal, which is so difficult if you don't have the right connection to it, occurs because, for Beatrice, no real transformation has to occur at all. It's just a coming home. I love that speech because it quite clearly shows where her heart is, and where her heart has been for years.

What these plays seem often to come back to is a requirement for balance and harmony. The tragedies end with disharmony, and the comedies with harmony, and the establishment of harmony is something to be aspired to. The marriages which close the comedies exist in many different forms, and so you could say that marriage per se isn't the ultimate goal, but balance, and love that is reciprocated, and love that exists between equals.

Indeed, Shakespeare questions the use of marriage as a comedic narrative device through marriages which are not quite as in tune. With Hero and Claudio, as with Bertram and Helena in *All's Well That Ends Well*, we are left with the questions: What kinds of relationships are these? And how will these couples really fare? One of the reasons that *Much Ado About Nothing* is such a lovely play to do is that Beatrice and Benedick seem to be two of the best-matched lovers in all of literature—certainly in comedy, and in tragedy they are in the company of Antony and Cleopatra and, at the beginning of their play, Macbeth and Lady Macbeth.

Like several Shakespearean heroes, Benedick is sometimes accused of not being quite of the vitality and strength of his heroine. Beatrice tells Don Pedro, "There was a star danced, and under that was I born" (2.1.232–233). Certainly in terms of wit she manages to run rings around Benedick for much of the play. But whereas Orlando or Orsino will never be a verbal match for Rosalind or Viola, Benedick does have enough weight for Beatrice. And he has a line which at least approaches hers in beauty: "Serve God, love me and mend" (5.2.62), which is perhaps about the best love poem anybody could say to anybody— it's certainly good enough for her.

* * *

Lady Macbeth and Beatrice—perhaps as characters not so very different after all. Both are haunted by a sadness which is the remnant of a difficult past: Beatrice's heart has been broken, Lady Macbeth has lost a child. What makes their stories so very different—more than anything else, perhaps—is their circumstances. What would have happened had Beatrice been transposed to Scotland, in the dark and the cold, and suffered the death of a child? How would Lady Macbeth have been in the sunshine, with nothing much to do but sit about and eat the oranges? As women, they certainly share many qualities: intelligence, feistiness, grit, greatness, and the strength to fight tooth and nail for survival in what is very much a man's world. While the way they're fighting is very different, Beatrice in an intellectual way and Lady Macbeth in a visceral way, they are united, I think, by something else. In both of them, deep down, I felt some fundamental longing, a deep-rooted desire to end the fight. It is more than a desire, though: it seems to be a need for harmony, for connection. And ultimately, for love.

Dame Harriet Walter

TWO LOVES,
OR THE ETERNAL TRIANGLE

DAME HARRIET WALTER, CBE, DBE, is an English actor whose performances, many of which were at the Royal Shakespeare Company, the Royal National Theatre, and the Donmar Warehouse, include *The Three Sisters, Hedda Gabler, Ivanov, The Duchess of Malfi, Arcadia, Mary Stuart,* and *Women Beware Women,* in addition to the Shakespeare *All's Well That Ends Well, Cymbeline, Twelfth Night, Macbeth, Antony and Cleopatra,* and *Much Ado About Nothing.* She has won many awards, including an Olivier for her portrayal of Viola. The stage production in which she played Lady Macbeth, with Sir Antony Sher as Macbeth, was made into a film. Her other films include *Sense and Sensibility, Onegin, Bright Young Things, Babel, Atonement, Cheri, The Young Victoria,* and *The Wedding Video;* her television appearances have included *Lord Peter Wimsey* and *Law and Order: UK.* She has also written the books *Macbeth* (in the Actors on Shakespeare series), *Other People's Shoes,* and *Facing It: Reflections on Images of Older Women.*

Two loves I have of comfort and despair,
Which like two spirits do suggest me still:
The better angel is a man right fair,
The worser spirit a woman coloured ill.
(Sonnet 144)

It has been, and probably ever will be, up for debate as to whether Shakespeare's Sonnets are autobiographical, but Sonnet 144 gave rise to a line of thought in my own mind whilst I was playing many of Shakespeare's heroines. In all but a few cases, I found myself as a character in competition with a man for the love of the hero. I decided to try and chart the variations in this triangular tension through the plays I had performed in and perhaps even get closer to Shakespeare's own feelings.

*   *   *

Romeo and Juliet was the earliest of Shakespeare's plays that I played in, by which I mean the earliest written (1593–1595) rather than the first one I performed. I played the part for BBC Radio when I was thirty but could *sound* a convincing thirteen. However young, Juliet seems more mature throughout the play than Romeo, who is to a certain extent dragged back by the boy culture which he is part of. Mercutio and his band of friends mock him for his lovesick moping over a woman, Rosaline, as he will later over Juliet. Mercutio says:

> Alas, poor Romeo, he is already dead, stabbed with a white wench's black eye, run through the ear with a love-song, the very pin of his heart cleft with the blind bow-boy's butt-shaft . . .
>
> (2.3.12–14)

Romeo is seen as deserting the gang, and this theme is developed further in the later play *Much Ado About Nothing* when Benedick's soldier companions ridicule his succumbing to love and marriage with Beatrice. In both these examples there is a tinge of jealousy and a fear of losing their mate to a mysterious other world that they do not understand and therefore need to despise—the world of women and marriage, which they feel necessarily leads to a betrayal of the buddy culture in which they are stuck.

Dame Harriet Walter as Beatrice in the Royal Shakespeare Company production of Much Ado About Nothing, *2002.*
Photograph by Tristram Kenton.

Much Ado was written in 1598, at about the same time that Sonnet 144 is thought to have first been circulated amongst Shakespeare's closest friends. When I played Beatrice at the Royal Shakespeare Company in 2002, I felt very aware of the tussle that Benedick was going through between the strong male bonding to his army mates and his tentative gropings towards a complicated grown-up heterosexual love for Beatrice. Shakespeare deliciously plays with Benedick's pride in his soliloquy in Act 2, Scene 3 when he has just overheard that Beatrice is in love with him: "I have railed so long against marriage. But doth not the appetite alter? A man loves the meat in his youth that he cannot endure in his age" (2.3.171–173). And then he wriggles out of the audience's (and his own) tacit reminder of his past pledge with: "When I said I would die a bachelor, I did not think I should live till I were married" (2.3.174–175).

Even at this point he does not quite admit that he could possibly love Beatrice but couches his change of heart from male love to female in the more or less honourable excuse: "No, the world must be peopled" (2.3.174). Maybe this was the philosophy of Shakespeare's day. Physical love could be homo- or heterosexual, but the latter had to be surrendered to in the end in order to keep the species going. Marriage was a biological duty or imperative, while one's true tastes and heart might lie elsewhere.

With this thought in mind, I found a way through the almost impossible "Kill Claudio" moment in Act 4, Scene 1. At the prompting of the malevolent Don John, Claudio has slandered Hero and left her at the altar. Beatrice is distraught for her friend's sake, and when Benedick entreats, "Come, bid me do anything for thee," she responds with the unexpectedly harsh, "Kill Claudio" (4.1.285–286). For me, rather than it being simply an irrational incitement to murder, the line became a different kind of test whose subtext was: "Prove to me that you are willing to cut out from your heart the strutting misogynist ethos of Claudio and your old gang." At the same time, I had to confront the fact that Beatrice is no pacifist saint. She herself would show no mercy to Claudio—"O God, that I were a man! I would eat his heart in the market-place" (4.1.300–301)—or at least this is her boast, whose main purpose is to throw down a gauntlet to Benedick challenging him to be a "proper" man, to be as brave and avenging as she would be if she could.

Benedick passes his test with flying colours and without having to actually kill Claudio. All the worlds are reconciled and the villain Don John is punished in the end. Only the ambiguous figure of Don Pedro, whose love for both Benedick and Beatrice is never quite expressed, remains unresolved. Benedick thinks he has the solution: "Prince, thou art sad: get thee a wife, get thee a wife" (5.4.115–116).

* * *

"Sad" is the word that strikes one when considering Antonio in *The Merchant of Venice* (1596). It is thought that Shakespeare played this eponymous role in a play where the other characters, especially Shylock, eventually eclipse what had started out as the central figure. In fact, Antonio opens the play with, "In sooth I know not why I am so sad" (1.1.1). Here again is a triangular relationship between an older man, a younger man, and a woman.

Antonio and the heiress Portia, whom I played in 1987, are both in love with Bassanio. Bassanio himself is caught between his loyalty to a man who has mentored and cherished him, and whom he knows fairly intimately, and a woman whom he finds beautiful and amazing (and yes, who is extremely rich), and who has the mystery of a distant shimmering object that he knows very little about.

The adventurer in him is what both his lovers like about him. Bassanio dares to have a go at Portia's dead father's test—a suitor is presented with three caskets; if he chooses the right one he wins Portia's hand, and if he does not he must remain celibate for the rest of his life—and he chooses the right casket. Just as he and Portia are about to celebrate his success, he hears of Antonio's plight—the merchant has lost his ships and is being held to ransom by Shylock to pay him what he owes. Without a moment's hesitation, Bassanio rushes to Antonio's side. Portia, hurt by this but nothing daunted, decides to disguise herself as a lawyer and defeat Shylock in court. The realization is painful to her that it is only by saving Antonio that she will find the way to Bassanio's heart.

After her success in the courtroom, there is a key scene between the disguised Portia and Bassanio where she tries to get him to give her the ring which he has promised Portia never to remove. He manages to hold out and refuse to surrender it, and then Portia leaves, presumably well pleased that her betrothed has kept his pledge.

Seconds later, Gratiano, Bassanio's friend, runs after her with the ring. Bassanio has changed his mind. Portia's disappointment is for the actress to play. All Antonio had had to say was, "My lord Bassanio, let him have the ring, / Let his deservings and my love withal / Be valued against your wife's commandment" (4.1.458–460). It hadn't taken much to swing Bassanio's loyalty back to the other man in the triangle.

In the fifth act of *The Merchant*, the intricate web of complex loyalties, and the unraveling of who was who, and the revealing of who thought who was who, is spun out deliciously, thereby making it one of the more enjoyable scenes to play. Enjoyable but not painless, as one of the strands is the revelation to Portia that her husband still feels enough love for Antonio to surrender her precious ring. Bassanio has to face his own confusion of emotions vis-à-vis his admiration for a young boy lawyer who showed exceptional skill, initiative, courage, and intelligence, and to whom he is indebted for the life of his friend, and he must digest the fact that this boy was one and the same as his supposed golden wife in her gilded Belmont cage. Antonio has to stand by and witness and eventually bless the heterosexual bond between his beloved Bassanio and the woman who saved his life. And to think that the great late-nineteenth- and early-twentieth-century actor-producer Henry Irving cut Act 5 because Shylock is no longer featured!

* * *

With *Hamlet* and *Troilus and Cressida* (both written in or around 1601), Shakespeare enters a darker, more misogynist phase. Imagine playing Cressida, reviled for her betrayal of Troilus, with no self-justifying speech to explain her actions to the audience or to posterity. It is as if Shakespeare abandons his own feisty creation like an unforgiving parent who has changed his mind about her worth.

Imagine then being on stage and playing Ophelia, as I was in Richard Eyre's 1980 production for the Royal Court, and being told that "the power of beauty will sooner transform honesty from what it is to a bawd than the force of honesty can translate beauty into his likeness" (3.1.117–119), or, "If thou dost marry, I'll give thee this plague for thy dowry: be thou as chaste as ice, as pure as snow, thou shalt not escape calumny. Get thee to a nunnery: go, farewell" (3.1.136–138). Imagine that you are portraying a woman in love with the speaker (Hamlet), who has become, in most cultures of the world, the most eloquent voice of humanity's psychological condition, and imagine being given practically nothing to say in your own or in Ophelia's defence. Knowing, moreover, that "the noble" Hamlet's treatment of Gertrude is similar, you can see how one starts to wonder whose side Shakespeare is really on.

In fact, I have turned down the part of Gertrude more than once because she seems to me to be even more muzzled than Ophelia, who at least breaks out into a form of self-expression in her madness. Gertrude is told by her son that she is too old for sex: "You cannot call it love, for at your age / The heyday in the blood is tame, it's humble, / And waits upon the judgement" (3.4.75–77). With these words the child seeks to control the mother. This is a love triangle with an Oedipal slant. Hamlet wishes to kill his rival Claudius for usurping his dead father's place not only on the throne but also in his mother's bed. Not able to deal with his own complex emotions, he is vicious and oppressive towards both the women he loves, and in the most famous play in the world the woman's voice is barely heard.

So it is that sometimes, while "inhabiting" a Shakespearean heroine, one feels to be on the receiving end of a comment about one's own sex that is distancing and alienating. Almost worse are the times when these comments are forced out of our own mouths. We are required to say, for example, as Viola, "How easy is it for the proper-false / In women's waxen hearts to set their forms! / Alas, our frailty is the cause, not we, / For such as we are made of, such we be" (*Twelfth Night*, 2.2.24–27), or, as Cressida, "Ah, poor our sex! This fault in us I find, / The error of our eye directs our mind" (*Troilus and Cressida*, 5.2.124–125). Even Cleopatra chides herself for being "No more, but e'en a woman" (*Antony and Cleopatra*, 4.15.85). With these self-condemnatory words, we and our characters endorse a negative male attitude which is never quite disowned by Shakespeare himself.

* * *

Maybe I should give him a break here. In *As You Like It* (1599), the older male cynic, Jacques, is marginalized at the end and Shakespeare seems genuinely to love Rosalind. Likewise, in *Twelfth Night* (1601), he spreads his gentle ridiculing of the madness of love evenhandedly between both sexes and gives Viola the voice of insight among the self-deluded. She is the fresh breath of air in a pit of insanity. She has the audience's ear and they are always on her side, and so when I played her for the RSC in 1987–1989 I felt Shakespeare's approval carrying me along.

In *Twelfth Night*, Shakespeare reaches a kind of apotheosis in his expression of sexual ambiguity. It is not so much a case of a love triangle as of several overlapping and contiguous love triangles. Viola is in love with Orsino and, disguised as his page Cesario, she must woo her own rival, Olivia; Olivia falls for the "boy" Cesario and meanwhile Orsino, who is supposed to be in love with Olivia, must face his ambisexual attraction to his page. The play is often blissfully funny. It is painful and perfect.

I wasn't thinking along those lines at the time, but the paradox is that as the disguised Viola I was acting out the young man in the triangular tussle between an older man (Orsino), a young man (Cesario), and a woman (Olivia). I even spoke lines that echo the recurrent theme of the Sonnets when Viola/Cesario chastises Olivia with "Lady, you are the cruell'st she alive, / If you will lead these graces to the grave / And leave the world no copy" (1.5.174–176).

The beauty of it is that Viola uses her insight into the female condition to get close to Olivia and it is that which draws Olivia to fall in love with her. The apex moment of the scene is Viola/Cesario's imaginative and rather girly reply when Olivia asks "Cesario" what *he* would do to woo her. Listening to and watching the passion in Viola's answer that she would "Make me a willow cabin at your gate, / And call upon my soul within the house" (1.5.201–202), we recognize that the chemistry changes and Olivia is hooked.

Of all the roles I have played, I felt Shakespeare's understanding of women to be fullest in Viola. She is the catalyst by which Orsino shifts from his unrequited objectifying and idolizing of Olivia to a more open-eyed, mature love for Viola. That this transition has to be worked through the agency of a boy catalyst is a bittersweet solution. Having acted out a kind of man-to-man intimacy, Viola has had a privileged glimpse into the male world and knows Orsino thoroughly. Orsino looks at women with a fresh eye on learning that the boy he favoured and confided in was actually a woman. A real woman. By becoming her own rival in the guise of a young man, the woman achieves her love, and despite an unresolved twinge of pain, with Viola knowing Orsino almost too well, this marriage looks to be set fairer than most.

* * *

A few years before I played Viola, I was cast as Helena in the RSC's *All's Well That Ends Well* in a production that began in Stratford-upon-Avon and then went to Broadway. It was a big break for me, my most meaty role to date, with the most stage time and the greatest range of emotions. To make the high stakes even higher, the director was Trevor Nunn and Dame Peggy Ashcroft was to play the Countess.

Trevor was being quite bold in attempting this play, which was written in 1601 but which, by the twentieth century, had acquired a negative reputation as a "problem play." In preparing for the role, it was alarming to read among other negative literature that the role of Helena was "unplayable."

Although the "problem" label has somewhat withered as a result of a handful of successful productions of the play in recent years, when we embarked on it in the early 1980s it was still going to be hard to win an audience over to a "heroine" who seemingly forces an unwilling young man with a promising future to marry her simply because *she* feels he is her destiny.

It is impossible to know how Shakespeare viewed his own creation, or whether he intended to challenge his audience with a particularly problematic love story. Reverse the role gender in this scenario and no one would bat an eyelid. But Helena is intense, a quality that signals danger to young men. She is strange, possibly gifted with healing powers, the orphaned daughter of a brilliant doctor (as usual with Shakespeare, no information on her mother—but that is another essay); she is the protégée of an aristocratic family who gets access to the King, miraculously cures him of his disease, and is given the hand of her beloved Bertram as a reward.

To be fair, Shakespeare shows little sympathy for the two men that complete the love triangle in the play. Bertram is an arrogant, privileged young pup, and Parolles, his best friend and accomplice in deserting Helena, while enjoying the audience's affection and laughter for much of the play, is finally shown up as a shallow swindler. With the more revered and upright characters—the Countess, the King, Lafeu the old courtier, and even the fool Lavache, not to mention all the characters she meets in Italy—all endorsing Helena's cause and expressing approval of her character, it would seem that Shakespeare himself was on her side.

To inhabit a heroine created by Shakespeare is a curious experience. To begin with, there is the inescapable fact that he never intended a woman to play the role. As I mentioned earlier, there is sometimes a feeling of discomfort at being the object of misogyny, where presumably a boy player would have felt none.

There is one scene in *All's Well*, for example, in which Parolles speaks to Helena with a disinhibited crudeness quite unlike any other I can think of outside the brothels of *Measure for Measure* or the Boar's Head in Cheapside. Perhaps because Helena is not wellborn herself, Parolles feels he can speak to her with an indelicacy he would not have used with a noblewoman. He tells her, for instance: "Virginity breeds mites, much like a cheese, consumes itself to the very paring, and so dies with feeding his own stomach. . . . Keep it not, you cannot choose but lose by't" (1.1.116–119). He continues with: "And your virginity, your old virginity, is like one of our French withered pears: it looks ill, it eats dryly. Marry, 'tis a withered pear. . . . Will you anything with it?" (1.1.128–130). Helena is not devoid of quips and parries to Parolles's digs against her virginity, but to sit and listen to such lines is to feel mocked, insulted, and dirty—but also it is to feel in a strange way more equal, to be let in to the secrets of a club, albeit a pretty horrible one. From one of his closest associates, Helena is being usefully educated as to the male ethos which Bertram is a part of, and it is all useful stuff to a sheltered girl.

Eventually Parolles is exposed as a coward in a scene which completely opens Bertram's eyes as to the true nature of the man he has been emulating, and from this point onwards, uncoupled from his blokeish partnership, Bertram is set free on the long (and still tricky) path to redemption and into the arms of his loving wife.

* * *

Imogen, whom I played in the RSC's 1987–1989 production of *Cymbeline* (1609), is more cruelly duped by the jealous Iachimo, who sets out on a quest to prove to her exiled husband, Posthumus, that all women, including Imogen, whom Iachimo has never met, are flakey and cheap. Iachimo travels all the way from Rome to Britain and introduces himself to Imogen as a messenger from her beloved. In the brilliant scene that ensues, Iachimo sews doubts in Imogen's heart similar to those with which Iago (same derivation of the names Iachimo and Iago) works on Othello's jealousy.

Unlike Othello, Imogen is not such easy game. After a momentary wobble, she manages to thwart Iachimo's plan. He makes the mistake of coming on to her, insinuating that the two of them should sleep together as a way of avenging what he alleges to be Posthumus's infidelity. She sees this for the trick it is and confronts Iachimo with it. Her righteous passion and fury are so formidable that Iachimo is forced to pretend that he had invented the whole thing in order to test her loyalty. They end the scene reconciled and friendly.

Iachimo changes tack and secretes himself in Imogen's bedchamber and then watches her as she sleeps. To complicate our feelings about him, Iachimo utters the most sublime erotic poetry over her sleeping form:

> But kiss, one kiss! Rubies unparagoned,
> How dearly they do't! 'Tis her breathing that
> Perfumes the chamber thus: the flame o'th'taper
> Bows toward her . . .
>
> (2.2.19–22)

Neither he nor his (almost) namesake Iago is indifferent to the goodness and beauty of the woman he is intent on destroying. Iachimo takes notes in a notebook of the bedroom furnishings and the mole on Imogen's breast so he can more convincingly persuade Posthumus that he has slept with his wife.

All comes out well in the end, but one asks oneself: How could Posthumus so easily believe the worst of his wife and decide to have her killed without ever giving her the chance to defend herself? And what motivates Iachimo? He has nothing personal against Imogen, never having met her when he forges his plan, and he barely knows Posthumus. One asks the same questions of the Othello/Iago/Desdemona triangle in *Othello* (1602) and to some extent of the Polixenes/Leontes/Hermione triangle in *The Winter's Tale* (1609).

The answers must lie somewhere in the mutual ignorance

of men and women as to the nature of the other. The physical attraction or biological compulsion towards someone one barely understands leaves great opportunity for suspicion, and for the projection of one's own self-hatred on to the "other." The man can too easily blame the woman for his uncomfortable feeling of powerlessness.

* * *

In *Antony and Cleopatra*, Cleopatra and Enobarbus are in competition for the soul of Antony. In many ways they are mirror images of one another. Both love the powerful Antony; both witness his deterioration with sadness; one deserts him and one has a mind to.

Enobarbus is a shrewd social observer and the chronicler of his age, a satirist who often expresses the misogyny of the times and in particular that of an army man: "between them [women] and a great cause they should be esteemed nothing" (1.2.133–134). He later claims that "there is never a fair woman has a true face" (2.6.122). Yet he is also a wise and broadminded man who finds Cleopatra infuriating but captivating and understands her in a way that Antony doesn't quite:

ANTONY: She is cunning past man's thought.
ENOBARBUS: Alack, sir, no: her passions are made of
    nothing but the finest part of pure love.

(1.2.138–140)

Indeed, their love of Antony unites Cleopatra and Enobarbus and, in Act 3, Scene 13, the only scene in which they are alone together, it is as though Cleopatra has sought him out deliberately to ask, "What shall we do, Enobarbus?" (3.13.1). She then

goes on to ask Enobarbus who is to blame for Antony's shameful
rout at Actium, herself or Antony, to which Enobarbus replies:

> Antony only, that would make his will
> Lord of his reason. What though you fled
> From that great face of war, whose several ranges
> Frighted each other? Why should he follow?
> The itch of his affection should not then
> Have nicked his captainship . . .
>
> (3.13.4–9)

Despite the rather belittling "itch of his affection," Enobarbus
does not blame the woman. Antony, by contrast, certainly does.
He is more involved in the shame of the defeat than the observer
Enobarbus, and because he cannot face it in himself, he blames
Cleopatra: "O, whither hast thou led me, Egypt?" (3.11.53).

> . . . thou knew'st too well
> My heart was to thy rudder tied by th'strings
> And thou shouldst tow me after.
>
> (3.11.60–62)

By calling her "Egypt," he endows her with the full force of her
realm and thus emphasizes his helplessness.

Neither Enobarbus nor Cleopatra can bear this falling off
of a great man. Enobarbus has many a soliloquy directed to the
audience to express his sadness, his reasons for desertion, and
his pre-suicidal regret of it. For Cleopatra there is no such direct
audience connection. For me as an actor, one of the most complex scenes to play was Act 5, Scene 2, when Cleopatra, knowing that Antony is a spent force politically, flirts with Caesar's
envoy and we are not quite sure whether or not she would fol-

*Dame Harriet Walter as Cleopatra in the Royal Shakespeare
Company production of* Antony and Cleopatra, *2006.
Photograph by Tristram Kenton.*

low through with Caesar's offer and betray Antony. Enobarbus
certainly interprets what he sees as a betrayal by Cleopatra and
fetches Antony in to see it for himself. Antony's resultant loss
of control, physical cruelty (he has the envoy flogged to within
an inch of his life), and the combination of ranting accusation
and whingeing at Cleopatra, is enough to unseat anyone's love.

But Antony and Cleopatra are codependent and she, by
protesting rather too much at how little he must think of her,
and how outraged she is at the insult of his even beginning
to believe that she would ever betray him, convinces and qui-
etens Antony so that he is soon back on best braggadocio form,
determining to get back at Caesar once again. Cleopatra cheers
him on with "That's my brave lord!" (3.13.208). She is grateful
for the brief restoration of her admiration for her fallen idol.

Enobarbus is more honest, but there is room in the scene for wordless play between the two characters who have invested so much in Antony.

As a vulnerable aging woman and the queen of a moribund Egypt, Cleopatra needs to cling to her belief in Antony far longer than the less self-deluding Enobarbus does. I used to listen with particular attention to Enobarbus's speeches to the audience, as they are a clue to what the intelligent politician in Cleopatra knows deep down, but is not ready to admit.

Another thing struck me as I listened in the wings. Enobarbus's language becomes more feminine (the simple "This blows my heart" [4.6.37] always got to me) and, as he prepares to kill himself, his language seems to point to a reconciliation with the feminine, and therefore somehow with Cleopatra. He invokes the traditionally female moon and needs her forgiveness:

> Be witness to me—O thou blessèd moon—
> . . .
>   . . . poor Enobarbus did
> Before thy face repent!
>
> > (4.9.9; 11–12)

And again:

> O sovereign mistress of true melancholy,
> The poisonous damp of night disponge upon me,
> . . .
>   . . . Throw my heart
> Against the flint and hardness of my fault . . .
>
> > (4.9.15–16; 18–19)

Enobarbus is one of my favourite characters, and in my role as Cleopatra I found that both the character and the actress wanted his approval.

* * *

I want Shakespeare's approval too. Shakespeare is supposed to be invisible and undetectable within the lines of his plays, but there is a little sense in which an actor can feel that she or he has been inside the playwright's head and felt the muddle of his sexual ambivalence.

He was a product of his time as well as a unique genius, but which is he being, and when? Is the "real" Shakespeare to be found in the Sonnets? I know better than to look for definitive biographical answers within his work. I want to talk to him; I want to ask him so much. I want him to rubber-stamp twenty-first-century feminism and to be reassured that were he living now he would happily adopt our contemporary culture's demystifying of the opposite sex. I need to believe that he includes women in his embrace of humanity. But the truth is that I have to lay aside my aching curiosity and accept that I can never know the man whose words I (mostly) love to speak and hear.

Jane Smiley

ODD MAN OUT

JANE SMILEY is an American author. She has written novels, short stories, and volumes of nonfiction; her works include *Barn Blind*, *The Greenlanders*, *Private Life*, and *13 Ways of Looking at the Novel*. Her novel *A Thousand Acres*, subsequently developed into a feature film, was awarded the Pulitzer Prize for Fiction. Other distinctions include an O. Henry Award and election into the American Academy of Arts and Letters.

When I was a child, I felt a lot closer to Shakespeare than I do as an adult. That I would feel at all close to Shakespeare is clearly absurd, and yet the experience of poring over the texts of plays, understanding very little of what you are reading, but being compelled to go on, is, paradoxically, an activity of great intimacy. I went to a private secondary school, and our English curriculum was organized systematically—we read a Shakespeare play every year from seventh through twelfth grade, beginning with *Twelfth Night* and ending with *King Lear*. We discussed the plays for about two weeks each, and we read sections of the plays aloud. They seeped into my brain rather like other barely understood (or frankly misunderstood) sets of words (think "round John virgin" as opposed to "round yon virgin"). Being difficult to understand was something adults specialized in; our job as children was to decipher the code.

The effort demanded concentration, and concentration resulted in contemplation—I pondered the bits of *Hamlet, A*

Midsummer Night's Dream, and the others we read over and over, so that when I finally did see a performance, the summer after twelfth grade (Sam Waterston in *Hamlet* at the Washington Monument), I was thunderstruck. The play seemed to coalesce right before my eyes; the play belonged to me somehow.

In college, of course, we read more Shakespeare plays, and the one I loved most was *Measure for Measure*. The one I loved least was *King Lear*. I read *King Lear* five times in the course of high school, college, and graduate school, and I never reconciled myself to what my friend William Shakespeare seemed to wish to teach me. Whereas in *Measure for Measure* fairness won out and the hypocritical tyrant was revealed and punished, in *King Lear* tyranny went unexplored. In fact, tyranny seemed to be embraced, and for no reason that I could discern. Was I supposed to pity Lear because he was a father? Because he was the king? Because he was foolish and/or senile? In *Measure for Measure*, the female characters were appealing in their intelligence. I didn't understand the female characters in *King Lear* at all.

Also in college, I took Old English. It is probable that Shakespeare was unaware of the history of the English language, that he did not know that William the Conqueror was both French and Scandinavian, that England itself was a map of the infusion of Old Norse into Anglo-Saxon—up in the northeast, where the Vikings held sway for several generations, the pronoun identifying a woman was "she." Down in the southwest, where the Nordic influence never arrived, the pronoun was "oo." Everywhere, the upper classes spoke a type of French while the lower classes spoke Germanic (pork in the dining hall, swine in the farmyard). The history of the language only started to form itself as a field of study in the eighteenth century, long after Shakespeare stopped writing, but even though he might not have known it, I could hear the competing languages in his plays (in just a few lines of Hamlet's famous soliloquy, we have "fardels," old French; "death, grunt, and sweat," Old English; "dream," Old Norse; "perchance," Middle French; and "shuffled," a neologism, possibly related to Low German, in the 1530s). For the rest of college, and into graduate school, I read *Hamlet* in one class, *Beowulf* in another, *A Midsummer Night's Dream* in one class and *Egil's Saga* in another. Fascinated with the sagas, I went to Iceland for a school year. Most of the time I was there, it was dark. I delved deeper. A friend reminded me of the Norse colony on the southern tip of Greenland. I found the whole enterprise so astonishing that I became obsessed with it, and after four or five years of ruminating upon it, and visiting Greenland, I produced *The Greenlanders*.

One thing I loved about literature was its strange and mutually exclusive forms—comedy, tragedy, epic, romance. Shakespeare was one of the few writers, maybe the only one, game enough to try each one, and versatile enough to make each effort seem radically different from the others. A romance, like *The Tempest*, had a whole different feel from the tragedy *Macbeth*, even though *Macbeth* was full of romantic elements. That impressed me, as it was supposed to. There were no plays in Shakespeare that appeared to stem directly from the saga tradition, but there was one play that seemed to hail from the north rather than the south or the east, and that was *King Lear*. There was nothing Italian about the title, nothing Italian about the characters' names (Edgar, Edmund), and nothing Italian about the chilly implacability of the enmities within Lear's family: these were grudges long nurtured, feelings expressed only bitterly and tersely—"What need one?" (2.2.452) says Regan.

I was living in north central Iowa. We were driving home from Minneapolis, surrounded by a northern gloom and a prairie emptiness. I looked into the sky lowering over the flat earth, and I said, "This is where I should set that *Lear* book." Its ancestors were not only the sagas, but also *Giants in the Earth* by Ole Rølvaag, *The Emigrants* by Vilhelm Moberg, and *O Pioneers!* by Willa Cather.

I had not come to like Shakespeare's play any better, though. I still felt that Goneril and Regan had a point of view that somehow the play (or maybe the critics) had slighted. Even when Goneril and Regan note the faults in their father that are the source of his unhappiness ("he hath ever but slenderly known himself" [1.1.299]), they are expected to be loving and indulgent. So I set about correcting my friend William Shakespeare—something no sane adult would attempt. I gave the royal family a background. I gave the daughters a rationale for their apparently cruel behavior. I gave Goneril a voice and Regan a point of view. I was sure that if I was detailed enough, Shakespeare would see the daughters my way. And by the time I was finished with *A Thousand Acres*, I felt that in some ways Shakespeare and I were closer than ever. I knew that, like me, he had reworked found material, and that he had discovered the material to be more intractable than he expected it to be. I knew he had wrestled with the logic of the action and the motivation of the characters. I knew that there were places in the play where he had done the best he could to patch it all together. I experienced my friend William Shakespeare as a fellow toiler in the literary muck, and it was a heartening experience. But as I pondered those points in *King Lear* where motivation became action and action resulted in reflection, I also learned, maybe for the first time in my life, that William Shakespeare and I were not soul mates, that I was a twentieth-century woman and he was a sixteenth-century man. He expected the world to be a crueler place than I did—warlike rather than litigious, for example; he took for granted Lear's claims as a king and as a man; his poetry voiced feelings and perceptions that were specific to his time and place, as in Lear's disgust at his daughters' sexuality, and Gloucester's lament, "As flies to wanton boys are we to th'gods: / They kill us for their sport" (4.1.41–42). I could not, in fact, think like Shakespeare and he did not, in fact, foresee our world. In short, when I followed Shakespeare into the *Lear* material, I discovered that he was human.

And later, I decided that he changed his mind. In *The Winter's Tale* he returns to questions of love and loss, but his view of them is not apocalyptic, or, shall we say, Ragnarokian. After Leontes impetuously jails his wife for suspected adultery and has his newborn daughter exposed, thereby ruining his life in Act 3, he is allowed to redeem himself in Act 5, first through honest remorse—"I am ashamed. Does not the stone rebuke me / For being more stone than it?" (5.3.43–44)—then by means that might or might not be a miracle, but that certainly offer a definition of love much different from that expressed in *King Lear*. The end of the world is not the end of the world, but a mistake that a man, even a hot-tempered king, can learn from. I have often thought that a troupe should perform both plays on alternating nights, so that we can see the difference between Shakespeare in 1605 and Shakespeare in 1611. I think he, like most humans, got wise.

Dame Margaret Drabble

THE LIVING DRAMA

DAME MARGARET DRABBLE, OBE, CBE, is an English author. She has written seventeen novels, including *A Summer Bird-Cage*, *The Garrick Year*, *The Peppered Moth*, *The Witch of Exmoor*, and *The Sea Lady*. Her nonfiction features biographies of Arnold Bennett and Angus Wilson, as well as critical studies of Thomas Hardy and William Wordsworth. She edited the fifth and sixth editions of *The Oxford Companion to English Literature*. Her many awards include the John Llewelyn Rhys Prize, the Society of Authors Travelling Fellowship, the James Tait Black Memorial Prize, and the E. M. Forster Award from the American Academy of Arts and Letters. Before turning to writing, she was a member of the Royal Shakespeare Company.

My second novel, *The Garrick Year* (1964), was inspired by a couple of seasons as a spear carrier in the early 1960s with the Royal Shakespeare Theatre in Stratford-upon-Avon, and I wrote some of it while I was sitting in the dressing room. Night after night, Shakespeare's verse resounded over the Tannoy system, from *Cymbeline* and *King Lear*, from *A Midsummer Night's Dream* and *The Taming of the Shrew*, forming the backdrop of my fictional domestic comedy about an ambitious and frustrated young mother married to an actor. This was a vintage period for the RSC, when the great impresario Peter Hall was launching his theatrical career, and those of us who were there in those days recall them with a peculiar intensity. Hall's enchanting *Dream* (in which I played a fairy and an Amazon) was notable for a classic performance of Titania by Judi Dench, whose clear, moonlit, silvery intonations still echo through the corridors of our memories; she was quarrelling with her Oberon, just as my heroine Emma was quarrelling with her husband, David:

> And never since the middle summer's spring
> Met we on hill, in dale, forest or mead,
> By pavèd fountain or by rushy brook,
> Or in the beachèd margent of the sea,
> To dance our ringlets to the whistling wind,
> But with thy brawls thou hast disturbed our sport.
>
> (2.1.83–88)

I knew her lines by heart, and indeed was obliged to learn them, for I was her understudy. I can see her now, with her elfin face, her clouds of silvery hair, her green woodland dress, her wicked smile. She was magical, a perfect match of actress and of role, of director and of play.

I also understudied Diana Rigg as Cordelia in *Lear*, and I knew those lines too. This was one of Peter Brook's groundbreaking productions, as bleak and spare as Hall's *Dream* was rich and light. Again, I can hear Paul Scofield's deep gravel voice of angry suffering in phrase after phrase, speech after speech— and the voices of others too, for this was a fine cast without a weak link. Even the words of the bit-part servants ring in my ears. Brook had been deeply influenced by the Polish critic Jan Kott, who related Shakespeare's vision to the work of Ionesco and Samuel Beckett and the nightmares of twentieth-century history, and he directed the play with a minimalist severity. Brook was already moving towards his later experiments with the Theatre of Cruelty and the drama of madness. I hear Scofield's strong voice catching and breaking as he neared the unbearable ending:

> Pray, do not mock me:
> I am a very foolish fond old man,
> Fourscore and upward, not an hour more nor less,
> And to deal plainly,
> I fear I am not in my perfect mind.
>
> (4.6.62–66)

I cannot exaggerate the importance to me, through later years, of the experience of being so close to Shakespeare on stage. Shakespeare on the page I had loved since school, and I remember with intense pleasure our classroom readings of *Richard II* and *Henry IV*, which must have been set texts: I fell in love with the incantatory narcissistic verse of Richard, and according to my younger sister used to keep her awake at night when we shared a bedroom during our summer holidays by intoning "Down, down I come, like glistering Phaeton" and other melancholy outpourings. I was fortunate with Shakespeare even at school, where some children learn to hate him. We had fine English teachers with a good sense of theatre and drama, who put on some first-class school productions: as Titania, sixth-former Judi Dench gave a preview of her Stratford incarnation (and I previewed my role as fairy in her train), and she also played Ariel in *The Tempest*, with a sureness of phrasing that seemed almost supernatural. Nearly sixty years later I can hear her voice, as Ariel describes the pitiable state of the bewitched and shipwrecked king and his followers, and assures her master Prospero that if he were to see them now he would pity them:

> ... if you now beheld them, your affections
> Would become tender.
>
> (5.1.20–21)

Prospero responds, "Dost thou think so, spirit?" (5.1.22)—to which she replies, "Mine would, sir, were I human" (5.1.22–23). Judi Dench uttered that phrase, "were I human," with such unearthly yearning that whole vistas of depth beyond depth in the meaning of the play opened before us. Such moments of revelation a truly fine performance can offer. They are worth as much as many pages of critical analysis. And Judi was only seventeen.

Everyone knows that Shakespeare's heroines were originally played by boys with unbroken voices well under the age of seventeen, and much research has been done into the identities and fates of these boy actors. It is easy to imagine a boy playing Rosalind or Viola or tomboy Beatrice, and the plots of several of Shakespeare's comedies have many allusions to cross-dressing, indeed are heavily dependent on the conceit. It is harder to imagine a boy playing Cleopatra, a tragic heroine notoriously past her salad days, the full-blown rose who proclaims herself to be "with Phoebus' amorous pinches black / And wrinkled deep in time" (1.5.33–34): voluptuous maturity is her key note, her defining attribute, and the play stresses again and again her passion, her fecundity, her overwhelming sexuality. How did a young boy cope with the sensuous richness of the verse, with its repeated allusions to physical love? Shakespeare does not avoid the issue; he confronts it. Cleopatra, theatrically envisaging her fate should she be led to Rome in Caesar's triumph, recoils from the prospect of the mocking pageant:

> Antony
> Shall be brought drunken forth, and I shall see
> Some squeaking Cleopatra boy my greatness
> I'th'posture of a whore.
>
> (5.2.258–261)

These verses, spoken by a boy actor, fortify her to be absolute for death, and to nurse the asp that kills her—again, in words that stress her womanliness: "Dost thou not see my baby at my breast / That sucks the nurse asleep?" (5.2.348–349). What depths of erotic knowledge could beardless and breastless boys plumb to deliver such lines? And yet they did, they did. Eternity was in their lips and eyes, bliss in their brows' bent.

In his later plays, it is my perhaps eccentric and personal belief that Shakespeare increasingly and deliberately deconstructed the artifice of his own work. He saw himself as puppet master and magician, a Prospero marooned on a lonely island of unapproachable genius, and he played tricks with the illusions and realities he had created, with the form in which he had worked so successfully, so commercially, so abundantly, for so long. By revealing and confessing the tricks, he reinforced the reality. There is a prefiguring of Pirandello's modernist games with the nature of artifice in many of his speeches and dramatic situations: *Cymbeline* is particularly rich in self-referential comments on the plot's basic implausibility. Again and again, characters comment on the unbelievability of events, with remarks such as "This was strange chance" (5.3.55) or "Howsoe'er 'tis strange, / Or that the negligence may well be laughed at, / Yet is it true, sir" (1.1.73–75).

The impossibly mistaken identity of Cloten dressed as Posthumus and conveniently headless, as discovered by Imogen, is one
of Shakespeare's most extreme stage effects: the audience does not
know whether to laugh or cry when Imogen cries out, "O Posthumus, alas, / Where is thy head? Where's that? Ay me! Where's
that?" (4.2.385–386). Tragedy, comedy, or late romance?

Shakespeare's plays have deeply infiltrated my own work,
on many levels, and my most recent novel, *The Sea Lady*
(2006), is subtitled *A Late Romance*. It features a manipulative
Prospero-like theatre director, a production of *The Tempest*,
and an even more manipulative Public Orator at a new university, who carefully reunites the two principal characters of
the fiction at a degree ceremony, knowing that they have been
deeply and secretly involved with one another in the distant
past. The reunion, as theatrical and implausible as any organ-
ised by an Elizabethan or Jacobean deus ex machina, nevertheless leads to forgiveness and reconciliation. The Public Orator
is himself a novelist, although something of a novelist manqué,
and he cannot resist playing with his puppets.

Conflicting concepts of realism, verisimilitude, and fantasy war with one another in Shakespeare's late plays, producing some strikingly odd results. And yet some of these plays,
notably *Cymbeline* and *The Tempest*, remain lastingly popular
with performers, and Imogen and Prospero are coveted roles.
Vanessa Redgrave has played both. She played Imogen in the
1962 RSC season in which I was her understudy, and years later
she played Prospero at the reconstructed Globe. Shakespeare
on stage continues to offer infinite variety, infinite possibility. I
am fortunate to have been so close to the living drama.

Joyce Carol Oates

THE TRAGEDY OF IMAGINATION IN *ANTONY AND CLEOPATRA*

JOYCE CAROL OATES is Professor of the Humanities and Professor of Creative Writing at Princeton University. She has published more than fifty novels, as well as plays and books of poetry, nonfiction, and short stories, including *them*, *We Were the Mulvaneys*, *I'll Take You There*, *The Falls*, *The Gravedigger's Daughter*, *Carthage*, and *The Accursed*. She is the recipient of many honors, including the National Book Award, two O. Henry Awards, the PEN/ Malamud Award, the Chicago Tribune Literary Prize, a National Humanities Medal, and the PEN Center USA Award for Lifetime Achievement.

> Nature wants stuff
> To vie strange forms with fancy . . .
> (*Antony and Cleopatra*, 5.2.117–118)

*A*ntony and Cleopatra is about its hero and heroine creating, through words, their own glorious reality. It is a play about the nature of magic, where magic is lyrical language, strengthened by the will to believe in it. Although in form their story is a tragedy, it also illustrates a resounding triumph of the human spirit. Since 1964, when I first began reflecting on *Antony and Cleopatra*, I have been developing these themes both in relation to the play and in the creation of my own works of fiction.

Shakespeare's *Antony and Cleopatra*, as I have always read

it, illustrates the obsessive and self-consuming rage of a tragic figure as he confronts and attempts to define "reality." But this reality is extravagantly layered with masquerade, and forms that are often as lyric as they are brutal shift and change and baffle expectation. The constant refinement of brute reality into lyric illusion is not simply the work of Antony, Shakespeare's hero, but the lifelong work of Shakespeare himself. Thus there is a curious, rather decadent air in this play in which flamboyant desires have as much import—if not ultimately as much political strength—as events themselves.

The critic Lionel Abel has stated that among the characters of *Hamlet* there are four playwrights: Claudius, the Ghost, Polonius, and Hamlet.* Among the characters of *Antony and Cleopatra* there are any number of mythologizing poets and playwrights, including Octavius Caesar, Enobarbus, Philo, and Cleopatra herself. But the most important is Antony, who is snared within the net of appearances and forced by politics to break free. His agony is curiously muted for being that of someone who has achieved and lost so much—but this fact can be better understood if we examine the basis of the play and its relationship to tragedy.

The movement of most works of literature—whether the simple medieval morality play or the ambiguous *Troilus and Cressida*—is toward a dramatic confrontation with reality. The hero's downfall (or, in happier works, his conversion or enlightenment) is determined by the success with which reality overcomes appearances. If there is any great theme of literature, in my opinion, this is it: the destruction of the *faux-semblant* and attendant illusions by the intervention, bitter or glorious, of

---

* Lionel Abel, *Metatheatre: A New View of Dramatic Form* (New York: Hill & Wang, 1963), p. 50.

reality. Tragedy works with this theme and is inseparable from it. The orthodox tragedy we are familiar with involves a process of learning and culminates in a kind of exorcism, which is manipulated by the tragic figure himself, as in *Oedipus Rex*, or by surrounding characters who may or may not be fragmented aspects of the hero himself, as in *The Revenger's Tragedy*, or by fate or external social forces, as in Ibsen's *Ghosts*.

In *Antony and Cleopatra*, however, all exorcism fails. Exorcism works to dispel illusion, but the poetry of *Antony and Cleopatra* works to *create* illusion. Just as Antony cannot rid himself of his obsession with Cleopatra, so Cleopatra cannot quite rid herself of the earthbound and, in a crude sense, comic aspects of her own mortality. The play is sustained by words alone, for its plot is certainly incidental; we are never interested in what a character does, but only in how he expresses his consciousness of what he has done, and what this evokes in the mirroring rhetoric of his witnesses. Here reality does not defeat appearances. Appearances are made—through a pressure that approaches magic—to defeat reality, or at least to render it irrelevant.

* * *

The play doesn't even start out as a typical tragedy. The first act is comic in intention: the lovers insist upon their love's hyperbole and most specifically upon Antony's rejection of his former life:

> Let Rome in Tiber melt, and the wide arch
> Of the ranged empire fall: here is my space.
> Kingdoms are clay: our dungy earth alike
> Feeds beast as man.

(1.1.35–38)

The banter and playacting of the first scene show Antony and Cleopatra at their worst, and this self-caricaturing gives a credulity to Philo's opening description of Antony that would not ordinarily belong to it.

> Nay, but this dotage of our general's
> O'erflows the measure: those his goodly eyes,
> That o'er the files and musters of the war
> Have glowed like plated Mars, now bend, now turn
> The office and devotion of their view
> Upon a tawny front. His captain's heart,
> Which in the scuffles of great fights hath burst
> The buckles on his breast, reneges all temper
> And is become the bellows and the fan
> To cool a gipsy's lust.
>
> (1.1.1–10)

This is Philo's judgment of Antony, which may be equated exactly with the judgment of the Roman world. Antony, he concludes, is the "triple pillar of the world transformed / Into a strumpet's fool" (1.1.12–13). The central image here works for the Antony of the entire play, since what is unforgettable in this Antony is his heart: the organ of courage, of magnanimity, of loyalty, of love, of hysterical valor made possible only by a "diminution in our captain's brain" (3.13.230). Antony *is* his heart, as Caesar is his reason, and the heart, being blind, appreciates the complexities of the "tawny front" (Philo's description of Cleopatra) by other means. Antony is a man of complexity, a colossus and a ruffian who consumes himself in the love that, by devouring him, transforms him into a being the military Antony could never have imagined. The passage suggests, further, a shameful helplessness; it suggests entrapment, the commitment of the passionate being to his passion.

Common judgments of Antony are perplexed, or at best mixed, for he is not a tragic figure in any recognizable sense. As much as he reveals himself in his words—in his half-false sincerities and his half-truthful lies—there is mystery in him because he is in a process of change. His variety is suggested by the differing men who see him, and, most famously, by Cleopatra after his death. To his officer, Ventidius, he is a captain generous only to those who keep themselves, cautiously and wisely, inferior to him (Act 3, Scene 1); to Enobarbus, he is a "fool" (3.13.48) and yet a "mine of bounty" for whom one might give his life (4.6.35); to Caesar, the Antony of old was a great soldier who fought "with patience more / Than savages could suffer" (1.4.65–66), but who is now a man "who is th'abstract of all faults / That all men follow" (1.4.9–10). Caesar might have gone on to see that Antony is not flawed by his faults but rather *is* his faults; in him, as in Cleopatra, the vilest things become themselves. Yet to Lepidus, there are not "Evils enough to darken all his goodness: / His faults in him seem as the spots of heaven, / More fiery by night's blackness" (1.4.12–14). Antony is considered, frequently, in terms of light and dark imagery. What is perplexing is the ease with which the polar values of light and dark may be confused. Antony is, in Cleopatra's famous speech, light itself:

> His face was as the heavens, and therein stuck
> A sun and moon which kept their course and lighted
> The little o'th'earth.

> (5.2.96–98)

This cosmic light blinks good and evil; when one leaves the atmosphere of the human condition, the two become indistinguishable.

* * *

The relationship of Antony and Cleopatra is as ignoble as nobility will allow. We see them as lovers in fragments: they wander through the streets and "note / The qualities of people" (1.1.58–59); they lie brilliantly and passionately to each other; they swear their love in impossibly exaggerated terms; they do not trust each other. Above all, they are not youthful lovers: Cleopatra sees herself as "with Phoebus' amorous pinches black / And wrinkled deep in time" (1.5.33–34); Antony speaks angrily of sending to "the boy Caesar . . . this grizzled head" (3.13.21). But, in them, surface conventions and the reality of spirit are blurred, just as the good and evil of Antony become one in the dazzling light he embodies.

So Cleopatra, with "wann'd" lip, is still the queen of her exotic land, and is evoked in the famous set piece of Act 2, Scene 2 in which Enobarbus describes her to an awe-stricken Roman as an impression rather than a reality—and it is the impression, finally, that matters. The scene upon the barge— the air lovesick with perfume, the rich imagery of gold and purple and silver, the transformation of attendants into cupids and mermaids, most of all the transformation of the perhaps desperate Cleopatra into Venus—may just miss being absurd. But Enobarbus, whose sense of reality we are to trust, understands that she does "make defect perfection" (2.2.267) and that, given this alchemy, the logical Roman world and its judgments are irrelevant. The paradox Cleopatra embodies is suggested most succinctly in Agrippa's exclamation, "Royal wench!" (2.2.261). Cleopatra's majesty is such that so crude a comic scene as the one in which she assaults the messenger of ill news does not destroy it; she is described in terms of food and eating, and describes herself so, but this counts, ultimately, as one of the symptoms of her complexity and not simply of her baseness. Recurring in her, even at her death, is a propensity to view matters comically.

Similarly, the play itself is not a typical tragedy, for it lacks a consciousness of either fate or divine intention. At a certain point Antony's god, Hercules, deserts him, but Antony registers no consciousness of this symbolic act. It does not work to relate directly to the hero's interpretation of his plight or to add to the audience's understanding of its dimensions. It is eerie; it is mystical; it is a possibility—just as anything in the enchanted Egypt is a possibility—but its suggestion of divine force or fate is never taken up by anyone in the play. *Antony and Cleopatra* is the most godless of Shakespeare's plays, because it is about human beings for whom anything less than self-divinity will be failure.

* * *

Another form of appearance the lovers indulge in is ceremony. *Antony and Cleopatra* is as ceremonial a play as *Richard II* and *Troilus and Cressida*, but though in the end all of these ceremonies come to nothing, the abandonment of these forms in *Antony and Cleopatra* does not constitute the education it does in the other plays. The people of both worlds, Roman and Egyptian, live according to ceremony. Caesar, disgusted, scorns Antony's vulgar performance when Antony at last flees back to Egypt:

I'th'market-place, on a tribunal silvered,
Cleopatra and himself in chairs of gold
Were publicly enthroned: at the feet sat
Caesarion, whom they call my father's son,

And all the unlawful issue that their lust
Since then hath made between them.

(3.6.3–8)

But then, minutes later, Caesar bitterly attacks the manner of
the arrival of his sister, Antony's lawful wife, because it has not
enough of show in it:

> You come not
> Like Caesar's sister: the wife of Antony
> Should have an army for an usher, and
> The neighs of horse to tell of her approach
> Long ere she did appear: the trees by th'way
> Should have borne men, and expectation fainted,
> Longing for what it had not . . .
> . . . But you are come
> A market-maid to Rome, and have prevented
> The ostentation of our love, which, left unshown,
> Is often left unloved.

(3.6.47–53; 55–58)

There is no distinction on this level between the Roman and the
Egyptian: for both, reality loses itself in appearance.

Later Antony, preparing for his suicide, will dream of his
reunion with Cleopatra after death in terms of this "show." It is
not enough for the lovers to dwell together in romantic bliss for
eternity. Their love exists, clearly enough, at least in part in the
awe of witnesses:

> Where souls do couch on flowers we'll hand in hand
> And with our sprightly port make the ghosts gaze.

Dido and her Aeneas shall want troops,
And all the haunt be ours.

(4.14.59–62)

This does not subtract from their love, but rather qualifies it as a particular sort of love. It's a love that can give more of itself to supposed irrelevancies than romantic love can afford to surrender.

∗ ∗ ∗

The several climaxes of the play baffle expectation. If the processes of exorcism are to be completed, Antony as the deluded lover must collide with reality and must see his folly. But the movement toward tragic enlightenment is always thwarted, and Antony withdraws from these encounters with his faith untouched. So after the battle at Actium when Antony seems a defeated man—"I am so lated in the world that I / Have lost my way forever" (3.11.3–4)—he rebounds thanks to the totality of his commitment to Cleopatra. He is able to say to her:

Fall not a tear, I say. One of them rates
All that is won and lost. . . .
Love, I am full of lead. Some wine
Within there and our viands! Fortune knows
We scorn her most when most she offers blows.

(3.11.76–77; 80–82)

After the defeat at Actium, with their world shaken and its vastness for the first time questioned, Antony and Cleopatra become recognizably human. Ceremony is forgotten in the urgency of the moment, and they are reconciled.

The next climax comes when Antony sees Caesar's messenger kissing Cleopatra's hand; he does not see that she is acting a part. His judgment on her turns back upon himself in a passage that should work as a catharsis of his love and liberate him from his bondage:

> But when we in our viciousness grow hard—
> O, misery on't!—the wise gods seel our eyes,
> In our own filth drop our clear judgements, make us
> Adore our errors, laugh at's while we strut
> To our confusion.
>
> (3.13.135–139)

He is maddened by Caesar's "harping on what I am, / Not what he knew I was" (3.13.169–170) as if his life were over. But he is again reconciled to Cleopatra, whose dignity grows when his diminishes, and he believes that they will yet do well. His bravado, however, has a new sound of hollowness:

> I will be treble-sinewed, hearted, breathed,
> And fight maliciously. For when mine hours
> Were nice and lucky, men did ransom lives
> Of me for jests. But now I'll set my teeth
> And send to darkness all that stop me. Come,
> Let's have one other gaudy night: call to me
> All my sad captains . . .
>
> (3.13.209–215)

The apparent change of fortune that follows (they beat back Caesar's men) makes the final catastrophe the more complete.

After the last defeat, Cleopatra's men desert to the enemy

and, for Antony, her apparent betrayal constitutes a betrayal of
all appearance:

> Sometimes we see a cloud that's dragonish,
> A vapour sometime like a bear or lion,
> A towered citadel, a pendent rock,
> A forkèd mountain, or blue promontory
> With trees upon't that nod unto the world
> And mock our eyes with air. Thou hast seen these
>   signs:
> They are black vesper's pageants.
>   . . .
> That which is now a horse, even with a thought
> The rack dislimns and makes it indistinct
> As water is in water.
>
> (4.14.3–9; 11–13)

For Antony, reality is defined by the protean condition of man
and his world, a vision presented here with deadly vividness—
but this glimpse of reality is again discarded. He is brought the
false report that Cleopatra has killed herself, and his commitment to love is again realized as he prepares for death.

*   *   *

It is the final restoration of his faith in love that justifies the
expenditure of passion the play has permitted. His death is
neither escape nor self-punishment; it is, of course, a mistake,
yet it is at the same time a willful surrender to something very
like love. Eros is Antony's knave and Antony's god: Antony will
"make death love me" (3.13.225) and will "run into't / As to a
lover's bed" (4.14.117–18). Brutus dies because he has awakened
from delusion; Othello dies when freed from the delusion of

what he is; Troilus, not a tragic figure, perhaps, nevertheless goes into battle to die when confronted with the prospect of a world totally corrupted. But Antony dies with his faith in love renewed. This long death scene avoids a ghastly sentimentality, partially by Cleopatra's unromantic wariness (fearing capture, she will not leave the monument to come to the dying Antony), partially by the confidence with which the lovers affirm themselves and their love, and partially by the sheer hyperbolic force of the poetry itself.

* * *

The play is conceived in hyperbole. In the controlled hysteria of Renaissance language, Shakespeare created a world to which no real world could ever be equal. The confines of the Roman-Egyptian horizons are, by necessity, without limitation. Even though the known world is collapsed into Antony, Cleopatra, and Caesar, nothing is missing from it, since they combine among them all its brilliance and all its stupidity.

As a result, Antony can say of himself that with his sword he "Quartered the world" (4.14.67). Even Caesar can say that "The death of Antony / Is not a single doom: in the name lay / A moiety of the world" (5.1.20–22). And Cleopatra can say of him that he destroys with his death all order in the world:

> . . . young boys and girls
> Are level now with men: the odds is gone
> And there is nothing left remarkable
> Beneath the visiting moon.
>
> (4.15.74–77)

These lines begin the extended re-creation of her lover—an act of love and poetry which must be unmatched in literature for

its audacity and its beauty—and they culminate in the speech
toward which all the earlier poetry moves:

> His legs bestrid the ocean, his reared arm
> Crested the world: his voice was propertied
> As all the tunèd spheres, and that to friends:
> But when he meant to quail and shake the orb,
> He was as rattling thunder. For his bounty,
> There was no winter in't: an autumn it was
> That grew the more by reaping. His delights
> Were dolphin-like: they showed his back above
> The element they lived in. In his livery
> Walked crowns and crownets, realms and islands were
> As plates dropped from his pocket.
>
> (5.2.100–110)

The play is finally Antony's, and Cleopatra is priestess to his
apotheosis. The wonder of these flights of poetry is that it is not
possible that Antony could have been as he is dreamed.

Throughout the play, Shakespeare balances hyperbole with
comic suggestion: the Antony as colossus and the Antony as
ruffian, the Cleopatra equal to all visions of herself and the
Cleopatra raging at the servant who has betrayed her. But the
counterpoint neither qualifies the grandeur of these people nor
cheats them of their incredible dignity. Instead, it suggests by
contrast the range of behavior this dignity allows itself, and the
heights to which it succeeds. Thus Cleopatra becomes unforgettable precisely because she is a woman, and at times a small
woman; what is insisted upon is her humanity, the ascent of
angels or demonic gods being too easy. The baseness of Cleopatra does not preclude her greatness but assures it, since without this her presence would be no more than a flight of words.

This magic, admittedly, will not work for everyone. Though the modern temperament admires passion and individuality more than the older virtues of prudence, modesty, and chastity, Cleopatra may still be interpreted as Shakespeare's Romans see her, and Antony's death may be seen as simply the necessary result of his having surrendered his reason to immoral passion. But the magic works for Antony and Cleopatra themselves, and it need not do more.

The denial of prosaic reality and its metamorphosis into something rich and strange are possible through the language Shakespeare uses. Thus the chilling vision Antony has of the cloud formations that baffle the eye and that extend, in their impermanence, into the lives of men is a vision that may be utilized profitably by the victims of this world of appearances. Antony dies with his belief in Cleopatra and himself secure (and it is surely Shakespeare's Antony that William Carlos Williams has in mind in his whimsical poem "To Mark Anthony in Heaven," the sense of the poem being that Antony's experience and his commitment to love are "heaven," man's highest achievement). Cleopatra asks, after her envisioning of Antony as a colossus, whether there was such a man as that of whom she speaks; when told there was not, she replies:

> You lie up to the hearing of the gods!
> But if there be nor ever were one such,
> It's past the size of dreaming.
>
> (5.2.115–117)

These lines propose a question they do not answer: Who was this man? Clearly there has been an Antony, but if there has been this Antony then he has fallen beyond man's capacity for understanding. At her own death Cleopatra is able to use her

imagination to transform the snake into a "baby at my breast /
That sucks the nurse asleep" (5.2.348–349). This final alchemy is
no more wonderful than that which has lighted the entire play.
We must turn to a Prospero to encounter equal omnipotence.

It is reality that is defeated in this play, and its defeat goes
unmourned. The uses of poetry are nowhere in Shakespeare
so well imagined as in this work about godly creatures who
delight in their humanity, and who leave their traces upon all
corners of their gigantic world. Illusion could not be sustained
in Hamlet's gloomy Denmark, or on the wild fields of Scotland.
It requires the light-drenched world of old Egypt—a world
that exists nowhere except in this play and then only within its
words, by the strenuous magic of its language.

Maxine Hong Kingston

WAR AND LOVE

MAXINE HONG KINGSTON is Professor Emerita at the University of California, Berkeley. She is the author of *The Woman Warrior*, for which she won the National Books Critics Circle Award, and *China Men*, for which she received a National Book Award. She is also the author of *To Be the Poet* and *The Fifth Book of Peace*, and editor of *Veterans of War, Veterans of Peace*. Her work has been recognized with a Guggenheim Fellowship and two National Endowment for the Arts Literature Fellowships, as well as the National Humanities Medal.

When America began fighting in Vietnam, I was teaching *Romeo and Juliet* to high school students who were not much younger than I. Of course, whether or not one has read or seen that play, we know it in our minds and hearts as the ultimate love story. We want to love and be loved as Romeo and Juliet loved each other. The high point of the story would be the balcony scene; everything else is background, everyone else unimportant.

It is a long, delicious scene, and it includes not just some of the most beloved lines of the English language, but some of the most yearned-for feelings of the human heart. Juliet appears at the window and Romeo exclaims,

> But, soft, what light through yonder window breaks?
> It is the east, and Juliet is the sun.

> (2.1.47–48)

He continues,

> It is my lady, O, it is my love!
> O, that she knew she were!
>
> (2.1.55–56)

And concludes, reminding us in his curious flight of fancy that Shakespeare was a glover's son,

> See how she leans her cheek upon her hand!
> O, that I were a glove upon that hand,
> That I might touch that cheek!
>
> (2.1.68–70)

Still unaware that he is below, Juliet speaks her thoughts out loud:

> O Romeo, Romeo, wherefore art thou Romeo?
>
> (2.1.80)

"Wherefore" means "why"—"why art thou Romeo?"—she wishes he had a different name because it is unthinkable for her to marry into his family. She muses,

> What's in a name? That which we call a rose
> By any other word would smell as sweet . . .
>
> (2.1.90–91)

He swears his love; she responds,

> O, swear not by the moon, th'inconstant moon . . .
>
> (2.1.158)

She is right, too; he has loved before. But this is a true love story because Juliet is no ordinary heroine. As she says,

> My bounty is as boundless as the sea,
> My love as deep: the more I give to thee,
> The more I have, for both are infinite.
>
> (2.1.184–186)

Her charm extends even to her famous parting words,

> Goodnight, goodnight! Parting is such sweet sorrow,
> That I shall say goodnight till it be morrow.
>
> (2.1.239–240)

If you're short of time, just study that one scene. If you're teaching and the students can't read at class level, let alone read Shakespeare, tell them the story in your own words. I had to make sure that school was interesting so the boys wouldn't drop out and join the Army, and so that they would learn as much as possible before they got drafted.

Here is part of a story I wrote about this time in my life and in the life of our country.

FROM "THE BROTHER IN VIETNAM"
China Men (1977)

The brother tried to get into the Coast Guard, which he thought rescued surfers and sailboats and directed traffic around buoys. He drove to Santa Cruz and Monterey, and there were no openings; everybody else who did not want to go to war had had the same idea. Then the Coast Guard were sent to Vietnam to fight on the rivers there.

The Japanese and Chinese Americans warned one another

what would happen if they got captured: the Vietnamese would flay Asian Americans alive. Unless you die of shock, you're still alive after being skinned. You had to die fighting. Imagine the eyes looking out of a skinless body. During World War II the United States had tactfully sent the 442nd Go-For-Broko AJA's to Europe, not Asia or the Pacific. But for this war, there was not that special consideration.

The rumor also went that the brother's draft board was channeling hippies and blacks into the infantry. And "Orientals" belonged over there in Asia fighting among their own kind. The only way that he would be able to get classified as a Conscientious Objector was to have a religion, and he did not have one. He did not want to end up a medic in this immoral war anyway.

While deciding what to do, as time ran out, the brother did his job, which was teaching high school. He had been teaching for months, but had not gotten over his surprise at how dumb the students were. Most of them had an I.Q. of 100, the average, which permitted them to read by sounding out each word. The human race was not smart.

During Current Events, he told his class some atrocities to convince them about the wrongness of war. The students looked at the pictures of napalmed children and said, "Sure, war is hell." Where had they learned that acceptance? He told them the worst torture he knew: the Vikings used to cleave a prisoner-of-war's back on either side of the spine, and pull the lungs out, which fluttered like wings when the man breathed. This torture was called the Burning Eagle. The brother felt that it was self-evident that we ought to do anything to stop war. But he was learning that upon hearing terrible things, there are people who are, instead, filled with a crazy patriotism.

"Who owns the electricity?" a boy with an 85 I.Q. and a

third-grade reading level asked one day. The brother recognized a "teachable moment," as these happy seconds were called in college. He explained how water, electricity, gas, and oil originally belonged to nobody and everybody. Like the air. "But the corporations that control electricity sell it to the rest of us," he said. "Well, of course they do," said the student; "I'd sell the air if I had discovered it." "What if some people can't afford to buy it?" "Whoever discovered it deserves to be paid for it," said the stubborn boy. "It's Communist not to let him make all the money he can." Although the students could not read or follow logic, they blocked him with their anti-Communism, which seemed to come naturally to them, without effort or study. He had thought that it was self-evident that air, at least, belongs to all of us. The students' parents were on welfare, unemployment, and workmen's compensation, but they defended capitalism without knowing what it was called.

"Can you invent a plan where a person can always find a job, and with that job make a living?" the brother asked. "How do we go about making food instead of bombs?" "What steps can we take to stop the war in Vietnam?"

"You think like that because you're a Communist," the kids replied. "That's a Communist question." Any criticism he had of America they dismissed as his being gookish.

Students were dropping out, not in protest like college students but to volunteer for the Army, Navy, and Marines. He had a few months, a few weeks, days to educate them before they got killed or killed others in Vietnam. Or until he himself had to go. He had to make up words of advice on the spot. Supposedly men, the dropouts came back to the hallways to show off their sturdy uniforms and good shoes. They looked more substantial, taller, smoothed out, as if some kind of potential had been fulfilled. "Take care of yourself," he told them. To those who dropped out to work on assembly lines, he said, "Find out what you're making."

In the one class that wasn't remedial, strange things happened to the literature. After the lessons on how to fill out employment forms, checks, income tax forms, driver's license and health insurance applications, after reading and discussing the motor vehicle code, he introduced *Romeo and Juliet* with a movie of it, models of the Globe, role-playing, and the sound track from *West Side Story*. But upon its reading, *Romeo and Juliet* became a horror story about children his students' age whispering, tiptoeing, making love, and driven mad in the dark. They killed and were killed in dark streets and dark rooms. They married in the dark. Plague infested the country, and drugs poisoned instead of cured. Children were buried alive among their ancestors' bones, with which Juliet feared she would dash her brains. She was locked in a tomb with her dead husband, a young suicide, and her cousin festering green. The brother could not shift the emphasis; he felt he had spoiled the love story for a generation of students.

Between the classes he found secret torn books hidden underneath shelves and stuffed behind other books. Somebody had jammed books behind the radiator and up the air vent, "Fuck you, bastard" scrawled on their pages. Books that he had bought for a classroom library were ripped in half among the bindings.

* * *

If I were teaching the play now, I would have the students collect news stories about love between Muslim and non-Muslim, Jew and Palestinian, Hutu and Tutsi. I'd tell them love stories of my generation: Chinese marrying Japanese, Americans marrying Vietnamese, Catholics marrying Protestants. I'd assign the students—many of them biracial or multiracial—to write love stories set in our global times.

Just now I reread the ending of *Romeo and Juliet*. I see that the Capulets and the Montagues made "a glooming peace," as it is called by the Prince of Verona in those resonant closing lines:

> A glooming peace this morning with it brings,
> The sun, for sorrow, will not show his head.
> Go hence to have more talk of these sad things:
> Some shall be pardoned, and some punishèd,
> For never was a story of more woe
> Than this of Juliet and her Romeo.
>
> (5.3.315–320)

Although tragic, some good did come out of the suicides of the young people: they ended a war.

My students of the Vietnam War era could not bear an unhappy ending. I remember one of them writing that Romeo and Juliet died and went to heaven, where they lived happily ever after. When Shakespeare writes for all time, and makes promises of immortality, do we dare keep young readers from making up their own love scenes?

Peter David

ON THE TERRIBLE AND UNEXPECTED FATE OF THE STAR-CROSSED LOVERS

PETER DAVID is an American author who writes novels, including the *Star Trek* series; novel adaptations, including *The Rocketeer*, *Spider-Man*, and *Iron Man*; comic books, including *The Incredible Hulk*; scripts for movies and television; and scenarios for video games. His many honors include an Eisner Award, a Wizard Fan Award, a UK Comic Art Award, a Golden Duck Award for Young Adult Series, a GLAAD Media Award, and an Australian OZCon Award for Favourite International Writer.

Many years ago, I took my daughter Gwen, then aged fourteen, to see Baz Luhrmann's new *William Shakespeare's Romeo + Juliet*—which is kind of like saying *William Shakespeare's West Side Story*, because, although the basic elements are there, the film bears as much resemblance to a real staging of *Romeo and Juliet* as *Kiss Me, Kate* does to *The Taming of the Shrew*. Actually, now that I think about it, there was probably more actual Shakespearean dialogue in *Kiss Me, Kate*.

The *West Side Story* comparison is apt, since Luhrmann had set the story in the modern day, with the Montagues and the Capulets as warring corporations and the squabbling youngsters tooling around in hot sports cars, shooting at each other and blowing up gas stations. It starred the kid-friendly pairing of Leonardo DiCaprio and Claire Danes.

I must admit I had no intrinsic problem with even a gutted version of Shakespeare. *Anything* that has a *scintilla* of a chance at getting even one kid per audience genuinely interested in the Bard is something I heartily support. Bottom line is, we went to an afternoon showing and the place was packed with teenagers. Teens watching something purporting to be Shakespeare: hey, at least it's *something*. How many of them would have been inclined to see anything that even hinted of Shakespeare if it didn't look like an extended MTV video and feature familiar young actors?

So to a certain extent it didn't matter that Danes was, at most, adequate (nowhere near the level of brilliance that she would later display in *Homeland*); that DiCaprio, despite all his efforts, never managed to wrap himself around the dialogue. He said his lines, he was prettier than Juliet, he didn't bump into the furniture, and he was rather effective screaming *"I am fortune's fool!"* at the top of his lungs. But that was about it. And the actor playing Benvolio was on par with the jock who auditioned for the High School of Performing Arts in *Fame* by stumbling through Juliet's part in the balcony scene.

But this isn't intended as a commentary on the film. Rather, it was the audience that I found intriguing—to be specific, the audience as the film moved to its climax.

There was Juliet, laid out in the crypt, apparently dead. There was Romeo, crying his eyes out, about to down poison so he could join his love in death.

And I heard audience members muttering all around me, "Watch. She'll wake up just in time."

I couldn't believe it. I glanced around the audience, saw

them smiling, confident that everything would work out. And that's when I realized they didn't know how it ended. I was in an audience full of people who were utterly clueless as to what was about to happen. They figured it was going to have a happy resolution. They didn't know Romeo and Juliet both end up dead.

I was astounded. This goes beyond not knowing, say, the significance of "Rosebud." The average school system doesn't teach *Citizen Kane*. But how could they never have been exposed to one of Shakespeare's most renowned plays?

Not to mention that it went beyond cultural and/or scholastic ineptitude. I couldn't comprehend why they didn't know the fate of the lovers because *it's said right at the top of the film*.

In one of the movie's cleverest bits of business, the famed prologue was delivered via a news anchor as if she were reporting the eleven o'clock news. Dutifully describing the feuding households of Verona, the newscaster said:

> From forth the fatal loins of these two foes
> A pair of star-crossed lovers take their life,
> Whose misadventured piteous overthrows;
> Doth with their death bury their parents' strife.
>
> (Prologue 5–8)

And just to make sure that the point was not lost on anyone, the prologue was immediately *repeated* with the dialogue *printed on the screen*. You would have thought that key phrases such as "take their life" and "death" would have tipped the audience off.

But no, the viewers remained oblivious of the star-crossed lovers' fate. There were startled faces all through the theater as Romeo, with a final kiss, died. Then Juliet picked up Romeo's gun, to complete the "take their life" part of the prologue. And the audience, watching in confusion, muttered, "She's going to *shoot* him too?"

Well, obviously she didn't. And when the final credits began to roll, the audience dissatisfaction was audible. "Well, *that* sucked!" "They both died?" "What the hell—?"

And I stood up and faced the audience (because most of them were behind us) and I bellowed (since they apparently felt that talking in the theater as if they were at home was perfectly fine, so why not give them back in kind), "What part of 'star-crossed lovers take their life' did you *not get*? They did it twice! The newscaster said it, and then they printed it! On the screen! In huge type! What the hell is wrong with you?! Were you too busy talking to each other to pay attention?!?"

Which was pretty much the last time that Gwen went to the movies with me. Although she did spend the rest of the week muttering about "King Lear."

Conor McCreery

SHAKESPEARE AND
FOUR-COLOUR MAGIC

CONOR MCCREERY is a Canadian journalist, television writer, and coauthor of the comic book series *Kill Shakespeare*, which has been nominated twice for the Shuster Award for Best Writing and also for a Harvey Award for Best New Series. Volume 1 of the series has been named to the YALSA Great Graphic Novel for Teens list and been honored by the Maverick Awards as a selected graphic novel; it has also been chosen by the Canadian Children's Book Centre as one of the best graphic novels of the year for young adults, as well as by the *Toronto Star* and the *New York Times* for their recommended Christmas lists. McCreery and coauthor Anthony Del Col also adapted the project to the stage; it was mounted by Toronto's acclaimed Soulpepper Theatre Company as part of the Young Centre's Word Festival, and will be presented at the Shakespeare Association of America conference in Toronto as well as at universities and Comic-Cons throughout the United States and Canada. McCreery and Del Col are currently adapting *Kill Shakespeare* for the screen with the support of Telefilm Canada, the Harold Greenberg Fund, and Corus Entertainment.

W hen most people talk about the magic of the theatre the topic usually turns to Shakespeare, Brecht, Chekhov, Beckett—heck, even Andrew Lloyd Webber. But when I hear about the magic of the theatre my thoughts turn, almost paradoxically, to a different kind of magic—to the four-colour magic of comics.

I say "paradoxically" because while theatre is generally seen as high culture, the humble comic book is almost universally accepted as an inferior art form—a work for kids, or for those who can't handle the complex narratives of "real" literature.

Of course, I'm a bit different than the average theatre-goer, given that I'm also a comics nerd. To date, I have spent a decent portion of my adult life either selling or making the little suckers.

Like many of us, I grew up reading brightly illustrated stories designed to make me laugh and perhaps teach me a thing or two. My constant companions were Archie and Tintin, Asterix and Obelix, and later Spider-Man, the X-Men, and the members of Alpha Flight. And, like many of us, I reached an age when I put my comics away in a shoe box, filed them away somewhere safe (just in case that *Web of Spider-Man* #17 I had would one day pay for my first house), and more or less forgot about them except for lazy holiday afternoons when the familiarity of home made me crave a hot cocoa, an easy chair, and the heroes of my youth.

Years later I had co-created an animated series pitch that had gained some traction—all I needed was to find a day job that I could walk away from once Hollywood "inevitably" called. So I ended up working at the same shop that fed my adolescent habit: the Silver Snail in downtown Toronto. It was there that I was reintroduced to my childhood friends and found out that they had grown up while I wasn't looking. Whether it was the antiheroism of *Watchmen*, the sympathetic portrayal of the Devil in *Lucifer*, or the sexual and racial politics of *Love and Rockets*, I quickly saw that the straightforward stories I had read as a child had matured into something more: nuanced morality plays that were as satisfying as anything I had been handed while earning my minor in theatre at university.

And of course I had been taught in these hallowed halls that the absolute pinnacle of the footlights, the plain upon which no mortals dare stride, was the rarefied and consecrated ground that the Bard first trod upon, nay, floated above.

In short, I was taught that Shakespeare should scare the shit out of me.

So it is understandable that there was many a raised eyebrow when Anthony Del Col and I first announced plans for our comic series, *Kill Shakespeare*. Wasn't it odd enough that we planned to mix all of the Bard's characters into one world? Why would we then further handicap our story by putting it into comics?

But for us, it was an obvious decision to start *Kill Shakespeare*'s life as a comic. No other medium provides such a natural staging ground for Shakespeare's special brand of populism, magic, kinetic energy, humour, storytelling, and depth of character.

It is odd that what makes the stage inherently magical is almost the opposite of that which infuses magic into comics. To me, theatre gives you goose bumps because you have no control over it. It unfolds in front of you in the dark as you watch flesh-and-blood actors ply their craft. Each performance is different, and each holds the same potential to be an unmitigated triumph that sends you bounding into the streets, filled with energy, chattering about how strangely alive you feel, as it does to be a complete disaster (which also, funnily enough, fills me with energy and sends me bounding into the streets, if only to say, "You'll never guess what a train wreck I just watched!").

Meanwhile, comics give readers a unique opportunity to control the way they consume stories, and it's a medium that gives creators an almost unparalleled ability to take bold creative steps because of the unique marriage of art and literature,

"Will you save us from the tyranny of William Shakespeare?"
Richard makes his offer to a overwhelmed Hamlet.
Art by Andy Belanger. Copyright Kill Shakespeare, *published by IDW.*

the lower financial stakes, and the ability to borrow the type of magic that Shakespeare used so beautifully in his work—a suspension of disbelief that allows the reader to be transported to almost any reality, be it the magic of the faerie world, the private madness of a king, or a strange island where almost anything is possible.

* * *

It was travelling to that island that brought me my first encounter with the Bard's magic. The journey was a traditional one for high school students in southern Ontario. Like most of my teenage ilk from around the world, I was exposed to/forced to read the Bard in English class. Unlike most of my teenage ilk, I had North America's most prestigious Shakespeare festival, Stratford, a short yellow-bus ride away.

So, like thousands of other kids in the province, I was bundled up with my classmates and taken to the festival. Neatly scrubbed and squeaky clean in slacks, blazer, and tie, like all others of my private-school set, I got off the bus in Stratford to join the hundreds of other tragically attired children there to fulfill their English-class obligations. Then I cautiously made my way through the mix of crowds—the private and public school kids,* octogenarians and (presumably) out-of-work actors, incrementally expanding upon the safe little bubble of my world. Now I look back at this "clash of cultures" as wholly appropriate for the Bard. After all, no writer in human history has more successfully taken us into the minds and hearts of so

---

* I was keeping a sharp eye out for the public school kids. For some bizarre reason, they didn't instantly see the appeal of a bunch of kids dressed with the sartorial splendour of mini Warren Buffetts. The fact that our blazers said "Holy Trinity" on them probably didn't help our street cred.

many different humans—from Othello to Iago to Hamlet to Cleopatra to Poor Tom to Lady Macbeth. No writer has done a better job of making us see ourselves in the "other." Now, whether the "other" Shakespeare was foreseeing wearing a ripped Megadeth T-shirt is up for debate, but the point stands.

The Tempest wasn't the first play I studied in school, but it was the first play I remember going to see live and it was the first play that piqued my sensibilities as a teenage boy. The previous year's play, *Much Ado About Nothing*, with its clever meditations on love, couldn't compare to monsters, magic storms, plots of murder most foul, and a mad wizard. But still, I wasn't expecting to be blown away. Even though I had read, and enjoyed, *The Tempest*, Shakespeare was still confined in my mind to being dusty words on a page—cooler than I'd been led to believe, granted, but still not as vibrant as *A Canticle for Leibowitz*, as relatable as *To Kill a Mockingbird*, or as vital as *The Handmaid's Tale*.*

Boy, was I in for a surprise.

Looking back, it seems sort of obvious that a tale with all the enchantment and mystery of *The Tempest* would catch a comic-loving, sixteen-year-old boy's attention, but it wasn't until I saw Wayne Best playing the half-man, half-beast Caliban with a languorous, menacing physicality that something clicked inside my feverish, four-colour brain.

Caliban was Wolverine.

I mean he wasn't *quite*—there were no claws, and, unlike everyone's favourite Canadian sociopath, Caliban was clearly a victim, trapped both by Prospero and by his own cowardly nature—but if you squinted hard enough you could see how

---

* Admittedly, I was a weird kid. My other favourite books at the time were Robert Asprin's *Myth* series and a series of pulp sci-fi thrillers that concerned a character named the Stainless Steel Rat.

Caliban *could* be Wolverine, one of the most beloved characters in modern comics.

Like Caliban, Wolverine was a feral creature cursed with a berserker's rage. And like Caliban, Wolverine was imprisoned and tortured, having been captured by a shadowy U.S. military organization (aren't those the best ones?) and forced to undergo painful experiments that fused his skeleton with an unbreakable metal. In Act 1, Scene 2, Prospero describes, at length, the pains and tribulations that he will punish Caliban with unless the beast obeys him:

> For this, be sure, tonight thou shalt have cramps,
> Side-stitches that shall pen thy breath up: urchins
> Shall, for that vast of night that they may work,
> All exercise on thee: thou shalt be pinched
> As thick as honeycomb, each pinch more stinging
> Than bees that made 'em.
>
> (1.2.382–387)

And also like Caliban, Wolverine had a tenuous connection with his family. Caliban's mother was imprisoned by Prospero (though there was evidence she wasn't a kind mother) and Wolverine, as a teenager, was rejected by his mother after he accidentally killed the man who may have been her lover.

Unlike Caliban, however, Wolverine eventually found peace and personal salvation, first as a member of the Canadian superhero team Alpha Flight and later with his lifelong mentor, Professor X, the leader of a "pro-mutant" school and founder of the X-Men. From there, Wolverine experienced the sort of growth that Caliban might have engaged in if Shakespeare had elected to continue *The Tempest*. Wolverine learned to control his animal passions, and eventually to realize that he was not a monster but a man who deserved love like all other men.

In that sense I understood that Shakespeare had not gifted Caliban with the same mercies that writers like John Byrne and Chris Claremont gave to Wolverine. While our misfit Canadian eventually finds some semblance of happiness with his love, Jean Grey (before she dies),* Caliban does not get this sort of personal affirmation. As the final exchange concerning him in Act 5 shows, while Caliban is forgiven for his actions he is still seemingly judged for his form by his "master" Prospero, and even Caliban chides himself not for having served another but for having served the wrong master—he remains a trapped outsider to the very end.

> ALONSO: This is a strange thing as e'er I looked on.
> (*Points to Caliban*)
> PROSPERO: He is as disproportioned in his manners
> As in his shape. Go, sirrah, to my cell:
> Take with you your companions: as you look
> To have my pardon, trim it handsomely.
> CALIBAN: Ay, that I will: and I'll be wise hereafter,
> And seek for grace. What a thrice-double ass
> Was I to take this drunkard for a god
> And worship this dull fool!
>
> (5.1.323–331)

Once I had connected the fantastic world of my favourite monthlies, *X-Men*, *Alpha Flight*, and *Spider-Man*, and the oper-

---

* Well, before her first death anyway. Comic characters are notorious for the Twain-like nature of the reports of their death generally being greatly exaggerated.

atic tone of the Silver Age* runs of *Daredevil, Fantastic Four, Captain America*, and *Thor*, to the similarly fantastic worlds and operatic tones of Shakespeare's works, the works suddenly pulsated with new vitality.

Of course, it didn't hurt that the next play we read in class was the supremely bloody and melodramatic *Julius Caesar*. Nor that soon after that I was introduced to Puck, Oberon, and Titania from *A Midsummer Night's Dream*. Those plays had a grandiosity and a sense of being rooted in something other than the boring, everyday world that thrilled me. They reminded me of the Thunder God's battles with Loki, or the strange powers of the Purple Man, or the grandiose and oddly sympathetic plans of Doctor Octopus. Heck, my favourite character in *Alpha Flight* was *named* Puck. I mean, how could I ignore a sign like that?** Shakespeare was definitely for geeks.

* * *

Through this I was able to see that Shakespeare's work had a special magic. It was not just the literal magic of plays like *The Tempest* or *Macbeth* that hooked me but that every one of his tales had a richness, a vibrancy, and a certain disregard for plot that swept me along and made me accept whatever it was he was proposing. Was I really supposed to believe that nobody could ever tell that Rosalind and Imogen and Viola were actually women? How *exactly* did the Prince of Denmark charm a boatload of bloodthirsty pirates and get them to deliver first his mail and

---

* The Silver Age of comics is generally considered to be from the mid-1950s to 1970.

** To be fair, "Puck," who was stubby and hirsute and happened to have a demon trapped inside of him, was probably called that because he bounced around like the little piece of black rubber we Canadians smack about in our national game—still, the connection was made.

Kill Shakespeare's *jumping-off point finds Hamlet alone in
the waves, not back in Denmark, after the Act 4 attack of the Pirates.*
Art by Andy Belanger. Copyright Kill Shakespeare,
published by IDW.

then his person back home? And what decision did Isabella *really*
make about marrying the somewhat capricious Duke of Vienna
in *Measure for Measure*? Weren't these somewhat significant plot
points? Shouldn't I get to see how all that happened? Or, as in the
case of *Measure*, shouldn't I get to know *what* happened? As far as
Shakespeare was concerned, the answer was: "No."* Shakespeare
taught me an important lesson as a storyteller—that little things
like the occasional lapse of logic or a plot hole or two aren't
important—it's the magic of the tale that counts.

One of my favourite "gaps" in Shakespeare's work comes in
Act 1, Scene 7 of *Macbeth*, in which Lady Macbeth talks of her
child:

I have given suck, and know
How tender 'tis to love the babe that milks me:

---

* And, as far as I was concerned, the response was: "Okay, cool!"

I would, while it was smiling in my face,
Have plucked my nipple from his boneless gums,
And dashed the brains out, had I so sworn as you
Have done to this.

(1.7.58–63)

Yet never is the child mentioned again—not as a motivation for their ambition, nor as a reason for Macbeth to get cold feet, nor as a part of the tragedy of Lady Macbeth's death. It is introduced to us as a way to show Lady Macbeth's commitment to the plot to kill King Duncan: she would have happily killed the child she loved before breaking her word. Such strong feeling indicates that the child must have been important to Lady Macbeth, yet that strong motivation is never touched on again, not even to confirm the child's (supposed) death.

Or, staying with *Kill Shakespeare* characters, there are two massive elements that happen off stage and are, as such, relatively unexplored: Richard's final wooing of and marriage to Lady Anne (a woman who despises him so much that after she dies she returns just to haunt him), and the manner of her death itself. It's not clear whether she died by Richard's hand or, in some mysterious way, because of the curse she unwittingly laid upon herself in Act 1 of *Richard III*:

If ever he have wife, let her be made
More miserable by the death of him
Than I am made by my poor lord and thee.

(1.2.26–28)

It is a credit to the force of Shakespeare's magic that such pivotal moments can remain murky while the story is undiminished.

To be clear, when I'm talking about "magic" I mean the

magic we find in stories that supersedes reality. These are stories that turn up their noses at narrative convention and stories
that take readers out of their usual points of view. This magic is
what makes stories fantastical, regardless of whether they are in
the fantasy genre, and such stories have the rare power to carry
us along so that we disengage the critical part of our brains and
immerse ourselves entirely.*

*　*　*

When I began reading the work of Alan Moore (*Watchmen*)
and Neil Gaiman (*Sandman*), I realized that I wasn't the only
one who had seen the connection. These authors wove Shakespeare's words and works intimately throughout their worlds,
borrowing from a master as Shakespeare himself had borrowed
from his forefathers. And while their homages were the most
direct, they were hardly the only ones. I suspect I've missed
twice as many Shakespeare references as I've caught in comics. In chatting with Doug Lanier, a professor of English at the
University of New Hampshire who studies Shakespearean references in comics, I found out that the 1950s had been a heyday
for the Bard being "borrowed" in the comic medium, especially
in the horror genre, where the tales of ghosts, spirits, and tragedy made perfect fodder, while the 1960s and 1970s represented
a drop-off in using Shakespeare until the Bard began appearing in comics in new ways in the 1990s and in the new century. Gaiman's aforementioned *Sandman* series (1989–1996)
uses Shakespeare as a character in his own right, as do Peter
David's *Marvel 1602: Fantastick Four* (2006) and Alan Moore's
League of Extraordinary Gentlemen: The Black Dossier (2007). In

---

* Or, to put it another way that would have saved a few words, "suspend our
disbelief."

this last work, Moore imagines a world in which his Victorian-age "super-team" was founded by Prospero. *The Black Dossier* even features the first act of a "lost" Shakespearean play, *Fairy's Fortunes Founded*, allegedly begun in the year of Shakespeare's death, 1616.

Add that all up and I was more than a little surprised that when co-creator Anthony Del Col, series artist Andy Belanger, and I started to produce *Kill Shakespeare*, people thought Shakespeare and comics were such an odd match. We even had to defend ourselves from real venom, as when Kimberly Cox, the Shakespearean scholar and girlfriend of comic legend Frank Miller, opined that we should be "bitch slapped" for daring to attempt our tale.* For us, the tale of a civil war between the Bard's characters, with Shakespeare himself as the ultimate prize, seemed uniquely suited to the medium. The more we worked, the more it became obvious to me that, in general, comics and Shakespeare were perfect bedfellows.

The main problem with reading the Bard's work is that you don't get to see it. Until I watched Caliban hang by one arm from the stage, rocking dangerously as he challenged Prospero's rule and threatened to perpetrate unspeakable acts on the wizard's daughter, Miranda, I hadn't been able to fully grasp the dynamism of the scene. And even if I still didn't quite understand what Caliban was saying, hearing and especially watching him say it made all the difference. Seeing Shakespeare's work made his stories exciting and relatable to me in a way that the words on the page could not.

Which leads us back to comics—the medium that shares theatre's kinetic energy. The best comics, like the best theatre,

* Ms. Cox also helpfully commented that the book made her throw up in her mouth.

straddle the line between the literary and the visual in a way that gives us a visceral rush—in many ways the two art forms are close substitutes for each other. But comics hold a creative advantage over theatre, one that allows them to be perhaps the most innovative visual medium. While film and theatre are limited by financial and business concerns, comics are pretty much bound only by the writers' and the artists' imaginations. And now, with the ability to use the Internet as a delivery mechanism, the reach of comics is greater than ever.

Because of the lesser financial constraints which help spur blue-sky thinking, the comics form became a natural medium for larger-than-life characters and stories. The most obvious example of this is the superhero genre, which the medium invented. In a comic book, nobody questions the ability of Superman to "leap tall buildings in a single bound," or the fact that Peter Parker was bitten by a radioactive creepy-crawly and suddenly became Spider-Man. Comic readers accept that the worlds they enter when reading comics will be somehow bigger, brighter, and more vital than what they experience around them. They are prepared for the magic of the tale.

Both Shakespeare and the best of the superhero genre often capture all that is most enjoyable about spectacle, while somehow avoiding the shallowness that the term implies. In addition, most Shakespearean tales and superhero comics were constructed to be entertainment for the masses.* Currently, superhero comics are facing a bit of a backlash within the industry. "The stories have become derivative," critics say; "the

---

* Although one could argue that comics as a medium are considered to be for the masses only because they are usually thought of as "kid stuff," that's a little ironic in that I wouldn't be handing any eight-year-old the first issue of DC's relaunched "52" version of *Batman*, or Mark Waid's *Irredeemable*, anytime soon.

content can't match the 'reality' that non-genre comics bring to the table," others proclaim; "they're just being used as farms for films," still others scoff. But these poor, maligned heroes show just what a natural pair Shakespeare and the medium truly are. Brightly coloured costumes? Check. Rich backstories steeped in mythology? Check. Operatic plots rife with backstabbing, comedy, romance, bawdy humour, and larger-than-life heroes and villains? Double check.

* * *

But say *The Tempest* and *Richard III* are not your favourite works—too many ghosts and sorcerers kicking about for your liking. Say you prefer the realism of *Othello* or the funny-sad rhythms of *Much Ado About Nothing*. How do comics capture the unique magic that Shakespeare put into those plays—a magic that isn't literal?

The answer is, "Quite well, actually." The medium of comics goes much deeper than the superhero genre and "kids' stories." It stretches into a general surrealism that permeates most comics. Rarely is a comic tale ever told completely "straight." It's a waste of the form's peculiar strengths to not engage in some sort of metaphor, visual or otherwise.

Let's take Andi Watson's *Little Star* as an example. Set in Britain, it follows Simon as he balances his relationship with his wife, his career ambitions, and his three-year-old daughter. In many ways it's a simple tale about how parenthood is more overwhelming than anyone expects. As a film or a novel it would be a bittersweet continuing-to-come-of-age tale. But as a comic, because of the nature of the medium, it branches beyond that. Watson uses his art to create dreamy starscapes to encapsulate how small Simon feels as a father, how much he has to learn about the ever-changing world of parenthood, and how his daughter, in her own way, is like an alien creature, with wants and personality traits that neither he nor his wife could ever have predicted.

Or, for something even more grounded in reality, yet with a far greater dose of that "comic surrealism," I present to you Ho Che Anderson's *King*, a comic book biography of Martin Luther King Jr.* Anderson tells the civil rights activist's story with gravity and delicacy. He captures King's legendary ability to inspire people, while he refuses to shy away from the leader's fractured relationship with his wife and his appetite for other women. Yet even in telling the story of a man so revered, a story that resonates so deeply with so many, Anderson uses the comics medium to make his version of King's life transcend even the extraordinary source material. The most notable effect comes when his art style changes dramatically midway through the tale. For the first half of the story, Anderson uses fairly sharp black-and-white line work, occasionally adding a splash of colour. He keeps the page layouts relatively unadorned and traditionally organized, sometimes even relying on the classic, and seen by some as dated, nine-panel page structure. But then the U.S. president, and King's ally, John F. Kennedy, is assassinated, and everything changes. Anderson's art becomes more hallucinogenic, colours bleed into the pages, and characters' faces are distorted or rendered in a far less realistic manner. Even the panels, the backbone of the story, become distorted. Gone are the carefully drawn borders. Instead, as King's life descends into bedlam, Anderson makes the panels seemingly lose all sense of order by having them encroach upon each other and some-

---

* And there is nothing more awesome than a tale about an American icon written by a Canadian who was born in England and whose parents named him after Ho Chi Minh and Che Guevara.

times disappear entirely. In short, it is chaos, representing how King's bloody destiny, once his White House protector had been killed, becomes inevitable. The change in artistic style is jarring but effective—fully capturing the operatic nature of King's life.

In a film, this abrupt artistic shift would more than likely instantly give the piece art-house status, with no chance of real commercial success or of attracting the wide audience that goes with more mainstream films. At worst, it would seem hopelessly over-the-top or showy. Even for the stage, Anderson's abrupt, theatrical, and somewhat horrific change of style would be unsettling and unnerving. And while for a first-time reader of comics Anderson's story is a challenge, the medium's unique structure softens the blow and allows the reader to enjoy this lack of reality.

Similar changes can be found in Shakespeare's work. One obvious example is in *Henry IV, Part 1* and then in *Part 2*. In *Part 1*, the play starts out as a comedy, following Prince Hal and his scoundrel mentor and foil, Sir John Falstaff. As the story continues, Hal rises above the earthly distractions that Falstaff provides him with and becomes a man worthy of nobility. The tone of the story changes again in *Part 2* as Falstaff struggles to redeem himself, knowing instinctively that the time of his death is approaching. Many consider *Part 2* to be elegiac in nature, making it distinctly different from the two major tones found in *Part 1*. An example of this shift can be seen in how the rebels are defeated in each play. In *Part 1*, Prince Hal helps his father, the King, defeat his enemies through (presumably) noble combat. In *Part 2*, the King's enemies are undone not through battle, but through double-dealing and political machinations.

Romeo and Juliet is another play that sees a marked shift. It starts very much in the vein of Shakespearean comedy: we have two young lovers, a case of mistaken identity, and the meddling of two initially helpful-seeming go-betweens, Friar Laurence and the Nurse. But after Mercutio is killed in Act 3, Scene 1, the play pivots. Romeo is banished, which sets the stage for the tragedy to come, and Friar Laurence and, to a lesser extent, the Nurse make disastrous decisions that ensure that the two lovers die.

While these stories are seen as classics, this sort of dramatic shift in tone, common in Shakespeare's work,* is far less usual today, if only because of the pressure on writers and filmmakers to construct clear narratives that attract as many paying customers as possible. This is where comics' "small money" status again comes in handy, as several titles successfully bounce back and forth between very different tones, be it the comedy and paranoia of Garth Ennis's *The Boys* or the continual, and enjoyable, genre-switching mayhem found in Bill Willingham's excellent *Fables*.

Part of this structure concerns the way an artist can alter the reader's experience by playing with the language of film (close-ups, wide shots, distorted angles) and a language unique to comics (panel borders, panel placements, splash pages).** Together, these elements give comics a visual depth that Shakespeare might have envied. Furthermore, the combination of these devices makes comics inherently "unreal" or magical. And the fact that only a pen and paper are needed to create comics encourages the sort of imaginative thinking that makes full use of these tools.

---

* Susan Snyder's *The Comic Matrix of Shakespeare's Tragedies* discusses how *Romeo and Juliet*, *Hamlet*, *King Lear*, and *Othello* are all tragic stories grafted on top of Shakespeare's comedic structures.
** Although it's important to note that a comic's visual vocabulary doesn't quite work like a film's. For example, in a film a series of quick cuts speeds up the action, while in a comic a run of small panels serves to slow down the story.

Because of this, new comics readers can quickly sample a collection of these tactics, often in the same book, in a way that allows them to quickly learn the medium's conventions. Since it takes a lot less time to, say, read an issue of *Batman* or *Bone* than it does to watch *Lord of the Rings* or *La Dolce Vita*, comics readers can either take in a greater range of storytelling tactics in the same amount of time that moviegoers can, or, as was the case with my own experience of *La Dolce Vita*, at least spend less time being confused.*

That later point isn't just made to reveal that I struggle with Italian Cinema (damn you, Fellini); I think it highlights an underappreciated aspect of comics. Because they are often serialized, they give readers more time to contemplate what it is they just read, allowing any frustration or confusion with the story to melt away with a postreading cup of tea, or a beer.

* * *

That leads me to my final point: beyond the visual aspects, what makes the magic of comics work is the medium's unparalleled democracy. In a film, or on TV, the viewers have almost no control over how they consume the story. A shot is on screen for exactly as long as the director and editor has decided it should be; if we want more, or become bored—tough cookies. But in the humble comic, we, *the readers*, choose the pacing. Unlike in film, where an editor chooses how long we watch a moment, and unlike in theatre, where actors and directors do the same,

---

* This may explain my troubled relationship with *La Dolce Vita*, by the way—the whole thing just takes so damn long. I know, I'm a classless lout, but in a three-hour film shouldn't something, you know, *comprehendible* happen? But I digress. . . .

in comics we're empowered to linger for as long, or as little, as we like on each and every panel. Comics readers decide which parts of the story most intrigue them, and how much time to dedicate to absorbing each beat.

In addition, unlike a novel, a comic is relatively easy to reread. That rereadability allows the writer and artist to layer the story in more complex ways because they know that if readers are confused they can easily go back to find the hints, allusions, and foreshadowings the creators have layered into their art and words. That easy readability also lets readers follow the ins and outs of stories that spawn a dozen or more volumes.*

It's also important to note that comics, like theatre, are collaborative. While there are many fantastic works that are written and drawn by the same person, most titles on the shelves are the products of many minds. In this way, comics seem to go out of their way to resist the cult of the auteur. Take *Kill Shakespeare*: without Andy Belanger's art and illustrative storytelling skills, half of the visual metaphors and almost all of the hidden Easter eggs wouldn't exist. Andy isn't the creator, but his storytelling abilities have dramatically enhanced the ways our fans have interacted with the narrative.

In the end, comics provide an envious degree of flexibility and freedom for both the consumers and the creators.

When Anthony, Andy, and I tell people (as we often do) that if Shakespeare were alive today he would be in the comics

---

* The *Matrix* trilogy of films is famous for intricate plotting and layering, but in order for a fan to absorb all that nuance it requires serious commitment to take in the films enough times to try to catch all of their hidden fruits. While good comics such as *Watchmen* and *Sandman* refuse to yield their secrets so easily either, it is a far less intimidating proposition to reread three comics versus rewatching three two-hour-plus movies.

industry, they often laugh. But we're not joking. At the beginning of *Henry V*, Shakespeare wishes he had a "muse of fire" to show his audience the parts of the story he has been unable to stage:

O, for a muse of fire, that would ascend
The brightest heaven of invention,
A kingdom for a stage, princes to act
And monarchs to behold the swelling scene!

(Prologue 1–4)

Had Shakespeare's medium of choice been comics, he wouldn't have needed such a muse—Shakespeare, with a talented artist's brush, could have staged anything his mind imagined. And while all of us are richer for joining our imaginations to the more perfect imaginings of the Bard, it would have been interesting to see what fresh mysteries Shakespeare would have left us with and what new things he would have shown us using comics' unique freedom.

It's also worth wondering how, if Shakespeare *had* made his home in the medium of comics, we would look at the graphic novel today. Would it have a higher literary status? Would he have inspired generations of genius comics creators who would have secured the medium's reputation as high art? And then how would we look at the other art forms? Would theatre be seen as the kinetically richer but inspirationally poorer cousin of the graphic novel? Would the great masters of painting and sculpture have been lured into creating breathtaking works that supported the words of men like Shakespeare? If the graphic novel had been claimed by Shakespeare and then by the many geniuses he inspired, would we still look at the novel as the pinnacle of human expression? I suspect that having a famous father figure would have gone a long way in improving the humble comic's profile.

And maybe he would have brought us Wolverine a few centuries earlier.

Julie Taymor

ROUGH MAGIC

JULIE TAYMOR is an American director of theater, film, and opera. Her films include *Frida, Across the Universe, Titus, The Tempest*, and the upcoming *The Transposed Heads*, a musical based on Thomas Mann's novella. She has additionally directed *The Tempest* on stage twice, as well as *The Taming of the Shrew, Juan Darién*, the musical *The Lion King*, and several operas, including *The Magic Flute, The Flying Dutchman, Oedipus Rex*, and an original opera, *Grendel*. She will be directing *A Midsummer Night's Dream*, opening November 2013: it will be the inaugural production of Theatre for a New Audience's first permanent home, a center for Shakespeare and classical drama, in Brooklyn, New York. Her work has been recognized with two Tony Awards, two Obie Awards, a Drama Desk Award, an Emmy Award, and an Academy Award nomination, as well as MacArthur and Guggenheim Fellowships.

D riven by the bitterness and fury of its lead character, the sorceress-scientist Prospera, *The Tempest* is at once a revenge drama, a romance, and a black comedy. It is the mother's protective love for her daughter, Miranda, that fuels the tempest she has conjured and all the subsequent events on the island in the space of a day.

Shakespeare was the ultimate screenwriter. More of his plays have been made into movies than any other writer's. His palette was immense, limited only by the boundaries of his imagination. In *The Tempest*, he wrote of real and fantasy worlds, of philosophies, both lofty and poetical, juxtaposed with rock-bottom crude and scatological fare. Young lovers in the mode of Romeo and Juliet are scripted with an understanding of the delicate, vulnerable, and awkward comedy that comes with first love. Smashed up against these scenes stumble the abominations of three of Shakespeare's best and bawdiest low-lifes. And mirroring this comic trio's treacherous escapades are the wicked, cynical, and corrupt lords, whose lives get turned upside down in the maelstrom of Prospera's fierce vengeance. In addition to the human characters, Shakespeare created a most singular and complex being in the form of the spirit Ariel.

The Tempest, in other words, offers a great opportunity for a film director—from its wondrous and diverse parts for actors to its visual dimensions and challenges that are ripe to be realized through extraordinary locations and experimental visual effects.

* * *

The Tempest is the second of Shakespeare's plays that I've directed for film: the first was Titus, which featured the great Anthony Hopkins. Titus Andronicus (1591–1592) was among Shakespeare's earliest plays, and The Tempest (1610–1611) was among his last. Titus is messy, raw, a young man's cynical, mad, and outrageous first tragedy, and, like a pearl in an oyster, it has its own perfection which one has to mine to reveal.

The Tempest, in contrast, is more neatly tied up in terms of its themes—and yet it's still not what could be called a conventional drama. It's more of a philosophical treatise, or a state of being, and so it's very difficult to make work as a film, a medium in which audiences expect stories to unfold in a linear way. Since this narrative is constantly moving from one group of players to another around the island, it doesn't provide the same feeling of satisfaction as those plays, such as *Romeo and Juliet*, which follow the main characters more closely.

My first Shakespeare to direct in the theater was *The Tempest*. It was on a small stage in New York City in 1986: the play began with the silhouette of a young girl building a sandcastle on the top of a black sand hill. Suddenly a stagehand, garbed in black and holding a large watering can, ran to the girl and started to pour water on the castle. As the lights shifted focus, illuminating only the castle and the falling water, this mundane image was transformed into a "rainstorm" that dissolved the fragile castle into the earth. Though Prospero's "magic" was exposed through the art of theater lighting, the audience was invited to believe that the tempest had begun. In this moment of theatrical conventions, the rules of the production were laid out. The form and style of theatrical storytelling illuminated the substantive meaning of the piece—Prospero was the ultimate puppet master, the string-puller and engineer of illusions.

Revealing the mechanics of the theater creates its own alchemy, its rough magic, and the audience willingly plays "make-believe." In cinema, however, where one can actually film on real locations and create seemingly naturalistic events, the temptation is to throw away the artifice and go for the literal reality. There is something inherently sad about this. Even in fantasy cinema the audience expects the worlds that are created to feel "real," or at least plausible, and it is not required of viewers that they fill in the blanks or suspend their disbelief.

In the film of *The Tempest*, I had an opportunity to act on these two impulses: to combine the literal reality of location—its natural light, winds, and rough seas—with conjured visual effects that subvert the "natural" and toy with it. As in the theater version, we begin the film with the close-up image of a black sandcastle. The camera pulls away, and we realize that the castle is tiny, fitting onto the palm of a hand. Rain begins to fall and the castle dissolves through fingers as the camera finally reveals the surprised expression of the young girl belonging to the hand, Miranda. Lightning cracks, and we cut to what she sees: the wide roiling sea and a distant ship caught in a ferocious storm. The long shot of the tempest looks like a Turner painting come to life. The juxtaposition of these two moments and the play with perception and scale signals the style of the film: from visceral reality to heightened expressionism.

At the start of the drama, one of the major themes of the play is posited: Nature versus Nurture. In one brief ideograph, civilization, represented by the simple form of a child's sandcastle, is destroyed in a downpour. The perilous storm that destroys the ship also establishes this theme, by exposing the fact that the lofty position of the King of Naples on board is rendered meaningless when Nature is in control. The irony is that it is Prospera who, at this moment in time, is in control of Nature. Her conflict with the abuse and renunciation of such power unfolds as another critical theme of *The Tempest*.

THE PLAYERS

I have chosen to discuss three of the main characters in this essay, as they proved to be the most conceptually challenging. The decision to switch the gender of the lead character, Prospero, renamed Prospera, was a diving board to a whole new appreciation of the play. Shakespeare's unique creations Caliban and Ariel are ripe for endless interpretations. Emblematic and surreal, they require total invention in shaping and designing the presentation of their natures. In terms of alchemical symbolism, Prospera's two "servants" represent opposites, the earth and the air, within and without, that she struggles to unite and ultimately to release.

Prospera

Having twice directed the play with Prospero as the principal
character, I made subtle discoveries with the gender change to
Prospera. The reason I decided to make the switch had everything to do with Helen Mirren and a coincidental exchange that
we had while I was mulling over possible actors for the part. It
was not that I wanted to do the play with a woman in the lead,
it's that I wanted to do it with this particular actor. There are
very few roles for women over forty in Shakespeare, and I was
intrigued by the possibility of discovering a new one in Prospera, while still being true to the essence of the original play.
Once I fixated on Helen Mirren for the role, examination of the
text and how it would change became illuminating. Except for
the obvious "he" to "she" and "sir" to "mum" or "ma'am," very
little of the text would need to be altered to accommodate the
change. Curiously, we discovered that one word that couldn't
be changed was "master," since in the English language "master"
does not equate with "mistress."*

The major adjustment to the text was in the reshaping of the
character's backstory, which was reconceived and put into verse.
In the original *Tempest*, Prospero lost his dukedom because he
hadn't been paying it proper attention; he confesses that the liberal arts had been all his study and that he had neglected all
worldly ends, "dedicated / To closeness and the bettering of my
mind" (1.2.105–106). In our backstory, Prospera's husband, the
Duke of Milan, being quite liberal, has allowed her to practice in
secret the arts of alchemy, midwifery, and herbal medicine—a

---

* There are two distinct ways of using a female lead in *The Tempest*. The
first is to have Prospero played as a woman, Prospera; the second is to
have a woman playing the role as a man, as with the gender reversal of
Shakespeare's boy actors performing the female parts.

path of study usually forbidden to women. When her husband
dies, Prospera becomes heir to his dukedom. Antonio, her ambitious and treacherous brother, seizes the opportunity to accuse
her of witchcraft, which was punishable by death at the stake—a
much heavier charge than being accused of political negligence.
Here we resume the original text, which describes how the faithful councilor, Gonzalo, helps to save Prospera and her four-year-
old daughter, Miranda, by secreting them aboard a small bark
and sending them out to sea. Their survival is a miracle.

Julie Taymor directing Helen Mirren as Prospera in
The Tempest, *2010.*
© *2010 Tempest Production, LLC. All Rights Reserved.*
Photograph by Melinda Sue Gordon.

When we first meet Prospera, she has already suffered
twelve years of exile. As sole ruler on an almost deserted island,
she is at once the master despot and the vengeful mother. Her
source of power stems from a mother's natural and ferocious
protective passion and a scholar-scientist's obsession with the
ability to control Nature for both dark and benign purposes.

The themes of power, revenge, compassion, and forgiveness

become more complex in the relationships that Prospera has with Miranda, Ferdinand, Ariel, and Caliban. Prospera's protective feelings for her daughter are quite different from those of a father. There is no male ego involved, no competition with the young suitor, and no "honor" defiled as in most attempted rape scenarios. But instead, Prospera's actions are a direct result of her knowing intimately what Miranda is experiencing as a young virginal woman and where the dangers lie. Moreover, similar to the way that a tigress takes care of her cubs—a metaphor which characterizes Tamora in *Titus*—there is no fiercer parent than a mother. In this gender twist, it is because Prospera is a woman that her dukedom could be stolen from her, and the bitterness of this fact infiltrates her relationships with those characters who affect her daughter.

These are subtle nuances that in no way alter the essence of Shakespeare's play, but rather give it another layer of depth and a new way to experience a familiar tale. In doing research on the play I was surprised to discover that the well-known speech of Prospera's in which she describes her "rough magic" is almost identical to the witch Medea's speech in Ovid's *Metamorphoses*. Here is Prospera:

> Ye elves of hills, brooks, standing lakes and groves,
> And ye that on the sands with printless foot
> Do chase the ebbing Neptune, and do fly him
> When he comes back: you demi-puppets that
> By moonshine do the green sour ringlets make,
> Whereof the ewe not bites: and you whose pastime
> Is to make midnight mushrooms, that rejoice
> To hear the solemn curfew, by whose aid—
> Weak masters though ye be—I have bedimmed
> The noontide sun, called forth the mutinous winds,

And 'twixt the green sea and the azured vault
Set roaring war: to the dread rattling thunder
Have I given fire, and rifted Jove's stout oak
With his own bolt: the strong-based promontory
Have I made shake and by the spurs plucked up
The pine and cedar. Graves at my command
Have waked their sleepers, oped, and let 'em forth
By my so potent art.

(5.1.38–55)

Although Shakespeare knew Latin and could have read Ovid
in the original, he might have modeled his wording on the first
English translation of Arthur Golding, published in 1567 as *The
Fifteen Books of Ovid's Metamorphoses*. The passage begins in
Book 7, at line 265:

Ye Ayres and Windes: ye Elves of Hilles, of Brookes, of
   Woods alone,
Of standing Lakes, and of the Night approche ye
   everychone
Through helpe of whom (the crooked bankes much
   wondring at the thing)
I have compelled streames to run cleane backward to
   their spring.
By charmes I make the calme Seas rough, and make
   the rough Seas plaine,
And cover all the Skie with Cloudes and chase them
   thence againe.
By charmes I raise and lay the windes, and burst the
   Vipers jaw.
And from the bowels of the Earth both stones and
   trees doe draw.

Whole woods and Forestes I remove. I make the
    Mountaines shake,
And even the Earth it selfe to grone and fearfully to
    quake.
I call up dead men from their graves: and thee O
    lightsome Moone
I darken oft, though beaten brasse abate thy perill
    soone.
Our Sorcerie dimmes the Morning faire, and darkes
    the Sun at Noone.

The identification and accusation of Prospera as a witch begins
in the Milan flashback. Yet she sees herself as an alchemist, a
scientist, engaged in the study of Nature in order to understand
and control its positive forces. Given that Nature is identified
as "the Mother," knowledge of the medicinal elements of the
earth has traditionally been the purview of women. The battle,
however, between white and black magic in our story begins on
the island, with the enslavement of Caliban. It is brought into
sharp focus as Prospera spews her disdain for the "foul witch,
Sycorax," the mother of Caliban and the torturer of Ariel. At the
top of the story, Prospera does not yet recognize or acknowledge her own dark side, but as the play progresses Prospera and
Sycorax become mirrors to one another in their malignant and
abusive use of the black arts.

Helen Mirren brings many conflicting characteristics to
her Prospera, and this makes her a classic protagonist in Shakespeare's canon. With her erratic fury, cruelty, maternal warmth,
cold authority, and poetic introspection, she plays the witch,
the scientist, the poet, the ferocious tiger protecting her cub, the
steely leader, and more. It is not neat. She is neither perfect nor
benign, but twisted by a tempest within that stems from guilt

over being the cause of her innocent daughter's exile and the urgency to exact revenge on those also responsible.

To Miranda, in explaining the tempest she has conjured:

> I have done nothing but in care of thee—
> Of thee, my dear one, thee, my daughter—who
> Art ignorant of what thou art: nought knowing
> Of whence I am, nor that I am more better
> Than Prospera, master of a full poor cell,
> And thy no greater mother.
>
> (adapted from 1.2.19–24)

And later, concerning her enemies:

> I will plague them all,
> Even to roaring.
>
> (4.1.208–209)

Prospera is complex, in a way similar to Titus. Shakespeare enjoys setting up his characters one way and then almost immediately controverting them. Prospera's kingdom has been usurped, but then she usurps Caliban's island kingdom; Caliban seems like a wronged innocent, but then we learn that he has attempted to rape Miranda. They all abuse; they've all been abused. Shakespeare's characters are so multilayered that you find yourself loving, disliking, admiring, and disrespecting them, potentially all at the same time.

Prospera believes in her own positive and benevolent nature until the end of the drama, when she finally acknowledges her magic as black, as "rough"—it has become perverse and twisted through her dark fury: "But this rough magic / I here abjure" (5.1.55–56).

Helen Mirren as Prospera and Ben Whishaw as Ariel
in Julie Taymor's The Tempest, *2010.*
Photograph by Melinda Sue Gordon.

In this speech of renunciation, she finally acknowledges that her own vengeful needs have pushed her over the top and caused her to misuse her power. With her spirit Ariel's help, she then gives up her power and finds her way back to compassion.

Once Prospera's mission is accomplished, her enemies punished and her magic renounced, she asks Ariel to help attire her so that she can "myself present / As I was sometime Milan" (5.1.90–91). As Ariel straps her into a tight corset, the court costume she arrived in, which is much more constricting than the free, androgynous clothing she had fashioned for herself on the island, her pained face reveals her sacrifice. In the original play, Prospero is being reinstated as the Duke with his fancy hat and robes; he will have his authority restored and will resume his lofty status in society. But with Prospera re-garbed in woman's dress, I wanted to emphasize the decision she makes in returning to her woman's place in Milan society—that the power and freedom she has wielded on the island will now be subject to the rules of the society to which she returns. This choice to return to Milan is made out of the great love she has for her daughter.

In the design concepts for both the landscape of the cell and her magical robe, we tapped the essence of Prospera herself as a living volcano, burning from within, primed to erupt and destroy, but ultimately to redeem and regenerate.

Ariel

Ariel is the embodiment in spirit of human emotion, vulnerability, and compassion. How does an actor play pure spirit, both and beyond male and female, appearing and disappearing on command, able to change shape and size, and yet able to move the audience to laughter or tears? In the theater I utilized the art of puppetry in the form of a disembodied mask that could be moved in any direction, defying gravity and human limitations. The purely theatrical choice was quite moving precisely because the artifice was so blatant, yet could project subtle emotions. In the film, however, the character of Ariel was conceived as an actor's fully human performance treated with the use of cinematic visual effects. The challenge was to retain the visceral, nuanced performance that only a human can give, while transforming his physical presence into the essence of light, fire, wind, and water, and the corporeal manifestation of harpies, frogs, stinging bees, and bubbling lava.

Ben Whishaw plays an androgynous Ariel, simultaneously evincing both the feminine and the masculine without diminishing either, which produces an ethereal but intense sexuality. Since in my previous theatrical productions I had always had a female Ariel to the male Prospero, this gender change to

Prospera added a different dynamic to the subtle erotic pull
between the two characters.

In casting Ben, I had to accept a significant condition:
he would be unavailable until the end of the shoot and thus
never on location with us in Hawaii. That meant that Helen
would have to film most of her Ariel scenes without Ariel. It
was a daunting, yet fortuitous, challenge. After all, Ariel is not
human, does not walk on the ground, and is constantly transforming. This limitation was an invitation to Kyle Cooper, the
visual effects designer, and myself to invent an entirely new way
of combining a live actor's performance with CGI. Because of
Ben's limited availability, most of his performance was filmed
in the studio, in front of a green screen, making it possible for
us to manipulate his image in postproduction and place him in
the pre-shot backgrounds with Helen.

Not all of his scenes were shot this way, however. It was
important for some of their most intense exchanges that Helen
and Ben be able to act together. We were then left to alter his
arrivals and exits, his physical form, whether it be translucent,
grossly deformed, or multiplied, with the help of postproduction effects. A few scenes, such as his appearance as a sea nymph
with Ferdinand, were shot through a large glass containing a
few inches of water. Ben was underneath, able to move freely
and speak his lines, yet his image appears to be fractured and
distorted through the lens of water—the miracle is that the
effect is live, in camera, and not computer generated. It was
extremely liberating to be able to preserve a great actor's performance and yet transform him into the various elements and
creatures that are delineated by the text.

There is one scene, however, in which I purposefully left
Ariel untreated, corporeal. It is an intimate scene with Prospera

in her cell. Her enemies have been brought low and she asks
Ariel how they are faring.

> ARIEL: . . . Your charm so strongly works
>   'em
> That if you now beheld them, your affections
> Would become tender.
> PROSPERA: Dost thou think so, spirit?
> ARIEL: Mine would, master, were I human.
>   (adapted from 5.1.19–23)

Because this is the first time that we see the fully human being
of Ariel, every little nuance of expression becomes that much
more intense and felt. This is the scene that finally leads Prospera to understand that "the rarer action is / In virtue than in
vengeance" (5.1.31–32). It's an extraordinary shift to the realization of what she has done, of how far she has abused her power
and taken the revenge and anger—it's an ennobling awareness,
a true moment of grace. And it is the spirit, Ariel, as an agent of
reconciliation, who signifies this compassion, forgiveness, and
ultimate redemption.

Caliban

He is addressed or described as "thou earth thou," a foul-
smelling "plain fish," a "puppy-headed monster," a "poisonous
slave," the bastard of an evil witch, and one guilty of the near
rape of Miranda, Prospera's precious daughter. Caliban may
also be perceived as simply a native of this remote island, and
the above depictions as a product of the prejudicial point of
view of the Europeans who are shipwrecked on it, in particular
those of Prospera, who now governs the island and Caliban as

her own. In casting an African in this role, one automatically brings to the forefront the obvious themes of colonialization and usurpation that clearly were part of Shakespeare's world-view, derived from stories culled from journeys of exploration to Africa and the New World.

But in order to truly serve Shakespeare's unique vision of this character, one must go beyond sociopolitical commentary achieved through a casting choice. Djimon Hounsou went through a four-hour makeup ordeal every day to achieve the look of his Caliban. His skin was made to resemble the island's cracked red earth and black volcanic rock, with raised scars of obscenities he had carved into his flesh. He says to Prospera:

> You taught me language, and my profit on't
> Is, I know how to curse. The red-plague rid you
> For learning me your language.
>
> (1.2.423–425)

The nickname "Moon-calf," endearingly coined by Stephano for Caliban, suggested the white circular moon that frames his one blue eye, which in itself was motivated by the notion that he is the whelp of that "blue-eyed hag," Sycorax. The "calf" part of the equation is delivered in the maplike patches of white on black skin that add to the "otherness" of this unique racial mash-up. This Caliban—half black, half white, with the one blue eye—partakes of both races and yet is an outsider to both. The webbing between his fingers and the long nails that can dig pignuts adds that touch of monster fantasy that speaks to the "strange fish," as Trinculo calls him. All in all, this Caliban, both beautiful and grotesque, is the island: Nature personified. And Djimon's athletic and antic movement, inspired by the Japanese dance form Butoh, completes his physical embodiment.

In casting Djimon Hounsou in this role, we were privileged to have not only a great actor but one who brought with him experience, belief, and respect for the power of white and black magic. His personal stories of sorcery in his country, Benin, were both inspiring and harrowing.

There was never any question in Djimon's mind that the figure Helen was playing, the sorceress, could control Caliban. He is the "natural" that Prospera tries and fails to reform in her nurturing. Their clashes leave the audience discomforted, unsure as to whom to root for, as Shakespeare never chooses sides. Djimon's Caliban is multifaceted: he can be physically threatening and violent in one scene and naïve and puppylike in another. He is comedic, foolish, elementally human, and profoundly tragic, bestowed with the innate intelligence to speak some of the most elegant and moving poetry of *The Tempest*:

> Be not afeard, the isle is full of noises,
> Sounds and sweet airs, that give delight and hurt not:
> Sometimes a thousand twangling instruments
> Will hum about mine ears; and sometime voices,
> That if I then had waked after long sleep,
> Will make me sleep again, and then in dreaming,
> The clouds methought would open and show riches
> Ready to drop upon me, that when I waked
> I cried to dream again.
>
> (3.2.118–126)

In these lines, famous because of their ethereal beauty, Caliban gives voice to something of Ariel's otherworldliness—and Ariel, who is air, who is transparent, who is the soul and spirit, is also, at times, bawdy, mischievous, and earthly. Everything in Shakespeare has duality. None of his characters exist on just one level, since even his inhuman beings are reflections of human complexities.

At the end of the original, Caliban begs for mercy, Prospero dismisses him, and it is sorrowful and unresolved, for there is no apparent understanding and Prospero seems to feel no remorse. I wanted to make it clear that Prospera realizes what she has done to Caliban, and so included an intense and silent moment when Caliban fearfully looks at Prospera's staff, knowing full well that if she raises that staff he will indeed be "pinched to death" (5.1.311)—but she doesn't move it. They simply look at each other with a complete understanding of what has passed between them, and then Caliban climbs up the stairs and out of the cell without looking back: he is free.

* * *

The word "free" becomes the most significant word of the play. Caliban is free, Ariel is free, the court is free, and the only one who is not going to be free is Prospera, since she must return to that rigid Milanese society, stripped of her liberating power. Although the initial decision came from the desire to work with Helen, I discovered that the story arc is in some ways more intense with a female lead, since what Prospera will be giving up is that much more keenly felt.

Shakespeare's characters are already full of contradictions, and changing the gender of the lead allowed us to participate in that creative process with Shakespeare himself to explore new ways of portraying all the complexities of the human condition. We all have that rough magic within us, and—as Shakespeare knew—the question for each of us is when to use it, when to abjure it, and when to transform it into the liberating white magic of the imagination.

James Franco

MY OWN PRIVATE RIVER

―――――――

JAMES FRANCO is an American actor, director, and author. His films include *James Dean* (which earned him a Golden Globe), the *Spider-Man* trilogy, *Pineapple Express* (recognized with a Golden Globe nomination), *Milk* (for which he won Independent Spirit and Broadcast Film Critics Association Awards), *Howl*, on the poet Allen Ginsberg, *127 Hours* (honored by many awards, including the Independent Spirit Award, as well as Academy Award, Golden Globe, BAFTA, and many other nominations), *The Broken Tower* (a film which he also wrote and produced, on the poet Hart Crane), *Return of the Planet of the Apes*, and *Oz: The Great and Powerful*. His television credits include *Freaks and Geeks* and *General Hospital*. He is the author of the collection of short stories *Palo Alto*. Gus Van Sant and James Franco created the exhibit *Unfinished* for the Gagosian Gallery in 2011.

I recently created a film called *My Own Private River*, which was shown at the Gagosian in Los Angeles alongside paintings done by Gus Van Sant, the director of the original *My Own Private Idaho*.

It was a very unusual project. I loved *My Own Private Idaho* when I was growing up. Before I even started acting, I used to watch it repeatedly: there was something about the emotion of it, its aesthetic, and the makeshift family that the characters create which spoke to my teenage self. There is Bob Pigeon, played by William Richert, who can be traced back to Shakespeare's Falstaff; Scott Favor, played by Keanu Reeves, who can be traced back to Prince Hal; and Mike Waters, played by River Phoenix, who can be traced back to the character of Poins. They find each other on the margins of society, and help each other through that time in their lives with an intricate combination of humor, aggression, and understanding.

When I had the chance to work with Gus Van Sant years later on *Milk*, we did premieres in New York, San Francisco, and Los Angeles. Then Gus wanted to do a premiere in his hometown, Portland, Oregon, and none of the other actors wanted to go. He knew I was obsessed with the film and he said, "James, if you come to Portland I will give you a tour of all of the *My Own Private Idaho* shooting locations"—as, curiously enough, none of the film was actually shot in Idaho. It was a dream come true, and so together we spent an entire day in Portland driving to the various sites, and along the way he told me stories about that filming experience.

"You know," he confided, "I kept all the old editor's film reels from the movie." It had been filmed in 1990–1991, so they had cut it on actual film, which meant that Gus had hundreds of rolls of film in storage.

"Are we gonna watch it?" I asked.

"No," he replied.

But several months later we spent two days watching as much of the twenty-five hours' worth of material as we could. It was a project just to watch it—and it was incredible. Gus hadn't watched it since he'd made the movie, and his style of making movies had changed in the intervening two decades. He had made a huge change in his aesthetic midcareer, having been influenced by minimalistic films, and his later films were characterized by minimal dialogue, fewer cuts, and very long takes. So, when we were watching those *Idaho* rushes again after those two decades, the question became, "What if you had cut this movie now?" For instance, there is a scene early on where it is just Keanu Reeves and River Phoenix walking down the street, and we found ourselves wondering, "What if you just held on that shot, and you stay on River's head, and then you continue with him for much longer? What would that give to our sense of his character?"

They were intriguing questions, and after we got the reels digitized and I had my own copy of the material, I asked Gus if I could play around with it myself. When I suddenly had that uncut film from what had been such a huge part of my teenage years right in front of me, it was poignant and exhilarating: we mark our memories by the cultural artifacts that we were engaged with when we were younger. I'd done similar work before, taking somebody else's material that was formerly a part of one project and then using it for a completely different project—but this was special, since I felt like the material was incredibly valuable because of the film's place in cinema history, and in River's life. For those reasons, I didn't want to go in there in a disruptive way: I wanted to go in there in a respectful way. To me, the archive had an inherent value, for every take was one I could just *watch*. It was difficult to cut any of it out, and in the end I did two films. From the original twenty-five hours, I cut one film that was twelve hours long and another that was 102 minutes. In the twelve-hour version there are multiple takes of the same shot, by means of which I could deliver the material in a way that made it feel like it was an archive and yet also a portrait of the filmmaking process. In the 102-minute cut I found a way to work so that it wasn't me trying to impose myself on it, but rather me playing Gus, as though he were making the movie now.*

---

* And then, for the Gagosian show, Gus ended up not cutting anything himself. He ended up doing *paintings*. Curiously, he went back to a version of himself before he had even made the movie, when he was a painter.

When Gus wrote the script it was a compilation of three previous scripts. One was a movie that was about street kids in Portland; one was a movie about two Hispanic kids looking for their parents who eventually go to Europe; and then one was mostly Shakespearean dialogue in a contemporary setting. This last was based on Orson Welles's *Chimes at Midnight*, which was a compilation of all the Falstaff sections of the *Henry IV* plays.

River Phoenix as Mike Waters, a character based on Henry IV's Poins, *in the footage of Gus Van Sant's* My Own Private Idaho, *1991, which was refashioned by James Franco into* My Own Private River, *2012.*

The other thing that Gus did, and which I pushed to the extreme, is that he focused on the Poins character, in this case Mike Waters, played by River Phoenix. Ned Poins is one of Prince Hal's sidekicks: he masterminds the double robbery of Falstaff in the comic Gad's Hill scene, but other than that plot function his purpose in the play is to bring the detail of character into that seedy but exuberant underworld. Shakespeare created 1,222 characters, and none of them are incidental: all are fully individuated. It is very moving to think about a side character, one out of all of these Shakespearean characters, being given the spotlight. This attention is made even more poignant by Phoenix's incandescent performance. Whether he was revealing himself through the role or not is made moot by the fact that it is arguably his best performance and that he was dead two years later. The performance caught on film is now infinitely more valuable because it captured the best actor of his generation at the peak of his powers. By cutting together outtakes of the unused material of the film, I was able to give more emphasis to the essential beauty of Phoenix and his work. Phoenix, in my remix film *My Own Private River*, is singled out from all other actors—and film performances, for that matter—because he can be presented in such an unflinching way, just as Van Sant was able to single out Poins in his original film.

Now the significance of *Idaho* has changed because River is gone, but you want him to just be there, you want him to keep going, you want to see what he can do, and you want to find all that is still alive and is still around that exists of him. Consequently, those moments that would immediately pull you *out of* a normal film pull you *into* this film—at least they pulled me in—because River is walking around, and he is alive again. What I mean is that you just want anything you can have of him. That sense of wanting time to stop goes back to the original too: *Henry IV* is, among other things, a coming-of-age story. Prince Hal's growing up is at once necessary and deeply poignant, and in many ways we want him to be able to remain a fun-loving, irresponsible kid with Falstaff forever. In a way, the length of the footage of the film I was able to cut, especially the longer version, serves to extend that moment indefinitely—since in an awful way River did grow up, and in another way he's still in that happy hour before the end. Since I didn't have all the economic burdens of the initial film, I was able to make a film with a much looser narrative. So whereas the original was driven by the need to tell a certain story, the film I made was driven just by River's presence.

Shakespeare creates such a vivid, rich, and complex world that we can fruitfully focus on just one part of it and find inspiration for a whole variety of artistic endeavors: in this instance, the result consisted of two new films, created by the act of cutting and shaping a film (*Idaho*) about a film (*Chimes*) about a couple of plays (*Henry IV, Parts 1 and 2*). It's an artistic genealogy, but at the same time we each bring something from outside and from ourselves to the relationship. As Shakespeare used British history for his material, Orson Welles used Shakespeare. Van Sant used Welles, Shakespeare, and his own experiences to create his film. In turn, I humbly used Van Sant and Phoenix to reveal how much I love them.

Isabel Allende

ENAMOURED WITH
SHAKESPEARE

ISABEL ALLENDE is the author of eighteen fictional works, including *The House of the Spirits*, *The City of the Beasts*, *The Stories of Eva Luna*, and *Maya's Notebook*. She is a member of the Academy of Arts and Letters and a Chevalier des arts et des lettres; her more than thirty awards include Chile's National Literature Prize.

M y love affair with Shakespeare started at age nine, when my stepfather gave me Shakespeare's complete works in Spanish. *It's a wise father that knows his own child*;* it was the perfect gift for me, for I was a *night owl* that read in bed until dawn with a flashlight. It was an expensive edition and a sloppy translation but then I didn't know that and, in any case, it didn't matter because I was not in a position to judge the beauty of the language or the psychological insights of the Bard; I only cared about the stories. Ah, those stories! *Such stuff as dreams are made on!* I skipped the Sonnets and plunged into the plays, especially the tragedies. At nine I was a *stony-hearted* kid with no sense of humor who disliked happy endings; given a choice

---

* Editor's note: We have left the quotations without references, since Ms. Allende is illustrating how these lines have jumped their plays and found their way into her, and our, language.

I preferred blood to comedy. My childhood was *the winter of my discontent.*

I was not a bad reader, yet I could hardly follow the plots in my leather-bound book: too many people behaved erratically; too many nobles were murdered *at the crack of doom*; there were too many turns *of giddy Fortune's furious fickle wheel*, not to mention an abundance of cross-dressers which placed the gender of all characters under suspicion. Shakespeare sounded like the Chilean radio soap operas, in which everybody suffered *the slings and arrows of outrageous fortune* and eventually ended up dead. I sensed there was *madness, yet there was method in it.* So I drew and cut out the characters in cardboard, glued them to matchsticks, and moved them about to act out the plays. The characters *had seen better days* by the time they appeared on my miniature stage, but they served my purpose. Once I unraveled the plots, I surrendered completely to Shakespeare's madness and genius.

At nine I couldn't imagine that one day I would become a writer and that Shakespeare would be my companion and mentor in the bumpy journey that is literature. From him I learned about love, betrayal, hatred, death, revenge, greed, jealousy, courage, and despair—all the great stuff of life. I learned that the characters drive the plot, not the reverse, and that the villain is always the most important character, although sometimes the villain is not a person but Fate. Without a villain there's no suspense and without suspense there's no story, except in minimalist contemporary literature in which nothing really happens anyway. Only critics care for it.

Shakespeare was a master storyteller: he used turns and twists in every story, and he had an uncanny instinct for rhythm and suspense, an incomparable talent to develop characters, and a prodigious sense of the unexpected and of mystery. Language was his only tool and he used it wisely but without being constrained by it. If the term he needed didn't exist, he invented it, and thus he contributed three thousand new words to the Queen's English. Early in my life he gave me a love of words and a passion for storytelling; later he helped me train my *mind's eye* to see the hidden motivations of the heart.

The writer is like God, master of his own creation, but Shakespeare's lesson is: *This above all: to thine own self be true.* One has to write what one knows to be true to the human condition and true to oneself. The fiction writer can use every trick under the heavens, rewrite history, plagiarize, and steal other people's lives, but without truth the story is neither believable nor memorable. *I will wear my heart upon my sleeve.* Shakespeare charmed the audience like an illusionist, he could *shame the Devil* in that sense, but he did it with the themes of emotions and relationships. *This is the short and the long of it*: people have found truth in his writing everywhere in the world since the sixteenth century because the human condition is common to all and remains unchanged.

Some are born great, some achieve greatness, and some have greatness thrust upon them, and Shakespeare fits into all three categories. A perfect story, timeless and universal, is almost impossible to achieve because it's the product of neither talent nor hard work; it's a stroke of luck, it happens by chance. The fact that only a handful of authors in the history of literature have reached immortality should make the rest of us very humble, but that's not the case: everybody I know is writing a novel. My neighbor, a snotty adolescent, is writing his memoirs.

Of course, I don't even dream of emulating Shakespeare. I am happy to tread along the path he opened, keeping in mind that writing fiction is first and foremost fun. I believe that in spite of the fathomless depth of his work, which has kept thou-

sands of scholars and millions of readers busy for more than
four centuries, he didn't take himself too seriously. How he
must have enjoyed frolicking with his robust muse!

One of my favorite movies of all time is *Shakespeare in
Love*. I have watched it whenever I have needed to charge my
batteries, more or less twenty-seven times up to the present.
In every instance, I have abandoned myself completely to the
magic of the story-within-a-story, the incurable addiction to
the stage, the charm of the young lovers, and the authority of
bejeweled Elizabeth I. *It is the east and Juliet is the sun. . . . See,
how she leans her cheek upon her hand. O that I were a glove
upon that hand, that I might touch that cheek.* Every single time,
I again fall for the actor, Joseph Fiennes, and cry inconsolably
with the ending. I imagine Shakespeare exactly like the character in the movie, eternally young, hot-blooded, unstoppable,
curious, and wildly creative. In my mind he will always have
ink-stained fingers and dirty clothes, he will always be writing,
fighting, drinking, and in love and haunted by his characters.

As a daughter of diplomats I spent my childhood traveling,
later I became a political refugee, and now I am an immigrant
in the United States. I have moved and started from scratch too
many times in my life, but I have retained that leather-bound
edition of Shakespeare's work by my side. I keep it on my night
table as other people keep the Bible. The pages are yellowish,
the gold letters have faded, and one of my dogs chewed the
cover, but the content is intact and it still speaks to my heart
with the voice of a snake charmer.

INDEX

All's Well That Ends Well: 230, 387,
  398–400
  Bertram: 387, 399, 400
  Countess of Rossillion: 398, 399
  Helena: 387, 398–400
  King of France: 399
  Lafeu: 399
  Lavache: 399
  Parolles: 399–400

Antony and Cleopatra: xii–xiii, xxvii,
  30, 34, 143, 325, 396, 402–406, 415–
  416, 418–432
  Agrippa: 423
  Caesar's Messenger: 423, 427
  Cleopatra: ix, xxiv, 34, 324, 387,
  396, 402–406, 415–416, 418–432,
  449
  Enobarbus: 402–406, 419, 422, 423
  Lepidus: 422
  Mark Antony: 34, 387, 402–406,
  418–432
  Octavius Caesar: 404, 416, 419, 421,
  422, 423, 424–425, 427, 429
  Philo: 34, 419, 421
  Ventidius: 422

As You Like It: x, xxiii, 39, 187, 202–203,
  207, 219, 300, 348, 350, 371, 373–
  376, 396
  Celia: 39, 187, 375–376
  Duke Frederick: 375, 376
  Duke Senior: 202, 350, 375, 376
  Jacques: 362, 396
  Le Beau: 187
  Orlando: 39, 202, 373, 388
  Phoebe: 202–203

Rosalind: x, 39, 187, 202–203, 209,
  348–349, 373–376, 388, 396, 415,
  452
  Silvius: 203
  Touchstone: 360, 365, 369

The Comedy of Errors: 353, 354, 355,
  366, 374
  Antipholus: 354

Coriolanus: xxiii, xxvi, 209–210, 211–
  216, 219, 220–227, 310
  Caius Martius Coriolanus: xxvi, 210,
  211–216, 220–227, 310
  Citizens: 214
  Menenius Agrippa: 209, 214–215
  Tullus Aufidius: 213, 215, 222–223, 224
  Tribunes: 214
  Volumnia: 215–216, 223–225

Cymbeline: xxv, 76, 190, 275–289, 308,
  317–318, 338–339, 348, 400–401,
  412, 416, 417
  Arviragus: 280, 285, 338–339
  Belarius: 278, 280, 283*n*; *also as*
  Belaria: 280, 282, 283*n*, 285
  Caius Lucius: 76
  Cloten: 276, 278, 280–282, 283*n*,
  286, 417
  Cornelius, the Doctor: 288
  Cymbeline: 276, 287*n*, 288
  Guiderius: 280–281, 283*n*, 285
  Iachimo: 276, 279, 280, 284, 338,
  400–401
  Imogen/Fidele: 276–282, 285*n*, 286,
  338, 348, 400–401, 417, 452
  Jupiter: 190, 277, 286–287, 287*n*

Cymbeline (continued):
  Pisanio: 283*n*, 286, 348
  Posthumus: 276, 278, 280, 284, 286,
    400–401, 417
  Queen: 276, 278, 283*n*, 338

Hamlet: viii, x–xi, xv, xix, xxiii, xxv,
    13, 21, 30, 31, 32, 33, 35–36, 37, 38,
    50–55, 58, 67–70, 72–73, 76, 77–86,
    90–93, 96–103, 107, 160, 180–186,
    188–189, 190, 191–193, 197, 236,
    314–315, 333, 342, 360, 364–365,
    374, 395–396, 407–408, 409, 419,
    452–453, 461*n*
  Claudius: xi, 31, 36, 51, 72, 83–84, 85,
    97, 107, 109, 192, 396, 419
  Fortinbras: xi, 37, 54, 85–86, 91–92
  Gertrude: xi, 31, 51, 81, 160, 192, 327,
    333, 395–396
  Ghost of King Hamlet: xi, xix, 35,
    82–83, 85, 91, 419
  Guildenstern: x, 80, 83, 92, 181, 359
  Hamlet: ix, x–xi, xii, xxiv, xxv, 5, 13,
    15, 31, 32, 35–36, 37, 38, 40, 42, 49–
    55, 67–68, 70, 72–73, 76, 77–86, 89,
    91–93, 96–103, 126, 160, 181–186,
    191–193, 240, 314, 321, 327, 332, 333,
    342, 374, 381, 395–396, 409, 419,
    432, 447, 449, 452–453
  Horatio: xi, 32, 35, 78, 90
  Laertes: 38, 76, 77, 92, 333, 374
  Marcellus: 35
  Ophelia: 35–36, 38, 81, 82, 83, 84–85,
    92, 185, 186, 191, 333, 374, 395
  Osric: xi
  Polonius: 32, 38, 51, 73, 81, 83, 84–85,
    92, 97, 181, 191, 419
  Rosencrantz: x, 52, 80, 83, 92, 181, 359

Henry IV, Parts 1 and 2: ix–x, xix, xxvi,
    87–88, 236, 414, 460, 483–484, 486,
    487–488
  Falstaff: ix–x, xii, 36, 306, 460, 483,
    486–488
  King Henry IV: 460
  Mistress Quickly: x

  Poins: 484, 486, 487
  Prince Hal: x, 36, 87–88, 236, 460,
    483–484, 487, 488

Henry V: x, xxv, 4–5, 13, 88, 106–107,
    113, 226, 303–315, 339, 374, 464
  Archbishop of Canterbury: 226
  Bardolph: 311–312
  Chorus: 4–5, 309–310, 464
  Duke of Bedford: 374
  Falstaff: x, 306
  Fluellen: 304, 305–307
  Governor of Harfleur: 303
  Gloucester: 374
  Katherine/the Princess: 304, 305
  King Henry V: 28, 36, 87, 106, 226,
    303–308, 311–314, 339, 374
  MacMorris: 304, 305, 307
  Michael Williams: 106–107, 305,
    307–308, 313
  Pistol: 305, 306, 311–312

Henry VI, Parts 1, 2, and 3: 291, 303

Henry VIII: 339

Julius Caesar: xxi, 104, 142–144, 228–
    250, 310, 452
  Caius Cassius: 142, 229, 233, 240, 241,
    243, 244, 246, 249
  Casca: 242, 249
  Cicero: 242–243
  Julius Caesar: xxvii, 31, 143–144, 145,
    229, 231–232, 233, 235–236, 240,
    243–249
  Lepidus: 243
  Marcus Brutus: 142, 143, 229, 231–
    232, 233, 235–236, 240–250, 428
  Mark Antony: 31, 104, 142–144, 145,
    233, 235–236, 243, 244, 247–250
  Messala: 241
  Octavius Caesar: 233, 236, 243
  Portia: xxvii, 240–242
  Titinius: 240

King John: 291

King Lear: viii, xii–xiii, xix, xxiii, xxiv,
    xxv, 13–14, 15, 25, 30, 31, 32, 34–35,
    36–37, 42, 56–66, 69–74, 127, 128–
    130, 132, 163, 188, 207–209, 218–219,
    230, 291, 303, 322–324, 369, 373–376,
    378, 383, 407–411, 412, 413, 461*n*
Cordelia: 31, 37, 38, 62, 64, 66, 209,
    252, 373–376, 413
Duke of Cornwall: 32
Edgar/Poor Tom: viii, xxv, 60–61,
    69–74, 129, 209, 409, 449
Edmund: 34, 72, 362, 409
Earl of Gloucester: 32, 34, 61, 63, 70,
    73, 411
Fool: xxiii, 14, 15, 17, 25, 59, 60, 62,
    64, 66, 188, 360, 365, 383
Goneril: 31, 42, 59, 127, 374, 376,
    410–411
Earl of Kent: 34, 59, 60, 62
King of France: 62
King Lear: 4, 14, 15, 17, 25, 28, 36–37,
    40, 58, 59–64, 66, 72, 107, 109, 127,
    128–130, 132, 163, 207–209, 218,
    322–324, 360–365, 408–411, 443
Oswald: 42
Regan: 31, 59, 127, 374, 376, 409–411

Love's Labour's Lost: xxv, 290–298, 300–
    301, 304, 315
Anthony Dull: 296
Berowne: 291, 293, 296
Costard: 293, 296
Don Adriano de Armado: 296
Ferdinand, King of Navarre: 291–
    295, 297
Holofernes: 295–296
Jaquenetta: 296, 297
Moth: 296
Sir Nathaniel: 295
Princess of France: 291–293, 297
Rosaline: 291

Macbeth: ix, xii–xiii, xviii, 3, 19–21,
    33, 214–215, 219, 230, 349, 371,
    373, 379–382, 387, 388, 409, 452,
    453–454

Banquo: 42
King Duncan: 19, 382, 454
Lady Macbeth: ix, xxiv, 7, 20, 42,
    214–215, 252, 371, 379–382, 387, 388,
    449, 452, 453–455
Macbeth: ix, xxiii, 17, 19–21, 28, 36,
    107, 109, 214–215, 216, 349, 381–382,
    387, 454
Macduff: 324
Weird Sisters: 373

Measure for Measure: xii, xxv, 76–77,
    80, 106, 230, 346–347, 399, 408, 453
Abhorson: 106
Angelo: xxv, 76–77, 80, 89
Duke: 230, 346–347
Lucio: 76

The Merchant of Venice: xxi, xxiii, 6–8,
    16, 124*n*, 188, 199, 230, 251–261,
    262–274, 348, 361, 373, 378, 393–394
Antonio: 255–257, 264, 265, 393–394
Bassanio: 393–394
Duke of Venice: 8
Gratiano: 8, 394
Jessica: 260, 263
Launcelot Gobbo: 188
Leonardo, Bassanio's Servant: 199
Lorenzo: 263
Portia: 7–8, 252, 253–256, 348, 361,
    369, 393–394
Salerio: 260
Shylock: xxiii, 7–8, 16, 117, 124*n*, 251–
    252, 254–257, 259–261, 262–267,
    270, 271, 393–394
Solanio: 260
Tubal: 263–265

The Merry Wives of Windsor: x, 189–
    190, 193, 195

A Midsummer Night's Dream: xxiii, 14,
    45–46, 47, 49, 95–96, 107, 188, 194,
    203–204, 207, 219, 338, 339, 357, 371,
    374, 407–408, 409, 412–413, 452
Demetrius: 45, 49, 204

A Midsummer Night's Dream
(continued):
Helena: 204, 374
Hermia: 204, 374
Hippolyta: 95, 203–204
Lysander: 204
Nick Bottom: xix, 188, 204
Oberon: 107, 194, 204, 371, 413, 452
Puck: 14, 194, 338, 357, 452, 452n
Theseus: 95–96, 203–204
Titania: 45–46, 203–204, 338, 371, 413, 414, 452

Much Ado About Nothing: 7, 188, 374, 379, 383–388, 390–393, 449, 458
Antonio: 382
Beatrice: xxiv, 374, 379, 381, 382–388, 390–393, 415
Benedick: 374, 382–388, 390–393
Claudio: 387, 392
Dogberry: 188
Don John: 7, 392
Don Pedro: 387, 393
Hero: 374, 382–384, 387, 392
Leonato: 382

Othello: xii, xxii–xxiii, 21–22, 42, 107–128, 130–140, 145–161, 162–177, 196, 216–217, 219, 318, 401, 458, 461n
Bianca: 162
Brabantio: 22, 109–110, 132, 147–150, 153, 163, 167
Cassio: 107, 108, 113–114, 118, 126, 133, 134, 139, 146, 153, 163–164, 167, 171, 172, 176; *also as Dilip*: 168–174
Desdemona: 22, 31, 38, 107n, 108, 109–110, 112, 114–115, 116–117, 122, 128, 130, 132, 136, 139, 145–146, 147, 150–156, 157–159, 160, 162–165, 167, 172, 174, 401; *also as Lushin*: 166–174
The Duke: 151, 163; *also as Daniella/ the Director*: 166–173, 175
Emilia: 22, 38, 128, 156, 158, 164
Iago: xii, xxiii, 7, 15, 21–22, 107n, 108, 113–114, 116–128, 131, 132, 133–140, 146, 148, 153, 155–157, 160, 162–164, 166–168, 172, 175, 176, 216–217, 248, 400, 401, 449; *also as Barry*: 167–174
Othello: xxiii, 22, 31, 107–128, 130–140, 145–161, 162–176, 216–217, 324, 400, 401, 428, 449, 540; *also as Adil*: 167–174
Roderigo: 132, 146, 163

Pericles: 339, 353
Pericles: 353
Marina: 353

Richard II: xxv, 77, 86–89, 195, 225–226, 414, 424
Bishop of Carlisle: 88
Duke of Aumerle: 88
Henry Bolingbroke: xxv, 77, 86–89, 195, 226
Richard II: 28, 87–89, 225–226, 414

Richard III: 13, 15–16, 49, 75, 360, 374, 454, 458
Duke of Buckingham: 75
Prince Edward: 374
Lady Anne: 454
Richard III: xxiii, 15–16, 31, 43, 374, 447, 454
Queen Margaret: 15

Romeo and Juliet: xviii, 37, 38, 48, 93–95, 96, 280, 291, 342–343, 371, 390, 433–435, 438–439, 440–443, 460–461, 461n, 468
Benvolio: 94, 441
Capulet: 37
Friar Laurence: 461
Juliet: x, xxiii, xxiv, 37, 38, 93–94, 342–343, 346, 348, 374, 390, 433–435, 438–439, 441–443, 467, 492
Mercutio: x, 94, 280, 390, 461
Nurse: 38, 94, 461
Paris: 37

Romeo and Juliet (continued):
 Romeo: x, 37, 93–94, 100n, 342–343,
  346, 347, 348, 374, 390, 433–435,
  438–439, 441–443, 461, 467
 Tybalt: 280

The Sonnets: xi–xii, xxi, 30, 40, 179n,
  317, 330–334, 390, 397, 406
 73: 31
 129: xii, 331–332
 144: 389–390, 391

The Taming of the Shrew: xxiii, 40, 75,
  76, 204–207, 219, 370–371, 373–376,
  412, 440
 Baptista Minola: 40, 375
 Bianca: 204, 370–371, 373–376
 Hortensio: 205
 Kate/Katharine: 40, 204–207, 209,
  370–371, 373–376
 Petruchio: 40, 75, 204–207, 214
 Tranio: 76

The Tempest: viii, xxv, 12, 22–24, 33,
  37–38, 49, 59, 76, 190, 339, 340, 353,
  355, 371, 374, 409, 414–415, 417,
  449–451, 452, 458, 466–482
 Alonso: 451
 Antonio: 374, 471
 Ariel: 24, 49, 59, 339, 355, 414–415,
  467, 469, 472, 474, 476, 477–479,
  481, 482
 Caliban: 24, 33, 76, 190, 371, 449–451,
  456, 469, 472, 474–475, 479–482
 Ceres: 340
 Ferdinand: 37, 472, 478
 Gonzalo: 471
 Miranda: 37–38, 456, 466, 469, 471–
  472, 475, 479
 Prospero: 12, 22–24, 37–38, 59, 190,
  349, 353, 374, 415–416, 417, 432,
  449–451, 456, 468, 469–471, 477,
  482; *also as Prospera*: xxv–xxvi,
  466–467, 469–482
 Stephano: 33, 480

Titus Andronicus: xxiii, 21, 210–212,
  218–219, 236, 372–373, 467, 472
 Aaron: 21
 Tamora: 472
 Titus Andronicus: 21, 210–212, 475

Troilus and Cressida: xii, 75, 225, 303,
  395, 396, 419, 424
 Cressida: 395, 396
 Pandarus: 75
 Troilus: 395, 429
 Ulysses: 225

Twelfth Night: xix, 3–4, 33, 39, 42, 54,
  100, 187, 326, 348, 352–355, 356, 360–
  363, 365, 367–368, 378, 396–398, 407
 Antonio: 39
 Feste: xix, 50, 54, 187, 188, 356, 359–
  365, 367–369
 Malvolio: 42, 361, 362, 365, 367
 Olivia: 42, 367, 397
 Orsino: 187, 352, 354, 362, 363, 388,
  397–398
 Sebastian: 39, 354
 Sir Andrew Aguecheek: 33
 Sir Toby Belch: 33, 326
 Viola/Cesario: xxiv, 42, 187, 348, 353,
  354, 356, 364, 365, 367–369, 388,
  396–398, 415, 452

The Two Gentlemen of Verona: 339, 348
 Julia: 348
 Proteus: 348

The Two Noble Kinsmen: 194–195, 339

The Winter's Tale: 18–19, 21, 128, 230,
  337–338, 346, 353, 401, 411
 Florizel: 346
 Hermione: 401
 Leontes: xxiii, 17, 18–19, 20, 128, 401,
  411
 Perdita: 337, 346, 353
 Polixenes: 401

ACKNOWLEDGMENTS

Grateful acknowledgment is made to the following for permission to reprint previously published and unpublished material:

F. Murray Abraham: "Searching for Shylock," copyright © 2013 by F. Murray Abraham.

Isabel Allende: "Enamoured with Shakespeare," copyright © 2013 by Isabel Allende. This essay, originally written for *Shakespeare & Me*, first appeared in *Folger Magazine* (Spring 2013).

Jessie Austrian, Noah Brody, and Ben Steinfeld: "Boldness Be My Friend," copyright © 2013 by Jessie Austrian, Noah Brody, and Ben Steinfeld.

Cicely Berry: "*King Lear* in Retrospect," from *From Word to Play*, by Cicely Berry, copyright © 2007 by Cicely Berry, Oberon Books, London. Reprinted by permission of Oberon Books.

Eve Best: "A Star Danced," copyright © 2013 by Eve Best.

Eleanor Brown: "Shakespeare's Siblings," copyright © 2013 by Eleanor Brown.

Stanley Cavell: "Saying in *The Merchant of Venice*," copyright © 2013 by Stanley Cavell.

Karin Coonrod: "Killing Shakespeare and Making My Play," copyright © 2013 by Karin Coonrod.

Brian Cox: "I Say It Is the Moon," copyright © 2013 by Brian Cox.

Peter David: "On the Terrible and Unexpected Fate of the Star-Crossed Lovers," copyright © 2013 by Peter David.

Dame Margaret Drabble: "The Living Drama," copyright © 2013 by Dame Margaret Drabble.

Dominic Dromgoole: "Playing Shakespeare at the Globe," copyright © 2013 by Dominic Dromgoole.

David Farr: "The Sea Change," copyright © 2013 by David Farr.

Ralph Fiennes: "The Question of *Coriolanus*," copyright © 2013 by Ralph Fiennes.

Angus Fletcher: "Tolstoy and the Shakespearean Gesture," copyright © 2013 by Angus Fletcher.

James Franco: "My Own Private River," copyright © 2013 by James Franco.